# THE SELF-HELP GROUP SOURCEBOOK

*Your Guide to Community and Online Support Groups*

## 7th Edition

Compiled and edited by

*Barbara J. White and Edward J. Madara*

American Self-Help Group Clearinghouse
100 E. Hanover Ave., 2nd fl
Cedar Knolls, New Jersey 07927

Phone: 973-326-6789
Website: www.selfhelpgroups.org

**THE SELF-HELP GROUP SOURCEBOOK:**
**YOUR GUIDE TO COMMUNITY AND ONLINE SUPPORT GROUPS**

Library of Congress Card Catalog Number: 97-075663
ISBN: 1-930683-00-6
ISSN: 8756.1425

Published by Saint Clares Health Services

*The logo on the cover was specifically designed for*
*our Self-Help Clearinghouse in 1981 by Ben Ruiz.*

# ~ Dedication ~

To all the self-help group founders who have had the courage to take those first steps, as well as those group members who are ever giving of themselves. Very real heroes...ordinary people who so often do such extraordinary things. Helping to make self-help groups into the truly unique, caring communities that they come to be. This work is dedicated to their spirit... those whose efforts may never be fully acknowledged, because in very selfless or often anonymous ways, they placed group needs ahead of personal recognition. May their initiative, dedication, and tireless volunteer efforts be an inspiration to others who follow.

# ~ In Memory ~

This edition of the Sourcebook is in memory of Al Katz, DSW. From his 1961 book _Parents of the Handicapped_ wherein he first described them as "self-organized groups," to his creation of the _International Journal of Self-Help and Self-Care_ at the turn of the millennium, he was a pioneer in promoting the increased awareness and understanding of self-help groups across the world.

# ACKNOWLEDGMENTS

First, we wish to express our sincerest and continued appreciation to all the **mutual aid self-help group members** who contributed information on their work in order to make this resource guide possible.

We extend our heartfelt appreciation to each of our outstanding volunteers--**Joanne Bessor, Dolores Bruzzi, Pat de la Fuente, Lois Fallat, Perry Frantzman, Esther Foster, Pat Heller, Anisha Jhaveri, Chris Hennessy, Ken Keuhlen, Marie Lattari, Barbara Laurenzi, Howard Lerner, Pete Lodato, Trudy Lonetto, Wendy Lubin, Lorraine McKinley, Caroline Myers, John and Shirley O'Loughlin, Adrienne Rothblatt, Harry Salle, Jenna Seigel, Barry Vogel,** and **Berit Wenner.** We also extend our gratitude to staff members **Mary Ellen Kerin, Jeanne Rohach** and **Wendy Rodenbaugh.** Without their hard work and consistent efforts, this edition of the Sourcebook truly would not have been published. Through their continued updating, handling of referrals, detective work in tracking down new groups, and related support efforts, they continue to give of themselves to help so many others.

We would also like to acknowledge **Jeffrey Schiller** who has spent countless hours upgrading our software program, MASHnet.

Appreciation is also given to the **New Jersey State Division of Mental Health Services** for their funding of the first statewide self-help clearinghouse in the country and the development of our national database that has helped so many hundreds of New Jersey residents start new self-help groups.

Finally, we wish to thank **Hoffmann La Roche, Inc.** for their support which made the first Self-Help Sourcebook a reality and an on-going resource to communities across the country--as well as their initial support over twenty-two years ago that resulted in publishing the first Directory of Self-Help Groups in New Jersey.

ଓ ଞ

# FOREWORD
*- Alfred H. Katz, DSW*

The biennial publication of this Sourcebook has been an extremely useful service for many people with diverse interests - individuals who are looking for a group to meet their special needs, professionals seeking an appropriate referral point for a client, or information about a problem, academics and researchers who want local or national self-help group contacts and information, policy-makers at all levels of government, media people seeking personal reactions to recent crises.

But the significance and value of this publication exceeds the simple purpose of providing accurate information on the growth and ever-widening scope of the world of self-help, mutual aid groups. It marks the growing maturity and acceptance of a dynamic social movement that is increasingly seen as an integral part of the American culture, way of life and ethos, and as an important social resource. The values of cooperative self-organization, non-bureaucratic mutual helping methods exemplified by the hundreds of organizations listed in this Sourcebook have penetrated the general culture inescapably and irreversibly. Self-help is seen as a social resource so that people no longer have to suffer in isolation or feel despair that they can find no help in confronting and coping with their problems.

Self-help mutual aid groups provide an accepting environment of social support that may not be available from other sources--family, neighbors, friends, work-mates and social institutions, such as religious, human service and educational organizations. Their help can have the intimacy and informality of the best family and neighborly assistance to those with short-term or longer needs. There is usually no financial barrier to joining them and using their services--need, and a wish to participate are the only criteria for membership.

They usually bring together accurate, up-to-date information on resources and methods for coping with the problem; they often include people at different stages of dealing with it, so that newcomers can learn from the more experienced.

Both the 12-step groups on the A.A. model and non-12-step groups provide philosophies and methodologies for personal growth and change, role models of people who successfully cope, recognition for personal effort and achievement, and opportunities to contribute to the well-being of others. Many groups also engage in education and actions and advocacy that have furthered and often led to change in government and private institutional policies and programs. A result of these varied activities and interactions in the self-help groups is a growth in self-confidence, self-esteem and psychological well-being for the individual member, and of confidence, cohesion and effectiveness of the group. In these ways, the self-help movement can be viewed as an important contributor to social development--the historic process of growth toward a positive, humane, people-oriented society. Self-help's philosophy is that of working with people in a mutually helping way, that is non-bureaucratic, holistic, open to change, and that recognizes and seeks to optimize the inherent strengths and capacities of individuals, families, community groups and institutions.

This is not to imply that self-help is a panacea for all problems--material, environmental, political, of the society, or that self-help groups are without many difficulties--internal strains of growth, lack of resources, personality and program conflicts, leadership burnout, and so on. Like all human organizations, they are subject to human weaknesses, and do not always overcome them.

But as the vast variety and continuing dynamic growth of groups this Sourcebook illustrates, in last years of the 20th century America (and elsewhere in the modern world), they are an indispensable human resource, a permanent and major social utility.

ଓ ଓ

*The late Dr. Katz served as Professor (Emeritus) in the U.C.L.A. departments of Medicine, Public Health, and Social Welfare. His twelve books, and more than one hundred professional articles, have included Parents of the Handicapped (1961), wherein he was the very first to describe the phenomena of self-help groups as "self-organized groups," The Strength in Us: Self-Help Groups in the Modern World (1976), Helping One Another: Self-Help Groups in a Changing World (1990), Self-Help: Concepts and Applications (1992), and Self-Help in America; A Social Movement Perspective (1993). In regards to promoting an increased recognition and understanding of self-help group efforts, he has been a consultant to the World Health Organization, the Ford Foundation, and many government and voluntary agencies.*

*Dr. Katz planned and developed the world's first journal focused specifically on self-help groups, The International Journal of Self-Help and Self-Care, being published by Baywood Publishing Company, 26 Austin Ave., Amityville, NY 11701, phone: 1-800-638-7819.*

*"Self-help through natural or created 'lay' groups and networks is both the oldest and most pervasive system of care for human ills."*
*- Alfred Katz, DSW*

# TABLE OF CONTENTS

# TABLE OF CONTENTS

**HEALTH (Cont'd)**

## HEALTH (Cont'd)

**HEALTH (Cont'd)**

**HEALTH (Cont'd)**

# TABLE OF CONTENTS

## HEALTH (Cont'd)

# TABLE OF CONTENTS

# HOW TO USE THE SOURCEBOOK

## TO FIND A GROUP

To find a mutual aid self-help group for your concern, you may want to begin by glancing over the section on **Self-Help Clearinghouses** to see if there is a clearinghouse which serves your community. Self-help clearinghouses can provide you with information on existing local self-help groups, especially on many of those local "one-of-a-kind" groups that are not affiliated with any of the national self-help organizations listed in this directory.

If there is no self-help clearinghouse in your area, or a local clearinghouse has no group information, go to the **key word index** at the end of the book to find page references for a specific self-help group issue. The index will refer you to pages in the directory where any groups related to that listing will be found. If you know the name of the group that you are looking for, look in the Addendum under **Group Names** that will refer you to the page number where that group is listed.

While looking for an appropriate group, you may want to check several types or categories of groups to find the various groups that may be helpful to you. As an example, if you are looking for a group for a parent who is raising a child with a rare illness, you may want to first look under the specific disorder (e.g. Aarskog Syndrome, Fragile-X Syndrome, etc), then look under the groups dealing with any traits associated with the disorder (e.g. craniofacial disfigurement, visual impairment, etc). You then might also check the generic groups for parents of disabled children, general parenting groups, and so on. You might also want to look through the Toll-Free Specialty Helplines to find other agencies that may be of assistance (e.g., education, equipment, literature, referrals, etc). For your reference, there is a list of U.S. state and Canadian abbreviations in the Addendum at the back of the book.

In the self-help group listing section, please note the various types of entries included. Most of the entries are for **national or international self-help organizations**. At the right of the group name, we have noted the scope of the group (e.g., national, international, model, online, or resource). In italics we have indicated the number of affiliated groups (if applicable) and the year founded. You can then use the information in the group listing to contact these national groups to determine if they have any local meetings or chapters in your area. Even if they have no group in your area, you may want to subscribe to their newsletter or participate in any other mutual support activities they offer (e.g. correspondence or phone network, conferences, etc). In addition, they may be able to provide you with information on starting a group in your area.

We also refer to **support networks** which are mutual help exchanges that often, because the condition is rare, don't have face-to-face groups, but do have interactive correspondence exchange, phone networks, national or regional conferences, or newsletters. In addition, we have included some **Online** groups and resources, especially when knew of no face-to-face group available. These online groups are marked with the symbol ▣.

20

We have also included **model** groups which have only one meeting or are limited to one geographic area. **We have included the model groups primarily to help persons who may be interested in starting such a group in their local community,** so they do not have to "reinvent the wheel." We kindly request that you only contact model groups if you are interested in developing a group in your community, since model groups often are very limited in their ability to respond to more general inquiries.

There are some issues for which we have been unable to identify any national, or model self-help groups (e.g. rape). However, there are resources available to help those persons interested in developing support systems around such issues. Entries entitled **Resource** are organizations that provide technical support and/or information and referrals and have a 📰 symbol. **How-To Guides** (manuals or how-to material) are indicated by a 📖 symbol.

If you are interested in finding support groups online, also look at Chapter 3.

## TO FORM A GROUP

If you are interested in starting a new group in your local area, we have included some suggestions in Chapter 2 on **"Starting Community Self-Help Groups**." In that same chapter we have included some separate guidelines for the professional who seeks to help start a self-help group, ideally serving as an "on tap, not on top" consultant to persons interested in developing a group. If you are interested in forming a group, check with the national and/or model groups listed herein, as well as with any local self-help clearinghouses, to learn more about how they might assist you in starting the new group. In most cases, national groups can provide you with assistance and printed guidelines for starting a local affiliated group or chapter.

In addition, Chapter 3, **"Finding and Forming Online Support Groups"** offers suggestions for persons who are interested in starting an online network or group.

## IN CONTACTING ANY GROUP BY PHONE OR MAIL

When writing to a group, always include a **self-addressed stamped envelope** to make it easier for them to respond. Consider sending a small donation. Many of the national group headquarters actually operate out of "kitchen table offices" and most run on "shoestring budgets." When phoning a group, keep in mind that many of these phone contacts are home numbers so please be considerate of the hour at which you phone, and keep in mind the different time zones. Please understand that several tries may be necessary.

## OTHER SOURCEBOOK SECTIONS

If you would like to read more about self-help groups, there are a number of references in the Bibliography section. For persons who are interested in **empirical research** on the effectiveness of self-help groups, Chapter 4 reviews the various research findings on the effectiveness of self-help groups.

Just as self-help groups provide free information on resources and ways that help people deal with a wide variety of human problems, there are an increasing number of national toll-free helplines that help reduce the frustration in finding such information. Although most of these helplines are not run by self-help groups, we continue to include a listing of **National Toll-Free Helplines** (Chapter 7) since they can be helpful, cost-free sources of information for individuals and groups alike.

## PLEASE NOTE:

The Clearinghouse has made every effort to include as many different self-help groups as possible. However, the Clearinghouse reserves the right to include or exclude any names, groups or telephone contacts at its absolute discretion. Omission of an organization does not signify disapproval. Inclusion of an organization does not signify approval. The use of any of the materials herein is entirely the responsibility of the reader. The Clearinghouse further disclaims any and all liability for any use or non-use of the materials herein. There are no warranties implied or expressed in any of the data provided herein. The information provided herein is based upon data supplied by the groups themselves. The Clearinghouse is not responsible for printing, insertion or deletion errors.

## DO YOU KNOW OF A NATIONAL OR MODEL GROUPS THAT SHOULD BE INCLUDED IN THE NEXT EDITION OF THE SOURCEBOOK?

We would be most grateful if you would let us know about any new or existing groups that you suggest be included in the next edition of the Sourcebook or included in our database. We also would appreciate your comments and suggestions as to how the Sourcebook may be improved. Simply advise us by writing to us at: American Self-Help Clearinghouse, 100 E. Hanover Ave., Suite 202, Cedar Knolls, N.J. 07927-2020.

ଔ ଔ

*"Though you have lost your dearest treasure, a child, your mate, your sanity, reputation, riches, position, health, self-control, you have received a special talent. You can say, 'I've been where you are. Let me help'... Wounded folks in self-help groups provide a unique source of hope, encouragement, love and purpose... Some of us stay, even for a lifetime to share this precious gift."* – Barbara Rehberg Fox, Founder (1964) of Self-Help Information Services of Nebraska, the very first self-help group clearinghouse.

# ABOUT THE AMERICAN AND NEW JERSEY CLEARINGHOUSES

The Sourcebook is the result of two self-help clearinghouse programs. Work in supporting self-help group efforts first began in 1978, when here at Saint Clares Health Services we started to pull together a listing of "hard-to-find" self-help groups for a wide variety of stressful life problems. Most hospital and mental health center staff knew of only a few groups. When we advised them of others, they reported back how grateful their patients were to find out that they were not alone and that there was such a support group available. In 1979, we compiled the first directory of self-help groups in New Jersey. Unlike other directories, we added national and model groups that didn't exist in New Jersey, in order to show people what new self-help groups they could develop if they were willing to join with others. At the same time, we had seen how easy it was for us to link interested people together resulting in the development of many new groups.

In 1980, we submitted a proposal to the New Jersey State Division of Mental Health Services to establish the first statewide self-help clearinghouse in order to increase the awareness, utilization, and development of self-help groups. Subsequently, in January of 1981, the New Jersey Self-Help Clearinghouse was started. With additional new state directory editions, our listings of national and model groups grew - as did the number of people who were able to start new groups throughout the state with assistance from a national or model group listed in the directory. Since its start, the New Jersey Self-Help Clearinghouse has assisted in the development of over one thousand new groups in the state. A wide variety of consultation, training, information and referral services are available to persons in New Jersey by calling us at 1-800-FOR-M.A.S.H. (Mutual Aid Self-Help).

In 1982, we began to share our national listings with other self-help clearinghouses through our MASHNet computer program and database which has been used by 18 other self-help clearinghouses in the U.S. and Canada. Our M.A.S.H. Networking Project service was then started in 1984 to help individuals outside New Jersey start new networks that didn't previously exist anywhere in the country. Names of persons interested in starting new types of groups were listed on that same database alongside existing groups. In that way, interested callers could be referred to help those starting groups. Over a dozen new "first-of-their-kind" groups or networks were started as a result.

The Clearinghouse listing of national and model groups had proved so helpful to others outside New Jersey, that with funding from Hoffmann La Roche, Inc., the first edition of the Self-Help Sourcebook was published in 1986 to make that information on those groups more widely available and known.

One way that we have sought to help more people learn about self-help groups is through our outreach efforts to the media. Prior mailings of the Sourcebook, with cover letters suggesting coverage of self-help groups, resulted in significant articles in Psychology Today, USA Today, American Health, FIRST for Women, Parade, New Age, New

Physician, Better Homes and Gardens, and many other national magazines, books, and professional newsletters.

In 1990, with funding from Saint Clares Health Services and the Saint Clares-Riverside Foundation, along with the help of additional volunteers, the American Self-Help Clearinghouse program was added. In addition to the Sourcebook, it provides the following services:

**Information and Referral:** For information on a group, we can be reached at (973)326-6789, Monday-Friday, 9:00am-5:00pm Eastern time. Staff and volunteers can provide callers with information and contacts on many national self-help groups that deal with their particular concern. If no appropriate national group exists and the caller is interested in the possibility of joining with others to start a local group, we can often provide information on model groups operating in other parts of the country, or individuals who are starting networks and seeking others to help develop them. We also provide callers with information on any local self-help clearinghouse that may exist to serve them in their area. We also have a website: http://www.selfhelpgroups.org

**Consultation:** If there is no group or support network that exists anywhere in the country for your problem and you are interested in starting a mutual help group or network, contact the Clearinghouse for help with suggestions, materials, and networking.

We firmly believe **the most powerful potential of self-help is in the ability of people who are in need to come together and start needed new groups and networks.** Through the work of both self-help clearinghouses, we strive to help more people tap that potential for the benefit of themselves and for so many others.

‎ଓ ଚ

In 1987, when then Surgeon General C. Everett Koop held a national two-day conference at UCLA to develop national recommendations for tapping the benefits of self-help support groups for Americans, some 200 health and human service professionals, scholars, and self-help group leaders participating in the "Surgeon General's Workshop on Self-Help and Public Health" recommended that a national registry or "centralized information center for referral to existing self-help groups and clearinghouses, and for assistance in the formation of new groups" be established. (Recommendation #1, The Surgeon General's Workshop on Self-Help and Public Health, U.S. Dept. of Health & Human Services, 1988, p. 30)

**Chapter 1**

# UNDERSTANDING
# SELF-HELP GROUPS

---

*"Friendship is born at the moment when one person says to another,*
*"What! You too? I thought I was the only one. "*
*- C.S. Lewis*

---

## AN INTRODUCTION TO SELF-HELP GROUPS
*Phyllis Silverman, Ph.D.*

It has always been important to me to be able to bring the personal and the professional together. I believe that very often what excites us in our work is connected to the experiences of our daily life. People who work in the mental health field are expected to keep these lives very separate. I don't think this works in reality. These two worlds are not distinct; each informs and enriches the other. Thus, my sustained interest over the years in self-help was fed by my appreciation of the help I received as a new mother from the La Leche League. I was having difficulty in nursing my first child. She slept very little, required frequent feedings, and fussed when left alone in the crib. A mother of ten, the local La Leche League leader said to me, "Get an infant seat for the kitchen table so she can watch and be part of the family, and when you nurse lie down in bed with her." With those two statements, she changed my entire relationship with my newborn and made the first year of our life together a very wonderful and exciting period. That experience introduced me to the value of "mutual help" and the knowledge gained from experience that no physician could provide me with. My gratitude remains to this day, and one of my most satisfying activities is to share with new mothers what I learned to this day. My experience with La Leche League led me to be more open to a finding in the research I was doing to learn more about the experience of newly widowed women. This finding pointed to another widow as the most appropriate helper at this time in a woman's life. In light of my experience as a new mother, this made very good sense and it led to the demonstration project called Widow to Widow that laid the foundation for what became known as the Widowed Persons Service sponsored by the American Association of Retired People.

The word self-help may be a misnomer. What I saw was an exchange; the helper was often helped as much as the person who was the recipient. It is often difficult to find the right word for something that is not always easily defined. Basically, we are talking about an exchange that occurs when people, who share a problem or predicament, come together to help one another. Mutual help may be a more appropriate name for this phenomenon. In the broadest sense, life as we know it is not possible without some exchanges of resources and mutual aid. Usually this aid is casual and informal and is the essence of what has been called natural helping networks. In this source book the focus is on organizations that provide people with opportunities to come together to help each other with a common problem. They have moved beyond the informal to make their services available to a larger audience. Alcoholics Anonymous is one of the oldest organizations of this sort. As you will see in glancing over the pages of this directory, in our heterogeneous, mobile society in this new millennium, the number and variety of organizations is quite extensive. In part, this is a result of the growing consumer movement that in some ways is a response to the depersonalization of consumers in the delivery of human services. To some extent, mutual help organizations have helped to "humanize" the human service system by helping their members become more informed consumers, and by lobbying for change in the formal health care and human service system. However, the development of these organizations is mainly due to people's need to find others like themselves who have experienced a similar problem. There is a growing awareness in our society that there is something special that people who share a common problem or difficult experience have to offer each other. Mutual help groups are especially attractive to persons undergoing a transition that requires a shift in social roles whether they are recovering alcoholics, former mental patients, new parents or tragically today, survivors of violence and terrorism.

There are many groups that are small (10-20 people) and constantly struggling to survive. They meet in people's homes or in other centers in their communities. They may list their activities in the local newspaper but would not find their way into this directory. Most groups mentioned here have, over time, incorporated and acquired non-profit status and their membership extends beyond their own communities. Some have been in existence for a long time. Whatever their history, these organizations do not follow one model for governing themselves. Some groups govern themselves wholly by consensus, sacrificing efficiency for maximum participation, making the rules up as they go along. Other groups follow parliamentary procedures, establishing committees and electing officers. Some set themselves up as service delivery systems with authority vested in a national office and leadership recruited through an elaborate ascending hierarchy. Some national organizations have a name that applies to a loose network of autonomous groups. The most common is an association supported by dues from affiliated local branches or chapters that are authorized to use its name. Many of these national associations have paid staff that develop program materials for the local groups and provide consultants from regional offices. Regardless of the way the association is organized, the member's common problem is the driving force in what these organizations do.

In these organizations, the helper and the beneficiary are peers. Learning is made easier when the teacher is a peer. His or her knowledge is something that does not require a special education or unique credentials. Helpers are qualified by virtue of having grappled with the common problem and is readily available to those who are in the recipient role. In this kind of relationship, the participants are not bound to the role of either helper or recipient. They are members, not clients. They can move between roles and this in itself can have therapeutic value. Discovering that others have the same problem, members no longer feel alone. Their feelings and experiences are legitimized; they no longer feel defective or deficient. Given the circumstances, their experience can be seen as typical and there are things that can be done about it. They are provided with a framework for coping: "The most important thing for me was finding someone like me. When I walked into the room and found 50 other widows, I can't explain the good feeling it gave me." Once having established the common groups for discussion, they can now expand their options about what can be done about it.

Each organization develops a body of relevant information and strategies: "When I get nervous now I follow the guidelines I learned at the meeting; it really works." The best known of these is the "Twelve Steps" of Alcoholics Anonymous, which have been adapted to the needs of many other anonymous groups that you will find in the directory dealing with problems such as gambling, overeating and drug abuse. Groups concerned with disabilities or with such universal problems as bereavement use a more flexible approach. The wisdom of experience amassed in these organizations provides a unique contribution distinct from the professional knowledge learned in schools. One member of such a group commented, "When she said she understood I knew she meant it. I needed to hear how she managed before anything else." Another person said, "I needed to have a name for what was bothering me. I could figure out what to do when someone explained what I needed, given my situation." A woman with crippling arthritis found a way to eat in a restaurant, "I learned that I could ask to have my food cut up in the kitchen and I didn't have to be embarrassed having someone else do it at the table. It was so simple but it would never have occurred to me."

There is no one way of helping in these organizations. The assistance provided by mutual help groups may include educational seminars, one-to-one exchanges and social gatherings, in addition to the basic sharing of personal experiences and small informal meetings. Some organizations have hotlines, others have outreach programs in which members make unsolicited offers of help, and others publish a regular newsletter. Today the use of the Internet makes geographic distances between members shrink. Many organizations have formal orientation or training programs for outreach volunteers, facilitators in small group discussions, and for officers and leaders. There are no fees for services. If money is exchanged it is for membership dues, for supporting a particular event or activity.

The role of professional in these organizations varies. Some organizations have professional advisory committees that provide medical information enabling members to become competent consumers of the services they need. Others use professionals to facilitate support groups they sponsor as part of their programs. Resources and policy however, is controlled by the membership. Some organizations choose not to involve professionals.

The American Self-Help Group Clearinghouse has been instrumental in promoting increased awareness and utilization of groups through their information, referral and consultation services, and by continuing to make this directory available to a national audience. They are helping people develop new self-help mutual aid organizations as witness their activity following the tragedy of September 11. They are encouraging and supporting survivors as they develop their own mutual help networks.

The organizations listed in this directory remind us that the basic dignity of each of us is expressed and affirmed in our capacity to be involved in these reciprocal helping exchanges. Out of this compassion comes cooperation and enhances the caring we want to encourage in our own community. We live in a society in which there is a tendency to abdicate responsibility for many human problems to professionals. We often accept that we do not have the training and qualifications to help others. Sometimes this is true, but as we learn more about the organizations listed in this source book, we come to appreciate the vast amount of experience most of us amass as part of living, and the special value there is in making it available to each other. In a sense, they speak for all of us since even those of us who study these groups as professionals are consumers.

*Dr. Silverman is a Professor Emeriti at the Institute of Health Professions of Massachusetts General Hospital. She also holds an appointment in the Department of Psychiatry at Harvard Medical School. She has served as consultant to several task forces on bereavement, mutual help and prevention. She developed the concept of the widow-to-widow program and directed the research that demonstrated its effect. Her most recent research was a longitudinal study of the consequences of the death of a parent for children between the ages of 6 to 17. In addition to her social work degree from Smith College of Social Work, she holds an MS in hygiene from Harvard School of Public Health and a Ph.D. from the Florence Heller School for Advanced Studies in Social Welfare at Brandeis University. She has published extensively and her works include* Helping Each Other in Widowhood; If You Will Lift the Load, I Will Lift It Too; Mutual Help Groups: A Guide for Mental Health Professionals, Mutual Help Groups: Organization and Development, Helping Women Cope with Grief, *and* Widow to Widow. *She is co-editor with D. Klass and S. Nickman of* Continuing Bonds: A New Understanding of Grief. *Her most recent book,* Never Too Young to Know: Death in Children's Lives *reports on her research with bereaved children that includes a section on how the bereaved help each other.*

୬ ଏ

*" If someone listens,
or stretches out a hand,
or whispers a kind word of encouragement,
or attempts to understand a lonely person,
extraordinary things begin to happen. "*

*- Loretta Girzatlis, P.H.O.B.I.A., (a panic and anxiety support group, NJ)*

## TO BETTER UNDERSTAND THE TERM
## "SELF-HELP GROUP"

Have you ever noticed when you have a problem, how it helps to talk with someone who has had a similar problem? Simply finding others who have "been there" and then realizing that "you are not alone" can be very comforting and helpful. The <u>Sourcebook</u> has been compiled to help you more easily find and form a self-help group--one that can provide such needed support, as well as practical information, education and sometimes advocacy.

The self-help groups listed on the following pages can better be described as "Mutual Aid Self-Help" groups because they derive their energy from members helping one another, without forms or fees. In examining the hundreds of national organizations, societies and foundations that exist for different illnesses, addictions, parenting and other stressful life situations and transitions, we have sought to identify those organizations that provide these mutual help opportunities. In addition to **"mutual support,"** three other key characteristics of self-help groups that constitute our general criteria are: that the group be **composed of "peers,"** people who share a common experience or situation; that the group or network be primarily **run by and for its members**, who therefore have a sense of "ownership" for the group or network; and that the group be **voluntary, non-profit**, i.e., they can "pass the hat," charge dues, or fundraise, but there are no fees for services.

Dr. Silverman, in her introduction to self-help groups, describes some of the characteristics and dynamics of self-help groups, and how these differ from professionally-run groups and services. Self-help groups can provide benefits that professional services cannot. However, self-help groups are not meant to replace needed professional services, although they supplement, support and sometimes even develop them, as well as often prevent the very need for them.

We should point out that there are other types of community organizations that are sometimes described as self-help, including civic, housing, fraternal, business, ethnic, church and political groups. However, these groups, by their very numbers and broader focus, would warrant or already have separate directories of their own.

Also, please understand that the quality of individual self-help groups differ, sometimes even among those with the same name. Contact and visit the group to see if it is for you. While initial research reflects the value of self-help groups, the ultimate evaluation and very survival of any self-help group is determined by those who attend it and decide to stay and contribute to it.

*"Self-help is when a person takes responsibility for themselves. But we cannot take responsibility for ourselves in a vacuum."*

*Betsy Wilson,"Let's Face It" in the USA, and former Chairperson of the National Council on Self-Help and Public Health*

## UNDERSTANDING WHAT SELF-HELP GROUPS DO
## AND HOW THEY DO IT

Self-help groups help their members cope with a wide variety of illnesses, disabilities, addictions, bereavement, parenting and many other stressful life problems. From groups for parents of children born prematurely to those families caring for an elderly-frail parent, there are hundreds of self-help groups listed within these pages that address different problems but function in very similar ways.

### WHAT THEY DO

Mutual help groups, as often reflected in their written mission statements, usually have three or four basic functions or purposes in that they provide:

1.    **Social Support** - relief from isolation, experiencing the stress-reducing support of others who truly understand. As one group leader expressed it..."The heart of our message is: 'You Are Not Alone.' Our strength has come from sharing our hardship and giving hope to others." In some groups, this support represents genuine "community." Duke University researchers who studied the value of social support to the life expectancy of cardiac patients (as reported in New York Times of Feb. 5, 1992) concluded, "A support group may be as effective as costly medical treatment. Simply put, having someone to talk to is very powerful medicine."

2.    **Practical Information** - on the problem or disorder, how to cope on a 24-hour a day basis (sometimes using a particular "program," e.g. the 12-steps), what professional services and other resources are available, alternatives, self-care techniques, research, etc. These help people to recognize that they are not helpless.

3     **Education** - primarily derived from the pooling of members' experiences and coping skills, as well as information on and familiarity with professional services; referred to as **"experiential knowledge"** (Dr. Thomasina Borkman, 1975). Secondarily, their ability to attract professionals to share their **professional knowledge** (e.g., to speak at meetings, workshops and/or contribute to newsletter), often leading to collaboration in **joint learning, education, treatment and research** development efforts.

4.    **Advocacy** (an optional function) - advocating to address problems or deficiencies that the members cannot resolve within in their group, but exist in the larger society. Historically, theses groups are the seeds for the development of many long-standing health foundations, societies, and movements dealing with various illnesses, disabilities, and health concerns. Not all groups (e.g., 12-step groups) involve themselves in pursuing an advocacy purpose and activities.

### HOW GROUPS DO IT

Some of the specific principles and group dynamics to be found at work within mutual-help groups and networks are:

30

1. **The "Helper Therapy" principle** - wherein those who help others are themselves helped (Dr. Frank Riessman, 1965). As heard in some groups, "if you help someone up the hill, you get closer to the top yourself."

2. **Positive Role Models** - those, who have been through it, demonstrate to new members that success, coping and/or recovery is possible ("do-able"). Their example and actions often provide needed encouragement and hope not otherwise available.

3. **Accessibility** - there are no fees, so they are financially more accessible. They are also psychologically more accessible in several ways: in that they require no forms be submitted; often, as in the many "anonymous" groups, no names need be given; and one can go to a group simply to learn, and does not have to assume "patienthood" to get help. Many groups also have convenient meeting sites in the community, at times that are more convenient than most professional services.

4. **Pooling of Knowledge and Resources** by members, so that all can take advantage of the experiences of many.

5. **Acceptance** - being accepted and understood, often for the first time.

6. **Empowerment** of members by their taking a more active rather than a traditional passive role.

7. **Normalization** - when they see how their experience is similar to others, they finally feel "normal." For what range of differences do exist, their basic human need for feedback (as to how they are doing) is finally met.

8. **Anonymity** is provided by many groups.

9. **The Prevention Equation** (of psychologist Dr. George Albee, 1982) reflects how groups contribute to the prevention of psychopathology and stress-related illness:

    a.  Incidence of        Stress + Constitutional Vulnerabilities
    b.  Dysfunction   =     Social   Support   +   Coping   Skills   +
        Competence

10. Groups provide **social support, coping skills**, and **increase competence**, thereby reducing incidence. To varying degrees, self-help groups serve a prevention function by enhancing social ties and connections that can serve as a buffer to stress, and by promoting the competency of people to cope with stress and adversity for a full spectrum of life transitions and crises. Dr. Phyllis Silverman (1985) of Harvard University points out that many stressful life transitions cannot be prevented, but that mutual help groups may be "one of the more powerful modalities" for facilitating the learning of coping skills subsequent to stress.

11. **Options** and **alternatives** are generated for resolving or coping with problems. Where previously a new member was despairing, thinking they had no options, other

31

members often provide a range of strategies and solutions, based upon their own experiences.

12. Groups are a source of **altruism** and **meaning** because many human beings seek needed meaning in their lives and find it in helping other through their personal and group efforts. This accounts for why many experiences members remain after they are helped. Yet self-help groups are a neglected form of volunteerism.

13. Groups **turn** what society considers **a liability** (e.g. one's experience as an addict, widow, etc.) **into an asset** (their unique ability to provide understanding and help others).

Unfortunately, an understanding of these functions and dynamics traditionally has been missing from most professional training curriculum. In 1987, then Surgeon General C. Everett Koop held a national conference that explored the value and potential of self-help groups to public health. The recommendation given the highest priority of over 60 developed at the two-day conference was the need to educate professionals to self-help groups. Dr. Koop later noted:

> *"My years as a medical practitioner, as well as my own first-hand experience, has taught me how important self-help groups are in assisting their members in dealing with problems, stress, hardship and pain... Today, the benefits of mutual aid experienced by millions of people who turn to others with a similar problem to attempt to deal with their isolation, powerlessness, alienation, and the awful feeling that nobody understands... Health and human service providers are learning that they can indeed provide a superior service when they help their patients and clients find appropriate peer support." - Former Surgeon General C. Everret Koop (in his 1992 foreword to Self-Help: Concepts and Applications, edited by Dr. A. H. Katz et. al., p. xviii).*

## References:

Albee, G.W., "Preventing Psychopathology and Promoting Human Potential" in American Psychologist, 37 (9), pp. 1043-1050, 1982.

Borkman, Thomasina, "Experiential Knowledge: a New Concept for the Analysis of Self-Help Groups" in the Social Service Review, vol. 50, number 3, pp. 445-456, 1975.

Riessman, Frank, "The Helper Therapy Principle" in Social Work, vol. 10, pp. 26-32, 1965.

Silverman, Phyllis, "Tertiary/Secondary Prevention - Preventive Intervention: the Case for Mutual Help Groups" in The Group Workers' Handbook, R. K. Conyne (Ed), Springfield, Il: Charles C. Thomas, pp. 237-258), 1985.

## TEN BENEFICIAL WAYS PROFESSIONALS
## INTERACT WITH GROUPS

1.  **Identify and refer** to local groups in your community. They often will reciprocate.

2.  **Communicate/collaborate with local groups,** e.g., identify contact person, request their literature, keep brochures on hand, subscribe to their newsletters, liaison, etc.

3.  **Involve groups in your training and conferences,** e.g., as speakers at in-service trainings, workshops and conferences; or host group demonstration/presentation at staff meeting or for clients.

4.  **Provide speaking engagements and/or training** that local groups desire.

5.  **Offer actual agency support,** e.g., meeting room, mailings, copying, clerical aid, etc.

6.  **Identify need for new groups** in your community and educate others to the potential for developing a specific group based upon a particular national model.

7.  **Identify and encourage potential "group starters,"** possibly from veteran patients.

8.  **Provide networking help** to meet their needs for speakers, advisors, consultants, referrals, researchers, special services or training, loan of newest equipment, etc.

9.  **Educate other professionals** to the availability and value of groups, e.g., report upon what you've learned here at agency meetings or professional conferences.

10. **Advocate for increased awareness** and understanding of groups, e.g., development of a local listing or directory that includes them, presentations before agency coalitions or associations, etc.

> *"Mutual support groups, involving little or no cost to participants, have a powerful effect on mental and physical health... The psychological and physical health importance of this diffuse community is striking... The self-help movement, both in face-to-face and virtual arenas, has tremendous therapeutic potential." - February, 2000 issue of American Psychologist feature article Who Talks?: The Social Psychology of Illness Support Groups, by K.P. Davison, H.W. Pennebaker, and S.S. Dickerson. (55) 2, pp. 205-217.*

## PUBLICATIONS BY PROFESSIONALS
## ON SELF-HELP

Most of the books and references that best describe mutual aid self-help groups can be obtained from the self-help group contacts listed in this directory. Their materials can often express the purpose and value of the group better than any textbook can. Here are some references, which, for the most part, examine self-help groups in general and are written primarily for a professional audience.

The International Journal of Self Help & Self Care, Fred Massarik, Editor. While not a book, this journal is a unique resource with a broad range of articles by both professional and self-help group writers. It was the brainchild of the late Dr. Alfred Katz. Go to www.baywood.com and click on "Journals" to learn more, review abstracts of past articles, read author's guidelines for writing and submitting articles, and more.

Understanding Self-Help/Mutual Aid: Experiential Learning in the Commons by Thomasina J. Borkman, based upon her years of working with and researching groups, it examines the increased popularity of self-help groups, who participates and why, and their relationships with professionals. Rutgers University Press, 1999.

Self-Help and Support Groups, by Linda Farris Kurtz, is an excellent classroom text since it provides discussion questions, classroom exercises and assignments for most of the eleven chapters that provide scholarly overviews of group dynamics, membership professional relationships, and other related issues. Published in 1997 by Sage Publications, 2455 Teller Rd., Thousand Oaks, CA 91320.

Redefining Self-Help: Policy and Practice, by Frank Riessman and David Carroll, reflects how people with problems can be viewed as resources through self-help groups. With illustrations from various groups, the authors demonstrate how health and human service agencies can benefit from their tapping into the power of self-help organizations. Concepts such as the helper therapy principle, self-determination, and consumer as producer are updated. Published in 1995 by Jossey-Bass, 350 Sansome St., San Francisco, CA 94104.

Understanding the Self-Help Organization, edited by Thomas J. Powell, includes 17 chapters on research on self-help groups and professionally-run support groups. Published in 1994 by Sage Publications, P.O. Box 5024, Beverly Hills, CA 90212.

Self-Help: Concepts and Applications, edited by Alfred Katz, H.L. Hedrick, D.H. Isenberg, L.M. Thompson, T. Goodrich, and A.H. Kutsche, is an informative collection of over 30 perspectives on self-help group dynamics and professional interface. Several chapters examine the value of groups for conditions like AIDS, hearing loss, cancer, death of a child, lupus, and others. There are several chapters that look at professional and self-help group relationships, including the first chapter on empowerment that provides and extensive and updated review of policy and partnership developments. The book, published in 1992, is available from Charles Press, P.O. Box 15715, Philadelphia, PA 19103.

The Self-Help Way: Mutual Help and Health by Jean-Marie Romeder with contributions from Hector Balthazar, Andrew Farquharson, and Francine Lavoie, provides an overview of the growth and development of the self-help groups, while probing the dynamics of "the self-help way." With an introduction by former U.S. Surgeon General Koop, it provides a variety of views and insights that would be of interest to both the general public as well as professionals. This 158 page book, published in 1990, is available from Canadian Council on Social Development, P.O. Box 3505, Station C; Ottawa, Ontario K14 4Gl, Canada.

Helping One Another: Self-Help Groups in a Changing World, by Alfred Katz and Eugene Bender (22 chapters examine specific types and general development of self-help groups in relationship to changing social, economic and political scene), 1990, 266 pages, Third Party Publishing, Oakland, CA 94661.

Working With Self-Help, edited by Thomas Powell, includes 17 chapters written primarily for professionals that vary from a look at 12-step programs to self-help and Latino communities, from bereavement groups to parents of the mentally ill in Israel. Printed in 1990, 338 pages, American Association of Social Workers, 7981 Eastern Ave., Silver Spring, MD 20910.

Rediscovering Self-Help: Its Role in Social Care, edited by Diane Pancoast, P. Parker and C. Froland, 1983, SAGE Publications, P.O. Box 5024, Beverly Hills, CA 90212.

The Surgeon General's Workshop on Self-Help and Public Health, printed by the U.S. Department of Health and Human Services, Public Health Service, (summary of presentations and recommendations), printed 1988, 60 pp. (Check with any local self-help clearinghouse serving your area to determine if they can provide a copy).

Self-Help Organizations and Professional Practice, by Thomas Powell, 1987, 366 pages, National Association of Social Workers, 7981 Eastern Ave., Silver Spring, MD 20910.

Helping People To Help Themselves: Self-Help and Prevention, edited by Leonard Borman, Leslie Borck, Robert Hess and Frank Pasquale, 1982, 129 pages, Haworth Press.

Mutual Help Groups: Organization and Development, by Phyllis R. Silverman (guide to starting groups, with attention of professional relationship and roles), 1980, 143 pages, SAGE Publications, P.O. Box 5024, Beverly Hills, CA 90212.

The Self-Help Revolution, by Alan Gartner and Frank Riessman, (Series of 18 essays that review particular groups, professional interface and evaluation), 1984, 266 pages, Human Sciences Press, 72 Fifth Avenue, New York, N.Y. 10011.

Rediscovering Self-Help: Its Role in Social Care, edited by Diane Pancoast, P. Parker and C. Froland, 1983, SAGE Publications.

Helping People to Help Themselves: Self-Help and Prevention, edited by Leonard Borman, Leslie Borck, Robert Hess and Frank Pasquale, 1982, 129 pages, Haworth Press.

Self-Help Groups for Coping with Crisis, by Morton A. Lieberman and Leonard D. Borman (review of literature and research on groups), 1979, 462 pages, Jossey Bass Publishers, San Francisco, CA.

"Hospitals and Self-Help Groups: Opportunity and Challenge" by E. Madara and W.D. Neigher, Health Progress, Vol. 67, No. 3, April, 1986, pp. 42-45.

Mutual Help Groups: Organization and Development, by Phyllis R. Silverman (guide to starting groups, with attention to professional relationships and roles), 1980, 143 pps, SAGE Publications, P.O. Box 5024, Beverly Hills, CA 90212.

Self-Help in the Human Services, by Alan Gartner and Frank Riessman (reviews range, variety and principles of groups), 1977, Jossey Bass Publishers, San Francisco, CA.

Support Systems and Mutual Help: Interdisciplinary Explorations, edited by Gerald Caplan and Marie Killilea, (contains excellent chapter on literature review by Marie Killilea), 1976, 325 pages, Grune and Stratton, Inc.

The Strength in Us: Self-Help Groups in the Modern World, edited by Alfred H. Katz and Eugene I. Bender (history, typology, political aspects), 1976, 258 pages, New York: New Viewpoints Press.

The Recovery Resource Book, by Barbara Yoder (Describes different self-help groups, agencies, books, and other resources dealing with various addictions and dependencies - providing samples of groups' materials), 1990, New York: Simon and Schuster, 314 pages.

"Clergy and Self-Help Groups: Practical and Promising Relationships" by E. Madara, and B.A. Peterson, The Journal of Pastoral Care, Vol. 41, No. 3, September, 1987, pp. 213-220.

"Introducing and Tapping Self-Help Mutual Aid Resources," by C.J. Paskert, and E.J. Madara, Health Education, (written for school personnel), Vol. 16, No. 4, Aug/Sept., 1985, pp. 25-29.

"The Self-Help Clearinghouse Operation: Tapping the Resource Development Potential of I & R Services," by E. Madara. Information and Referral: The Journal of the Alliance of Information and Referral Systems, (written primarily for I & R agencies) Vol. 12, No. 1, Summer, 1985, pp. 42-57.

"Self-Help and How We Teach Tomorrow" What's New in Home Economics, (written primarily for teachers), Vol. 17, No. 4, December, 1983, pp. 1 and 4.

*"When the wise healer's work is done, the people say,
'Amazing. We did it all ourselves.'"*
- Lao Tze

## A Self-Help Story... "Self-Help – What It Means to Families of Children With Special Needs"

*Beth Randall, President, Mothers from Hell 2*

I had a lot of great ideas backed up by impressive research findings for this my writing short piece on why self-help is crucial for families of children with special needs—really I did! I also had good intentions of polishing it up.

But, the day I set aside to start work on it I....
attended our local family support group meeting where a mom whose child was recently diagnosed with a neurological disorder asked, "What is respite care?" Ever the optimist I replied that surely hadn't the child's physician, nurse, case manager, teacher, schools social workers, *someone* explained how a respite caregiver funded through the state Department of Human Services could give her family precious hours of relief from the intense care her child needs 24 hours a day, seven days a week? A bewildered look was her response. I offered to gather information on the local respite care resources for her, and while I'm at it why don't I prepare some respite information for those professionals, too? "That's great!" she says, "and by the way, the speech therapist suggested we look into something called sensory integration. Do you have anything on that?" Why, of course. Another batch of information to prepare for this parent and the aforementioned professionals. While I'm at it, I better pull together stuff on educational rights, as this child is obviously not receiving all of the services he is entitled to.

Then, the next day that I set aside I....
sat in on an Individual Education Program meeting at a parent's request. Apparently, her child had been spending less and less time in the regular education classroom, as he wasn't quite working at grade level and there were some new behavior concerns. So I ask what strategies have been employed for the behaviors, what has been done to adapt the curriculum and that supports are in place for the child to receive an appropriated education in his Less Restrictive Environment of the regular education classroom? Hearing stammering and vague responses I offer to provide the team with information on inclusive education, related services and supports and behavior management.

Trying again, I....
end up chasing my nine-year-old son down the street as he tries to "run away to New York City" (we live in Illinois!) for the fourth time this week. He is wearing only underwear. I am dragging him home; kicking, screaming, biting, (him) and crying (me). I restrain him for about an hour until we are both sweaty, sobbing and exhausted. He says, ""I'm sorry Mommy." I tell him I am sorry, too. We collapse in a heap and watch cartoons. I contemplate installing one of those "invisible fences for dogs, but reconsider because there is no place on my little Houdini that the collar would stay on. Instead I call that parent I met at a conference on my child's disability who mentioned a heavy duty spring loaded door lock—for the *inside* of the door and only when we are home, of course. Really now, who else besides other parents of "runners" that fear nothing and have no concept of danger would understand the sheer terror a mother feels as she hears the door slam just as she thought it was safe to take a two-minute shower? With whom

else could you discuss in all seriousness seeking AMA approval of tranquilizer darts for children?

I will get this done!!! But first I....
call my best friend to whine about how this is the fourth week I have set aside an afternoon to write this article, and it still isn't done! When she says, I know how you feel. I don't wince like I usually do when the nurse at the clinic says it. She really does know— her three kids have special needs, two of my four do. I wonder aloud if this wouldn't be the perfect time to commit a crime, a small one mind you, but one severe enough to warrant a few days of incarceration. No phone, no fax, no computer, no cooking,....no *kids*! She says it sounds too good to be true. She suggests that I better not chance it.

Anyway, I would have loved to express how valuable opportunities for self-help are to families of children with special needs. How they allow for the exchange of information parents glean from personal experience, professional contacts, support group and committee meetings, etc. as well as the very unique support only those who have "walked the walk" can give, but I guess it'll just have to wait for another afternoon....

"Mothers From Hell 2" is a national grassroots parent's organization facing the unique challenges of raising children with special needs with combustible humor; and advocating for disability rights...we will not be silenced!

ೞ ಐ

## A Self-Help Story... "The Rewards of A Personal Touch"
*- Contributed by Nancy H. Patterson, Grave's Disease Foundation*

The Graves' Disease Foundation provides a personal touch that is sorely needed by those when the diagnosis of a hyperactive thyroid comes along. Many of those people feel alone and frightened. In addition to the many physical changes that are ravaging their bodies, the emotional imbalance caused by the overactive thyroid hormones can cause tremendous upheaval. Many of our phone calls are late in the evening, take a long time, and the person on the other end is quite grateful. However, we do not always hear from them again. That makes the following e-mail a special indication of what we do:

*"I think it was you I spoke to on the phone a couple of months ago when I called the NGDF. I just wanted to say how wonderful you were, through my very hysterical time. I had been crying and unable to function for over three days due to false information I had been given. After my phone conversation with you, I felt a thousand times better and was able to calm down right away. Just wanted to thank you again for your calm, kind, and excellent information."*

This note was forwarded to one of our Board of Advisors at the Mayo Clinic, and his reply is the kind of thing that keeps us going on: "What a lovely indicator of the value of your work."

ೞ ಐ

# Chapter 2

# HOW TO START A SELF-HELP GROUP IN YOUR COMMUNITY

---

*"Never doubt that a small group of thoughtful, committed citizens can change the world: indeed it's the only thing that ever has."*
*- Margaret Mead*

---

## BASIC STEPS & SUGGESTIONS

Self-help groups offer people who face a common problem the opportunity to meet with others and share their experiences, knowledge, strengths and hopes. Run by and for their members, self-help groups can better be described as "mutual help" groups. Hundreds of these groups are started each week across the nation by ordinary people with a little bit of courage, a fair sense of commitment, and a heavy amount of caring. The following guidelines are based on our experience at the Self-Help Clearinghouse helping hundreds of individuals to start groups. While there is no one recipe for developing a group (different national groups offer different model approaches), here first is an overview of the general steps and strategies.

1.  **Don't Re-invent the Wheel.** If you are interested in starting a group around a particular concern or problem, find out what groups already exist for it. Check first in the Sourcebook for any national self-help groups that address your concern. Contact and ask them for what help and "how-to" starter packet information they can provide, and which of their groups might be closest to you. Then check with local community helplines serving your area to confirm there are no existing local groups that may address your issue, but are not affiliated with a national group (you can often find your local community helplines by calling your United Way at 1-800-411-8929). If you do have a local self-help clearinghouse in your area (see Chapter 6), contact them and learn how they can help you in starting a group

2.  **Think "Mutual-Help" From the Start.** Find a few others who share your interest in starting (not simply joining) a self-help group. Starting a group should not be on one person's shoulders alone. So, put out flyers or letters that specifically cite your interest in hearing from those who would be interested in "joining with others to help start" such a group. Include your first name and phone number. Make copies and post them at places you feel most appropriate, e.g., library, community center, or post office. Mail copies to key people whom you think would know others like yourself. When, hopefully, you receive calls, discuss with the caller what their

interests are, share your vision of what you would like to see the group do, and finally ask if they would be willing to share the work with you for a specific period of time to try to get the group off the ground. Suggest that their work could be greeting people at the door and introducing new members, bringing refreshments, making coffee, co-chairing or helping to run the meeting, etc. Once a couple of people have said yes, you have a "core group" or "steering committee" - and you won't have to do it alone. It's much easier to start a group if the work is shared. But most importantly, if several people are involved in the initial work at that first meeting (refreshments, publicity, name tags, greeting new people, etc.), you will model for newcomers what your self-help mutual aid group is all about - not one person doing it all, but the volunteer efforts and the active participation of all the members.

3.  **Find a Suitable Meeting Place and Time.** Try to obtain free meeting space at a local church, synagogue, library, community center, hospital or social service agency. If you anticipate a small group and feel comfortable with the idea, consider initial meetings in members' homes. Would evening or day meetings be better for members? Many prefer weeknights. It is also easier for people to remember the meeting time if it's a fixed day of the week or month, like the second Thursday of the month, etc.

4.  **Publicize & Run your First Public Meeting.** Reaching potential members is never easy. Depending upon the problem area, consider where potential members go. Would they be seen by particular doctors or agencies? Contacting physicians, clergy or other professionals can be one approach to try. Posting flyers in post offices, community centers, hospitals, and libraries is another. Free announcements in the community calendar sections of local newspapers can be especially fruitful. Consider simply calling the paper and asking to speak with an editor to suggest an article on the group and the issue. Editors are often grateful for the idea. The first meeting should be arranged so that there will be ample time for you to describe your interest and work, while allowing others the opportunity to share their feelings and concerns. Do those attending agree that such a group is needed? Will they attend another meeting, helping out as needed? What needs do they have in common that the group could address? Based on group consensus, you can make plans for your next meeting.

    If your group intends to have guest speakers, another idea for a first meeting is to arrange for a good speaker and topic that can be publicized well in advance. But be sure to build in time for people to discuss the speaker's points in light of their own experiences, i.e., after questions and answers with the speaker, have a discussion group or (if a large turnout) break into smaller discussion groups. Then come together as a full group and present the idea of continuing discussions as an ongoing self-help group.

5.  **Identify and Respond to the Felt Needs of Your Members.** If your group is new and doesn't follow a set program for helping members help one another, always

remember to plan your groups' activities and goals based upon the expressed needs of your members. Share your vision. At the very first meeting, go "round-robin" permitting each member an opportunity to say what they would like to see the group do. Then discuss these needs and come to a consensus as to which ones you will address first. Don't make the same mistake that some professionals make in professionally-run groups--of thinking that you know the members' needs without ever asking them. Remember to regularly ask your new members about their needs, and what they think the group might do to meet those needs. Similarly, be sure to avoid the pitfall of the core group members possible becoming a clique. The welcoming of new people into the group is a process that continues well beyond welcoming them at the door.

6.   **Future Meetings.** Other considerations for future meetings may be the following:

   -   *Defining the purpose(s) (mission) of the group in no more than two sentences.* Is it clear? You may want to add it to any flyer or brochure that you develop for the group. Some groups also include any guidelines that they have for their meetings right on their flyer or brochure.

   -   *Membership.* Who can attend meetings and who cannot? Do you want regular membership limited to those with the problem and an associate membership for spouses and family?

   -   *Meeting format.* What choice or combination of discussion time, education, business meeting, service planning, socializing, etc. best suits your group? What guidelines might you use to assure that discussions be non-judgmental, confidential and informative? Topics can be selected or guest speakers invited. A good discussion group size may be about 7 to 15. As your meeting grows larger, consider breaking down into smaller groups for discussion.

   -   *Ongoing use of professionals.* Consider using professionals as speakers, advisors, sources of needed space and services, educators, helpful gatekeepers, advocates, possible trainers, researchers, consultants to your group, or simply as sources of continued referrals. All you have to do is ask.

   -   *Help between meetings.* Many groups encourage the exchange of telephone numbers or a telephone list to provide members with help over the phone when it is needed between meetings. Older groups have a buddy system that pairs newcomers with veteran members.

   -   *Projects.* Begin with small projects, e.g. developing a flyer, obtaining newspaper coverage by calling editors, beginning a newsletter, etc. Rejoice and pat yourselves on the back when you succeed with these first projects. Then, if the group desires, work your way up to more difficult tasks and projects, e.g. planning a conference, advocating the introduction of specific legislation, developing a visitation program, etc.

- *Sharing responsibilities and nurturing new leaders.* You will want to look for all the different, additional roles that people can play in helping other members and making the group work, e.g., group librarian, arranging for speakers, greeter of new members, group liaison with an agency, etc. In asking for volunteers, it's easier to first ask the group what specific tasks they think would be helpful. If you haven't yet experienced it, you'll come to know the special "helper's high" satisfaction of helping others. Don't be selfish. Remember to let your members feel the fine satisfaction of helping others in the group. By sharing responsibilities you help create opportunities for others to become key members and leaders in the group.

- *Lastly, expect your group to experience regular "ups and downs"* in terms of attendance and enthusiasm. It's natural and to be expected. You may want to consider joining or forming a coalition or state association of leaders from the same or similar types of self-help groups, for your own periodic mutual support and for sharing program ideas and successes.

The suggestions above are the basic ones you need to know. We've added on the following pages other ideas related to starting and running a group.

*"Start your own community... It won't be easy. You'll be scared. You will often feel that you don't know what you're doing. You'll have a difficult time persuading people to join you...there will be anger, anxiety, depression, even despair. But keep going into the night. Don't stop halfway. It may seem like dying. But push on. And then suddenly you will find yourself in the clear of the mountaintop, and you'll be laughing and crying and feeling more alive than you have in years—maybe more alive than you've ever been. "*

- *M. Scott Peck, The Different Drum, 1987*

## ADDITIONAL IDEAS FOR RECRUITING GROUP CO-FOUNDERS AND/OR MEMBERS

In addition to those we suggested earlier, you and your group co-founders can consider these ideas for publicizing your group. Select which ones will be tried and who will be in charge of carrying each out.

- *Contact local agencies and associations* that address your area of concern, e.g., county office on aging or disability, United Way, YMCA, mental health association, etc. Ask if they would please mention your group at their next staff meeting. If they print a newsletter, ask if they would kindly mention your group in it.

- *Contact key professionals*: doctors, agency directors, social workers, clergy, media representatives, i.e., anyone who would be sympathetic to your need. Ask for their support and any ideas they may have for publicizing your group, e.g. their writing letters to other professionals or agencies or, if they have expertise or experience in your area, their willingness to be interviewed by a reporter.

- Simply pick up your phone and *call the local weekly/daily newspaper*, ask for an editor or reporter, request they consider doing an article, cite how unique and helpful your group will be, mention any professionals who support your work and would be willing to be interviewed too. If they only ask you to send them more information, include a double-spaced press release as an attachment that says:

    "SUPPORT GROUP ORGANIZING - Persons who/with _____ are invited to participate in a self-help support group that is being organized for the _____ area. Members of the group would share their experiences, coping skills, hopes, and successes. A meeting date and location will be determined by the response of interested participants. To become involved, or for more information, call (phone number) by (date)."

- If health related, *contact your local hospital's departments* that see members, e.g., social services dept., community health education dept., oncology dept., etc.. As with other professionals whom you contact, consider asking for their outreach suggestions, too.

- *Write a brief 10 second radio spot* and send it to local radio stations requesting they please air it as a public service announcement, or include it in their "Community Calendar" announcements.

- *Write a very brief community announcement ad* and send it to the *local cable TV* company(s) for posting on their community notices channel.

- If you know of any *websites* that publicize local events in your area, write the webmaster or post a message on any related message board. If you are developing a local group of a national organization, ask the national to list you at their website.

- *Talk to persons who have started similar groups* and ask what methods and contacts they found especially helpful in recruiting new group members.

- *Design and have printed a brochure* that explains the group's purpose and activities in greater detail than your flyer.

- *Call your local community helpline(s)* - make sure they know about, and have your group listed in their database.

- *Contact local churches* and ask that they please post a flyer or mention your group in their bulletin/newsletters.

- *Write a "letter to the editor"* describing your group (it is more likely to be printed if you comment on a current article or editorial that relates to your issue).

- Finally, ask yourselves, *"Is there another good way we can reach potential members?"*


*"You alone can do it —
but you can't do it alone."*
*- O. Hobart Mowrer*


*"None of us is as smart as all of us."*
*-Ziggy*

## SUGGESTIONS FOR LOCATING A MEETING SPACE

The most obvious place to have a small meeting, especially a first meeting of your core group, is in someone's home. If you expect more people than such a space can hold, or if you personally prefer not to open your home to people who are (initially) strangers, consider the possibilities listed below:

- *Churches* are the most common public meeting place for self-help groups and seem the most cooperative. In requesting space, a personal connection is the best (know anyone who is a member?), and could mean no charge initially - so work through personal contacts you or your core group may have (the pastor or rabbi ). Otherwise, just phone local churches. More and more churches have been requiring a minimal donation to go towards heating and utilities.

- *Hospitals* are another option, especially if your group is health related. An advantage is that hospital space is usually free, but for this reason space on a regular basis is in short supply Begin by contacting the administrative office or the community relations department to request a meeting space.

- *Community organizations or agencies* such as community centers, counseling centers, YMCA/YWCA, Red Cross, Salvation Army, veterans organization hall, senior citizens centers, and others will sometimes provide space free of charge for self-help group meetings. Your local library or daycare centers and schools, bank, municipal town hall or community college are other facilities where self-help groups hold meetings. Again, if anyone in your initial group personally knows a staff member or officer, it helps.

Availability of a kitchen or a sink with running water is desirable for making coffee or other refreshments. It is helpful to place chairs in a circle or around a table. In this way, members may face each other and the atmosphere is friendlier and more supportive. A table can serve to display books, pamphlets, announcements and other printed materials. A small storage space can also be helpful for storing supplies, etc., if one could be made available.

When inquiring about a meeting place, be sure to communicate the fact that your group is a voluntary, non-profit organization that intends to provide a service to the public free of charge. Be clear on the specific nights that you would like your meetings to take place, how long they will be, and who will be responsible for opening and closing the facility. Such attention to detail will serve you and your group well!

> *"If they're anything, support groups are low maintenance. They don't require a lot of equipment, or complicated setups, or specially-designed facilities. Basically they call for a bit of quiet, a bit of privacy, and a few people who are ready to say something meaningful to one another. Consequently, support groups can function fairly well in a variety of places."*
>
> - James E. Miller, <u>Effective Support Groups</u>, p. 23.

45

## IDEAS FOR STRUCTURING YOUR GROUP MEETING

Meeting formats for self-help groups vary from loosely structured discussion groups to more formally structured meetings that follow the traditional program of the national group (e.g., "12-Step groups"). There is no one right way to plan a meeting. The following activities are common to some self-help group meetings and can be used as an initial guide for structuring your meeting. It's not necessary to incorporate every activity mentioned here in each meeting agenda.

As people arrive at the meeting room, be sure that at least one member is there to...

**Welcome New Members:** It is a practice of many self-help groups that a volunteer member greets and welcomes new members at the door when they arrive, introducing them to other members, especially those who are in a similar situation.

1.  **Start the Meeting:** Shortly after the agreed upon time, the meeting should be called to order by the leader for that night. Some groups open their meetings with a welcoming statement, a reading of the group's purpose and/or a meeting guidelines, and/or an outline of what the agenda is for that meeting.

2.  **Introduction of Members or "Check-In":** Going around the room, each member can introduce himself/herself briefly (often just giving a first name) and may state their reason for coming to the group or, if not the first meeting, how they have been doing since the last meeting.

3.  **Basic Discussion or Another Activity:** For a first meeting, members can take turns (going around in a circle) indicating what they would like to see this group do, the key topics they would like to see discussed, any group speakers they would like to hear on those issues, and other major activities or problems that they would suggest the group address. Be aware of the fact that often those people, who bring up a special issue, may be knowledgeable enough to share with members what they know about the topic. In other words, you might ask if they would spend time talking about what they know the topic at a future meeting.

    - **Regular Group Discussion and/or Guest Speaker.** For discussion, selecting one or more discussion questions ahead of time is one possibility (see separate handout, "Possible Discussion Topics & Questions"). Another idea, you could have a book or an article reviewed by a member who reports on it, and then the group might discuss any questions raised. Playing a short but good tape recording of a presentation, TV or radio program is another way to trigger group discussion. If you decide to have a guest speaker at one of your meetings, consider having time for group discussion that would give members an opportunity to comment upon on the speaker's points that, based upon their experience, they found most important.

- **Goal Setting** Some groups set aside some time after discussion for goal-setting - that is, each member who is willing, sets a personal goal that they they hope to meet by the next meeting. Then at the next meeting, they can report back on how they did.

4. **Business/Planning Portion**: If included, this time could be set aside for any business the group wishes to take up, such as planning or reporting upon projects or activities (to include any advocacy efforts by the group or members), arranging for future meetings (choosing discussion topics/guest, speakers, etc.), making announcements, and collection of any dues or voluntary contributions by "passing the hat."

5. **Wrap-Up or "Check-Out"**: This is an opportunity for the leader of this meeting to summarize the meeting discussion and ask if any members need to say anything left unsaid from the meeting, whether it be an insight or an expression of thanks. Members are then reminded of time and place of next meeting.

6. **Formal Closing:** It is helpful when you have some signal or tradition that the meeting is formally closing, e.g., a closing statement, or other ritual at the end of each meeting, e.g., joint reading of the serenity prayer, "God grant me the Serenity to accept the things I cannot change, the courage to change... etc.".

7. **After the meeting, refreshments** are often served, providing an opportunity for informal but often very helpful conversations. After the meeting, in some groups, members have the opportunity to go to a diner for coffee. If this is the case, always invite new members and avoid the appearance of cliquishness that turns off newcomers.

*"The major reason for meeting is sharing. You may not want to do this all the time, but never stray too far or too long from this simple and basic function of the meetings... While every person should have the chance to talk, those with the greatest need will use a greater share of the time. Others should be encouraged to provide feedback including any similar experiences, alternative solutions, and support. Those providing advice and support will surely feel helped by virtue of their having been helped themselves... Some groups designate certain meetings for discussions of topics or special educational programs. .. There is no correct answer about what is the best format for a particular group's meetings. The group must decide for itself what is best for them. No two groups are alike; therefore their needs and goals will differ."*

*- Wendy Miller Resnick, The Manual for Affective Disorder Support Groups, The Depression & Related Affective Disorders Association, 1988.*

47

## SAMPLE GUIDELINES FOR GROUP DISCUSSION

Self-help groups should provide an atmosphere of caring, sharing and support for their members. In help , here are some basic guidelines used by groups. Choose or adapt any of those below. To insure that all members are familiar with them, some groups have a member briefly read the main points (in bold below) at the start of each meeting.

- **We start and end our meetings on time.** We try to arrive on time, because people arriving late can sometimes be disruptive. We also need to respectful of people's time and also end the meeting on time.

- **We keep confidential all personal information shared in the group.** What we share about our personal lives and experiences is to be kept absolutely confidential by all members. So, "what is said in the group stays in the group."

- **No interrupting or side conversations.** It is important that we actively listen when someone is talking and avoid interruptions or side conversations (so no "crosstalk").

- **Use "I" statements.** We encourage all members to speak in the first person, using "I" statements, because we know that we learn when each of us shares our different experiences.

- **Don't give advice.** We do not prescribe, diagnose, judge, or give advice. Rather we respect each member's right to reach and make their own personal decisions. So we listen, we speak as to what has worked for us in similar circumstances, and we help members to recognize and explore their options.

- **Share what helps you.** While we present the special problems we face, we all make a special effort to share our successes, coping skills, insights, strengths, and hopes - no matter how small.

- **No monopolizing the group's time.** By talking for long periods of time or talking too frequently, we are disrespectful of the need for all members to participate.

- **Members have the right not to speak.** In our group discussions, each person always has the right to pass on any question that he or she prefers not to answer.

*"To deal with any controversial issues that might divide a group, we should begin by clearly stating the purpose of the group and the way this group goes about its interaction. For example, a parents' support group might have this as part of their purpose; 'Our Parents' Mutual Aid Group meets to aid parents in dealing with their unique concerns as parents. In that spirit, we are not here to take positions about what is right or wrong for another parent. Rather, our purpose is to help all parents examine the implications of the decisions they choose to make. Room for a variety of points of view and ways of doing things will always be provided.'"*     - Ted Bowman, national group trainer

# DISCUSSION TOPICS

While well-established groups usually have developed structured exercises to help members share their experiences, strengths, hopes, coping skills, and practical information, other groups simply plan initial group discussions on the basis of their members' common needs and interests. Consider surveying the members and have them name those topics that interest them the most. Then members can take turns at different meetings to simply introduce a chosen topic by giving a brief summary of the issue and then introducing discussion questions. If they need to prepare, they can read up on the topic or ask other members about their experiences or perspectives on it. Topics could range from education to advocacy issues, but the most important point is that the topic be based on the needs of your members.

Discussion can also be based on a specific question, as determined by members beforehand. Some sample questions are provided here. Members may want to review them and pick those they would most like to schedule for discussion. For the discussion, members can go "round-robin," taking turns answering, following a clockwise motion around the room. Another way is the "popcorn" approach, when members simply speak up when they feel ready to speak (or "pop") until everyone has had a chance to respond. Also, it's important that the group shouldn't be too large, to be sure to allow each person the opportunity to talk. If you feel your group is too large, consider breaking into smaller groups.

Remember that the purpose of asking these questions is to help individuals share, think about, and learn from each others' experiences and insights. There are no right or wrong answers, only answers reflecting the different personal responses and perspectives of people coping with the stresses and challenges. The following questions are just examples. The best questions are ones your members develop. Try to phrase questions so they will reveal positive answers.

1. Who has been most supportive to me in helping me deal with this situation? What have they done or said that has helped me the most? What has been the worst advice given me.

2. How do I handle the issue of whether and when to tell others about my situation - in social situations, the workplace, and elsewhere?

3. What did I used to think about people who had this problem before I knew I had it? What's the most important point that the public should know about this that they don't know now? How can or should they best be taught?

4. What am I most proud of, as it relates to my coping with this situation - either personal traits, coping skills, or accomplishments that help me deal with the small (and large) problems.

5.  What would I say in a note or a letter to someone (or their spouse/family) who was facing what I have faced?

6.  Generally, how has my life changed? What new values and priorities do I have now that I did not have before?

7.  In what ways does the life event or illness control my life? In what ways have I learned ways to regain control of my life?

8.  For what in my life am I most grateful? What do I now like most about my life?

9.  What long term goals have I set for my life? What is the major goal and how do I plan to reach it?

10. If I have learned anything special about life or human nature as a result of my situation, what is it?

*"The best way to have a good idea is to have a lot of ideas."*
*-Linus Pauling, M.D.*

*"Don't ever forget the power of listening and the strength it takes to be there - not curing but caring... The world is in need of listeners."*
*- Bernie Siegel, M.D.*

*"With the gift of listening comes the gift of healing, because listening to your brothers or sisters until they have said the last words in their hearts is healing and consoling."*
*- Catherine de Hueck Doherty*

*"Mutual empathy is the great unsung human gift."*
*- Jean Baker Miller, MD & Irene P. Stiver, PhD*

## "ONE PERSON ALONE SIMPLY CANNOT DO IT"
## SHARING THE WORKLOAD

You know you can't do everything, and in a "mutual aid" group you shouldn't - unless you want to set yourself up for probable burnout. Also, if you have been helping people, you already know how good you feel after you help them - so don't be selfish and keep all those good feelings to yourself! Other members need to become involved and share the work. Research shows that the longer-lasting self-help groups are the ones where the responsibilities are shared. Be sure to remind members that "The responsibility for running our group can't be just on one person's shoulders, we all need to help out." Others can co-lead the meeting with you, greet people at the door, and bring refreshments.

The key to getting people involved and helping out in your group can be expressed in one word, "ownership." Who owns the group? The extent to which people perceive the group as truly "their group," will influence how much they will invest their time and efforts in helping their group to survive and prosper. But if they view the group as belonging to just one person, be that person a lay leader or a professional, they will tend to be passive and let that person continue to do all the work. When several people are seen helping out at meetings, they model for newcomers what your self-help mutual aid group is all about - not one person doing it all, but a group that depends on the active participation of its members. This is why, if you're starting a group, it's especially important to seek out a couple of other people who will help out in promoting and running that first meeting.

In delegating responsibility, you always run the risk that the work may not be done, or done quite the way you would do it. But if you don't delegate, you run an even greater risk of not believing in or nurturing the abilities of your members.

If you have an existing group, a first step in getting more help is to identify, name and describe the jobs that will help your group fulfill its purpose. Write them down (see samples under "Volunteer Opportunities With Our Group," p. 55). In each description, be clear as to what tasks are involved. "*Fear of the unknown*" is one of man's greatest fears. The clearer the job duties, the easier it is to get people to accept responsibility for doing "*that*". But recognize, too, that not all jobs have to be written down. There are always a good number of short-term project opportunities that will arise.

### WAYS TO GET MEMBERS TO HELP OUT

1.  **Ask them personally on a one-to-one basis in private.** Ask if they would like to serve in a specific job. Be sure to indicate why you think they would be good for that position, and how you or someone else will help them if they have a question or problem. If they give you a time-limited excuse (e.g., a family obligation over the next two months), note it, and approach them again after the given time.

2.  Whenever possible, **give members a choice of two jobs,** but allow them to volunteer for another job.

3.  Always **specify how long** they will be expected to serve, e.g., until the end of the year. You may want to consider a fixed term of service for all jobs, e.g., one year.

4.  If you encounter problems in finding someone to do a specific job, **ask for two people to volunteer to share the responsibility** of that job. Some people will more willingly accept if they know the work won't be all on their shoulders.

5.  Similarly, some groups have difficulty getting someone to volunteer to be the "president." **Having two "Co-leaders"** may be less intimidating to reluctant group members. On the other hand, we know of at least one group that attracts members by giving everyone who volunteers for a job the title of "vice-president of ........."

6.  Be sure to continuously **acknowledge people publicly** for the jobs/tasks accomplished. This can be done at meetings, through newsletters, on a web page, or by awarding certificates of appreciation.

7.  While not as good as a request in person, you can consider **circulating a sign-up sheet** at a meeting, or in a mailing (see "Volunteer Opportunities With Our Group" section). But don't depend on that one method alone.

8.  In addition to a "sign-up sheet" above, another idea is a **skills/contacts sheet**. Members could list any special skills or knowledge they have (worked with media, computer techie, typing, etc.), and any special personal contacts (brother is a printer, son is a lawyer, etc.). Use the list to tap members for jobs and projects. The skills category may provide new and exciting positions (e.g., if someone writes "give great parties" sign them up for being the Holiday party chairperson!).

9.  **When people resign from their volunteer position, ask them to suggest a good replacement.** Also, ask them for feedback on how they would evaluate their experience. Their positive comments could be used to encourage others to take the position; and any suggestions they offer should be seriously considered.

10. **Always nurture new potential volunteers.** Find small jobs (e.g., handing out brochures, doing photocopying, etc.) that will give people a small but initial opportunity to help out in the group.

*"Expect people to be better than they are; it helps them to become better.*
*But don't be disappointed when they are not; It helps them to keep trying."*
*- Merry Browne*

*(Following is a sample Handout - Rewrite it to Meet Your Group's Needs)*

## VOLUNTEER OPPORTUNITIES WITH OUR GROUP

Every self-help support group depends upon its members' involvement to keep the group running. Please help us to continue our meetings by offering to volunteer for any of the following tasks (check any you would be willing to serve in). You would be volunteering to serve in a position until (date)_____. If you have any questions or need further information, just speak to _____ .

❑ **Greeter** - Arrives early to welcome new members at the door, explains how the meeting will run, tries to answer any questions, introduces them to the other members - especially those with similar experiences. Handles name tags, if group decides they want to use them.

❑ **Refreshments Coordinator** - Arranges for refreshments at meetings, makes coffee (if desired by group), arranges for and sets out "goodies" and hospitality supplies. Initially, this job might be combined or shared with "greeter."

❑ **Phone Contact person(s)** - Ideally, we should have two or three people taking calls from our group flyers, ads, etc. The contact person gives potential members meeting time, location and directions, basic information, and encourages caller to come to the meeting to see how the group works. Be prepared with local helpline numbers and/or other resources, if caller needs any immediately.

❑ **Outreach/Publicity Coordinator** - Gets the word out! Arranges for meeting notices in newspapers, distribution and posting of flyers; does special mailings, press releases, etc. Might occasionally speak before community groups or at professional agency staff meetings.

❑ **Librarian** - Arrives a few minutes early to put out materials or copies of information, resources and events (which might be stored at meeting site, if possible); replenishes literature as needed, checks out books, collects payment/donations for materials.

❑ **Liaison person(s)** - Maintains contact with a specific local, state or national organization (ideally with a staff member at that organization), receives their newsletter, updates members on the news, events and services. For which organization(s): _____ .

❑ **Newsletter Editor** - Compiles newsletter with help of co-leaders and other members, writes/finds articles or help with the writing, organizes the printing and mailing.

❑ **Webmaster** - maintains the group's website, providing information on the group and its work, best website links, future events, recognition, projects, newsletter, etc. Self-

53

help groups can sometimes get free web space from newspaper or community websites.

❑ **Secretary** - Keeps list (maybe computer list) of active members, mails out meeting notice reminders with any topic before each meeting, composes and mails out any letters to include "thank you" notes if speakers are used, handles any responses. Works with treasurer.

❑ **Treasurer** - Collects/deposits contributions (passing a donations basket around towards end of meeting) or collects/deposits dues if there are any. If group needs a checking account, writes checks, and reconciles any monthly bank statement. Works with secretary.

❑ **Co-Leader** - A Co-Leader shares or rotates the responsibility for running the meetings. They arrange for the meeting space. They stay in touch with national office (if there is one). May assume any of the duties below when there is no member yet assigned.

❑ **Other** (handling special projects or events): _____ (fill in space as needed by your group).

> *"No one can be the best at everything.*
> *But when all of us combine our talents,*
> *we can and will be the best at virtually anything."*
> *- Dan Zadra*

---

## A CAUTION

As a founder of a new group, members naturally will look to you for answers and guidance. Be careful not to become "the expert." Redirect questions put to you to the group. Remember that's why they call it a "support group," and not a "support person." Work to pull together the collective wisdom that can be found in mutual aid self-help groups when members pool together their experiences, resources and insights. You can take great pride and satisfaction in your volunteer work when you see members helping one another through the group you started.

If you are looking for additional reading, one of the better references is <u>Effective Support Groups: How to Plan, Design, Facilitate and Enjoy Them</u> by James E. Miller, Willowgreen Publishing, 1998, 64 pages, $6.95.

---

## DEVELOPING SELF-HELP GROUPS:
## TEN STEPS & SUGGESTIONS FOR PROFESSIONALS

Among the variety of roles that professionals play in support of self-help groups - which range from providing referrals, to being a guest speaker or serving as a group advisor - no role is more challenging and productive over the long term than that of helping to create a new, free, on-going self-help group. It appears that about one out of every three self-help groups is started with some help from a professional. By the very nature of his or her work and specialty, the professional is in a favorable position to identify and link persons who have the potential to start a mutual help group.

For most professionals helping to start a free, on-going self-help group, the task involves their assuming what very well may be a new type of professional role--that of a consultant in a group organization. The following serves as an overview of ten basic steps that the professional can follow in helping self-help groups organize. These are suggested guidelines that have proven helpful to many professionals. It represents one general approach. Actual group development and the sequence of steps may vary slightly, based upon choice of a particular self-help group model or other special circumstances, preferences or opportunities. The ten steps are to:

1.  Acquire a Basic Understanding of Self-Help Group Dynamics and Benefits. The professional who contemplates starting a self-help group is probably already aware of the general needs for such a group (e.g., social support, experiential knowledge, normalization, shared coping skills, helper-therapy, positive role models, etc.) and has recognized the way in which the group could supplement professional services. The professional needs to familiarize him/herself with the basic understanding of self-help group dynamics, and how they differ from professionally-run therapy or support groups. For a better understanding as to how self-help groups operate as mutual help organizations, the professional can refer to readings on mutual help (see bibliographical section). An excellent way to learn is simply to attend a local group that has meetings open to professionals.

2.  Assess Current Groups and Models. If you have determined that a need exists for a particular type of self-help group, check as to what national or model self-help groups may already exist for that problem. At the same time, you also want to confirm that there is no local chapter or similar group already existing in your immediate area. A variety of these national and model self-help groups print development manuals or helpful "How to Start" guideline materials that you should obtain and review.

3.  Identify Persons Interested in Starting a Group. Identify at least two former/current patients or clients who have experienced the problem, and who express an interest "in starting" a group. Simply having persons interested "in joining" a group is not sufficient. Ideally you will want to include "veterans" who have had greater experience at coping with the problem and are willing to help others. Some opportunities for locating potential group founders include: contacts with other professionals and agencies; announcements at the conclusion of educational

55

programs or conferences on the topic; and registration of your specific group interest in starting a group with your local self-help clearinghouse if there is one.

4.   Form a Core Group. Once several persons have been identified, the next step is to have a preliminary meeting to organize these persons into a "core group." The professional will want to confirm their interest and emphasize that this is a "mutual help" effort to create a mutual help group. All members of the core group should be expected to contribute in some way to the development of the group by sharing in the work. They should make this commitment to one another, possibly for a specific period of time.

5.   Clarify and Negotiate the Relationship. It is important at this preliminary meeting to clarify the professional's role in relationship to the development of the group. The most appropriate role for the professional to assume at this stage is that of a consultant. A common pitfall for professionals is to continue at this time to play the traditional role of leader, which promotes ongoing dependence on the professional, while also stifling the member's own sense of responsibility and ownership that spark the very energy and dynamics of most mutual help groups. The role of the consultant, the types of assistance available, and a time frame for providing consultation, should be explained and agreed upon with members of the core group. The consultation would focus primarily on group organization, but also might include help in resource identification, skills building, program development, and collaboration in problem solving. As in the case of any consultant, the professional provides advice and counsel, but does not assume responsibility for leadership, decision making or group tasks, unless the group requests such assistance. Some groups refer to this as being "on tap, not on top." The importance of the members themselves taking responsibility for the group, and the professional serving in an ancillary role, is key.

6.   Advise on Planning and Publicizing First Public Meeting. With the consultative relationship established, members of the core group should turn their attention to their first project - the first general meeting of the self-help group. Core group members should share responsibilities for the meeting. This they can do by sharing tasks such as serving as co-chairpersons, making arrangements for the meeting space, serving as greeter, making refreshments and coffee, etc. Shared responsibilities reduce the high risk of "one leader burn-out" that is often faced when only one person assumes the responsibilities. More importantly, at that first meeting core members will "model," by their shared volunteer activities, what mutual help is--not one person doing it all, but shared responsibilities and contributions by members. Core group members can begin work on publicity, letters to the editor, putting notices in church bulletins, printing and distribution of flyers, etc. The professional can assist in promoting referrals to this first meeting by contacts with other key professionals, agencies and associations.

7.   Assist at the First Meeting. A professional's participation in the first meeting may vary from providing moral support to core group members who are chairing the meeting to addressing the group as a speaker, or possibly even being a co-leader if

56

necessary. The role should be minimal in order to allow the group to exercise and develop its own group competencies. Time should be allowed for all members to introduce themselves and describe the needs they feel the group might address. It will take several meetings of trust-building before members take more initiative in contributing to group discussion and work. At the close of the first meeting there should be general consensus on the needs for a group and agreement on a suitable site and time for a second meeting. It is easier for people to remember future meeting times if it is held on a particular day of the week or month, e. g., the second Thursday of the month.

8.  Advise on Plans for Subsequent Meetings and Continued Organizational Development. The format for future meetings should include a portion of time devoted to the "business" of developing the organization, as well as discussion. Many groups include guest speakers, films, or special service projects as part of their educational program for members. For example, one service would be the establishment of an audio tape library of guest speaker presentations. Another would be development of a lending library of books and medical articles on the specific problem the group addresses. Future projects may include community education and visitation programs. The organizational structure for the group may be as formal or informal as members prefer--with or without elected officers and written by-laws. But general guidelines for group meetings and discussion, which the professional can help the group develop, are often helpful. Another helpful resource that the group can begin to develop is that of a professional advisory committee. The group itself may decide to establish several working committees, e.g., program, publicity, or study committees, to examine needs that were prioritized at the first meeting.

9.  Identify and Address Any Special Problems. With any consultation there often is the need to "trouble-shoot" or address new problems as they arise. The professional, as a consultant, can be very helpful in advising the group of solutions to problems that they may encounter, e. g., handling a member who dominates discussion, or increasing membership through better publicity. Problem solving should usually be a collaborative effort with members. It is also important to note the responsibility for addressing these problems should continue to be focused on group competencies, rather than too quickly providing professional intervention at times critical to group development.

10.  Review and Evaluate Role. At the conclusion of the consultation time period, an assessment of the consultation and a reassessment of the professional role should take place jointly between the consultant and consultee. If the group is operating without problems, the consultation may be terminated. At the request of the group, the professional may remain available on an ad hoc basis as a consultant. He or she may also assume a somewhat different role, such as a resource or agency liaison person who may continue to attend meetings to answer questions related more to their expertise rather than group process issues. At other times the professional may be called upon to assume additional temporary roles, such as serving as a trainer in skills-building.

In summary, an important factor in the development of a viable and self-sustaining mutual help group is the need for the professional to assume a consultation role. This permits the group members to assume responsibilities for the operation of the organization, for exercising and developing group competencies, and for addressing the felt and unmet needs of its members. The extent to which members perceive the group as "their own" will directly determine the amount of responsibility they take for it and the amount of investment they make in it. The importance of self-help, as ultimately reflected in the members' ability to take responsibility for the group, is crucial to developing and realizing many of the unique benefits that self-help groups have to offer.

C3 80

*"Today, the benefits of mutual aid are experienced by millions of people who turn to others with a similar problem to attempt to deal with their isolation, powerlessness, alienation, and the awful feeling that nobody understands...The future of health care in these troubled times requires cooperation between organized medicine and self-help groups to achieve the best care for the lowest cost...Health and human service providers are learning that they can indeed provide a superior service when they help their patients and clients find appropriate peer support."*

Former Surgeon General C. Everett Koop, for the Forward of the book, Self-Help: Concepts and Applications, Charles Press, 1992, p. xviii.

## LEARNING FROM "THOSE WHO HAVE BEEN THERE" A FEW STORIES ABOUT GROUP DEVELOPMENT

Here are stories of ordinary people who, after facing adversity, started self-help group. If not for the dedication and compassion of such persons, self-help groups could not exist. It is through such commitment and perseverance that our face-to-face communities and cybercommunities continue to grow to help so many in extraordinary ways.

### "Support Groups: Building a Bridge of Hope"
*Linda S. Webb, Southern District Director/BEBRF, Inc.*

Seven years ago, I was diagnosed with benign essential blepharospasm, a rare disorder. It is a chronic, unremitting, bilateral, forceful closure of the eyelid. It is due to involuntary muscle contractions caused by misfiring of neutrons within the central nervous system, and involves the fifth and seventh cranial nerves. At this time, there is no known cause nor cure. The spasms are out of a person's control and can render them functionally blind.

For two years, I suffered not knowing what was wrong with me and neither did the physicians I saw. Once a person is diagnosed with this disorder, it takes time to recover from the hurt, anger and frustrations of such a baffling condition. I decided that I was not going to sit on my good intentions while others were sitting there in the dark like myself.

I began to talk with churches, the library, and finally my physician, who helped me get in touch with the right person at the local hospital. After much searching, we found a place to have a support group meeting. Support groups are very healthy, and I found that I was with individuals, like myself, who understood and knew what I was going through. Having this devastating disorder helped me realize how important support from family, friends and groups can be.

I have used this as a tool rather than an adversity; whereby, I have received so many blessings from others by just reaching out. Through much thought and effort by a great "pioneer," Mattie Lou Koster, who founded the Benign Essential Blepharospasm Research Foundation, Inc. (P.O. Box 12468, Beaumont, Texas 77726-2468). Mattie Lou's great endeavors instilled in me the willingness to help others. I was asked to become Alabama's State Coordinator and Southern District Director for BEBRF, Inc. I began my journey upward rather than being just a sinking vessel.

I have started the Blepharo Buddies Awareness Support Group of Alabama. Our support group meets quarterly in Huntsville, AL. From there, several groups began to spring up, created just by caring people.

A very important thing to remember is publicity plays one of the greatest parts in finding new patients, as well as informing physicians and lay community.

In starting a support group, two essential elements are needed: a *caring heart* and *helping hands*. We each have gifts that have been given to us, and we need to step out on faith and put those to good works.

By relating patient-to-patient, we soon build a bridge of *hope*, where we can walk hand-in-hand with each other. Support groups teach us to believe in ourselves. We must first love "me" before we can love "others." Through all of this, I have found a few pearls along the way; some have stayed and some have gone, others have left "footprints" on my heart.

Ralph Waldo Emerson said, "A friend is the hope of the heart." Being with other individuals, we bring hope to one another and the bridge gets easier to cross.

Emily Dickinson said, "Hope is the thing with feathers that perches in the soul, and sings the tunes without the words, and never stops at all."

I thank God every day for support groups, where they have helped me become focused and positive in my every day walk of like.

In closing, no, I do not have PMS,. I have PMA (Positive Mental Attitude).

రాజ ౬౦

## "From Out of Despair Emerges a Self-Help Group"
*Terry S., Cleptomanics And Shoplifters Anonymous*

Hi, my name is Terry and I'm a recovering shoplifter. I began shoplifting in my late teens in reaction to increasing anger and depression, and specific and general feelings of life being unfair. My father was alcoholic and my parents divorced when I was ten. My father never really worked through his disease and I felt I was always living on the edge. I felt the shame of having an alcoholic father and a divorced family. I tried to grow up early and take care of my mother and younger brother and ended up co-dependent, always trying to help others and neglecting my own needs and stuffing my anger.

I felt like my childhood was stolen from me. In addition, I also had several important items (comic books, bikes, skateboards) stolen from me when I was a teen. I was a time bomb and the explosion would take the form of stealing. I stole a few comic books to try to get back what was stolen from me. By senior year of high school I was devastated when a girlfriend broke up with me. I also had a bad case of acne and was anxious about going to college. I started shoplifting, followed by a feeling of guilt and shame. A cycle developed. I knew it was wrong but I felt compelled to engage in this behavior and develop a secret life. It was as if a dam had broken loose, like Mr. Hyde had to have his say just as my Dr. Jekyl had.

I stopped when I got into college. Wanting to turn over a new leaf but midway through I experienced another romantic rejection and generalized depression. I started to engage in some employee theft and then back to shoplifting. I was soon arrested and was terrified. I was given little punishment and thought I was cured. Six months later, after I was off probation, I was out shoplifting again almost daily. I was shoplifting mainly small things (magazines, cassette tapes, food, toiletries). But I was getting a high from it and, again, found it hard to stop.

Three years later I was out of control. I hit bottom after another romantic break-up and felt suicidal. I told my parents I needed to see a counselor. I also told them I'd been shoplifting over the last six years. Thus began the long road to recovery. It was through therapy that I began to understand that the shoplifting was actually an addictive behavior. I was using it to avoid feelings and dealing with underlying issues. I started attending other support groups because there were no groups in the Detroit area for shoplifting addicts. I knew, one day, I'd have to start my own. In 1992, I started C.A.S.A. (Cleptomaniacs And Shoplifters Anonymous), and independent, weekly self-help group. Apparently, there are only a handful of such groups in the U.S. (or around the world for that matter). I started a webpage five years ago (www.shoplifteranoymous.com) and have received nearly a thousand inquiries during this time and several thousand website hits in the last year alone. I have been in the local and national media to bring this subject out into the open. I have written a book which I hope to get published one day.

Starting a group was not easy. I knew I had to be well enough and committed enough to make it work. I secured a meeting place at a local church, reassuring them that the group was legitimate. I then made up a flyer and distributed it to all the local courts and many counseling offices, attorney's offices and churches. It is important to include your first name and telephone number on the flyer in case anyone wants to verify information. I also got an article in the local paper around December 1992 to promote the group I have found that the media pays attention more during the holiday season.

Our favorite group saying is, "There's no such thing as something for nothing; there's always a cost in the end."

CS ଠD

## "You Don't Have to Do It Alone"
*Sue Schoenfeld, Endometriosis Support Group Leader*

Living in constant pain and not having anyone to talk to can certainly get the best of anyone. When I first began having severe pain a few days a week, and then every day, I thought I was going to lose my mind. Sure, I had support from family and friends, but even some of them were skeptical. And why shouldn't they be? After all, the doctors were telling me that I was fine and there was nothing wrong with me. Yet I had been convinced for the 5½ years before I was diagnosed that I had endometriosis.

Although I had a supportive husband, family members, and friends I could talk to, it certainly wasn't the same as talking to another woman who had endometriosis and could really empathize with what I was going through. Let's face it—unless they are going through it themselves, they don't really understand the pain and the anguish you are going through. I also found that a lot of people got irritated if I brought it up too much. They would listen for short periods of time but would then get aggravated at me. Not to mention that talking about the disease and the symptoms are so personal. It certainly wasn't easy to just talk to anyone about it.

Shortly after I was diagnosed, I became a member of the International Endometriosis Association. Reading the newsletter and realizing that so many women had dealt with or were dealing with the same things I was going through, gave me an incredible sense of relief. I no longer felt so alone and could now dismiss the myth that all women were going through this. Naturally, I wish I had found the association during the years I was struggling to be diagnosed. I believe it would have helped tremendously with my mental state.

A year later, I decided to start up a support group. Being a shy and private person my whole life, I certainly wasn't sure if I could do it but I wanted to make the effort. I had been through so many ups and downs in my life and was at a point where I really needed to do something positive. I wanted to provide an atmosphere where women could talk about the disease and not feel like they were constantly being judged. And I hoped that I could spare some women the emotional turmoil I felt when I kept being told that there was nothing wrong with me.

Of course, not everyone is comfortable speaking about their problems in front of groups. For those who feel that this is not a feasible option for them, there are other ways for you to receive support from others. There are e-mail support groups and online chats that serve the same purpose. There are also plenty of individuals who are willing to provide support. There is certainly no reason for you to have to do it alone. There is help out there!

C3 80

## An Inner Voice and a Promise Kept
### *- Mary Slaman-Forsythe, TTTS Foundation*

My advice to another who is drawn and pulled to start a support group is to trust your inner voice. God bless women with intuition that men don't have. That inner voice inside is God speaking to you, and you must trust it. If you can dream it, the rest will be easy. You will find a way even if the path is yet paved.

I know this to be true because I started an international non-profit organization from a promise to my twins Matthew Steven and Steven James on the day they born December 7, 1989. Promised them that they would be known and remembered and that I would find the answers. I had a placental disorder called twin to twin transfusion syndrome (TTTS) during my pregnancy with them. The babies are perfectly normal and healthy, but there is an abnormality in how the placenta nourishes them. Matthew Steven survived; Steven James did not. My love for them both will always be; I knew that I could never bare another family hearing that nothing could be done as I heard. When I thought to do a fund-raiser for the disease, a friend told me I could do it. It was the emotional support that I needed to truly make my promise come true. I did not know how to start a non-profit but did it anyway. The passion was there and that is truly all you need. We have raised over $300,000 for the fight against this disease and have counseled thousands.

62

Because of two little boys, Matthew and Steven, this disease will be eradicated in my lifetime.

As I was gaining confidence and self-esteem after Steven passed away, I attended a bereavement group at a hospital. In the group were two other women who had lost a twin. Without any words, they understood my sorrow, the continued pain and anguish and joy from raising a surviving twin. Because of them I knew that I was not alone. I wanted my non-profit to give that back to the families, help them recognize that they were not alone going, nor were they just a "textbook pregnancy" going through this diagnosis, along with helping them learn that there were many things they could do to try to save their babies.

What is most ironic is that I did not know how to start a non-profit organization, I learned because my passion fueled me; my promise to my twin babies helped me never to give into the ultimate fear that I would not succeed. After five years of being up and running, I got my masters in non-profit management. I could have taught those courses from simple experience.

If it has never been done before, pave the path yourself. If you can dream it, you can make it happen. God will bring people into your life to help you.

The biggest benefit of being part of a support group: It is that feeling of aloneness that you get in the wee hours of the night when you can't sleep that you know you can turn to the internet and read letters from mothers who have been there before you. When you have no strength to make it through another minutes, those that have done before you give you strength.

C3 80

*"My husband was in the hospital for 15 years dying of a disorder called Huntington's Chorea, or Huntington's disease. It took several years before we even got a diagnosis. The family suffered; he suffered; there were many problems involved. When we got the diagnosis, I was told hopeless, helpless, go home - forget about it... I can say it now with a smile, but really down deep in my heart, I am kind of angry. I wish somebody could have told me, 'Well, it's true we don't know anything about it, but maybe someday we'll do something.' If somebody had only said a hopeful word, I might have started ten years before what I finally did get around to doing in 1967. But I was foolish like most young people and accepted the word of the authorities, of the medical profession, and went along thinking there was nothing I can do. And of course 15 years later, I woke up... I woke up and said no more. I am sure I can do something."*

*- Marjorie Gutherie, Founder, The Huntington's Disease Foundation (from: Explorations in Self-Help and Mutual Aid: Proceedings of the Self-Help Exploratory Workshop held June 9-12, 1974, Chicago, Illinois, under the auspices of the W. Clement and Jessie V. Stone Foundation, published by the Center for Urban Affairs, Northwestern University, Evanston, IL, 1975, pp. 101-113.)*

## A Self-Help Story...   Learning the Lessons of the Geese

Have you ever wondered why geese fly in a "V" formation? As with most animal behavior, there's a very practical reason for it. But there is even more that we can learn from their "mutual aid" group:

As each bird flaps its wings, it creates an "uplift" for the bird behind. By flying in their V group formation, the flock adds 71% more flying range than if each bird flew alone.

*Lesson #1: People who share a common direction and sense of community can get where they're going quicker and easier when they travel on the strength of one another.*

The hardest job indeed is that of the lead goose. So, after a while, when the lead goose eventually gets tuckered out, it's time for him or her to fall back in the formation, and for another goose to assume that point position.

*Lesson #2: Shared leadership and interdependence give us each a chance to lead as well as an opportunity to rest.*

Whenever a goose falls out of the group formation, it suddenly feels the drag and resistance of trying to fly alone, and quickly gets back into formation to take advantage of the "lifting power" of the bird immediately in front.

*Lesson #3: It's harder to go it alone, and easier if we learn from the experience of those ahead of us.*

The geese in formation honk from behind to encourage those up front to keep up their speed.

*Lesson #4: We all need to encourage each other by voicing our small successes and those of other members, and expressing our caring and appreciation.*

When a goose gets sick, wounded, or shot down, two geese drop out of formation and follow it down to help and protect it. They stay with the wounded goose until the goose is either able to fly again or dies. Then the two geese launch out on their own, join another group, or catch up with their flock.

*Lesson #5: A few of us may need extra help from time to time outside of our group. On a one-to-one individual basis, members can help those experiencing an especially difficult time through a buddy system, phone call follow-up, visitation, or needed referral to helpful professional resources.*

cx ත

**Chapter 3**

# HOW TO FIND OR FORM AN ONLINE SELF-HELP GROUP

*"There is tremendous satisfaction in being able to help others on this walk through hell."*

*- Dolly Campbell (who founded "CDJ Voice" website and mailing list shortly after her husband's death from an untreatable disease).*

Over the last decade, the number and variety of online mutual help groups has grown to provide a wealth of information, support, and comfort available through the Internet. While we have listed dozens of online groups here in the Sourcebook, primarily for those concerns or disorders for which we could not find a national or international support organization with face-to-face groups, you may want to also seek out any of the thousands of online support groups available on the Internet. In addition, new online groups are always developing, and you may even want to consider starting one of your own.

## UNDERSTANDING THE TYPES OF ONLINE GROUPS

For those unfamiliar with the Internet, here's a quick review of the primary forms in which online mutual help groups take.

- **Message boards** usually appear as part of a website. All the messages can be read here, usually with the latest messages appearing first. Sometimes messages are grouped by topic. You can go online to this site to read, post, and reply to the messages at your convenience. Many message boards require you to first register with them before you can post messages. The reason for this is to be able to disallow use by any person who might act inappropriately. Registering is simply a matter of reading and agreeing to the discussion rules or terms of service which outline the do's and don'ts.

- **Newsgroups** are one form of message or bulletin boards that are available on special news servers. You need to configure your browser to access newsgroups, and your internet service providers (ICP) needs to carry the newsgroup you want to access. For an overview of newsgroups, go to: http://www.finanisp.com/usenet.php

- **Chat rooms** allow people to "talk" with one another in real time through the keyboard (although there now exists the technology to allow people to speak directly into the computer). After someone types a questions or response, as soon as they push their enter key, they send it to the chat room where everyone else in that chat room reads it.

- **E-mail discussion groups** (sometimes referred to as a mailing list or Listserv) are similar to a magazine subscription. Each list has a particular theme or topic (e.g. cancer survivors, caregivers, persons with social anxiety, etc). Many mailing lists are independent of any website. Each subscriber (subscriptions are usually free) can post a message, comment or question to everyone else on the list by sending out just one e-mail message - which goes out to every other subscriber to that list. In essence, every message that is posted to that list by any member is sent to every other member. Some mailing lists allow the subscriber to opt for a condensed or abridged daily or weekly version since large mailing lists can generate an overabundance of e-mail messages.

## FINDING A GROUP

As reflected in the group descriptions that we provide here in the Sourcebook, most of the **established national and international self-help group organizations** have developed their own websites. Many of these sites provide interactive message boards or e-mail discussion groups, chat rooms, and links to other helpful sites that deal with their particular issue. So the websites of the face-to-face self-help groups would be one good place to start to check for an online discussion group. If the national self-help organization doesn't have a message board or an e-mail discussion group displayed at their website, send them an e-mail asking if they know of any good online groups that exist.

You can also begin with a search at **Google.com**. Click on their "Advance Search" and in the top box type in the problem or concern you are searching for; then in the "exact phrase" box type "support group" or "support network." But understand that Google.com will not give you all the groups. There are a significant number of online support groups that will not show up, including many of those groups that operate as an e-mail discussion group or listserv.

A second search engine is the **Open Directory Project** at: http://dmoz.org that can be similarly searched. You will find support groups under "Health," "Health Mental Health," and "Society." They also break out website by language.

For websites loosely linked together around particular issues, search at WebRing.org. In addition, SupportPath.com provides links to online message boards, mailing lists and newsgroups for some 300 illnesses and other problems.

Another way to find an existing online support group is to visit the any of the following websites that may deal with your concern. They will either have, or refer you to, multiple mailing lists or message boards for your particular issue.

- For **mental health groups - PsychCentral.com** at http://psychcentral.com Click on "Mental Health & Psychology Resources Online" for a comprehensive listing by subject. This database is maintained by Dr. John Grohol, who is a pioneer in the identification and development of online resources for mental health.

- For specific **neurological disorders - BrainTalk** (www.braintalk.org). There are over two hundred message boards. Chat rooms are also available. Previously known as the Neurology Web Forums at Massachusetts General Hospital, pioneered by John Lester. Similar neurology-related message boards are available on Med Help International in the Cleveland Clinic Neurology Forum (http://medhelp.org) hosted there.

- For specific **cancer groups - Association of Cancer Online Resources** (www.acor.org) is a non-profit patient/family-run organization that has over 130 e-mail discussion groups related to different forms of cancer and non-malignant tumors, both for patients and caregivers. They also help those seeking to start and run a needed new online support group for any type of cancer or tumor disorder for which there is no existing online group.

- For specific **12-step and other online recovery groups - Online Recovery** (onlinerecovery.org) lists hundreds of online recovery groups and websites dealing with a wide range of issues including addictions, mental health issues, survivors of abuse, and others.

- For **parents groups - Parents Place** (www.parentsplace.com/messageboards) has numerous message boards for specific parenting problems, issues and concerns.

For **older adults - SeniorNet** (www.seniornet.org) provides older adults with access to, and education about, computers. They also have discussions and chat rooms on dozens of different topics of interest to older adults.

- For **health issues**, the largest sites have different illness and health issue boards/forums. Consider checking www.MedHelp.org (which has a free patient-to-patient network that connects patients with same condition), www.boards.webmd.com, and www.drkoop.com. For other other issues, www.clubs.lycos.com and EZBoards' www.forumfind.com

If you decide you want to search newsgroups, good starting sites are http://groups.google.com (where you can search all past newsgroup's messages which can be especially helpful for identifying discussions of a rare illness or problem) and www.ibiblio.org/usenet-i/search.

## WHAT TO LOOK FOR

The quality of online groups varies greatly, much more so than community self-help groups. Here are some of the characteristics of a good online self-help group that you might look for.

- The first is to see if it's alive, i.e., **active and vibrant.** It's easy for anyone to hang out a shingle saying that there is an online support group when in fact there is little or no activity. Look for a fair number of people and recent postings. Just as in a community group, the life of an online group depends on the continued participation of people who have found it helpful. A good number of participants also help to correct misinformation. However, take into account that with rare disorders and concerns, the membership and message volume will often be naturally low.

- Message volume alone doesn't indicate quality. Look to see if people are actually **helping one another.** Beware of the "pity party" discussion groups where people mostly complain instead of helping themselves and each other to recover. Do different members who share their positive experiences, strengths and hopes answer questions and requests for help? Or is there just one person doing all the helping? Look for the multiple ideas and collective wisdom of a "support group," not just a "support person."

- Is the environment **non-judgmental and caring**? In viewing the messages, does it feel like a safe and welcoming place? Look for tolerance of different opinions and feelings, as well as ground rules that prohibit negative behavior like "flaming" (the use of abusive language used to demean a person or their idea).

- After you have had an opportunity to view messages and participate, do you feel a **sense of community**? Online self-help groups, run by and for people who share the same experience, provide an understanding ear that no one else in the world can provide. Newcomers often report that they feel an instant sense of belonging. This is one reason that many people stay active in the group, helping others after being helped themselves. Professionals may also be available at some online group sites as helpful resource people (online it's not unusual to see them as "guest speakers" for a full week). But it is important that they not dominate or take over the self-help group.

- Self-help groups are **non-proprietary**. Therefore, be sure that the online group has no explicit or hidden agenda of selling products or services. Some self-help groups may use a free online service that has general ads, e.g., Yahoo e-mail groups, which is normal and to be expected. But be beware of any groups or online sites that encourage purchases, especially of a quick-cure product.

Ultimately, the key to a good online self-help group is whether it **meets your needs**. There are a variety of groups available that have different values and personalities. A good group should match your needs and values.

Online networks provide individuals worldwide with the peer support, understanding, and information they seek. Some online groups also do a good job in promoting needed and timely advocacy efforts. The Internet overcomes barriers of distance, time, and disability. Overall, better understanding and use of the Internet will continue to expand mutual help networks to better meet people's needs and improve the overall quality of our lives.

## STARTING YOUR OWN ONLINE GROUP

As a result of the Dotcom bust in 2001, fewer online services provide free mailing lists or message boards. Many of the surviving online service providers, who once provided free community sites, now charge fees. However, there are a few free services still available at this time.

E-mail discussion groups are the most popular. Free mailing lists are still available from **Yahoo** (http://groups.yahoo.com/group) and **Topica** (www.topica.com). You just need to answer the questions, as you create the type of mailing list group you want to have (e.g., having an "open" group so anyone can join, or a "restricted" group where you approve each membership—see our website, under "How To Develop An Online Group," for an overview of how to create a Yahoo mailing list). Both Yahoo and Topica have an option for making your list a one-way e-mail newsletter.

Free chat rooms are still available at Yahoo.com (click on "create a room" after entering) and www.parachat.com. But like anything "free" on the Net these days, you have to put up with multiple ads that make these "free" online services possible.

The options for obtaining a free message board are more limited. **Delphi Forums** (www.delphiforums.com) and **MSN Clubs** (http://groups.msn.com/home) currently still provide free message boards but with multiple banner and pop-up ads. For access without ads, you would have to pay for their "Plus" membership, which is currently sixty dollars a year. Another alternative is to consider approaching any existing website that deals with your condition. Ask the webmaster if he or she would be willing to add a message board.

For building a free website (but with a variety of banner and possible pop-up ads), there's still **Angelfire** (www.angelfire.com). If you are seeking a free online website for your local self-help group, check if any of the daily newspapers in your area are providing free online community group web pages. Some newspaper syndicates provide free web pages, in exchange for having ads in one section of the screen. If available, they are usually easily built using templates. But if you do develop a website, remember that simply having a website doesn't automatically result in referrals. The number of referrals you get will depend upon how many other websites list yours. This means you should be contacting other websites related to your concern and asking them if they would create a link to your site.

For an update on free websites and chat rooms, go to **The Free Site** (www.thefreesite.com). Also see any applicable links at **Network for Good** (www.networkforgood.org/npo). For more detailed information on developing an online group, visit Dr. Grohol's **"Starting a New Online Support Group"** which he periodically updates at: http://psychcentral.com/howto.htm. If you are interested in developing an online group for a particular condition that doesn't yet have one online, contact our Clearinghouse for additional ideas (ed@selfhelpgroups.org).

&#x2767;

## A Self-Help Story...
## "It's a Relief to Hear That My Mom Isn't the Only One"

In August of 2000, Ann Hildegard started an e-mail group for families dealing with Lewy Body Disease, a form of dementia, representing about one fifth of all dementias, but *"still relatively unknown in both the medical and lay world"* as the group explains it. The cause of LBD is still unknown, and there is no known cure.

While she had discovered information on various web sites, Ann realized that it was no easy task for other families to find those sites, and she knew of no other families dealing with the disease. After she created the list, it very soon emerged that there were many in the same situation. Two months after creating the online group, Ann wrote: *"I had never heard about the disease... Then my sister-in-law was diagnosed with LBD, and it's been a big scramble for information ever since."*

The online group quickly grew in numbers and within a year there were ninety members, mainly from the USA, but also from Canada, Australia, the British Isles and the Channel Isles. Members exchange experiences and frustrations, give tips for dealing with situations and offer support to each other. When someone finds useful information about LBD they share it by posting addresses of websites or enclosing relevant articles. Many find "LBDcaregivers" an absolute lifeline.

While symptoms, rate of progress, degree of fluctuation, and effects of medications vary dramatically from person to person, many problems are common and the experiences of others have helped immeasurably, e.g.: *"It's a relief to hear that my mom isn't the only one with auditory rather than visual hallucinations.", "Thanks to you all for all the information. I never realized how I wanted to talk to someone else about LBD. When friends call, you try to explain what you found out, or how things are really going, but they are not truly interested in the details and do not understand. I have gleaned more information from all of you in the past three weeks than I ever could any other way."*

Sharing emotional feelings has also helped those on the site feel less alone: *"I miss the person my husband was when he was well, I'm sad our life has had to change so much. I miss having someone to share responsibilities, and I'm angry about the attitude I encountered from some health professionals in trying to find help. Some days he is responsive to my mother, sister and me; other days, he breaks our hearts."*

Furthermore, as one member put very succinctly: *"I want to see the public brought to focus on the social and economic issues of an aging population with serious degenerative diseases including LBD and fewer and fewer people to do the care giving. I want to see society get their heads out of the sand and start figuring out how we are going to manage. It's probably too late to help my mother. I want to see other families spared this grief. I want to stop feeling scared of the future."*

For all these reasons, the e-mail group took the first steps in creating the "Lewy Body Disease Association." Their first project was the creation of the group's website, www.lewybodydisease.org. Their efforts continue.

ʊ ꙮ

# Chapter 4

# A REVIEW OF RESEARCH ON THE EFFECTIVENESS OF SELF-HELP MUTUAL AID GROUPS

*Elaina M. Kyrouz, Ph.D., Keith Humphreys, Ph.D. and Colleen Loomis, Ph.D.*
*Veterans Affairs Health Care System*
*and Stanford University School of Medicine,*
*Palo Alto, California*

For the past few decades, researchers have been evaluating the effects of self-help/mutual aid groups on participants. Most research studies of self-help groups have found important benefits of participation. Unfortunately, few of these studies have gotten into the hands of self-help group members, clearinghouse staff and others who wish to advocate for self-help/mutual aid. The purpose of this chapter is to help correct this problem by summarizing the best research supporting the effectiveness of self-help groups in a brief and clear fashion.

As we read over research on the effects of mutual help groups, we noticed a common confusion. Many studies that claim to study self-help groups are actually studies of psychotherapy or support groups solely led by a professional who does not share the condition addressed by the group. We excluded such studies from this review. Instead, we focused on groups where the participants all shared some problem or condition and ran the group on their own. In a very few cases, we included studies where a group was co-led by a professional and by a self-helper. Professional involvement in an advisory or assistance capacity did not rule a study out of consideration, because in the real world, many member-run self-help groups use professional advisors.

We have been selective about the methodological strengths of the studies we chose to summarize. Many studies have demonstrated that if the current members of any self-help group are surveyed at any given time, the members will respond positively about the group and say that it helps them. Such studies (which are sometimes called "single-group cross-sectional surveys") have some value, but they do not tell us much about how members change over time, or whether members change more than non-members. For this reason, we focus here primarily on studies that compared self-help participants to non-participants, and/or gathered information repeatedly over time (that is, "longitudinal" studies). Because we focus on studies with these characteristics, the following is only a subset of research on self-help effectiveness. At the same time, relative to the research literature as a whole, it is a methodologically stronger subset of studies. Hence, this should make the results presented here more convincing to people outside and inside of the self-help movement.

In the brief summaries below, we have tried to use as little jargon as possible. One exception to this rule is to use the scientific convention of using the letter "N" to refer to the number of people participating in each research project or group ("n"). For the sake of space and

71

simplicity, we have generally omitted most details about how the study was conducted and about secondary and non-significant findings. Readers who wish to have further details about any particular study can use the reference information provided to locate the original sources. Reviews are in alphabetical order by the first author's last name grouped into the following categories: Addiction related recovery, Bereavement, Cancer groups, Caregiver group, Chronic illnesses, Diabetes, Groups for elderly people, Mental health, and Weight loss.

# RESEARCH REVIEWS

### ADDICTION-RELATED GROUPS

**Alemi, F., Mosavel, M. Stephens, R., et al. (1996). "Electronic Self-Help and Support Groups." Medical Care 34 (Supplement): OS32-OS44.**

This was a study of 53 pregnant women who had a history of drug use. Participants, most of whom were African-American, were assigned either to attend face-to-face biweekly self-help group meetings (n=25) or to participate in self-help meetings operated over a voice bulletin board accessed by phone (n=28). In the bulletin board group, participants could leave voice mail messages for the entire group to hear. Significantly more women participated in the voice mail group (96% of those assigned) than in the face-to-face self-help groups (32% of those assigned). Bulletin board participants made significantly fewer telephone calls and visits to health care clinics than did individuals assigned to participate in the face-to-face group. Both groups had similar health status and drug use at the end of the study.

**Christo, G. and S. Sutton (1994). "Anxiety and Self-Esteem as a Function of Abstinence Time Among Recovering Addicts Attending Narcotics Anonymous." British Journal of Clinical Psychology 33: 198-200.**

Members of Narcotics Anonymous (NA) self-help groups (N=200) who stayed off drugs for three years or more while they were members showed no more anxiety and no less self-esteem than a comparison group of 60 never-addicted students. The longer people remained members while staying off drugs, the less anxiety and the more self-esteem they experienced.

**Emrick, C. D., J. S. Tonigan, et al. (1993). Alcoholics Anonymous: What is Currently Known? In Research on Alcoholics Anonymous: Opportunities and Alternatives, edited by Barbara S. McCrady and William R. Miller. New Brunswick, NJ: Rutgers Center of Alcohol Studies, pp. 41-75.**

Using meta-analysis of more than 50 studies, these authors report that AA members stayed sober more if they (1) had an AA sponsor, (2) worked the "twelfth step" of the program, (3) led a meeting, (4) increased their degree of participation over time, or (5) sponsored other

AA members. The study also found that professionally treated alcoholic patients who attend AA during or after treatment are somewhat more likely to reduce drinking than are those who do not attend AA. Membership in AA was also found to reduce physical symptoms and to improve psychological adjustment.

**Hughes, J. M. (1977). "Adolescent Children of Alcoholic Parents and the Relationship of Alateen to These Children." Journal of Consulting and Clinical Psychology 45(5): 946-947.**

This study compared 25 Alateen members with 25 non-members who had an alcoholic parent and 25 non-members with no alcoholic parent. Adolescents with an alcoholic parent who were members of Alateen experienced significantly fewer negative moods, significantly more positive moods and higher self-esteem than those who were not members. In fact, Alateen members had self-esteem and mood scores similar to those of adolescents who did not have an alcoholic parent.

**Humphreys, K., B. E. Mavis, and B. E. Stoffelmayr (1994). "Are Twelve Step Programs Appropriate for Disenfranchised Groups? Evidence from a Study of Post-treatment Mutual Help Involvement." Prevention in Human Services 11(1): 165-179.**

One year after being admitted to a public substance abuse treatment agency, Caucasian- and African-Americans were attending mutual help (Narcotics Anonymous, Alcoholics Anonymous) groups at the same rate. African-American participants (N=253) in NA and AA self-help groups showed significant improvements over twelve months in six problem areas (employment, alcohol, drug, legal, psychological, and family). African-American self-help group participants had significant more improvement in their medical, alcohol, and drug problems than did African-American patients who did not participate in self-help groups after treatment.

**Humphreys, K. and R. H. Moos (1996) "Reduced Substance-Abuse-Related Health Care Costs among Voluntary Participants in Alcoholics Anonymous." Psychiatric Services, 47, 709-713.**

Over a period of three years, alcoholics who initially chose to attend AA were compared to those who sought help from a professional outpatient treatment provider (N=201). Those who chose to attend AA had 45% ($1826) lower average per-person treatment costs than did those who chose outpatient treatment. Despite the lower costs, AA attendees also experienced significant improvements in alcohol consumption, dependence symptoms, adverse consequences, days intoxicated and depression. These outcomes did not differ significantly from those of alcoholics who chose professional treatment. This was true both at one year and at three years after the beginning of the study.

Humphreys, K. & Moos, R. (2001). Can Encouraging substance abuse patients to participate in self-help groups reduce demand for health care? A quasi-experimental study. Alcoholism: Clinical and Experimental Research, 25, 711-716.

Over a period of one year, low-income, US veteran men (N=1774) receiving substance abuse treatment in either a 12-step or cognitive-behaviorally oriented inpatient program were compared on participation in a self-help group, use and costs of inpatient and outpatient mental health services, and outcomes (abstinence from drugs and alcohol, substance abuse-related problems, psychological distress, and psychiatric symptoms). Those who received 12-step oriented treatment participated more frequently in self-help groups and used fewer professional services (almost half as many), with lower associated health care costs than did men who were inpatients in a program with a cognitive-behavioral orientation. Men treated in a 12-step oriented inpatient program also had higher rates of abstinence from drugs and alcohol. The two groups did not differ on psychological and psychiatric characteristics.

Humphreys, K. & Noke, J. M. (1997). The Influence of Post-treatment Mutual Help Group Participation on the Friendship Networks of Substance Abuse Patients. American Journal of Community Psychology, 25, 1-16.

Over the period of one year, the friendships of men (n=1,972) who participate in 12-step groups were compared to similar men (n=1,349) who did not participate. All men were discharged from inpatient substance abuse treatment and had very little or no prior involvement with a 12-step program. The friendship networks of 12-step group participants were larger and of higher quality, with more frequent contact, than those of men who did not belong to a 12-step group. Also, friends of 12-step group participants were less supportive of substance abuse.

Jason, L. A., C. L. Gruder, et al. (1987). "Work Site Group Meetings and the Effectiveness of a Televised Smoking Cessation Intervention." American Journal of Community Psychology 15: 57-77.

This study compared the effects of two smoking cessation programs at work. One hundred and ninety-two workers viewed a television program and used a self-help manual, while 223 workers had these materials supplemented by 6 self-help group meetings. Group meetings were led by recruited smoking employees who had been given a three-hour training session in how to lead groups. The two programs were implemented at 43 companies. Initial rates of quitting smoking were significantly higher for the 21 companies that used self-help groups (average of 41% vs. 21% of participants). Group participants also smoked significantly fewer cigarettes per day, with lower tar, nicotine and carbon monoxide content. Three months later, an average of 22% of group participants had continued not to smoke, compared to 12% in companies with no self-help groups.

**Kingree, J. B., & Thompson, M. (2000). Mutual Help Groups, Perceived Status Benefits, and Well-Being: A Test with Adult Children of Alcoholics with Personal Substance Abuse Problems. American Journal of Community Psychology, 28, 325-342.**

Over a period of six months in a residential treatment program, substance abusers who are adult children of alcoholics (randomly) assigned to ACOA were compared to those who attended substance abuse education classes (total N=78). Those who attended ACOA had increased perceived status benefits (personal strength, changes in life philosophy, and improved interpersonal relations) than did those who attended education classes both at one month and at six months after the study began. After six months, ACOA attendees had decreased depression and substance use than did individuals in classes.

**McAuliffe, W. E. (1990). "A Randomized Controlled Trial of Recovery Training and Self-Help for Opiod Addicts in New England and Hong Kong." Journal of Psychoactive Drugs 22(2): 197-209.**

This study randomly assigned volunteer graduates from substance abuse treatment programs (N=168) to participate in RTSH (Recovery Training and Self-Help), an aftercare program that combined professionally led recovery-training sessions with peer-led self-help sessions. Participants in the recovery program significantly reduced their likelihood of relapse into opiod addiction compared to those who received only referrals to other programs and crisis-intervention counseling. The RTSH program helped unemployed participants find work and reduced criminal behavior.

**McKay, J. R., A. I. Alterman, et al. (1994). "Treatment Goals, Continuity of Care, and Outcome in a Day Hospital Substance Abuse Rehabilitation Program." American Journal of Psychiatry 151(2): 254-259.**

Male substance abuse patients (N=180, 82% African American, mostly low income) who participated in self-help groups (Alcoholics Anonymous, Narcotics Anonymous) after treatment significantly reduced their frequency of alcohol and cocaine use by the 7-month follow up. Participants with high self-help attendance rates used alcohol and/or cocaine less than half as much as did those with low self-help attendance. This was true regardless of previous substance use and whether or not they completed a 4-week hospital rehabilitation program. Hence, the effects of self-help groups were not simply due to motivation or other characteristics of the individuals who participated.

**Pisani, V. D., J. Fawcett, et al. (1993). "The Relative Contributions of Medication Adherence and AA Meeting Attendance to Abstinent Outcome for Chronic Alcoholics." Journal of Studies on Alcohol 54: 115-119.**

A group of 122 mostly male, white alcoholic patients admitted to short-term hospital treatment programs participated in this study. In the 18 months following treatment, the more days the patient attended Alcoholics Anonymous self-help meetings, the longer their abstinence lasted. AA meeting attendance improved abstinence considerably more than did adherence to prescribed medication.

**Tattersall, M. L. and C. Hallstrom (1992). "Self-Help and Benzodiazepine Withdrawal." Journal of Affective Disorders 24(3): 193-198.**

This study followed members (n=41) of TRANX (Tranquilizer Recovery and New Existence), a British self-help organization that provided telephone counseling and support groups to its members. Members were mostly white women who had been addicted to tranquilizers for an average of 12 years. During a 9-month period, members of the group were more likely to stop using tranquilizers than were individuals (n=76) who made an initial telephone contact but did not become a member. Most members (73%) also reported that the symptoms for which they had initially been prescribed tranquilizers improved, and 65% reported that they were at least moderately satisfied with their withdrawal in terms of its effects on their subjective quality of life.

**Walsh, D. C., R. W. Hingson, D. M. Merrigan, et al. (1991). "A Randomized Trial of Treatment Options for Alcohol-Abusing Workers." The New England Journal of Medicine 325(11): 775-782.**

Workers assigned to participate in Alcoholics Anonymous self-help groups reduced their drinking problems over a two-year period. Furthermore, compulsory AA groups (n=83) did not significantly differ from compulsory inpatient treatment (n=73) in their effects on job-related outcomes of participants. Costs of inpatient treatment averaged 10 percent less for AA participants than for hospital rehabilitation participants.

**Watson, C. G., Hancock, M., Gearhart, L. P., Mendez, C. M., Malovrh, P., & Raden, M. (1997). A Comparative Outcome Study of Frequent, Moderate, Occasional, and Non-attenders of Alcoholics Anonymous. Journal of Clinical Psychology, 53, 209-214.**

Four groups of men were compared on alcohol consumption and quality of life (e.g., number of times jailed, re-hospitalization, detoxifications, lost jobs). Information was gathered monthly during one year. The men (N=150), recently discharged from a three-week substance abuse residential treatment program, were grouped by the number of Alcoholics Anonymous (AA) meetings attended during the first month after discharge. There were four groups: non-participants (no meetings), occasional (one to four), moderate (five to eight), and frequent (nine or more). Attending meetings frequently did not make a difference among the groups on the average amount of alcohol drank daily. Men with moderate attendance were more likely to be abstinent from alcohol than non-participants, and those who attended meetings occasionally or moderately drank less alcohol on average daily than non-participants. Participants who attended any AA meetings (occasional, moderate, or frequent) were jailed fewer times than non-participants; the four groups did not differ on the other quality of life indicators used.

## BEREAVEMENT GROUPS

**Caserta, M. S. and Lund, D. A. (1993). "Intrapersonal Resources and the Effectiveness of Self-Help Groups for Bereaved Older Adults."** Gerontologist 33(5): 619-629.

Widows and widowers over age 50 who participated in bereavement self-help groups (n=197) experienced less depression and grief than non-participants (n=98) if their initial levels of interpersonal and coping skills were low. Those with initially high interpersonal skill levels also benefited from participation if they participated in the groups for longer than eight weeks.

**Lieberman, M. A. and L. Videka-Sherman (1986). "The Impact of Self-Help Groups on the Mental Health of Widows and Widowers."** American Journal of Orthopsychiatry 56(3): 435-449.

This study followed 36 widowers and 466 widows, 376 of whom were members of the bereavement self-help group THEOS. Over a period of one year, THEOS members who formed social relationships with other group members outside group time experienced less psychological distress (depression, anxiety, somatic symptoms) and improved more in psychological functioning (well-being, mastery, self-esteem) than did non-members and members who did not form such relationships.

**Marmar, C. R., M. J. Horowitz, et al. (1988). "A Controlled Trial of Brief Psychotherapy and Mutual-Help Group Treatment of Conjugal Bereavement."** American Journal of Psychiatry 145(2): 203-209.

Bereaved women who sought treatment for grief after the death of their husband were randomly assigned to either professional psychotherapy (n=31) or self-help groups (n=30). Self-help groups worked just as well as the therapy. Participants and non-participants in the self-help groups reduced stress-specific and general psychiatric symptoms such as depression equally. They also experienced similar improvements in social adjustment and work functioning.

**Vachon, M.L.S., W.A.L. Lyall, et al. (1980). "A Controlled Study of Self-Help Intervention for Widows."** American Journal of Psychiatry 137(11): 1380-1384.

Women (N=162) whose husbands had died within the past month were studied over a two-year period. Half of these women were assigned to participate in a "widow-to-widow" program. After 6 months in the program, participants were more likely than non-participants to feel more healthy and to feel "better," and less likely to anticipate a difficult adjustment to widowhood. After 12 months, participants were more likely than non-participants to feel "much better," to have made new friends, and to have begun new activities, and were less likely to feel constantly anxious or to feel the need to hide their true emotions. Participation facilitated adjustment both inside the person (in their relationship with themselves) and outside the person (in their relationships with others).

**Videka-Sherman, L. and M. Lieberman (1985). "The Effects of Self-Help and Psychotherapy Intervention on Child Loss: The Limits of Recovery."** American Journal of Orthopsychiatry **55(1): 70-82.**

This study compared white, mostly female bereaved parents who had received psychotherapy (n=120) to those who attended a Compassionate Friends (CF) bereavement self-help group sporadically (n=81), actively (n=25) or actively with social involvement with group members outside the group (n=97). Active participation in the self-help group accompanied by involvement with group members outside the group increased bereaved parents' comfort in discussing their bereavement with others and reduced parents' self-directed anger. Psychotherapy did not have these effects. CF members reported that group involvement had increased their self-confidence, sense of control, happiness, and freedom to express feelings, and decreased their depression, anxiety, guilt, anger, and isolation.

## CANCER GROUPS

**Maisiak, R., M. Cain, et al. (1981). "Evaluation of TOUCH: An Oncology Self-Help Group."** Oncology Nursing Forum **8(3): 20-25.**

This study surveyed 139 members of TOUCH, a self-help group for cancer patients in Alabama. TOUCH focuses on teaching its members about cancer and training them to be peer counselors to help other patients. The longer members participated in a group, the more they improved their knowledge of cancer, their ability to talk with others, their friendships, their family life, their coping with the disease, and their following of doctors' orders. The percentage of people indicating their coping was very good after TOUCH was 59%, more than double the percentage indicating it was very good before TOUCH (28%).

**Spiegel, D., Bloom, J. R., Kraemer, H.C. and Gottheil, E. (1989). "Effect of psychosocial treatment on survival of patients with metastatic breast cancer."** The Lancet **October 14: 888-891.**

Participants in this study were 86 women undergoing treatment for metastatic breast cancer. A subset of these women (N=50) were randomly assigned to have their oncologic care supplemented with a weekly support group. The support groups were co-facilitated by a therapist who had breast cancer in remission and a psychiatrist or social worker. The sessions focused on living life fully, improving communication with family members and doctors, facing death, expressing emotions such as grief, and controlling pain through self-hypnosis. On average, support group participants lived twice as long as controls (an average of almost 18 months longer).

## CAREGIVERS GROUPS

Cook, J. A., Heller, T., & Pickett-Schenk, S. A. (1999). The Effect of Support Group Participation on Caregiver Burden Among Parents of Adult Offspring with Severe Mental Illness. Family Relations, 48, 405-410.

Parents caring for an adult child with severe mental illness who chose to attend NAMI-affiliated (National Alliance for the Mentally Ill) family support groups (n=86) were compared to similar parents who did not attend a support group (total n=34). Most groups met once a month, and the average number of months parents attended meetings was 46. The average size of the support group was 13 parents.  Those who attended a NAMI-affiliated group had less caregiver-related burden (e.g., guilt, shame, fewer leisure activities, financial strain) than parents who did not attend a support group.

Dunham, P. J., Hurshman, A., Litwin, E., Gusella, J., Ellsworth, C., & Dodd, P. W. D. (1998). Computer-Mediated Social Support: Single Young Mothers as a Model System. American Journal of Community Psychology, 26, 281-306.

Parenting stress levels of single mothers (N=42) with young infants were compared before involvement in a computer-mediated social support group and six months later.  Support was exchanged via public messages, private E-Mail, and text-based teleconferencing 24 hours per day.  Consistent participation decreased levels of parenting stress.  The messages exchanged provided mostly positive social support (98%) such as emotional, informational, and tangible support.  Mothers in the group developed close personal relationships and a sense of community among themselves.

Minde, K., N. Shosenberg, et al. (1980). "Self-Help Groups in a Premature Nursery--a Controlled Evaluation." Behavioral Pediatrics 96(5): 933-940.

Parents of premature infants were randomly assigned to participate in support groups in a hospital. The weekly groups (1.5 to 2 hours long) focused on coping and were co-led by a nurse and by a mother of a premature infant. Speakers were also brought in from outside periodically. Compared to 29 parents who did not participate, the 28 participants visited their infants in the hospital significantly more often, and touched, talked to, and gazed at their infants more often during visits. Participants also rated themselves more competent at infant care. Three months after their babies were discharged, group participants continued to show more involvement with their infants during feedings and were more concerned about their infants' general development.

Toseland, R.W., Rossiter, C.M., and Labrecque, M.S. (1989). "The Effectiveness of Two Kinds of Support Groups for Caregivers." Social Service Review, September: 415-432.

This study divided 103 adult women caring for frail older relatives into three conditions: participation in a peer-led self-help group, participation in a professional-led support group, and no participation in either group. Groups met for eight weekly two-hour sessions. Both groups focused on enhancing coping skills. Compared to non-participants, women who participated in either type of group experienced significantly greater (1) increases in the size of their support network, (2) increases in their knowledge of community resources, (3) improvement in their interpersonal skills and ability to deal with the problems of caregiving, (4) improvement in their relationships with their care receivers, and (5) decreases in pressing psychological problems.

## CHRONIC ILLNESS GROUPS

**Becu, M., Becu, N., Manzur, G. and Kochen, S. (1993). "Self-Help Epilepsy Groups: An Evaluation of Effect on Depression and Schizophrenia." Epilepsia 34(5): 841-845.**

Argentine researchers conducted a 4-month longitudinal study of 67 epileptic patients who participated in weekly self-help group meetings. Epileptic patients trained by psychologists led the groups. Group participants had decreased depression and other psychological problems over the course of the study.

**Hinrichsen, G.A., T.A. Revenson, et al. (1985). "Does Self-Help Help? An Empirical Investigation of Scoliosis Peer Support Groups." Journal of Social Issues 41(1): 65-87.**

Adults with scoliosis who had undergone bracing or surgery and participated in a Scoliosis Association self-help group (n=33) were compared to adults with similar treatment who did not participate in the group (n=67). Compared to non-participants, group participants reported (1) a more positive outlook on life, (2) greater satisfaction with the medical care they received, (3) reduced psychosomatic symptoms, (4) increased sense of mastery, (5) increased self-esteem, and (6) reduced feelings of shame and estrangement.

**Nash, K.B. and K.D. Kramer (1993). "Self-Help for Sickle Cell Disease in African American Communities." Journal of Applied Behavioral Science 29(2): 202-215.**

This study focused on 57 African Americans who had been members of self-help groups for sickle-cell anemia. The members who had been involved the longest reported the fewest psychological symptoms and the fewest psychosocial interferences from the disease, particularly in work and relationship areas.

**Sibthorpe, B., D. Fleming, et al. (1994). "Self-Help Groups: A Key to HIV Risk Reduction for High-Risk Injection Drug Users?" Journal of Acquired Immune Deficiency Syndromes 7(6): 592-598.**

Injection drug users (N=234) who had shared a dirty needle in the previous 30 days were followed over six months. Those who attended self-help groups (mostly Narcotics Anonymous and Alcoholics Anonymous) during that time were almost twice as likely to report reducing or eliminating their risk of exposure to HIV compared to those who did not attend such groups.

**Subramaniam, V., Stewart, M. W., & Smith, J. F. (1999). The Development and Impact of a Chronic Pain Support Group: A Qualitative and Quantitative Study. Journal of Pain and Symptom Management, 17, 376-383.**

Over a period of five months of participation in a Pain Support Group (PSG), individuals (N=13) with chronic low back pain attending a 2-hour monthly meeting reported significantly less functional disability and fewer visits to health care services after five months participation in the PSG than before joining. Seventy percent of the members said the PSG helped them in everyday life. Benefits noted by participants include the following: discussing with other members, gaining knowledge, adapting to life with pain, learning about and seeking alternative coping strategies, increasing motivation, having a sense of belonging, establishing new friendships, and helping others. Members' desired the PSG to enhance telephone support, informational resources, and public profile as well as increase the number of social events.

## DIABETES GROUPS

**Gilden, J.L., Hendryx, M.S., et al. (1992). "Diabetes Support Groups Improve Health Care of Older Diabetic Patients." Journal of the American Geriatrics Society 40: 147-150.**

Male diabetic patients were randomly divided into three groups. The first group (n=8) received no intervention. The second group (n=13) received a six-session education program on diabetes self-care. The third group (n=11) received the education program plus 18 meetings of a patient-led self-help group. The patient-led group focused on coping skills, group discussions, structured social activities, and continuing diabetes education. At the end of the study, those who participated in both the education program and the patient-led group had better diabetes knowledge and quality of life and lower depression than non-participants. The participants in the peer-led group also reported less stress, greater family involvement, and better glycemic control than the patients who received no intervention.

**Simmons, D. (1992). "Diabetes Self Help Facilitated by Local Diabetes Research: The Coventry Asian Diabetes Support Group." Diabetic Medicine 9: 866-869.**

Researchers assessed members of a self-help group for South Asian diabetics in England (N=53) for levels of glycated hemoglobin and knowledge about diabetes. Those who attended the group twice or more during a year had a significantly greater drop in glycated hemoglobin levels and a significantly greater increase in knowledge about diabetes. Although professionals helped start the group, it continues to operate independently, emphasizing education, mutual support, information sharing, and family social activities.

## GROUPS FOR ELDERLY PERSONS

**Lieberman, M.A. and Bliwise, N.G. (1985). "Comparisons Among Peer and Professionally Directed Groups for the Elderly: Implications for the Development of Self-Help Groups." International Journal of Group Psychotherapy 35(2): 155-175.**

This study compared participants (86 women and 22 men) in peer-led and professionally-led SAGE (Senior Actualization and Growth Explorations) self-help groups for the elderly to those who were on a waiting list to join the groups. Members of both types of SAGE groups felt they achieved their desired goals to a greater extent than those in the waiting-list group. Participation in either SAGE group also reduced psychological problems, such as nervousness and depression.

## MENTAL HEALTH GROUPS

**Edmunson, E.D., J.R. Bedell, et al. (1982). Integrating Skill Building and Peer Support in Mental Health Treatment: The Early Intervention and Community Network Development Projects. Community Mental Health and Behavioral Ecology. A.M. Jeger and R.S. Slotnick. New York: Plenum Press: 127-139.**

After ten months of participation in a patient-led, professionally supervised social network enhancement group, one-half as many former psychiatric inpatients (n=40) required re-hospitalization as did non-participants (n=40). Participants in the patient-led network also had much shorter average hospital stays (7 days vs. 25 days). Furthermore, a higher percentage of members than non-members could function with no contact with the mental health system (53% vs. 23%).

**Galanter, M. (1988). "Zealous Self-Help Groups as Adjuncts to Psychiatric Treatment: A Study of Recovery, Inc." American Journal of Psychiatry 145(10): 1248-1253.**

This study surveyed 356 members of Recovery, Inc., a self-help group for nervous and former mental patients, and compared them to a 195 community residents of similar age and sex. Although about half of the Recovery Inc. members had been hospitalized before joining, only 8% of group leaders and 7% of recent members had been hospitalized since joining. Members used more outpatient non-psychiatric resources than did the community sample.

**Kennedy, M. (1990). Psychiatric Hospitalizations of GROWers. Paper presented at the Second Biennial Conference on Community Research and Action, East Lansing, Michigan.**

This study found that 31 members of GROW, a self-help organization for people with chronic psychiatric problems, spent significantly fewer days in a psychiatric hospital over a 32-month period than did 31 former psychiatric patients of similar age, race, sex, marital status, number of previous hospitalizations and other factors. Members also increased their sense of security and self-esteem, decreased their existential anxiety, broadened their sense of spirituality, and increased their ability to accept problems without blaming self or others for them.

**Kurtz, L. F. (1988). "Mutual Aid for Affective Disorders: The Manic Depressive and Depressive Association." American Journal of Orthopsychiatry 58(1): 152-155.**

This study found that 82% of 129 members of the Manic Depressive and Depressive Association reported coping better with their illness since joining the self-help group. The longer they were members and the more intensely they were involved with the group, the more their coping had improved. Further, the percentage of members reporting being admitted to a psychiatric hospital before joining the group was 82%, but the percentage reporting hospital admission after joining was only 33%.

**Lieberman, M. A., Solow, N. et al. (1979). "The psychotherapeutic impact of women's consciousness-raising groups." Archives of General Psychiatry 36: 161-168.**

32 participants in women's consciousness-raising groups were studied over a 6 month period. Over the course of the study, participants reported decreased distress about their target problem, increased self-esteem, and greater self-reliance. They also reported greater identification with feminist values and politics.

**Powell, T. J., Hill, E. M., Warner, L., Yeaton, W., & Silk, K. R. (2000). Encouraging people with mood disorders to attend a self-help group. Journal of Applied Social Psychology, 30, 2270-2288.**

Patients (N=226) hospitalized for major depression or bipolar disorder randomly assigned an MDDA (Manic-Depressive and Depressive Association) sponsor were compared to those who were not assigned a sponsor. Volunteer sponsors with stabilized illnesses received training on introducing MDDA and accompanying an individual to a meeting. Researchers compared attendance at an MDDA meeting after an individual went with a sponsor. Individuals with sponsors were almost seven times as likely (6.8) to attend subsequent meeting(s) on their own than were those without sponsors. The proportion of individuals attending meetings was greater among persons with sponsors (56%) than those without sponsors (15%).

**Raiff, N. R. (1984). "Some Health Related Outcomes of Self-Help Participation." Chapter 14 in The Self-Help Revolution, edited by Alan Gartner and Frank Riessman. New York: Human Sciences Press.**

Highly involved members of Recovery, Inc. (N=393, mostly female and married), a self-help group for former mental patients, reported no more anxiety about their health than did the general population. Members who had participated for two years or more had the lowest levels of worry and the highest levels of satisfaction with their health. Members also rated their life satisfaction levels as high or higher than did the general public. Members who had participated less than two years, were still on medication, lived below the poverty level, or lacked social-network involvements also appeared to benefit from group participation, although to a lesser degree.

**Roberts, L. J., Salem, D., Rappaport, J., Toro, P. A., Luke, D. A., & Seidman, E. (1999). Giving and Receiving Help: Interpersonal Transactions in Mutual-Help Meetings and Psychosocial Adjustment of Members. American Journal of Community Psychology, 27, 841-868.**

Over a period of six to thirteen months (on average eight months) of participation in group meetings, individuals (N=98) with serious mental illness attending one of 15 different GROW self-help groups showed improved psychological and social adjustments. Helping others in the group improved members' social adjustment. Receiving help from those with closely integrated members was also related to positive adjustment. Receiving help from less closely associated members was related to adjustment that is more negative. Adjustment of members high in both giving and receiving help did not differ from those with lower levels of giving and receiving.

## WEIGHT LOSS GROUPS

**Grimsmo, A., G. Helgesen, et al. (1981). "Short-Term and Long-Term Effects of Lay Groups on Weight Reduction." British Medical Journal 283: 1093-1095.**

These researchers conducted three studies of mostly female participants in 8-week peer-led weight-loss groups in Norway (Grete Roede Slim-Clubs). The first study gathered information from 33 women before, during, immediately after, and 1 year after participation. Participants lost an average of 14.3 pounds while they were in the group, and had kept almost all of it from coming back by the end of the year (they had an average of 12.1 pounds less weight). The second study surveyed 1000 people who had completed the group from 1 to 5 years previously, and found that average weight loss remained stable for the first couple of years and was still 5 - 6% below starting weight after 5 years. The third study surveyed more than 10,000 participants before and immediately after participation, and found an average weight loss of 15.2 pounds.

**Peterson, G., D.B. Abrams, et al. (1985). "Professional Versus Self-Help Weight Loss at the Worksite: The Challenge of Making a Public Health Impact." Behavior Therapy 16: 213-222.**

This study compared 30 employees assigned to a professionally-led weight-loss group with 33 employees assigned to a peer-led group. Both groups used "Learn to Be Lean" workbooks based on behavioral therapy principles. Members of both groups lost weight in equal amounts over a six-month period. The peer-led group was only half as costly as the professional-led group.

---

*Note: This concludes the research review by Drs. Kyrouz, Humphreys, and Loomis. Their work was supported by the Department of Veterans Affairs Mental Health Strategic Health Group. Their review on research is in the public domain and can be photocopied.*

---

0ʒ  0ʒ

## Interested in Doing or Requesting Needed Research?

The **"Self-Help Group Research" Mailing List,** or "SLFHLP-L" Listserv, currently has over a hundred members, mostly from colleges and universities worldwide. They discuss various aspects of doing research with, and on, self-help groups. A few representatives of self-help groups are members too, and they are welcome to raise issues related to any type of research issue dealing with self-help groups.

To subscribe to SLFHLP-L, just send an e-mail message to:
   **listserv@listserv.utoronto.ca**
Type in the message text section:
   **SUB SLFHLP-L YourFirstName YourLastName**

For example if John Doe wants to subscribe, he will type in the message section:
   **SUB SLFHLP-L John Doe**
Note that anything typed in the "Subject" header line of your e-mail will be ignored.

After you send this e-mail, you will automatically receive back an e-mail acknowledgement that you are subscribed. You will also receive information on how to post a message and how to cancel your subscription. You will then receive any e-mail postings that are made to this listserv as others post them. You can also post a message to the listserv, introducing yourself and indicating what type of research information or interest that you or your group have.

# An Interesting Research Study...
## "Why Self-Help Groups May Be a Woman's Natural Response to Stress"

Although there is no empirical research showing that more women participate in self-help groups than men, there is now research reflecting why more women under stress might be more prone to seek out other women in a support group. The research study done by Dr. Shelly Taylor and others (see reference below) revealed that women have a **"Tend-and-Befriend"** response to stress rather than the male **"Fight-or-Flight."** response. The reason that this was only recently discovered is that prior to 1995, only 17% of participants in human stress experiments were women. The new research has revealed that women have a different inborn response to stress than men, one that is more calming and communal with two primary characteristics: "*Tending*" = nurturing activities to protect oneself and any children, and "*Befriending*" = **turning to a social network of supportive females for safety and to reduce stress.**

According to the study, the response appears to be based on the action of hormones (oxytocin produced in the brain by the pituitary gland) being released in high levels during stressful or painful situations like childbirth, thus producing a calming effect and facilitating social contact and bonding. Touching, hugging, stroking, and cuddling release oxytocin and its anti-stress properties. Both men and women secrete oxytocin. However, women's estrogen amplifies the effect and men's testosterone diminishes the effect.

So, while men have historically tended to form social groups more for purposes of aggression and war, we now see that women tend to form social groups during stressful periods (as typified by their asking others for directions when lost). They are more communal. This is an inborn tendency--it doesn't mean that women cannot be aggressive, or that men do not befriend others. Commenting on the findings, Drs. David Sobel and Robert Ornstein concluded in their Mind/Body Health Newsletter (IX, 3, 2000) that this style of coping may be related to the why women enjoy a seven year greater life expectancy over men. It may also explain why more women than men are apt to start self-help groups.

- Shelley E. Taylor, LC Klein, BP Lewis, TL Gruenewald; RA Gurung, & JA Updegraff (Dept. of Psychology, UCLA), "Biobehavioral Responses to Stress in Females: Tend-and-Befriend, Not Fight-or-Flight" Psychological Review, 2000, 107(3), pp 411-429.

**Chapter 5**

# SELF–HELP GROUP CLEARINGHOUSES

Self-help clearinghouses provide information on local support groups, especially the one-of-a-kind groups that are not affiliated with any national self-help organization. In addition, many of the clearinghouses listed below provide consultation to new and existing groups, directories of local groups, and other services of interest to self-help groups. To find a local self-help group for your concern, review the list of self-help clearinghouses below to see if there is one that serves your area.

# UNITED STATES

## ARIZONA

**Self-Help Umbrella**                                        **Central Arizona**
Provides information and referrals to support groups. Offers assistance in starting groups.
Self-Help Umbrella                   *Phone:* 602-231-0868
P.O. Box 97251                       *E-mail:* umbrella-az@juno.com
Phoenix, AZ 85060 7251

## CALIFORNIA

**SHARE! (Self-Help And Recovery Exchange)**                  **Los Angeles**
Provides information and referrals to local self-help groups. Offers technical assistance for new and ongoing self-help groups. Provides meeting space for various groups. 24-hr. voice-mail with information on the most requested groups.
SHARE!                               *Phone:* 310-305-8878
5521 Grosvenor Blvd.
Los Angeles, CA 90066

**Friends Are Good Medicine**                                **Modesto**
Provides information and referrals to local self-help groups. Publishes directory of self-help groups.                 *Phone:* 209-525-6239
Friends Network                      *Fax:* 209-525-5361
800 Scenic Dr.                       *E-mail:* chowlett@mail.co.stanislaus.ca.us
Modesto, CA 95350                    *Website:* http://www.co.stanislaus.ca.us

**Mental Health Association**                                **Sacramento area**
Provides information on local self-help groups. Provides training and technical assistance to people starting new groups. Conducts community education about self-help.

MHA                                     *Phone:* 916-366-4600
9719 Lincoln Village Dr., #130          *Fax:* 916-855-5448
Sacramento, CA 95827

**Self-Help Connection**                                    **San Diego County**
Provides information and referral to over 600 free or low cost support groups in San
Diego County. Also provides facilitator training for individuals who are interested in
starting and maintaining support groups. Publishes Directory.
Self-Help Connection                    *Phone*: 619-543-0412
c/o MHA in San Diego County             *Fax:* 619-543-0748
2047 El Cajon Blvd.                      *E-mail*: mhasd@flash.net
San Diego, CA 92104 1091

**HELPLINK**                                    **Greater San Francisco area**
Provides information and referral to support groups in an 11 county area. Assistance in
starting groups. Conducts community education. Also provides information and referrals
to local services and agencies. Accepts collect calls.
HELPLINK                                *Phone*: 1-800-273-6222; 415-772-4357
N. Calif. Council for the Comm.         *Fax:* 415-391-8302; *TTY:* 415-772-4440
50 California St., Suite 200             *E-mail*: nccchelp@pacbell.net
San Francisco, CA 94111                 *Website*: http://www.ncccsf.org

**Mental Health Association of Yolo County**                    **Yolo County**
Provides information and referrals to support groups in Yolo County. Offers assistance in
starting  and maintaining groups, training workshops, how to materials, directory of local
groups. Sponsors several self-help groups. Conferences, speakers bureau.
MHA of Yolo County                      *Phone:* 530-756-8181
P.O. Box 447
Davis, CA 95617

# CONNECTICUT

**Connecticut Self-Help Support Network**                          **Statewide**
Provides information and referrals to support groups. Offers technical assistance in
starting and maintaining groups, and group leadership training, educational workshops
and conferences. Publishes directory of self-help groups, newsletter, other publications.
Connecticut SH Support Network          *Phone:* 203-624-6982
c/o The Consultation Center             *Fax:* 203-562-6355
389 Whitney Ave.                        *E-mail:* info@theconsultationcenter.org
New Haven, CT 06511                     (attention: self help)

# HAWAII

**United Self-Help**                                              **Statewide**
Provide information and referrals to self-help groups. Assists persons in starting new
groups.                                 *Phone*: 1-866-866-4357 or 808-926-0466

United Self-Help                    *Fax*: 808-926-1651
277 Ohua St.                        *E-mail*: director@unitedselfhelp.org
Honolulu, HI 96815                  *Website*: http://www.unitedselfhelp.org

# ILLINOIS

**Information Line**                                              **Statewide**
Provides information about support groups. Publishes directory of local self-help groups.
Information Line                    *Phone*: 312-368-9070 ext. 10
c/o Mental Health Assn. in Illinois
188 W. Randolph, Suite 2225
Chicago, Il 60601

**Illinois Self-Help Coalition**                                 **Statewide**
Provides assistance in starting groups, training workshops, consultation to existing groups, how-to materials, conferences, speakers bureau, directory of support groups.
Illinois Self-Help Coalition        *Phone:* 773-481-8837
Zarem/Golde ORT Tech. Inst.         *Fax:* 773-481-8917
3050 W. Touhy Ave.                  *E-mail:* dipeace@aol.com
Chicago, Il 60645                   *Website:* http://www.selfhelp-illinois.org

**Self-Help Center**                     **Champaign and surrounding counties**
Provides information and referral to local support groups. Offers assistance in starting support groups, how-to materials, training workshops, directory, specialized group listings, newsletter, consultation to existing groups, and library of self-help literature.
Self-Help Center                    *Phone:* 217-352-0099; *Fax*: 217-352-9512
c/o Family Service                  *TDD:* 217-352-0160
405 S. State St.                    *E-mail*: selfhelp@prairienet.org
Champaign, IL 61820 5196            *Website*: http://www.prairienet.org/selfhelp

**First Call For Help**                                          **Macon County**
Provides information and referrals to local support groups. Publishes directory of local groups.
First Call For Help                 *Phone:* 217-475-2255
160 E. Main
Decatur, IL 62523

# INDIANA

**United Way of Bartholomew County**                    **Bartholomew County**
Provides information on local support groups. Online list of groups available.
United Way of Bartholomew Cty.      *Phone:* 812-376-6666 or 812-376-0011
522 Franklin St.                    *Fax:* 812-376-2217; *E mail:* uwbc@iquest.net
Columbus, IN 47202 0827             *Website*: www.unitedway.bartholomew.in.us/

**Riverwood Center For Self-Help                Southwest Michigan/Northern Indiana**
Provides information and referrals to support groups. Networks individuals, groups, professionals and agencies. Provides community education. Assists new groups in starting. Facilitates group meetings. Training workshops. Directory.

Riverwood Center for Self-Help        *Phone*: 1-800-336-0341 (in MI)
P.O. Box 547                          *Phone:* 616-927-6065 ext. 6 (outside MI)
Benton Harbor, MI 49023 0547

## KANSAS

**Self-Help Network of Kansas                                          Statewide**
Provides information and referral to self-help groups. Technical assistance and consultation to existing groups or persons interested in starting groups. Offers community education, training workshops and conferences. Self-help group leader handbook. Publishes directory of groups. Conducts research.

Self-Help Network of Kansas          *Phone:* 1-800-445-0116 or 316-978-3843
Wichita State University             *Fax:* 316-978-3593
Box 34, 1845 Fairmount               *E-mail:* selfhelp@wichita.edu
Wichita, KS 67260-0034               *Website:* www.selfhelpnetwork.wichita.edu

**Mental Health Association of the Heartland       Greater Kansas City area (KS/MO)**
Information and referral to local mental health services, including support groups. Speakers bureau, conferences, advocacy for mental health consumers, and educational workshops for self-help group leaders. Teen suicide and violence prevention program available. Directory of self-help groups.

MHA of the Heartland                 *Helpline:* 913-281-1234 (9am-9pm)
739 Minnesota Ave.                   *Admin:* 913-281-2221; *Fax:* 913-281-3977
Kansas City, KS 66101                *Warmline:* 913-281-2251

## MICHIGAN

**Michigan Self-Help Clearinghouse                                     Statewide**
Provides referrals to support groups statewide. Helps people to start new groups. Provides consultation to existing groups. Newsletter, speakers bureau, training workshops, written materials, and statewide directory.

Michigan Self-Help Clearinghouse     *Phone:* 1-800-777-5556 (in MI)
4095 Legacy Parkway #500             *Admin:* 517-484-7373; *Fax:* 517-487-0827
Lansing, MI 48911-4263               *Website:* http://www.mpas.org

**Riverwood Center For Self-Help                Southwest Michigan/Northern Indiana**
Provides information and referrals to support groups. Community education. Assists new groups in starting. Facilitates group meetings. Training workshops. Directory.

Riverwood Center for Self-Help       *Phone:* 1-800-336-0341 (in MI)
P.O. Box 547                         *Phone:* 616-927-6065 ext. 6 (outside MI)
Benton Harbor, MI 49023-0547

# MINNESOTA

**First Call For Help in Minnesota**                                    **Statewide**
Provides information and referral on all types of local self-help groups. Also provides information on other types of local agencies and services.
FCFH in MN                          *Phone*: 1-800-543-7709 (in MN)
P.O. Box 7519                        or 1-800-240-4334 (outside MN)
St. Cloud, MN 56302

# MISSOURI

**Mental Health Association of the Heartland**       **Greater Kansas City area (KS/MO)**
Information and referral to local mental health services, including support groups. Public awareness and education. Speakers bureau, conferences, and educational workshops for self-help group leaders. Teen suicide and violence prevention program available. Directory of self-help groups.
MHA of the Heartland                 *Helpline:* 913-281-1234 (9am-9pm)
739 Minnesota Ave.                   *Admin:* 913-281-2221; *Fax:* 913-281-3977
Kansas City, KS 66101                *Warmline*: 913-281-2251

**St. Louis Self-Help Clearinghouse**                                    **St. Louis area**
Provides information and referral to all types of support groups in the St. Louis area. Helps interested persons to start support groups. Provides consultation and technical assistance to new and existing groups. Directory available.
St. Louis Self-Help Clearinghouse    *Phone:* 314-773-1399
c/o MHA of Greater St. Louis         *Fax:* 314-773-5930
1905 S. Grand                        *E-mail:* mhagstl@aol.com
St. Louis, MO 63104                  *Website*: http://www.mhasstl.org

# NEBRASKA

**Nebraska Self-Help Information Services**                              **Statewide**
*(Founded 1964)* Provides information and referral to support groups. Offers assistance to new and existing groups. Acts as an answering service to groups. Presentations can be arranged for schools and other interested organizations.
Nebraska Self-Help Info. Services    *Phone:* Barbara Fox 402-476-9668
1601 Euclid Ave.                     *Fax:* 402-434-3972
Lincoln, NE 68502

# NEW JERSEY

**New Jersey Self-Help Group Clearinghouse**                            **Statewide**
Provides information and referrals to over 4500 self-help support groups statewide. Offers assistance to new and existing groups. Conducts workshops and conferences on starting groups, facilitation skills, and other issues. Publishes directory of local and national support groups.        *Phone:* 1-800-367-6274 (in NJ)

NJ Self-Help Group CH              *Phone:* 973-326-6789 (outside NJ)
100 E. Hanover Ave., Suite 202     *E-mail:* info@njgroups.org; *Fax:* 973-326-9467
Cedar Knolls, NJ 07927-2020        *Website:* http://www.selfhelpgroups.org

# NEW YORK

**Self-Help Resource Center**                                    **Broome County**
Provides information and referrals to local self-help groups. Publishes a directory of local groups. Works with established and prospective self-help group leaders to assist them in creating and/or developing their groups. Conducts needs assessment. Assist in organizing new groups. Presents free consumer conferences designed to educate public about psychiatric diagnoses and self-help methods for symptom management.
Self-Help Resource Center          *Phone:* 607-771-8888
c/o MHA                            *Fax:* 607-771-8892
82 Oak St.                         *E-mail:* mha@stny.rr.com
Binghamton, NY 13905

**Self-Help Clearinghouse of Cattaraugus County**          **Cattaraugus County**
Provides information and referral to local support groups. Offers assistance in starting new groups. Assistance with utility payments, disaster funding and assistance, various health and safety training classes, blood drives, and military emergency service (24 hrs).
American Red Cross                 *Phone:* 716-372-5800
SH Clearinghouse of Cattaraugus Cty.
452 N. Barry St.
Olean, NY 14760 2612

**InfoLine of United Way of Dutchess County**              **Dutchess County**
Helps connect individuals in the community with the services and/or information they need. Maintains a database on local, non-profit, human services providers and self-help groups. Publishes directories on human-services, self-help, and civic groups. Specialized directories are available.
InfoLine of UW of Dutchess County  *Phone:* 845-473-1500 (info and referral)
75 Market St., P.O. Box 832        or 845-471-1900 ext. 24 (directory orders)
Poughkeepsie, NY 12602

**Erie County Self-Help Clearinghouse**                          **Erie County**
Provides information and referrals to local self-help groups. Offers assistance to existing groups in the Buffalo area.
Erie County Self-Help Clearinghouse  *Phone:* 716-886-1242
c/o MHA of Erie County, Inc.         *Fax:* 716-881-6428
999 Delaware Ave.
Buffalo, NY 14209

**Clearinghouse for Self-Help Groups**                          **Monroe County**
Provides information and referrals to local support groups. Assistance in starting new groups, training workshops, how-to materials. Offers consultation to existing groups. Directory of local groups to be published online.

Clearinghouse for Self-Help Groups    *Phone:* 585-325-3145 ext 18; *Fax:* 585-325-3188
339 East Ave., Suite 201              *E-mail:* dsponable@mharochester.org
Rochester, NY 14604                   *Website:* http://mharochester.org

**Long Island Self-Help Clearinghouse**                    **Nassau and Suffolk Counties**
Referrals to local support groups. Assistance to new and existing groups.
LI Self-Help Clearinghouse           *Phone:* 516-626-1721
NY College of Osteopathic Med.       *Fax:* 516-686-7890
NY Institute of Technology           *E-mail:* egiannet@nyit.edu
P.O. Box 8000
Old Westbury, NY 11568

**New York City Self-Help Center**                                  **New York City**
Provides information and referrals to support groups in the five boroughs (Manhattan,
Bronx, Staten Island, Queens, and Brooklyn). Offers assistance to new and developing
groups. Publishes New York City Resource Guide ($10).
NYC Self Help Center                 *Phone:* 212-586-5770
850 7th Ave., Suite 1201             *Fax:* 212-399-2475
New York, NY 10019

**Niagara Self-Help Clearinghouse**                               **Niagara County**
Provides information and referrals to local support groups. Provides technical assistance
to new groups and group leader training. Publishes directory of self-help groups.
Maintains mental health video/book library.
Niagara Self-Help Clearinghouse      *Phone:* 716-433-3780
c/o MHA of Niagara County
36 Pine St.
Lockport, NY 14094

**Helpline/Rapeline**                                             **Orange County**
Provides information and referral to local support groups. Offers 24-hour crisis and rape
hotline. Referrals to local services and agencies. Publishes directory of local services.
Helpline/Rapeline                    *Phone:* 1-800-832-1200 (Orange County )
c/o MHA in Orange County             *Phone:* 914-294-9355 (outside Orange County)
20 Walker St.
Goshen, NY 10924

**The Self-Help Clearinghouse**                                 **Rockland County**
Provides information and referral concerning self-help groups. Offers consultation and
assistance to new groups that are forming. Publishes newsletter, self-help directory ($3).
Self-Help Clearinghouse              *Phone:* 845-639-7400 ext. 22
c/o MHA of Rockland County Inc.      *Fax:* 845-639-7419
20 Squadron Blvd.                    *E-mail:* selfhelp@mharockland.org
New City, NY 10956                   *Website:* http://www.mharockland.org

**Reachout of St. Lawrence County**                    **Saint Lawrence County**
Provides referrals to local support groups and other services and agencies. Also has
information on national organizations. Provides limited consultation to existing and new
groups. Acts as Alcoholics Anonymous answering service. Provides crisis intervention.
Reachout                          *Phone:* 315-265-2422; *Fax:* 315-265-1752
P.O. Box 5051                     *E-mail:* reachout@slic.com
Potsdam, NY 13676 5051            *Website:* http://pages.slic.com/reachout

**Mechanicville Area Community Services Center, Inc.**          **Saratoga County**
Provide information and referral to local self-help groups. Offers consultation and
technical assistance to existing groups.
Mechanicville Area Comm Svc Ctr.  *Phone:* 518-664-8322
P.O. Box 30                       *Fax:* 518-664-9457
Mechanicville, NY 12118           *E-mail:* macsc@albany.net

**Institute for Human Services/HELPLINE**   **Steuben, Allegheny, Chemung Counties**
Provides information and referrals to local services and agencies, as well as local support
groups. Assistance to new and existing self-help groups. Acts as 24-hour crisis and
referral line. Newsletter, information and referral.
HELPLINE/Inst. for Human Svcs.    *Phone:* 1-800-346-2211 (in NY)
6666 County Rd.                   *Phone:* 607-776-9467 (outside NY)
Bath, NY 14810-7722               *Helpline:* 607-776-9604

**HELPLINE Information and Referral Service**          **Syracuse/Onandaga County**
Provides information on area self-help groups. Also refers callers to other local services
and agencies. Publishes a Human Services Directory,
HELPLINE                          *Phone:* 315-474-7011 or 315-474-7013
c/o United Way of CNY             *TDD:* 1-800-662-1220
P.O. Box 2129                     *E-mail:* sstarr@unitedway cny.org
Syracuse, NY 13220 2129           *Website:* http://www.unitedway cny.org

**Mental Health Association in Tompkins County**          **Tompkins County**
Information and referral, education, advocacy, respite and family support concerning
mental health issues and services, including referrals to support groups and therapists.
Publishes a support group guide, a directory of local psychotherapists, and a newsletter.
MHA in Tompkins County            *Phone:* 607-273-9250; *Fax:* 607-272-5343
518 W. State St.                  *E-mail:* info@mhaedu.org
Ithaca, NY 14850                  *Website:* http://www.mhaedu.org

**Mental Health Association in Ulster County**          **Ulster County**
Provides information and referrals to local support groups. Offers assistance in starting
mental health support groups, training workshops, how to materials, and consultation to
existing groups. Directory, speakers bureau, and training programs for families of the
mentally ill, models for transitional groups.
MHA in Ulster County              *Phone:* 845-339-9090 ext. 113
P. O. Box 2304                    *Fax:* 845-339-9306
Kingston, NY 12401 0227           *E-mail:* olla70@hotmail.com

**Westchester Self-Help Clearinghouse**                    **Westchester County**
Information and referral to local support groups. Assists new and existing groups through leadership training, workshops and conferences. Publishes directory of self-help groups. Phone network for newly widowed persons and newly separated women.
Westchester Self-Help Clearinghouse    *Phone*: 914-949-7699 ext. 319
141 North Central Ave.                  *Fax*: 914-949-3224
Hartsdale, NY 10530

# NORTH CAROLINA

                                    **Cabarrus, Chatham, Durham, Gaston,**
**SupportWorks**                    **Mecklenburg, Orange, Rowan, Wake Counties**
Provides information and referral to support groups in eight county area. Networks persons seeking mutual support. Provides consultation to people developing face-to-face and telephone groups. Offers free or low-cost telephone conference calls available to non- profit organizations. Publishes how-to materials on starting groups.
SupportWorks                        *Phone:* 704-331-9500 (group information)
1125 E. Morehead St., Suite 209     *Admin*: 704-377-2055
Charlotte, NC 28204 2849            *Website:* http://www.supportworks.org

# NORTH DAKOTA

**FirstLINK**                                    **Fargo-Moorhead area**
Provides information and referral to self-help groups and other services and agencies. Publishes directory of local support groups, and provides limited consultation to new and existing groups. Also offers listening services and crisis intervention.
FirstLINK                           *Phone:* 701-293-6462 (admin)
P.O. Box 447                        *Helpline:* 701-235-7335
Fargo, ND 58107 0447                *Fax:* 701-237-0982

# OHIO

**Mental Health Association**                   **Greater Cincinnati area/northern KY**
Provides referrals to local self-help groups. Publishes directory and website listing. Provides assistance to existing groups.
MHA                                 *Phone:* 513-721-2910; *Fax:* 513-287-8544
2400 Reading Rd., Suite 412         *E-mail:* sgcmha@hotmail.com
Cincinnati, OH 45202                *Website:* http://www.mentalhealthassn.org

**Greater Dayton Self Help Clearinghouse**                    **Dayton**
Provides information and referral to self-help groups. Technical assistance and leadership training for new and existing group leaders. Self-help group directory upon request.
Greater Dayton Self-Help Clrnghs    *Phone:* 937-225-3004
c/o Family Service Assn.            *Fax:* 937-222-3710
184 Salem Ave.                      *TDD*: 937-222-7921
Dayton, OH 45406                    *E-mail:* community@fsadayton.org

**The Greater Toledo Self-Help Network**                                    **Toledo**
Provides information and referrals to local self-help groups. Assists area professionals in locating groups for their clients. Provides consultation to new and existing groups, training workshops, and how to guidelines.
Greater Toledo Self-Help Network     *Phone:* 419-475-4449
c/o Harbor Behavioral Health Care     *Fax:* 419-479-3230
4334 Secor Rd.
Toledo, OH 43623

## OREGON

**Northwest Regional Self-Help Clearinghouse**     **Northern OR/Clark county WA**
Maintains an extensive database of resources and self-help groups in Multnomah, Clackamas and Washington counties in Oregon, and Clark county in Washington. Publishes Resource File, Self-Help Group Directory, and Human Services Directory.
NW Reg. Self-Help Clearinghouse     *Phone:* 503-226-3099 (I&R)
c/o Guide Line, Inc.                       *Phone:* 503-499-5555 (admin)
621 SW Alder, Suite 400             *Fax:* 503-499-4301
Portland, OR 97205                   *E-mail:* rebecca@guidelineinc.org

## PENNSYLVANIA

**HELPLINE**                                                     **Allegheny County**
Provides general information and referrals for the Allegheny county area. Also makes referrals and provides support to local self-help groups in southwestern Pennsylvania.
HELPLINE                             *Phone:* 412-255-1155
c/o CONTACT Pittsburgh, Inc.         *Fax:* 412-820-0130
P.O. Box 111294                      *E-mail:* helpline@contactpgh.org
Pittsburgh, PA 15238

**SHINE (Self-Help Information Network Exchange)**     **Lackawanna County**
Information and referral to support groups in northeastern area. Sponsors workshops and special events for self-help advocates. Brochure. Community resource library.
SHINE                                *Phone:* 570-961-1234 (24 hrs) or 570-347-5616
538 Spruce St., Suite 420            *E-mail:* shine@vacnepa.org
Scranton, PA 18503                   *Website:* http://www.vacnepa.org

**Valley Wide Help**                                              **Lehigh Valley**
*(Bilingual)* Provides information on local support groups in the Lehigh Valley area (Allentown, Easton, Bethlehem, and Slate Belt areas). Also provides comprehensive information about non-profit agencies, programs and services.
Valley Wide Help                     *Phone:* 610-435-7111 (groups) or 610-865-4400
c/o American Red Cross               *TDD:* 610-866-0131; *Spanish:* 610-866-1089
2200 Avenue A                        *E-mail:* LewisCa@usa.redcross.org
Bethlehem, PA 18017 2181             *Website:* http://www.irissoft.com/vwhp

**Mutual Support Group Clearinghouse**                    **Susquehanna Valley**
Provides information on self-help groups in central region. Technical assistance to new
and existing groups. Workshops, newsletter, directory of regional self-help groups.
Mutual Support Group Clearinghouse    *Phone*: 1-800-874-8363 or 570-784-9583
c/o MHA                                *Fax*: 570-784-3220
37 W. Main St., Suite 204              *E-mail*: mhacsvi@netscape.net
Bloomsburg, PA 17815

## SOUTH CAROLINA

**Midlands Area Support Group Network**            **Richland/Lexington County**
Provides information and referral to self-help groups in Richland/Lexington County.
Midlands Area Support Group Ntwrk    *Phone:* 803-791-2800
2720 Sunset Blvd.
West Columbia, SC 29169

## TENNESSEE

**Mental Health Association of Greater Knoxville**        **Greater Knoxville area**
Provides information and referral regarding self-help groups in eastern Tennessee. Offers
consultation for persons interested in starting new groups and training for self-help group
leaders. Publishes directory of local support groups ($12).
MHA of Greater Knoxville            *Phone:* 865-584-9125 (Voice/Fax)
P.O. Box 52405                      *Website:* http://www.kornet.org/mha
Knoxville, TN 37950-2405

## TEXAS

**Texas Self-Help Information and Referral Service**              **Statewide**
Provides information and referral to local self-help clearinghouses and agencies
statewide. Offers consultation to persons interested in starting new groups. Publishes
technical manual for starting support groups and other manuals.
Texas Self-Help I&R Service        *Phone*: 512-454-3706 ext. 202
c/o MHA                            *Fax*: 512-454-3725
8401 Shoal Creek Blvd.
Austin, TX 78757

**Community Council of Greater Dallas**                        **Dallas area**
Provides referrals to mental health resources and support groups.
Comm. Council of Greater Dallas    *Phone:* 214-871-5065
400 N. St. Paul
Dallas, TX 75201-5065

*"What do we live for, if it is not for helping each other."*– George Eliot

**Self-Help Resource Center for Greater Houston**                    **Houston**
Provides information and referral services for self-help groups in the Houston area. Services provided for persons developing new groups and for persons who facilitate groups. Facilitation workshops, directory and newsletter are also available.

Self-Help Resource Ctr.            *Phone*: 713-522-5161 (groups) or 713-523-8963
c/o MHA of Greater Houston         *Fax*: 713-522-0698
2211 Norfolk, Suite 810            *E-mail*: jesse@mhahouston.org
Houston, TX 77098                  *Website:* http://www.mhahouston.org

**Self-Help Clearinghouse for Tarrant County**                **Tarrant County**
Promotes the awareness and development of mutual aid self-help groups throughout Tarrant county. Provides information and referrals to support groups.

SHC of Tarrant County              *Phone:* 817-335-5405
c/o MHA of Tarrant County          *Fax:* 817-334-0025
3136 W. 4th St.                    *E-mail:* mhatc@mhatc.org
Fort Worth, TX 76107 2113          *Website*: http://www.mhatc.org

# UTAH

**Information and Referral Center**                        **Salt Lake City area**
Information and referral to local self-help groups and other services and agencies. Limited consultation to new and existing groups. Publishes directory of local groups.

Info. and Referral Center          *Phone:* 801-978-3333; *Fax*: 801-978-9565
1025 S. 700 West                   *E-mail:* joshp@csc ut.org
Salt Lake City, UT 84104           *Website:* http://www.informationandreferral.org

# WASHINGTON

**Northwest Regional Self-Help Clearinghouse**      **Northern OR/Clark county WA**
Information on resources and self-help groups in Multnomah, Clackamas and Washington counties in Oregon, and Clark county in Washington. Publishes Self-Help Group Directory, and other directories.

NW Reg. SH Clearinghouse           *Phone*: 503-226-3099 (I&R)
c/o Guide Line, Inc.               *Phone*: 503-499-5555 (admin)
621 SW Alder, Suite 400            *Fax:* 503-499-4301
Portland, OR 97205                 *E-mail:* Rebecca@guidelineinc.org

# NATIONWIDE

**American Self-Help Group Clearinghouse**                      **National**
Maintains database of national self-help headquarters and model one-of-a-kind groups. Referrals to self-help clearinghouses worldwide. Offers assistance to persons interested in starting new national groups or networks. Publishes Self-Help Sourcebook.

American Self-Help Clearinghouse   *Phone:* 973-326-6789; *Fax:* 973-326-9467
100 E. Hanover Ave., Suite 202     *E-mail*: info@selfhelpgroups.org
Cedar Knolls, NJ 07927-2020        *Website:* http://www.selfhelpgroups.org

**National Self-Help Clearinghouse**                                      **National**
Information and referral to self-help groups and regional self-help clearinghouses. Conducts training and research on self-help groups. Publishes manuals and training materials.

National Self-Help Clearinghouse      *Phone:* 212-817-1822
CUNY Grad School & Univ. Ctr.         *E-mail:* ajgartner@gc.cuny.edu
365 Fifth Ave., Suite 3300            *Website:* http://www.selfhelpweb.org
New York, NY 10016

# CANADA

## ALBERTA

**Support Network Edmonton's Distress and Information Center**      **Edmonton**
Provides referrals to local self-help groups. Publishes directory of self-help groups.
The Support Network                   *Phone:* 780-482-4636 or 780-482-0198
301-11456 Jasper Ave.                 *E-mail:* admin@thesupportnetwork.com
Edmonton, AB T5K 0M1 Canada           *Website:* http://www.thesupportnetwork.com

## BRITISH COLUMBIA

**Self-Help Resource Association of B.C.**                            **Vancouver**
Provides support and resources to self-helpers, agencies, professionals, and others involved in the self-help/mutual aid community. Services and programs include: resource library, group development and facilitator training, public education and outreach, annual directory of local self-help groups, self-help community development, Youth Initiative Program which fosters the development of self-help circles for youth.
SHRA-BC                               *Phone:* 604-733-6186; *Fax:* 604-730-1015
306 1212 W. Broadway                  *E-mail:* shra@telvs.net
Vancouver, BC V6H 3V1 Canada          *Website:* http://www.vcn.bc.ca/shra

## MANITOBA

**SMD Self-Help Clearinghouse, Inc.**                                **Winnipeg**
Provides information on local self-help groups. Offers assistance to new and existing groups, training workshops. Directory of local groups.
SMD Self-Help Clearinghouse           *Phone:* 204-975-3037
825 Sherbrook St.                     *Fax*: 204-975-3027
Winnipeg, MB R3A1M5 Canada            *Website:* http://www.smd-clearinghouse.com

## NEW BRUNSWICK

**INFO line**                                                    **New Brunswick**
Provides information and referral on community services. Publishes a variety of human
service directories.                          *Phone*: 506-633-4636 (group info)
INFO line                                     *Phone*: 506-634-1673; *Fax:* 506-636-8543
c/o Human Development Council                 *E-mail:* hdc@nbnet.nb.ca
Box 6125 Station A                            *E-mail:* infoline@nb.aibn.com
Saint John, NB E2L 4R6 Canada                 *Website*: humandevelopmentcouncil.nb.ca

## NEWFOUNDLAND

**CHANNAL (Consumer Health Awareness
Network Newfoundland And Labrador)**                    **Newfoundland/Labrador**
Provides information and referrals to local self-help groups. Helps persons to start and
maintain self-help groups.
CHANNAL                                       *Phone*: 709-753-5111
P.O. Box 5788                                 *Fax:* 709-753-8537
St. John's, NF A1C 5X3 Canada

## NOVA SCOTIA

**Community Health Promotion Network**                              **Atlantic**
Shares health promotion information among individuals, groups and communities in
eastern Canada.                               *Phone:* 902-463-9885 or 1-866-872-4762
Canadian Health Promo Network                 *Fax:* 902-463-7885
14 Averill St.                                *E-mail:* chpna@echo-chn.net
Dartmouth, NS B3A 2H2 Canada                  *Website:* http://www.canadian-health-network.ca

**Clearinghouse - The Self-Help Connection**                        **Dartmouth**
Provides referrals to provincial self-help groups. Assistance to new and existing groups.
Publishes directory of local self-help groups.
Clearinghouse - SH Connection                 *Phone:* 902-466-2011
63 King St.                                   *Fax*: 902-466-3300
Dartmouth, NS B2Y 2R7 Canada                  *E-mail:* selfhelp@attcanada.ca

## ONTARIO

**CMHA Barrie Simcoe Branch**                              **Barrie Simcoe area**
Provides referrals to local self-help groups. Offers assistance to new and existing groups.
CMHA Barrie Simcoe Branch                     *Phone:* 705-726-5033
5 Bell Farm Rd.                               *Fax:* 705-726-0636
Barrie, ON L4M 5G1 Canada

**CMHA Durham Region**                                                    **Durham**
Provides referrals to local self-help groups. Offers assistance to new and existing groups.
Publishes directory of self-help groups.
CMHA Durham Region                    *Phone:* 905-436-8760
111 Simcoe St. North                  *Fax:* 905-436-1569
Oshawa, ON L1G 4S4 Canada

**AWARE (Action on Women's Addictions Research and Education)**          **Kingston**
Provides information and referrals to local self-help groups.
AWARE                                 *Phone:* 613-545-0117
P.O. Box 86                           *Fax:* 613-545-1508
Kingston, ON K7L 4V6 Canada           *E-mail:* aware@kos.net

**CMHA London Middlesex Branch**                              **London-Middlesex**
Provides referrals to local self-help groups. Offers assistance to new and existing groups.
CMHA London Middlesex Branch          *Phone:* 519-434-9191; *Fax:* 519-438-1167
648 Huron St.                         *E-mail:* mailbox@london.cmha.ca
London ON N5Y 4J8 Canada              *Website:* http://www.london.cmha.ca

**Rotary Club of Hamilton Self-Help Centre**              **New City of Hamilton**
Provides information and referrals to local self-help groups. Helps persons to start and
maintain groups.
Rotary Club of Hamilton SH Ctr.       *Phone:* 905-522-7353 ext. 300
255 West Ave. North                   *Fax:* 905-522-9374
Hamilton, ON L8L 5C8 Canada           *E-mail:* self.help.centre@hwcn.org

**Olde Forge Community Resource Center**                      **Ottawa-Carlton**
Provides referrals to local self-help groups. Assistance to new and existing groups.
Publishes directory of self-help groups.
Olde Forge Comm. Res. Ctr.            *Phone:* 613-829-9777
 2730 Carling Ave.                    *Fax:* 613-829-9318
Ottawa, ON K2B 7J1 Canada             *E-mail:* forge@ncf.ca

**Community Network Support Team**                              **Owen Sound**
Provides information, education and assistance in the development of local mental health
self-help groups. Maintains lending library of mental health books and videos. Operates
"Family Support Initiative" and "Consumer/Survivor Development Project" as well as
database of mental health and addiction programs.
Comm. Network Support Team            *Phone:* 519-371-4551; *Fax:* 519-371-6138
1139 Second Avenue East               *E-mail:* cnst@gbchc.healthserv.org
Owen Sound, ON N4K 2J1 Canada

**Oxford Self-Help Network**                                  **Oxford County**
Referrals to local mental health self-help groups. Publishes directory of resources and
other local self-help organizations. Lending library.

Oxford County Self-Help Network     *Phone:* 519-421-2980 or 1-877-464-3571
592 Adelaide St.                    *Fax:* 519-421-0826
Woodstock, ON N4S 4B9 Canada        *E-mail:* oshn@on.aibn.com

**Four Counties Self-Help Network**                          **Peterborough area**
Provides referrals to local self-help groups. Offers assistance to new and existing groups.
Four Counties Self-Help Network     *Phone:* 705-748-9144 ext. 305
201 Antrim St.                      *Fax:* 705-748-9177
Peterborough, ON K9H 3G5 CA         *E-mail:* nancym.pfrc@accel.net

**Self-Help Network of Sudbury Manitoulin**                  **Sudbury Manitoulin**
Provides information and referral to local self-help groups. Helps persons to start and
maintain groups.
Self-Help Network of                *Phone:* 705-677-0308
  Sudbury Manitoulin      *Fax:* 705-673-3354
199 Travers St.                     *E-mail:* selfhelp@isys.ca
Sudbury ON P3C 3K2 Canada           *Website:* http://theselfhelpnetwork.on.ca

**Self-Help Resource Center**                                **Greater Toronto area**
Provides referrals to local self-help groups. Offers assistance to new and existing groups.
Directory of self-help groups. Information on Ontario and national self help organizations
and special projects.               *Phone:* 416-487-4355 (Toronto area)
Self-Help Resource Center           *Phone:* 1-888-283-8806 (outside Toronto)
40 Orchard View Blvd., Suite 219    *E-mail:* shrc@selfhelp.on.ca
Toronto, ON M4R 1B9 Canada          *Website:* http://www.selfhelp.on.ca

**CMHA Waterloo Regional Branch**                            **Waterloo**
Provides referrals to local self-help groups. Assistance to new and existing groups.
Publishes directory of self-help groups.
CMHA Waterloo Regional Branch       *Phone:* 519-744-7645
c/o Centre for Mental Health        *Fax:* 519-744-7066
67 King St. East                    *E-mail:* cmhawrb@golden.net
Kitchener, ON N2G 2K4 Canada        *Website:* http://www.cmhawrb.on.ca

**CMHA Windsor Essex Branch**                                **Windsor-Essex**
Provides referrals to local self-help groups. Assistance to new and existing groups.
CMHA Windsor Essex Branch           *Phone:* 519-255-7440
1400 Windsor Ave.                   *Fax:* 519-255-7817
Windsor ON N8X 3L9 Canada           *E-mail:* bklingel@cmha-wecb.on.ca

**Self-Help Network of York Region**                         **York Region**
Provides information and referrals to local self-help groups. Helps persons to start and
maintain groups.
Self-Help Network of York Reg.      *Phone:* 905-780 0491
c/o Krasman Centre                  *Fax:* 905-780 1960
10121 Yonge St.                     *E-mail:* krasman@idirect.com
Richmond Hill, ON L4C 1T7 CA        *Website:* http://krasmancentre.com

# PRINCE EDWARD ISLAND

**Family Support and Self-Help Program**                          **Provincial**
Referrals to local self-help groups. Assistance to new and existing groups. Publishes directory of self-help groups.
Family Support & Self-Help Program     *Phone*: 902-628-1648
c/o CMHA                               *Fax*: 902-566-4643
P.O. Box 785                           *E-mail:* selfhelp@cmha.pe.ca
Charlottetown PEI C1A 7L9 Canada

# QUEBEC

**Centre d'Action Benevol du Quebec**                          **Provincial**
Provides information on local self-help groups. Helps to start and maintain groups.
Centre d'Action Benevol du Quebec     *Phone:* 418-681-3501
615 Pierre Bertrand Blvd S., #250     *Fax:* 418-681-6481
Vanier, PQ G1M 3J3

**Centre de Reference du Grand Montreal**                          **Montreal**
Provides referrals to local self-help groups. Offers assistance to new and existing groups. Publishes directory of self-help groups.
Ctr. de Ref. du Grand Montreal        *Phone:* 514-527-1375
801 Sherbrooke East, Suite 401        *Fax:* 514-527-9712
Montreal, PQ H2L 1K7 Canada

**West Island Volunteer Bureau**                          **West Island of Montreal**
Provides referrals to local self-help groups. Assistance to new and existing groups.
West Island Volunteer Bureau          *Phone*: 514-631-3720
750 Dawson Ave.                       *Fax*: 514-631-3024
Dorval, PQ H9S 1X1 Canada

# SASKATCHEWAN

**Saskatchewan Self-Help Network**                          **Saskatoon**
Information and referral to local self-help groups. Assistance with the development and maintenance of groups. Publishes directory of local self-help groups (printed version, CD Rom and online). Inexpensive server space and webpage development available. Training programs for professionals.
Saskatchewan Self-Help Network        *Phone*: 306-373-8908
315 28th St. West                     *Fax*: 306-665-3047
Saskatoon, SK S7L 0K6 Canada          *Website:* http://www.selfhelponline.ca

*"The greatest good you can do for another is not just share your riches,*
*but reveal to them their own."- Disraeli*

# INTERNATIONAL

## AUSTRALIA

**Collective of Self-Help Groups**                                         Victoria
Network of self-help and social action groups. Publishes directory of local groups.
Collective of Self-Help Groups        *Phone:* 9-349-301 (Wed., 2-4pm)
P.O. Box 251                           *E-mail:* coshgmelb@yahoo.com.au
Brunswick East, Australia 3057         *Website:* http://www.vicnet.net.au/~coshg

**Self-Help Queensland, Inc.**                                           Queensland
Provides information on local self-help groups. Helps persons to start and maintain
groups.
Self-Help Queensland, Inc.            *Phone:* (07)3344-6919
P.O. Box 353                          *E-mail:* qnosho@gil.com.au
Sunnybank, Queensland, Australia 4109

**WISH (Western Institute of Self-Help)**                        Western Australia
Supports self-help groups and identifies new groups. Publications.
WISH                                  *Phone:* +61 8   92 28 44 88
P.O. Box 8140                         *Fax:* +61 8   92 28 44 90
AUS Perth Business Centre             *E-mail*: info@wish.org.au
Western Australia 6849                *Website*: http://www.wish.org.au

## AUSTRIA

**Fonds Gesundes Osterreich**                                          Nationwide
Supports self-help groups nationwide. Aids in starting and maintaining groups, networks
regional clearinghouses, and acts as a liaison with political and administrative entities.
Fonds Gesundes Osterreich             *Phone*: +43 1 8 95 04 00 12
SIGIS                                 *Fax:* +43 1 8 95 04 00 20
Marianhilfer Strasse 176              *E-mail:* andrea.lins@fgoe.org
A 1150 Wien, Austria                  *Website*: http://www.fgoe.org

## BELGIUM

**Trefpunt Zelfhulp**                                              Flanders/Leuven
Information and referrals to Flemish and local self-help groups. Helps new and existing
groups. Education, crisis intervention, legal advice, advocacy.
Trefpunt Zelfhulp vzw                 *Phone:* +32/16 23 65 07 or +32/16 32 31 58
Dept. Sociologie                      *E-mail:* trefpunt-zelfhult@soc-kuleuven.ac.be
E. Van Evenstraat 2c                  *Website*: http://www.zelfhulp.be
B 3000 Leuven, Belgium

## CROATIA

**Al'drija Stampar School of Public Health**                         Zagreb
Provides referrals to local self-help groups.
Al'drija Stampar School of          *Phone:* 00385-1-4590100
  Public Health                    *Fax*: 00385-1-4648406
Rockefeller Str. 4
10000 Zagreb, Croatia

## DENMARK

**Faellesforeningen**                                               National
Provides referrals to self-help groups nationwide.
Faellesforeningen                   *Phone:* +45  62 20 11 30
c/o Mellem Mennesker                *Fax:* +45  62 20 11 13
Toldbodvej 5
DK 5700, Svendborg, Denmark

## ENGLAND

**Self-Help Nottingham**                                            National
Provides information and referral to self-help group nationwide. Publications, research.
Assistance in starting new groups, workshops.
Self Help Nottingham                *Phone:* +44 115 - 9 11 16 62
c/o Ormiston House                  *Phone*: +44 115 - 9 11 16 61 (infoline)
32 36 Pelham St.                    *Fax:* +44 115  - 9 11 16 60
GB Nottingham                       *E-mail:* enquiries@selfhelp.org.uk
NG1 2EG, England, UK                *Website*: http://www.selfhelp.org.uk

**Contact-A-Family**                                                National
*(Limited to illnesses/disabilities)* Provides help and advice to families of children and young people up to the age of 19 with illnesses or disabilities. Also provides information to adults affected by specific rare disorders. Hosts Rare Disorder Alliance. Maintains database of rare disorders. Publishes directory.
Contact-A-Family                    *Phone*: +44 (0) 20 7608 8700
209 211 City Rd.                    *Fax:* +44 (0) 20 7608 8701
London, England EC1V 1JN UK         *E-mail:* info@Cafamily.org.uk
                                    *Website:* http://www.cafamily.org.uk

🖳  **PATIENT UK**                                                  Online
Provides information on health related and bereavement self-help organizations serving the United Kingdom, which can then usually direct people to local support groups.
*Phone:* 0191 217 1536              *E-mail:* patientuk@btinternet.com
                                    *Website:* http://www.patient.org.uk

# FINLAND

**The Citizen Forum Association**                                    **Nationwide**
Coordinates contacts between self-help groups, clearinghouses, voluntary organizations
and professionals. Offers training, publications, information, research.
The Citizen Forum Association        *Phone:* +35/89 7 74 40 80
Sornaisten Rantatie 27A, 2nd floor   *E-mail:* marianne.nylund@helsinki.fi
SF  00500 Helsinki, Finland          *Website:* http://www.kansalaisareena.fi/

# GERMANY

**NAKOS (Nationale Kontakt)**                                    **Nationwide**
Distributes information on self-help groups nationwide. Assists new groups in starting.
Offers specialized publications, directory, and literature on starting and maintaining self-
help groups.
NAKOS (Nationale Kontakt)        *Phone*: +49 030  891 40 19; *Fax:*  893 40 14
Wilmersdorfer Strasse 65         *E-mail:* nakos@gmx.de
D 10709 Berlin, Germany          *Website:* http://www.nakos.de

**Deutsch Russischer Austausch e.V.**                                    **Nationwide**
Assists democratic development in Russia by cooperation with Russian non-government
organizations and independent media. *Phone:* +49/30/44/66  80 0 ext. 22
Deutsch Russischer Austausch e.V    *Fax:* +49/30/44/49 46 0
Brunnenstrasse 181                  *E-mail:* dra@austausch.com
D 10119 Berlin, Germany             *Website*: http://www.austausch.com

# HUNGARY

**Self-Help Information Centre**                                    **Budapest**
Provides referrals to local self-help groups.
Self-Help Information Centre    *Phone:* +36 1   3 41 06 75 or +36 1 3 11 40 09
Anrassy Street 82               *Fax*: +36 1   3 41 06 75
H 1068, Budapest, Hungary

# IRELAND

🖳 **Irish Medical Directory  Patient Support Organizations**        **Online**
Provides a list of self-help groups for a large variety of topics in Ireland.
                            *Website:* http://www.imd.ie/suppindx.htm

# ISRAEL

**Israel Self-Help Center**                                    **Nationwide**
Provides information and referral to self-help groups nationwide.

ISHC
37 King George St.
P.O. Box 23223
IL 61231, Tel Aviv, Israel

*Phone:* +972/3 6299389 or +972/3 6200259
*Fax:* + 972/3 5254486
*E-mail:* selfhelp@netvision.net.il
*Website:* http://www.selfhelp.org.il

## JAPAN

**Clearinghouse MUSASHI**                                    Nationwide
Provides information on self-help groups.
Clearinghouse MUSASHI
Omiya Nishi Post Office
331 0051, Japan

*Phone:* 048 297 9780 (Voice/Fax)
*E-mail:* info musshi@lycos.ne.jp

**Supporting Network for Chronic Sick Children of Japan**        Nationwide
Provides information and contacts to self-help groups nationwide. Provides some
international contacts.
Supporting Network for Chronic
  Sick Children of Japan
Bunkyo-Shogaku Biru 6F
1-15-4, Hongo, Bunkyo-ku
Tokyo 113-0033 Japan

*Phone:* 03 5840 5972 (office)
*Phone:* 03 5840 5973 (counseling)
*Fax:* 03 5840 5974
*E-mail:* ganbare@nanbyonet.or.jp
*E-mail:* toka@sophia.ac.jp (English)
*Website:* http://nanbyonet.or.jp

**Hyogo Self-Help Support Center**                              Hyogo
Provides information on self-help groups in the Hyogo area.
Hyogo Self-Help Support Center
1-8-22-203 Minamimachi Fuake
Higashinada-ku, Kobe City
Hyogo, 658-0022 Japan

*Phone:* +81-78-452-3082 (Voice/Fax)
*E-mail:* hyogosh@titan.ocn.ne.jp
*Website:* hyogo-selfhelp.hoops.ne/jp/

**Osaka Self Help Support Center**                              Osaka
Provides information on local self-help groups.
Osaka Self-Help Support Center
c/o Osaka Volunteer Association
1 5 27, Doshin, Kita ku
Osaka, 530 0035 Japan

*Phone:* +81 6 6352 0430
*Fax:* +81 6 6358 2892
*E-mail:* GHE01500@nifty.ne.jp

**Tochigi Self-Help Clearinghouse**                             Tochigi
Provides information on self-help groups in the Tochigi area.
Tochigi Self-Help Clearinghouse
Kyosei Bldg., 3rd floor
2-5-1 Hanawada, Utsunomiya
Tochigi, 320-0027 Japan

*Phone:* +81-28-621-7661 (Voice/Fax)
*E-mail:* tshc@blue.forum.ne.jp

*"You cannot talk about apple juice to someone who has not tasted it. No matter
what you say, the other person will not have the true experience of apple juice. The
only way is to drink it."– Thich Nhat Hanh*

## LIECHTENSTEIN

**Kontaktstelle SHG**                                                    **Schaan**
Provides referrals to local self-help groups.
Kontaktstelle SHG                    *Phone:* +423 79 419 1802
Postfach 1, FL 9494
Schaan, Liechtenstein

## NETHERLANDS

**Symboise**                                                           **Sittard**
Regional clearinghouse for self-help with nationwide contacts. Offers consultation to new
and existing groups. Provides information, training.
Symboise                             *Phone:* +31 46   4 20 80 80
Unit P.C.G., Postbus 5086            *E-mail:* pvdh@symboise.nl
NL 6130 PB Sittard, Netherlands      *Website:* http://www.symbiose.nl

## NORWAY

**Norsk Selvhjelpsforum**                                            **Nationwide**
National self-help clearinghouse. Provides information, literature, referrals, training.
Norsk Selvhjelpsforum                *Phone:* +47 22 92-50-30
c/o Professor Dahlsgl                *E-mail:* selvhjelp@selvhjelp.no
45 N 0367, Oslo Norway               *Website:* http://www.selvhjelp.no

## POLAND

**TOPOS Information Center**                                         **Nationwide**
Provides information on self-help groups to health professionals, local governments and
general public. Information and assistance for people starting new groups.
TOPOS Information Center             *Phone:* +48 22 8 31 22 12
Schroegera 82/100A                   *Fax:* +48 22   8 31 22 12
01 828 Warszawa, Poland              *E-mail:* topos@topos.pl

## ROMANIA

**Federatia Comunitatilor Evreisesti**                                **Bukarest**
Provides information on local self-help groups.
Federatia Comunitatilor Evreisesti   *Phone:* +40 1  3 13 32 25
Dept. Asistenta                      *Fax:* +40 1 3 22 40 67
Str. Dimistrie Racovita nr. 8
Sector 2, Cod 70307,
RO  Bukarest, Romania

## SWEDEN

**Distriktlakare**                                             **Lapland**
Provides information on self-help groups in Lapland. Can also provide information for other clearinghouses in Sweden.

Distriktlakare                 *Phone:* +46 961 14800; Fax: 14819
Villavagen 14,                *E-mail:* bo-henricson@nll.se
930 90, Arjeplog Sweden       *Website:* http://hem.passagen.se/snaps

## SLOVENIA

**Counseling Center for Children, Adolescents and Parents**     **Nationwide**
Supports self-help activities informally. Provides mental health counseling.

Counseling Center for Children,     *Phone:* +386(0)1/583 75 00
    Adolescents and Parents         *Fax:* 386(0)1/519 11 20.
1000 Ljubljana                 *E mail:* sc-oms.Ij@guest.arnes.si
Gotska 18 Slovenia             *Website:* http://www.szcoms.ij.si

## SPAIN

**Agencia Municipal de Serveis a les Associacions**           **Nationwide**
Information on self-help groups. Assistance, training and publications for groups.

Ajuntament de Barcelona       *Phone:* +34 4 407 10 22; *Fax:* +34 4 407 11 97
Agencia Mun. de Serveis a les Assoc.   *E-mail:* tjussana@mail.bcn.es
Torre Jussana                 *Website:* http://www.bcn.es/tjussana
Avinguda Cardenal Vidal i Barraquer 30
E 08035 Barcelona, Spain

## SCOTLAND

⌨ **Health Education Board for Scotland**             **Nationwide**
Information on local self-help groups. *Website:* http://www.hebs.scot.nhss.uk

## SWITZERLAND

**Stiftung KOSCH**                                     **Nationwide**
Nationwide coordinating organization for self-help groups. Umbrella organization for regional clearinghouses throughout Switzerland.

Stiftung KOSCH                 *Phone:* +41 61 - 3 33 86 01
Laufenstrasse 12              *Fax:* +41 61 - 3 33 86 02
CH 4053, Basel                *E-mail:* v.vogelsanger@kosch.ch
Switzerland                   *Website:* http://www.kosch.ch

*"To know the road ahead, ask those coming back." – old Chinese proverb*

## WALES

**Health Promotion Division**                                    **Nationwide**
Provides information on self-help groups. Website has information on groups.
Health Promotion Div.                *Phone:* +44 (029) 2075 2222
Nat'l Assembly for Wales             *Website:* http://www.hpw.wales.gov.uk/
Ffynnoalas, Ty Glas Ave.
Cardiff FF14 5EZ, UK

## A Self-Help Story: "WHY?"

*Pat Becker, Coordinator, The Self-Help Umbrella*
*A volunteer-run self-help clearinghouse for Arizona*

People sometimes wonder why I am so engrossed in the self-help community. For one thing, in this age of gangs, drive-by shootings and methamphetamine psychotics 'with eerie fire in their brains', it is a never-ending joy to be around folks who are doing positive things with their lives. The Self-Help Movement is no passing fad, but more of a cultural upheaval as major human needs are being met in its embrace. The most recent estimate is that 15 million Americans will attend a self-help/support/prayer group this week! These group members find, among many other things, a precious sense of community and almost always bring out the best in one another, thus strengthening their families, schools, work places and neighborhoods. I am frequently reminded of Victor Hugo's statement: "There is nothing so powerful in the world as an idea whose time has come!"

A few years ago, I saw a little paragraph somewhere about a new 12-step program called Violence Anonymous in San Diego. I called and spoke with the founder, Susan N., who said that she herself is the violent person. She told me she has been filled with rage most of her life and has left in her wake a trail of bloodshed, agony, prison and wasted years. Then, on the edge of suicide one terrifying dark night of the soul, Susan in anguish threw her life at God. She had a sudden flash of insight and came to understand that her energy was at the mercy of her rage, and that it might, with the help of the Great Spirit, one breath at a time, be used to build instead a life of some real value. In addition to taping a TV special, Susan visits local prisons sometimes giving talks that not only provide inspiration but many practical suggestions. She also now volunteers at a local mediation program.

I was fascinated with Susan as we talked for nearly an hour; and I wept for a l-o-n-g time after we hung up, overcome by the radiance of her moment of grace and pilgrim spirit. I was blessed with such a moment myself many years ago and it still illuminates every fiber of my being. I love to see the hand of the Great Spirit every now and then as someone begins to bloom, and occasionally I can be a catalyst in that process. As a sort of cheerleader for this vigorous movement, I find opportunities to touch many lives, enriching my own in the process. One morning soon after, I woke up humming an old hymn from my childhood: "Oh Love, that will not let me go . . ." THAT'S WHY!!!

**Chapter 6**

# SELF–HELP GROUPS

---

## ABUSE

*"You can clutch the past so tightly to your chest
that it leaves your arms too full to embrace the present."*
*- Admiral Grace Hooper*

---

### CHILD ABUSE
*(Also see Sexual Abuse)*

**Adult Survivors of Child Abuse**                                          **National**
*9 affiliated groups. Founded 1991.* Mutual support for adult survivors of physical, sexual, or emotional child abuse or neglect. Encourages victims to become survivors, then thrivers. Face-to-face and online support group meetings, newsletter, group starter manuals, and general information. Assistance in starting groups.

The Morris Center - ASCA            *Phone:* 508-835-6054
c/o George J. Bilotta, Ph.D.        *E-mail:* tmc_asca@dnai.com
173 Malden St.                      *Website:* http://www.ascasupport.org
West Boyleston, MA 01583

The Morris Center – ASCA            *Phone:* 415-928-4576
P.O. Box 14477
San Francisco, CA 94114

**Parents Anonymous, Inc.**                                                 **National**
*1000 groups. Founded 1970.* Country's oldest child abuse prevention organization. Opportunity for parents to learn new skills, transform their attitudes and behaviors, and create lasting changes in their lives. Group meetings offer free childcare or structured children's programs. Helps to develop new community groups by providing free consultation, training and technical assistance, materials and networking.

Parents Anonymous, Inc.             *Phone:* 909-621-6184; Fax: 909-625-6304
675 W. Foothill Blvd., Suite 220    *E-mail:* palmelendez@juno.com
Claremont, CA 91711-3416            *Website:* http://www.parentsanonymous.org

**VOCAL (Victims Of Child Abuse Laws)**                                     **National**
*150 chapters. Founded 1984.* To protect the rights of persons falsely and wrongly accused of child abuse. Aims to obtain more protection for children against abusers within the children's services system. Referrals to psychologists and attorneys. Newsletter. Chapter development guidelines. Dues $15/year.

VOCAL                               *Phone:* 303-233-5321
7485 E. Kenyon Ave.                 *Website:* http://www.nasvo.org
Denver, CO 80237

🖳 **MAMA (Mothers Against MSBP Allegations)**                    **Online**
Message board that provides support to families who have been falsely accused of
Munchausen's Syndrome by Proxy.
MAMA                                *Fax:* 662-562-6669
1407 Ranch Dr.                      *E-mail:* mama@msbp.com
Senatobia, MS 38669                 *Website:* http://www.msbp.com

🖳 **Shaken Baby Alliance**                                        **Online**
*Founded 1998.* Promotes public awareness and education about shaken baby syndrome.
Offers victim and family support, and victim advocacy, networking and literature. Dues
$30-50. Provides assistance in starting groups. Listserv.
Shaken Baby Alliance                *Phone:* 1-800-6-END-SBS or 1-877-636-3727
P.O. Box 150734                     *E-mail:* info@shakenbaby.com
Ft. Worth, TX 76108                 *Website:* http://shakenbaby.com

# SEXUAL ABUSE / INCEST / RAPE
*(Also see Child Abuse)*

**Adult Survivors of Child Abuse**                                **National**
*9 affiliated groups. Founded 1991.* Mutual support and information for adult survivors of
physical, sexual, or emotional child abuse or neglect. Encourages victims to become
survivors, then thrivers. Face-to-face and online group meetings, newsletter, and group
starter manual. Assistance in starting groups.
The Morris Center - ASCA            *Phone:* 508-835-6054
c/o George J. Bilotta, Ph.D.        *E-mail:* tmc_asca@dnai.com
173 Malden St.                      *Website:* http://www.ascasupport.org
West Boyleston, MA 01583

The Morris Center – ASCA            *Phone:* 415-928-4576
P.O. Box 14477
San Francisco, CA 94114

**False Memory Syndrome Foundation**                              **International**
*Founded 1992.* Research-oriented organization for persons falsely accused of childhood sex
abuse based on the recovered repressed memories of someone else. Also for persons
questioning their memories, and the professionals working with them. Information, phone
support, networking, and small group meetings. Newsletter. Conferences.
False Memory Syndrome Fdn.          *Phone:* 1-800-568-8882 or 215-940-1040
1955 Locust St.                     *E-mail:* mail@fmsonline.org
Philadelphia, PA 19103              *Website:* http://www.fmsonline.org

---

**▣  Incest Resources, Inc.**                                                   **Resource**
*Several groups in Boston, MA area. Founded 1980.* Educational and resource materials for survivors of childhood sexual abuse, and the professionals who work with them. International listing of survivor self-help groups, manual for starting groups, and many other resources. For information send self-addressed envelope with two stamps.
Incest Resources, Inc.
46 Pleasant St.
Cambridge, MA 02139

**Incest Survivors Anonymous**                                              **International**
*Founded 1980.* 12-step 12-tradition fellowship of men, women and teens who meet to share their experience, strength and hope so that they may recover from their incest experiences and break free to a new peace of mind. Not open to perpetrators or Satanists. Pen pals, quarterly letter, cassettes. Assistance in starting I.S.A. groups. When writing send a self-addressed stamped envelope (with 55 cents in postage).
ISA                                               *Phone:* 562-428-5599
P.O. Box 17245                                    *E-mail:* isa@lafn.org
Long Beach, CA 90807-7245                          *Website:* http://www.lafn.org/medical/isa/

**LINKUP**                                                                  **International**
*Independent groups. Founded 1991.* Mutual support for survivors of clergy abuse. Aims to educate victims, clergy, professionals and the public. Newsletter, advocacy, conferences. Assistance in starting independent groups. Dues $35.
LINKUP                                            *Phone:* 847-475-4622 or 270-788-6924
118 Chestnut St.                                  *E-mail:* ILINKUP@aol.com
Cloverport, KY 40111                              *Website:* http://www.thelinkup.com

**National Organization on Male Sexual Victimization**                          **National**
*Founded 1995.* Information and referrals for male survivors of sexual assault and the professionals working with them. Biennial conference, periodic regional retreats. Referrals to local resources. Newsletter. Online chat room.
NOMSV                                             *Phone:* 1-800-738-4181
PMB 103                                           *E-mail:* nomsv@malesurvivor.org
5505 Connecticut Ave., NW                          *Website:* http://www.nomsv.org
Washington, DC 20015-2601

**Parents United International**                                            **International**
*42 chapters. Founded 1972.* Provides treatment for perpetrators, non-offending spouses, and victims of child sexual abuse, including adults molested as children. Assistance provided through individual therapy, group therapy and guided self-help. Chapter development guidelines and training available for professionals wishing to start groups.
Parents United Int'l                              *Phone:* 209-572-3446; *Fax:* 209-524-7780
615 15th St.                                      *E-mail:* Parents.United@usa.net
Modesto, CA 95354-2510                             *Website:* http://srv2.ainet.com/parentsunited

113

**SARA (Sexual Assault Recovery Anonymous) Society**          **International**
*15 groups. Founded 1983.* Education and support for adults and teens who were sexually
abused as children. Group development guidelines and assistance for starting groups.
Literature on behavioral modification. Newsletter. Dues $10.
SARA Society                          *Phone:* 604-584-2626
P.O Box 16                            *Fax:* 604-584-2888
Surrey, BC V3T 4W4 Canada

**SESAME (Survivors of Educator Sexual**
**Abuse/Misconduct Emerge)**                              **National network**
*National network. Founded 1993.* Support and information network for families of children
(K-12) who have been sexually abused by a school staff member. Aims to raise public
awareness. Information and referrals, phone support, literature, advocacy, newsletter. Online
e-mail group.                         *Phone:* 518-329-1265 or 516-489-6406
SESAME                                *Fax:* 516-489-6101; *E-mail:* donses@earthlink.net
P.O. Box 905                          *E-mail:* Babe4justice@aol.com
Pahrump, NV 89041                     *Website:* http://www.sesamenet.org

**Survivor Connections, Inc.**                              **National network**
*Founded 1993.* Grassroots, activist organization for non-offending survivors of sexual
assault by family, ritual, youth leaders, counselors, doctors, clergy, etc. Newsletter, peer
support groups, information and referrals. Maintains database of perpetrators.
Survivor Connections, Inc.            *Phone:* 401-941-2548; *Fax:* 401-941-2335
c/o Frank Fitzpatrick                 *E-mail:* scsitemail@cox.net
52 Lyndon Rd.                         *Website:* http://www.angelfire.com/ri/
Cranston, RI 02905                    survivorconnections/

**Survivors of Incest Anonymous**                              **International**
*300 groups. Founded 1982.* 12-step program for persons 18 yrs. or older who have been
victims of child sexual abuse and want to be survivors. Newsletter ($15/yr), literature packet
($25), assistance in starting groups, volunteer information and referral line, speaker's
bureau. Send self-addressed stamped envelope when writing.
Survivors of Incest Anonymous        *Phone:* 410-893-3322
P.O. Box 190                          *Website:* http://www.siawso.org
Benson, MD 21018-9998

**VOICES In Action, Inc.**                              **International**
*Founded 1980.* Assists victims of incest/child sexual abuse in becoming survivors by
helping them locate local support services and treatment. Provides public education on
effects of incest. Newsletter. Guidelines on starting self-help groups. Special interest
correspondence groups. Conferences, publications. Dues $35/yr. (includes newsletter,
conference discounts).
VOICES In Action, Inc.               *Phone:* 1-800-7-VOICE-8
P.O. Box 13                           *Fax:* 847-498-0505
Newtonville, OH 45158                 *Website:* http://www.voices-action.org
114

**Molesters Anonymous**                                      **Model**
*Model. 10 groups in California. Founded 1985.* Provides support with anonymity and confidentiality for men who molest children. Use of "thought stoppage" technique and buddy system. Groups are initiated by a professional but become member-run. Group development manual ($9.95).
Dr. Jerry Goffman                      *Phone:* Dr. Goffman 909-355-1100
1850 N. Riverside Ave., #220           *Fax:* 909-370-0438
Rialto, CA 92376

**WINGS Foundation, Inc.**                                   **Model**
*Groups throughout Colorado. Founded 1982.* Provides healing for survivors of incest and childhood sexual abuse through facilitated support groups. Helps reduce the trauma of childhood sexual abuse. Information, referrals to therapists, support groups. Help in starting new groups.                          *Phone:* 303-238-8660 or 1-800-373-8671
WINGS Foundation, Inc.                  *Fax:* 303-238-4739
8725 W. 14th St., Suite 100             *E-mail:* wings@vs2000.org
Lakewood, CO 80215                      *Website:* http://www.wingsfound.org

🖳 **Able2SurvivorPartners**                                 **Online**
Support and understanding for partners and friends of survivors of sexual abuse, rape, incest, etc. Provides a safe place to communicate with others who understand that partners need support, too.                    *Website:* http://groups.yahoo.com/group/
                                        Able2survivorpartners/

🖳 **Healing Hopes**                                          **Online**
Support for sexual abuse, incest and rape victims diagnosed with dissociative identity disorder. Information for family and friends of the survivor. Provides newsletter, chat rooms and message boards.              *Website*: http://www.healinghopes.org

🖳 **Making Daughters Safe Again: Survivors of Sexual Abuse**  **Online**
*Founded 1999.* Extensive, private support forum for adult women who were victims of mother-daughter sexual abuse. Also provides public forums, pen pal program for female survivors, information, resources, artwork, and advocacy.
*Phone:* 1-877-735-5603                  *E-mail:* mdsa@comcast.net
*E-mail:* mdsasupport@mail.com           *Website:* http://mdsasupport.org
                                        *Website:* http://mdsa-online.org

🖳 **Parents and Loved Ones of Sexual Abuse and Rape Survivors**  **Online**
Online support group for the non-offending parents of sexually abused children. Also separate group for the loved ones of persons who were sexually abused or raped.
                                        *Website:* www.geocities.com/HotSprings/2656/

🖳 **Stop Prisoner Rape, Inc.**                               **Online**
Committed to fighting sexual violence against men, women, and children in all forms of

detention. Opportunity for victims of prison rape to exchange support and information through an e-mail discussion list. *Phone:* 323-653-STOP or 323-653-7867
Stop Prisoner Rape, Inc.                    *Fax:* 323-653-7870
6303 Wilshire Blvd., Suite 205              *E-mail:* info@spr.org
Los Angeles, CA 90048                       *Website:* http://www.spr.org/

💻 **Positive Partners of Survivors**                                    **Online**
Support and understanding for partners of persons who were sexually abused. Opportunity to talk with other support partners who understand that partners need support as well.
*Website:* http://groups.yahoo.com/group/Positivepartnersofsurvivors/

💻 **Stigma**                                                            **Online**
Support network for persons conceived in rape or incest. Message boards, chat room, contact list, and other online and offline resource. Opportunity for individuals discuss unique issues, and realize that they are not alone. Open to families, friends and other interested persons.                     *E-mail:* former_fetus@stigmatized.org
                                            *Website*: http://www.stigmatized.org

*Note:* **For Rape Victims Groups** that may exist, call your local helpline, self-help clearinghouse, rape crisis service, or women's center. We know of no national self-help group for rape victims at this time. If you can recommend a  local member-run group that can serve as a model, or know of any how-to group development guideline for rape victims, please let us know.

## SPOUSE ABUSE / DOMESTIC VIOLENCE

**Batterers Anonymous**                                                 **National**
*20 chapters. Founded 1980.* Self-help program for men who wish to control their anger and eliminate their abusive behavior toward women. Buddy system. Group starter manual ($9.95).
Batterers Anonymous                         *Phone:* Dr. Jerry Goffman 909-355-1100
1850 N. Riverside Ave., Suite 220           *Fax:* 909-370-0438
Rialto, CA 92376

**Domestic Violence Anonymous**                                         **International**
*32 affiliated groups. Founded 1983.* 12-step spiritual support for men and women who, through shared experience, strength, honesty and hope, are recovering from domestic violence. Whether the domestic violence happened as an adult or child, DVA welcomes anyone who wants to stop the emotional, physical or mental violence in their lives. Purpose is to carry the message of recovery to those who still suffer. Brochure on teen violence.
Domestic Violence Anonymous                 *Phone:* 415-681-4850
c/o BayLaw                                   *E-mail:* BayLaw1@ix.netcom.com
P.O. Box 29011                              *Website:* http://www.baylaw.org
San Francisco, CA 94129

**Pathways to Peace**                                                              **International**
*11 groups. Founded 1998.* Self-help group for anger management. Offers peer support, education, workbook ($24). Assistance in starting new groups.

Pathways to Peace                           *Phone:* 716-595-3884
P.O. Box 259                                *E-mail:* transfrm@netsync
Cassadaga, NY 14718                         *Website:* http://www.pathwaystopeaceinc.com

📖 *How-To Guide:* Talking It Out: A Guide to Groups for Abused Women. While we know of no national group to help with the development of a group for battered women, this book discusses how to start a group, how to lead it, group issues, group exercises, groups for specific populations, and how to prevent burnout. Authored by Ginny Ni Carty, Karen Merriam, and Sandra Coffman. Published by Seal Press, 3131 Western Ave., Seattle, WA 98121-1028.

*"Incest is like screaming
and not hearing an echo.
Support groups provide the echo."*
*- Anonymous*

ೞ ೲ

*"So often, a trauma survivor feels like the consummate outsider.
She has felt outside of her family, estranged from peers,
outside her community, and dissociated from her very self.
Healing connections are an essential part of any recovery and can
happen naturally as a group evolves and coalesces."*

*- Maxine Harris, Ph.D, Co-director of Community Connections mental health agency in Washington, DC, adjunct professor at Dartmouth Medical School, and psychological consultant to the Maryland Correctional Institute for Women. Author of Women of the Asylum and The Loss That is Forever.*

# ADDICTIONS

*"Our lives improve only when we take chances—*
*and the first and most difficult risk we can take is to be honest with ourselves."*
*- Walter Anderson*

## ADDICTIONS (GENERAL)
*(Also see specific addiction, Parents of Out-of-Control Kids)*

**16 Steps of Empowerment**                                    **National**
*100+ groups. Founded 1992.* Support for a wide variety of quality of life issues, such as addiction, codependency, abuse, empowerment, etc. The 16 Steps focus on a positive approach to help members celebrate personal strengths, have choices, stand up for themselves, heal physically, express love, and see themselves as part of the entire community, not just the recovery community. Online mailing list.

16 Steps of Empowerment            *E-mail:* empower16@yahoo.com
362 N. Cleveland Ave., #1           *Website: h*ttp://www.crosswinds.net/
St. Paul, MN 55104                  ~/empower16/steps.htm

**Anesthetists in Recovery**                          **National network**
*Founded 1984.* Network of recovering nurse anesthetists. Provides telephone support, information and referrals to groups and treatment.

AIR                                *Phone:* 215-635-0183
c/o Art Zwerling                    *E-mail:* a.to.z@comcast.net
8233 Brookside Rd.
Elkins Park, PA 19027

**ART (Academics Recovering Together)**               **National network**
*Founded 1989.* Multi-purpose, informal support network for academic professionals (college and university level) in recovery from alcohol/drug addiction. Exchange of information on day-to-day academic life, sabbaticals, relocation, issues surrounding promotion, tenure, etc. Newsletter, information and referrals, phone support.

ART                                *Phone:* Bruce Donovan 401-863-3831
c/o Bruce E. Donovan               *Fax:* 401-863-1961
Brown University                   *E-mail:* Bruce_Donovan@brown.edu
Box 1865
Providence, RI 02912

**Alcoholics Victorious**                                 **International**
*150 affiliated groups. Founded 1948.* Christian-oriented 12-step support for those recovering from chemical dependency. Information and referrals, literature, phone support,

conferences, group meetings, newsletter. Assistance in starting groups.

Alcoholics Victorious            *Phone:* 1-800-624-5156 or 816-471-8020
Assn. of Gospel Rescue Missions  *Fax:* 816-471-3718
1045 Swift St.                   *E-mail:* info@alcoholicsvictorious.org
Kansas City, MO 64116-4127       *Website:* http://alcoholicsvictorious.org

## Chemically Dependent Anonymous                                National

*65 affiliated groups. Founded 1980.* Purpose is to carry the message of recovery to the chemically dependent person. For those with a desire to abstain from drugs/alcohol. Information and referrals, phone support, conferences. Group development guidelines.

Chemically Dependent Anon.       *Phone:* 1-888-232-4673
P.O. Box 423                     *E-mail:* willie@atlantech.net
Severna Park, MD 21146           *Website:* http://www.cdaweb.org

## Families Anonymous                                            International

*500+ groups. Founded 1971.* 12-step self-help support fellowship for relatives and friends of persons with drug, alcohol, or behavioral problems. Members learn to achieve their own serenity in spite of the turmoil, which surrounds them. Besides many booklets, pamphlets, and bookmarks, publications include a daily thought book and newsletter.

F.A.                             *Phone:* 1-800-736-9805; *Fax:* 310-815-9682
P.O. Box 3475                    *E-mail:* famanon@FamiliesAnonymous.org
Culver City, CA 90231-3475       *Website:* http://www.FamiliesAnonymous.org

## Free-N-One Recovery                                           National

*30 affiliated groups. Founded 1985.* Group teaches people to be free mentally and spiritually, as well as free of drugs and alcohol. Information and referrals, phone support, literature, conferences. Assistance in starting local chapters.

Free-N-One Recovery              *Phone:* 310-764-4400
404 N. Rose St.                  *Fax:* 310-764-5439
Compton, CA 90221                *E-mail:* freenone@msn.com

## HESHE (Help Everyone Share Healthy Emotion) Anonymous         National

*Founded 1997.* 12-step fellowship that helps members recover from any addictive or abusive behavior. Helps members stay emotionally sober. Groups for adults and adolescents. Deals with any addiction, compulsion, abusive behavior, or dysfunction.

HE/SHE World Service             *Phone:* 802-447-4736 (eve)
P.O. Box 1752                    *E-mail:* heshe@together.net
Keene, NH 03431                  *Website:* http://www.berks.com/12step
                                 or http://homepages.together.net/~heshe

## Intercongregational Alcoholism Program                        International

*Founded 1979.* Network of recovering alcoholic women in religious orders. Helps Roman Catholic women who are, or have been, members of religious orders who are in need due to substance abuse. Information and referrals, networking, phone support, conferences, and newsletters.

ICAP                                    *Phone:* 708-445-1400
1515 N. Harlem Ave., #202               *Fax:* 708-445-1418
Oak Park, IL 60302                      *E-mail:* icapsrs@aol.com

**International Doctors in Alcoholics Anonymous**          **International network**
*175 affiliated groups. 6000 members. Founded 1949.* Opportunity for doctoral level health care professionals to discuss common problems and find common solutions to drug and alcohol problems. Annual meeting (1st week in Aug.), phone support, information and referrals, newsletter. Support group meetings at conferences of other organizations.
IDIAA                                   *Phone:* 636-482-4548 (day); *Fax:* 636-228-4102
P.O. Box 199                            *E-mail:* idaadickmd@aol.com
Augusta, MO 63332                       *Website:* http://members.aol.com/aadocs/

**International Lawyers in Alcoholics Anonymous**                    **International**
*40+ affiliated groups. Founded 1975.* Serves as a clearinghouse of support groups for lawyers who are recovering alcoholics or have other chemical dependencies. Newsletter, annual conventions. Group development guidelines.
ILAA                                    *Phone:* 702-455-4827 or 702-528-2677
P.O. Box 552212                         *E-mail:* webmaster@ilaa.org
Las Vegas, NV 89155-2212                *Website:* http://www.ilaa.org

**International Nurses Anonymous**                          **International network**
*Founded 1988.* Fellowship of RNs, LPNs, and nursing students who are in recovery from chemical dependency, co-dependency, or involved in any 12-step program. Newsletter.
INA                                     *Phone:* Pat G. 785-842-3893
1020 Sunset Dr.                         *E-mail:* Patlgreen@aol.com
Lawrence, KS 66044

**International Pharmacists Anonymous**                             **National**
*Founded 1987.* Fellowship of pharmacists and pharmacy students recovering from any addiction. Members must belong to a 12-step group. Newsletter, conferences, meetings. Networking.                                *Phone:* Mary Jo 308-284-8296
IPA                                     *E-mail:* mjcerny@megaviion.com
319 E. Fifth St.                        *Website:* http://mywebpages.comcast.net/
Ogallala, NE 69153-2201.                mitchfields/Ipa/ipapage.htm

IPA                                     *Phone:* Nan 908-537-4295
1 Dewey Lane                            *E-mail:* nandr@earthlink.net
Glen Gardner, NJ 08826-3102             *Website:* http://www.crml.uab.edu/~jah/

**JACS (Jewish Alcoholics, Chemically**
**Dependent Persons and Significant Others)**                      **International**
*Founded 1980.* For alcoholic and chemically dependent Jews, their families, friends, associates and the community. Networking, community outreach, retreats, newsletter,

literature, spiritual events and speakers bureau.

JACS
850 Seventh Ave.
New York, NY 10019

*Phone:* 212-397-4197
*Fax:* 212-399-3525

## LifeRing Secular Recovery                                    International

*Founded 1987.* Secular community of persons who are building lives free of dependency on alcohol and other drugs. Group activities are not associated with religion or spirituality. Members practice complete abstinence from alcohol and other addicting drugs. Peer support, literature, information and referrals, and advocacy activities. Large online e-mail support group and several smaller special interest groups (women, weight loss, stop smoking, etc). Online chats, forum. Publishes sobriety literature.

LifeRing Secular Recovery
1440 Broadway, Suite 10001
Oakland, CA 94612-2029

*Phone:* 510-763-0779; *Fax:* 510-763-1513
*E-mail:* service@lifering.org
*Website:* http//www.unhooked.com
*Website:* http://www.lifering.com

## Overcomers In Christ                                         International

*Founded 1987.* Recovery program that deals with every aspect of addiction and dysfunction (spiritual, physical, mental, emotional and social). Uses "Overcomer's Goals" which are Christ-centered. Resources, information and referrals. Assistance in starting new groups.

Overcomers in Christ
P.O. Box 34460
Omaha, NE 68134

*Phone:* 402-573-0966; *Fax:* 402-573-0960
*E-mail:* OIC@OvercomersInChrist.org
*Website:* http://www.OvercomersInChrist.org

## Overcomers Outreach, Inc.                                    International

*700 affiliated groups. Founded 1985.* Christ-centered 12-step support group for persons with any compulsive behavior, their families and friends. Uses the 12-steps of A.A. and applies them to the scriptures, using Jesus Christ as "higher power." Supplements involvement in other 12-step groups. Newsletter, group development guidelines, conferences.

Overcomers Outreach
P.O. Box 2208
Oakhurst, CA 93644

*Phone:* 714-491-3000 or 1-800-310-3001
*Fax:* 714-491-3004
*E-mail:* info@overcomersoutreach.org
*Website:* http://www.overcomersoutreach.org

## Psychologists Helping Psychologists                          National network

*Founded 1980.* For doctoral-level psychologists or students who have had a personal experience with alcohol or drugs. Aim is to support each other in recovery, and to educate psychology community. Regional get-togethers, newsletter.

PHP
3484 S. Utah St.
Arlington, VA 22206-1921

*Phone:* 703-578-1644 or 703-243-4470
*Fax:* 703-243-7125; *E-mail:* AnnS@Erols.com
*Website:* http://www.crml.uab.edu/~jah/php.html

**Rational Recovery Systems**                                                **International**
*Founded 1986.* Program of self-recovery from addiction to alcohol and other drugs through planned, permanent abstinence using Addictive Voice Recognition Technique (AVRT). Newsletter, political action guidelines. Online message/discussion forum.
Rational Recovery Systems          *Phone:* 530-621-4374 or 1-800-303-2873
P.O. Box 800                       *Fax:* 530-622-4296; *E-mail:* rr@rational.org
Lotus, CA 95651                    *Website:* http://www.rational.org

**Secular Organizations for Sobriety (Save Ourselves)**          **International**
*20000 members. Founded 1986.* Mutual help for alcoholics and addicts who want to acknowledge their addiction and maintain sobriety as a separate issue from religion or spirituality. Newsletter. Online chats. Guidelines and assistance in starting groups.
S.O.S.                             *Phone:* 323-666-4295; *Fax:* 323-666-4271
4773 Hollywood Blvd.               *E-mail:* sos@cfiwest.org
Hollywood, CA 90027                *Website:* http://www.cfiwest.org/sos/

**SMART Recovery Self-Help Network**
**(Self-Management And Recovery Training)**                      **National**
*275 affiliated groups. Founded 1994.* Network of self-help groups for individuals wanting to gain their independence from addictive and compulsive behaviors. An abstinence program based on cognitive behavioral principles, especially those of rational emotive behavior therapy. Newsletter, information and referrals, literature. Help in starting groups.
SMART Recovery                     *Phone:* 440-951-5357; *Fax:* 440-951-5358
7537 Mentor Ave., Suite 306        *E-mail:* srmail1@aol.com
Mentor, OH 44060                   *Website:* http://www.smartrecovery.org

**Social Workers Helping Social Workers**                        **National network**
*Founded 1980.* Supports social workers (BSW/MSW) or MSW matriculating students in their, or a loved one's, recovery from chemical dependence. Social workers with other addictions are welcome to attend meetings. Newsletter, annual conferences, regional retreats/meetings, continuing education, e-mail digest, group development guidelines.
SWHSW                              *Phone:* 641-422-7485 or 641-422-7797
P.O. Box 486                       *Fax:* 641-422-7516
Nora Springs, IA 50458-8883        *E-mail:* davidcm@omnitelcom.com

**Teen-Anon**                                                    **National**
*Founded 1999.* 12-step program for teens 12-19 who need help with their own abuse of alcohol or drugs, or with dealing with the addiction of a friend or family member. A behavioral and spiritual group supervised by caring, experienced, recovering adults. Assistance in starting new groups. Booklets available for $1 on kicking drugs and alcohol, or helping someone who abuses drugs or alcohol.
Teen-Anon                          *Phone:* 510-444-6074
267 Lester Ave., Suite 104         *E-mail:* webmaster@Teen-Anon.zzn.com
Oakland, CA 94606                  *Website*: http://www.teen-anon.com

**Veterinarians in Recovery**                                **National network**
*Founded 1990.* Support network for veterinarians in recovery from substance abuse problems. Information and referrals, phone support, and newsletter. Online listserv. Maintains database of members for support. Al-Anon members and recovering veterinarian staff welcome at meetings. Many VIR members also are members of Int'l Doctors in AA and meet during their annual conference.

VIR, Attn: Jeff H.                *Phone:* 205-875-2125 or 651-261-4029
104 Maple Trace                   *E-mail:* jah@crml.uab.edu
Birmingham, AL 35244              *Website:* http://www.crml/uab.edu/~jah/vir.html

**Young and Recovering**                                            **National**
*Founded 1999.* 12-step program for young adults 18-24 who need help with their own abuse of alcohol or drugs, or with dealing with the addiction of a friend or family member. A behavioral and spiritual group supervised by caring, experienced, recovering adults. Assistance in starting new groups. Booklets on kicking drugs and alcohol, or helping someone who abuses drugs or alcohol ($1).

Young and Recovering              *Phone:* 415-437-2235 or 1-866-884-7638
P.O. Box 191396                   *E-mail:* youngandrecovering@yahoo.com
San Francisco, CA 94119           *Website:* http://www.youngandrecoverung.com

**Chapter Nine Group of Hollywood, MD**                            **Model**
*1 group in Maryland. Founded 1989.* 12-step program of recovering couples (substance abuse) in which partners work together. Group name comes from chapter nine of the A.A. Big Book "The Family Afterward" based on the belief that members of the family or couples should meet upon the common ground of tolerance, understanding and love.

Chapter Nine                      *Phone:* Don .J. 410-586-1425
1168 White Sands Dr.              *E-mail:* justiced@chesapeake.net
Lusby, MD 20657

**Dentists Concerned for Dentists**                                **Model**
*1 group in Minnesota. Founded 1977.* Assists dentists with recovery from alcoholism or chemical dependency, or other human problems (family/marital, mental health, financial, etc). Group development guidelines.

Dentists Concerned for Dentists   *Phone:* 651-641-0730
450 N. Syndicate, Suite 117
St. Paul, MN 55104

**Hypoics Not Anonymous**                                          **Model**
*Founded 2000.* Mutual support for anyone with any type of addiction. Follows the philosophy that addictions are caused by a neurological mechanism. Offers networking, phone support, literature, advocacy, information and referrals.

HNA                               *Phone:* 516-763-1315
163 Hendrickson Ave.              *E-mail:* dumano@optonline.net
Rockville, NY 11570               *Website:* http://www.nvo.com/hypoism
                                  /hypoicsnotanonymous

**Realtors Concerned for Realtors**                                        **Model**
*20 groups in Massachusetts. Founded 1993.* Purpose is to assist real estate professionals, their families, associates, affiliates and employees regarding alcohol and drug abuse through education, support, prevention and recovery programs. Information and referrals, phone support, conferences, and networking. Assistance in starting similar programs.
RCR                                       *Phone:* John Walsh 1-800-854-7505
3 Oldham St.                              *Fax:* 781-293-4006
Pembroke, MA 02359                        *E-mail:* bonnieleebaird@compuserve.com

**Therapists In Recovery**                                                 **Model**
*Founded 1987.* Mutual support for licensed therapists in recovery from alcohol or drug addiction. Local group meetings, phone support, information and referrals. Assistance in starting similar groups. Dues $36/year.
T.I.R.                                    *Phone:* Mary Jo R. 760-944-8594
1840 Gatepost Rd.                         *E-mail:* MRush4681@aol.com
Encinitas, CA 92024

🖳 **Sober24**                                                              **Online**
Support for persons in recovery from chemical addictions and their families. Includes "Emergency Room" for persons in recovery and need someone to talk with, "Recovery Room" for 24-hour discussions focused on recovery, online meetings, and a family meeting room.                                  *Website:* http://www.sober24.com

## ADRENALINE ADDICTION

🖳 **Adrenaline Addicts Anonymous**                                         **Online**
Support for persons who use their own adrenaline as an addictive drug. For copy of the AAA "Big Book" send a self-addressed stamped envelope (donations appreciated).
AAA                                       *Website:* http://pw1.netcom.com/~periwink/
P.O. Box 626                              adrenanon.html
Ben Lomond, CA 95005

## ALCOHOL
*(Also see Addictions General)*

**Adult Children of Alcoholics World Services Org., Inc.**        **International**
*1500+ meetings. Founded 1977.* 12-step program of recovery for individuals who were raised in an alcoholic or dysfunctional households. Group development guidelines. Newsletter, literature.
ACA                                       *Phone:* 310-534-1815
P.O. Box 3216                             *E-mail:* info@adultchildren.org
Torrance, CA 90510-3216                   *Website:* http://adultchildren.org

124

**Al-Anon Family Groups, Inc. World Services**          **International**
*27103 groups. Founded 1951.* (Multilingual) 12-step fellowship of men, women, adult children and children whose lives have been affected by the compulsive drinking of a family member or friend. Opportunity for personal recovery and growth applying the 12-steps adopted from A.A. Guidelines for starting groups. Literature in 30 languages.
Al-Anon Family Groups, Inc.        *Phone:* 757-563-1600 or 1-888-ALANON
1600 Corporate Landing Parkway     *Fax:* 757-563-1655; *E-mail:* wso@al-anon.org
Virginia Beach, VA 23454-5617      *Website:* http://www.al-anon.alateen.org

**Alateen**                                              **International**
*2696 groups. Founded 1957.* (Multilingual) 12-step fellowship of young persons whose lives have been affected by someone else's drinking. An active adult member of Al-Anon serves as a sponsor for each group. Group development guidelines, newsletter. Literature available in 30 languages. Hotline in English, French and Spanish.
Alateen                            *Phone:* 757-563-1600 or 1-888-425-2666
c/o Al-Anon Family Groups          *Fax:* 757-536-1655
1600 Corporate Landing Parkway     *E-mail:* wso@al-anon.org
Virginia Beach, VA 23454-5617      *Website:* http://www.al-anon.alateen.org

**Alcoholics Anonymous World Services, Inc.**            **International**
*98000 groups worldwide. Founded 1935.* (Multilingual) 12-step fellowship of women and men who have found a solution to their drinking problem. The only requirement for membership is a desire to stop drinking. Supported by voluntary contributions of its members and groups, A.A. neither seeks nor accepts outside funding. Members observe personal anonymity at the public level, thus emphasizing A.A. principles rather than personalities. For more information check your local phone directory or newspaper.
AA General Service Office          *Phone:* 212-870-3400
P.O. Box 459 Grand Central Sta.    *Fax:* 212-870-3003
New York, NY 10163                 *Website:* http://www.alcoholics-anonymous.org

**Calix Society**                                        **International**
*52 chapters. Founded 1947.* Fellowship of Catholic alcoholics maintaining their sobriety through Alcoholics Anonymous. Concerned with total abstinence, spiritual development and sanctification of the whole personality of each member. Bi-monthly newsletter. Assistance in chapter development.
Calix Society                      *Phone:* 651-773-3117 or 1-800-398-0524
2555 Hazelwood Ave.                *E-mail:* calix@usfamily.net
St. Paul, MN 55109                 *E-mail:* dmhackl@ieee.org

**Men for Sobriety**                                     **International**
*3 affiliated groups. Founded 1976.* Purpose is to help all men recover from problem drinking through the discovery of self, gained by sharing experiences, hopes and encouragement with other men in similar circumstances. Recognizes men's complex role in today's society.

Men for Sobriety                    *Phone:* 215-536-8026; *Fax:* 215-538-9026
P.O. Box 618                        *E-mail:* NewLife@nni.com
Quakertown, PA 18951-0618           *Website:* http://www.womenforsobriety.org

**Moderation Management**                                           National
*50 groups. Founded 1993.* Support for problem drinkers who want to reduce their drinking
or quit, and make other positive lifestyle changes. For those who have experienced mild to
moderate levels of alcohol-related problems. Not intended for alcoholics. Literature,
handbook, group meetings. Assistance in starting new groups.
MM                                  *Phone:* 732-295-0949
c/o HRC                             *E-mail:* moderation@moderation.org
22 West 27th St.                    *Website:* http://moderation.org
New York, NY 10001

**Recovered Alcoholic Clergy Association**                          National
*Founded 1965.* Network of clergy of the Episcopal Church who support one another in their
recovery from alcoholism. Assistance to clergy, and their families, who are in trouble with
drinking issues. Semi-annual national gathering and local network groups. Quarterly
newsletter.
RACA                                *Phone:* 706-543-1294 ext. 202
c/o Father Courtney                 *E-mail:* petercourtney@home.com
Emanuel Episcopal Church            *Website:* http://www.geocities.com/racafool/
498 Prince Ave.
Athens, GA 30601

**Women For Sobriety**                                          International
*150 groups. Founded 1976.* A program designed specifically to help the woman alcoholic
achieve sobriety. Addresses the need to overcome depressed feelings and guilt. Monthly
newsletter, information and referrals, phone support, group meetings, pen pals, conferences,
and group development guidelines.
Women for Sobriety                  *Phone:* 215-536-8026; *Fax:* 215-538-9026
P.O. Box 618                        *E-mail:* NewLife@nni.com
Quakertown, PA 18951-0618           *Website:* http://www.womenforsobriety.org

# DRUG ABUSE
*(Also see Addictions General)*

**Co-Anon Family Groups**                                       International
*30 groups. Founded 1985.* 12-step program for families and friends of people who have
problems with cocaine or other drugs. Online e-mail meeting, and face-to-face meetings.
Provides assistance in starting new groups.
Co-Anon                             *Phone:* 520-513-5028
P.O. Box 12722                      *Website:* http://www.co-anon.org
Tucson, AZ 85732-2722

**Cocaine Anonymous, Inc.**                                   **International**
*2000 chapters. Founded 1982.* 12-step fellowship who share their experience, strength and hope that they may solve their common problem and help others to recover from addiction. Newsletter. Group starter kit.
Cocaine Anonymous
3740 Overland Ave., Suite C
Los Angeles, CA 90034-6337

*Phone:* 1-800-347-8998 (24 hour helpline)
*Phone:* 310-559-5833; *Fax:* 310-559-2554
*E-mail:* cawso@ca.org
*Website:* http://www.ca.org

**Crystal Meth Anonymous**                                        **National**
12-step fellowship for those in recovery from addiction to crystal meth. The only requirement for membership is the desire to stop using crystal meth, and to stay clean. Open to families and friends.
CMA General Service
8205 Santa Monica Blvd.
PMB 1-114
West Hollywood, CA 90046-5977

*Phone:* 213-488-4455
*Website:* http://www.crystalmeth.org

**Marijuana Anonymous World Services**                        **International**
*50+ groups. Founded 1989.* 12-step fellowship of men and women who desire to stay clean of marijuana. Literature, starter packets. Various online meetings.
M.A.
P.O. Box 2912
Van Nuys, CA 91404

*Phone:* 1-800-766-6779 (recorded message)
*E-mail:* office@marijuana-anonymous.org
*Website:* http://www.marijuana-anonymous.org

**Nar-Anon World Service Organization**                       **International**
*Founded 1967.* 12-step group offering self-help recovery to families and friends of addicts. Members share their experience, hope and strength with each other. Some Nar-Ateen and Nar-Atot programs available. Packet of information for starting new groups.
Nar-Anon
P.O. Box 2562
Palos Verdes, CA 90274-0119

*Phone:* 310-547-5800

**Narcotics Anonymous**                                        **International**
*21,000+ groups. Founded 1953.* (Multilingual) 12-step fellowship of men and women who come together for the purpose of sharing their recovery. There are no dues, fees, or registration requirements. The only requirement for membership is the desire to stop using drugs. Information is available in several languages, on audio tapes and in Braille.
N.A.
P.O. Box 9999
Van Nuys, CA 91409

*Phone:* 818-773-9999; *Fax:* 818-700-0700
*E-mail:* wso@na.org
*Website:* http://www.na.org

**National Family Partnership**                                  **National**
*55 affiliates. Founded 1980.* Provides drug prevention and education, information, networking, and guidelines for parents forming community groups to address drug prevention. Legislative advocacy on federal level and information resource for state and

local efforts. Newsletter. Annual Red Ribbon Campaign. Center for drug prevention and anti-tobacco resources.

Nat'l Family Partnership  
c/o Peggy Sapp  
2490 Coral Way  
Miami, FL 33145  

*Phone:* 1-800-705-8997; *Fax:* 305-856-4815  
*E-mail:* info@nfp.org  
*Website:* http://www.redribbon.org  
*Website:* http://www.nfp.org  

**Pill Addicts Anonymous**                                                **International**  
*3 groups. Founded 1979.* 12-step fellowship for all who seek freedom from addiction to prescribed or over-the-counter mood-changing pills. Sharing of experience, strength and hope to stay clean and help others achieve sobriety. Group development guidelines.  
Pill Addicts Anonymous  
P.O. Box 13738  
Reading, PA 19612-3738  

**Prescriptions Anonymous**                                                    **National**  
*8 affiliated groups. Founded 1998.* Provides support to persons who are addicted to prescription or over-the-counter medications. Members share comfort, support and understanding. Offers support to families and friends. Literature, phone support, networking, information and referral. Assistance in starting groups.  

Prescriptions Anonymous, Inc.  
P.O. Box 1297  
Powder Springs, GA 30127  

*Phone:* 770-428-1220 (Voice/Fax)  
*E-mail:* Cindy@prescriptionanonymous.org  
*Website:* http://www.prescriptionanonymous.org  

**Benzodiazepine Anonymous**                                                    **Model**  
*5 affiliated groups in California. Founded 1989.* Support for persons in recovery from an addiction to benzodiazepines (Xanax, Halcion, Valium, Ativan, Dalmane, Librium, etc) or other addicting prescription drug. Support for all with an honest desire to stop using these prescription drugs. Uses B.A. 12-steps. Open to families. Assistance in starting new groups.  

B.A.  
11633 San Vicente Blvd., #314  
Los Angeles, CA 90049  

*Phone:* 310-652-4100 (Voice/Fax)  

**Pills Anonymous**                                                              **Model**  
*2 groups in New York City.* Self-help, self-supporting, anonymous 12-step program based on A.A. for those who want to help themselves and others recover from chemical addiction.  
Groups meet in New York City.          *Phone:* 212-874-0700  

## FOOD ADDICTION / OVEREATING
*(Also see Addictions General, Eating Disorders, Overweight)*

**Compulsive Eaters Anonymous - H.O.W.**                                        **National**  
*250+ affiliated groups. Founded 1985.* 12-step fellowship who share experience, strength and hope in order to help themselves and others overcome compulsive eating. H.O.W.

(Honesty, Open-mindedness and Willingness) groups use a food plan that includes an abstinence from sugar and refined flour, and allows only three weighed and measured meals per day.

CEA-HOW
5500 E. Atherton St., #22715
Long Beach, CA 90815-4017

*Phone:* 562-342-9344 (day)
*E-mail:* gso@ceahow.org
*Website:* http://www.ceahow.org

### Eating Addictions Anonymous - SANE Fellowship                    National
*6 affiliated chapters.* 12-step recovery for men and women recovering from all forms of eating and body image addictions. Includes anorexia, bulimia, binge eating, overeating, etc. Focuses on internal growth and reclaiming bodies rather than weight or appearance.

EAA General Service Office
P.O. Box 8151
Silver Spring, MD 20907-8151

*E-mail:* 12n12@tidalwave.net
*Website:* http://www.eaagso.org
*Website:* http://dcregistry.com/users/
eatingaddictions/main.html

### Eating Disorders Anonymous                                  International
*Founded 2000.* Fellowship of men and women who share their experience, strength and hope with each other that they may solve their common problems and help others to recover from their eating disorders. Focuses on the solution, not the problem. EDA endorses sound nutrition. Literature, information and referrals, pen pals, phone support. Assistance in starting groups.

EDA
18233 N. 16th Way
Phoenix, AZ 85022

*Phone:* 602-788-4990
*Email:* info@eatingdisordersanonymous.org
*Website:* http://eatingdisordersanonymous.org

### Food Addicts in Recovery Anonymous                             National
*150 affiliated groups. Founded 1998.* Purpose is to help people with food addiction problems to recover from food addiction or bulimia. Open to persons with a desire to stop eating addictively. Newsletter, literature, phone support, conferences. Long-distance sponsors.

FARA
6 Pleasant St., Room 402
Malden, MA 02148

*Phone:* 781-321-9118
*Fax:* 781-321-9223
*E-mail:* famail@aol.com
*Website:* http://www.foodaddicts.org

### Food Addicts Anonymous                                      International
*141 affiliated groups worldwide. Founded 1987.* 12-step fellowship of men and women who are willing to recover from the disease of food addiction. Primary purpose is to maintain abstinence from sugar, flour and wheat. Information and referral, pen pals, online contacts, conferences. Assistance in starting groups.

F.A.A.
4623 Forest Hill Blvd., #109-4
W. Palm Beach, FL 33415

*Phone:* 561-967-3871; *Fax:* 561-967-9815
*E-mail:* info@foodaddictsanonymous.org
*Website:* http://www.foodaddictsanonymous.org

## O-Anon                                              International
*6 affiliated groups. Founded 1979.* 12-step fellowship of friends and relatives of compulsive overeaters. Group development guidelines.

O-Anon                     *Phone:* 559-877-3615; *Fax:* 559-877-3615
P.O. Box 1314              *E-mail:* oanon@netptc.net
North Fork, CA 93643       *Website:* http://www.oaregion6.org/0-anon.html

## Overeaters Anonymous                                International
*9,000 groups. Founded 1960.* 12-step fellowship of men and women who meet to help one another understand and overcome compulsive eating. Also groups and literature for young persons and teens. Monthly magazine, literature, group development guidelines.

O.A.                       *Phone:* 505-891-2664
P.O. Box 44020             *E-mail:* overeatr@technet.nm.org
Rio Rancho, NM 87174-4020  *Website:* http://www.overeatersanonymous.org

# GAMBLING
*(Also see Addictions General)*

## Gam-Anon Family Groups                              International
*500 groups. Founded 1960.* 12-step fellowship for men and women who are husbands, wives, relatives or friends of compulsive gamblers who have been affected by a loved one's gambling problem. Purpose is to learn acceptance and understanding of the gambling illness, to use the program to rebuild lives, and give assistance to those who suffer. A few groups have Gam-Ateen groups for children of gamblers.

Gam-Anon                   *Phone:* 718-352-1671; *Fax:* 718-746-2571
P.O. Box 5701571           *E-mail:* info@gam-anon.org
Whitestone, NY 11357       *Website:* http://www.gam-anon.org

## Gamblers Anonymous                                  International
*Approximately 1800 chapters. Founded 1957.* 12-step fellowship of men and women who share experiences, strength and hope with each other to recover from compulsive gambling. Monthly bulletin.            *Phone:* 213-386-8789
G.A.                       *Fax:* 213-386-0030
P.O. Box 17173             *E-mail:* isomain@gamblersanonymous.org
Los Angeles, CA 90017      *Website:* http://www.gamblersanonymous.org

## Bettors Anonymous                                   Model
*4 groups in Massachusetts. Founded 1990.* 12-step fellowship who share their experience, hope and strength with each other in order to help themselves and others recover from compulsive gambling. The only requirement for membership is the desire to stop gambling. Literature, information and referrals, phone support. Provides assistance in starting groups.

Bettors Anonymous          *Phone:* George 978-988-177 (day/eve)
P.O. Box 304
Wilmington, MA 01887

## MENTALLY ILL / CHEMICALLY ADDICTED
*(Also see Addictions General, specific addiction, specific disorder)*

**Double Trouble in Recovery, Inc.**                          **National**
*100+ affiliated groups. Founded 1989.* Fellowship who share their experience, strength and hope with each other so that they may solve their common problems and help others to recover from an addiction and a mental disorder. For persons dually-diagnosed with an addiction as well as a mental disorder. Literature, information and referrals, conferences. Help in starting new groups.

DTR, Inc.                              *Phone:* MHEP 518-434-1393;
c/o MH Empowerment Project             1-800-643-7462 or Howie 718-996-6324
261 Central Ave.                       *Fax:* 518-434-3823
Albany, NY 12206                       *Website:* http://www.doubletroubleinrecovery.com

**Dual Recovery Anonymous**                                  **International**
*400 chapters. Founded 1989.* A self-help program for individuals who experience a dual disorder of chemical dependency and a psychiatric or emotional illness. Based on principles of the 12-steps and the personal experiences of individuals in dual recovery. Literature, newsletter, assistance in starting local groups.

DRA                                    *Phone:* 1-877-883-2332; *Fax:* 615-297-9346
P.O. Box 218232                        *E-mail:* webmaster@draonline.org
Nashville, TN 37221-8232               *Website:* http://draonline.org

**Dual Disorders Anonymous**                                 **Model**
*28 groups in Illinois; 20 in other states. Founded 1982.* 12-step fellowship of men and women who come together to help those members who still suffer from both a mental disorder and alcoholism and/or drug addiction. Group development guidelines.

Dual Disorders Anonymous               *Phone:* 847-490-9379
P.O. Box 681264                        *E-mail:* DualDisorder@yahoo.com
Schaumburg, IL 60168-1264              *Website:* http://www.dualdisorder.anon

## NICOTINE / SMOKING
*(Also see Addictions General)*

**Nicotine Anonymous World Services**                        **International**
*500+ groups. Founded 1985.* 12-step program for people who want to recover from nicotine addiction and live free of nicotine in all forms. Welcomes all, including persons using cessation programs and nicotine withdrawal aids.

NAWS                                   *Phone:* 415-750-0328; *Fax:* 714-969-4493
419 Main St. PMB #370                  *E-mail:* info@nicotine-anonymous.org
Huntington Beach, CA 92648             *Website:* http://www.nicotine-anonymous.org

*"I used to be a hopeless dope fiend. Now I am a dopeless hope fiend."*
*- Author unknown*

# OVERSPENDING / DEBT
*(Also See Addictions General)*

**Debtors Anonymous General Service Board**                           **International**
*450 groups. Founded 1976.* 12-step fellowship that provides mutual help in recovering from compulsive indebtedness. Primary purpose of members is to stay solvent and help other compulsive debtors achieve solvency. Newsletter, phone support network.
DAGSB                              *Phone:* 781-453-2743; *Fax:* 781-453-2745
P.O. Box 920888                    *E-mail:* da-gso@mindspring.com
Needham, MA 02492-0009             *Website:* http://www.debtorsanonymous.org

**Spenders Anonymous**                                                  **National**
*4 affiliated groups.* 12-step program based on the principles of Alcoholics Anonymous for persons recovering from compulsive spending. Aim is to spread the message that overspenders are not alone. Website contains information on starting local self-help groups.
Spenders Anonymous                 *Phone:* 651-649-4573
P.O. Box 2405                      *E-mail:* info@spenders.org
Minneapolis, MN 55402             *Website:* http://www.spenders.org

# SEX / LOVE ADDICTION
*(Also see Addictions General)*

**Augustine Fellowship, Sex and Love Addicts Anonymous**            **International**
*1234 affiliated groups. Founded 1976.* 12-step fellowship based on A.A. for those who desire to stop living out a pattern of sex and love addiction, obsessive/compulsive sexual behavior or emotional attachment. Newsletter, journal, information and referrals, conferences, phone support. Group development guidelines ($6).
Augustine Fellowship                *Phone:* 781-255-8825; *Fax:* 781-255-9190
P.O. Box 338                       *E-mail:* slaafws@slaafws.org
Norwood, MA 02062-0338            *Website:* http://www.slaafws.org

**COSA (Codependents Of Sex Addicts)**                                  **National**
*50+ affiliated groups. Founded 1980.* A self-help program of recovery using the 12-steps adapted from A.A. and Al-Anon, for those involved in relationships with people who have compulsive sexual behavior. Help in starting new groups. Newsletter ($12).
COSA NSO, Inc.                     *Phone:* 763-537-6904
P.O. Box 14537                    *E-mail:* cosa@shore.net
Minneapolis, MN 55414             *Website*: http://www.cosa-recovery.org

**Love-N-Addiction**                                                 **International**
*73 chapters. Founded 1986.* Explores how loving can become an addiction. Builds a healthy support system to aid in recovery from addictive love into healthy love. Uses ideas from <u>Women Who Love Too Much</u> by R. Norwood. Chapter development guidelines ($15).

Love-N-Addiction                        *Phone:* Carolyn Meister 860-423-2344
P.O. Box 759
Willimantic, CT 06226

### S-Anon                                                             International
*100 affiliated groups. Founded 1984.* 12-step group for loved ones of persons with a sexual addiction. Assistance available for starting groups. Conferences. Quarterly newsletter ($10).
S-Anon                                  *Phone:* 615-833-3152
P.O. Box 111242                         *E-mail:* sanon@sanon.org
Nashville, TN 37222                     *Website:* http://www.sanon.org

### Sex Addicts Anonymous                                              International
*570 groups. Founded 1977.* 12-step fellowship of men and women with a desire to stop their addictive sexual behavior and to help others recover from sexual addiction. Newsletter.
ISO of SAA                              *Phone:* 713-869-4902 or 1-800-477-8191
P.O. Box 70949                          *E-mail:* info@saa-recovery.org
Houston, TX 77270                       *Website:* http://www.saa-recovery.org

### Sexaholics Anonymous                                               International
*700 chapters. Founded 1979.* Program of recovery for those who want to stop their sexually self-destructive thinking and behavior. Mutual support to achieve and maintain sexual sobriety. Phone network, newsletter, literature and books. Assistance in starting groups.
S.A.                                    *Phone:* 615-331-6230; *Fax:* 615-331-6901
P.O. Box 111910                         *E-mail:* saico@sa.org
Nashville, TN 37222-1910                *Website:* http://www.sa.org

### Sexual Compulsives Anonymous                                       International
*140+ groups. Founded 1982.* Fellowship of men and women who share their experience, strength and hope that they may solve their common problem and help others to recover from sexual compulsion. Newsletter, information and referrals, phone support, conferences.
SCA                                     *Phone:* 1-800-977-4325
P.O. Box 1585 Old Chelsea Sta.          *E-mail:* info@sca-recovery.org
New York, NY 10011                      *Website:* http://www.sca-recovery.org

### Sexual Recovery Anonymous                                          International
*32 groups. Founded 1990.* 12-step fellowship of persons who share their experience, strength and hope with each other that they may solve their common problem and help others to recover from compulsive sexual behavior.
SRA                                     *Phone:* 212-340-4650 (NY); 213-243-9438 (CA)
P.O. Box 73                             or 604-290-9382 (Canada)
New York, NY 10024)                     *Website:* http://www.sexualrecovery.org

*"While there's life, there's hope."*
*- Terence, comic dramatist*

## WORKAHOLICS

**Workaholics Anonymous World Service Organization, Inc.**          **International**
*100+ groups. Founded 1983.* 12-step fellowship for persons who feel their work lives have gotten out of control. Also for families and friends. Mutual support in solving problems of compulsive overworking. Weekly meetings. Group development guidelines.
Workaholics Anonymous                    *Phone*: 510-273-9253
P.O. Box 289
Menlo Park, CA 94026-0289

CG 8D

### An Interesting Research Study...

Participants in national self-help group for **parents of young drug and alcohol abusers** -- PRIDE (Parent Resources Institute for Drug Education) -- reported that their participation was associated with **improvement in their children's drug problem.** A majority of the participants also reported improvements in their children's general discipline problems and in adjustment outside the home. (Galanter, M.D., Gleaton, T., Marcus, C.E. & McMillen, J. Self-help groups for parents of young adults and alcohol abusers. American Journal of Psychiatry, vol. 141, no. 7, 1984.

---

### *Serenity Prayer*

*God grant me the serenity*
*To accept the things I cannot change,*
*The courage to change the things I can*
*And the wisdom to know the difference.*

---

# BEREAVEMENT

*"The world is round and the place which may seem like the end may also be the beginning."*
— Ivy Baker Priest

## BEREAVEMENT (GENERAL)
*(Also see specific situation/loss)*

**AARP Grief and Loss Programs**                                    **National**
*240 groups. Founded 1973.* Offers a wide range of resources and information on grief and loss issues to bereaved adults, and their families. Programs include one-to-one outreach support (e.g. Widowed Persons Services), a grief course, support groups, interactive online support groups, and informational booklets and brochures. Works with local organizations to develop community-based bereavement programs.

AARP Grief and Loss Program          *Phone:* 202-434-2260
601 E Street NW                      *E-mail:* griefandloss@aarp.org
Washington, DC 20049                 *Website:* http://www.aarp.org/griefandloss

**ACCESS (AirCraft Casualty Emotional Support Services)**      **National network**
Matches persons who have lost a loved one in an aircraft accident to volunteers who previously experienced a similar loss. Aim is to help fill the void that occurs when the emergency and disaster relief organizations disband, the initial shock subsides, and the natural grieving process intensifies. Persons communicate through e-mail or by phone.

ACCESS                               *Phone:* 1-877-227-6435
1594 York Ave., Suite 22             *E-mail:* info@accesshelp.org
New York, NY 10028                   *Website:* http://www.accesshelp.org

**COPS (Concerns Of Police Survivors), Inc.**                      **National**
*41 chapters. Founded 1984.* Provides resources for the surviving families of law enforcement officers killed in the line of duty according to federal criteria. Also offers law enforcement training, newsletter, departmental guidelines, peer support, and special hands-on programs for survivors. Offers summer camp for children ages 6-14 and their parent/guardian, retreats for parents and spouses, spouse's get-aways, Outward Bound experiences for young adults ages 15-20, sibling and adult children's retreat.

COPS, Inc.                           *Phone:* 573-346-4911; *Fax:* 573-346-1414
P.O. Box 3199, S. Highway 5          *E-mail:* cops@nationalcops.org
Camdenton, MO 65020                  *Website:* http://www.nationalcops.org

**Grief Share**                                                    **National**
*21 affiliated groups. Founded 1998.* Network of support groups to assist anyone who is grieving the loss of a loved one. Information, referrals, literature, Help in starting groups.

135

Grief Share                              *Phone:* 919-562-2112; *Fax:* 919-562-2114
220 S. White St.                         *E-mail:* info@griefshare.org
Wake Forest, NC 27587                    *Website:* http://www.griefshare.org

**National Donor Family Council**                                        **National**
*52 affiliated groups. Founded 1992.* Mutual support for families who donated the
organs/tissues of a loved one who died. Provides literature, programs and local resources.
Newsletter, pen pals, conferences, advocacy.
Nat'l Donor Family Council               *Phone:* 1-800-622-9010 or 212-889-2210
c/o Sarah Ockler                         *Fax:* 212-689-9261
30 E. 33rd St.                           *E-mail:* info@kidney.org
New York, NY 10016                       *Website:* http://www.donorfamily.org

**National Fallen Firefighters Foundation**
**Fire Service Survivors Support Network**                       **National network**
Provides emotional support for spouses, families, and friends of firefighters who have died.
Members are matched with survivors of similar experiences to help them cope during the
difficult months following the death.
Nat'l Fallen Firefighters Fdn.           *Phone:* 301-447-1365
Fire Svc. Survivors Support Network      *Fax:* 301-447-1645
P.O. Box Drawer 498                       *Website:* http://firehero.org
Emmitsburg, MD 21727

**RAINBOWS**                                                     **International**
*8500 affiliated groups. Founded 1983.* Establishes peer support groups in churches, schools
or social agencies for children who are grieving a death, divorce or other painful transition
in their family. Groups are led by trained adults. Online newsletter, information and
referrals. Many programs have concurrent groups for parents.
RAINBOWS                                  *Phone:* 1-800-266-3206 or 847-952-1770
2100 Golf Rd., Suite 370                  *E-mail:* info@rainbows.org
Rolling Meadows, IL 60008                 *Website:* http://www.rainbows.org

**TAPS (Tragedy Assistance Program for Survivors)**              **National network**
Provides support for persons who have lost a loved one while serving in the armed forces
(army, air force, navy, marine corps, national guard, reserves, service academies or coast
guard). Offers networking, crisis information, problem solving assistance, and liaison with
military agencies. Offers program for kids. Annual seminar.
TAPS                                      *Phone:* 1-800-959-8277 or 202-588-8277
2001 S St., NW, Suite 300                 *Fax:* 202-638-5312; *E-mail:* info@taps.org
Washington, DC 20009                      *Website:* http://www.taps.org

**TCF Sibling Pen Pal Program**                                  **National network**
*Founded 1969.* Opportunity for bereaved siblings of any age wishing to meet other siblings
with similar interests, hobbies, and whose sibling may have had a similar cause of death.

TCF Sibling Pen Pal Program
P.O. Box 3696
Oak Brook, IL 60522-3696

*Phone:* 1-877-969-0010
*Fax:* 630-990-0246
*Website:* http://www.compassionatefriends.org

**Twinless Twin International**                    **International network**
*Founded 1985.* Mutual support for twins who have lost their twin or multiple(s). Information and referrals, phone support, conferences. Parents of infant/child age survivor twins welcome. Publishes <u>Twinless Times</u> ($18/yr). Group development guidelines. Assistance in starting local groups. Videos.

Twinless Twin Support Group
P.O. Box 980481
Ypsilanti, MI 48198-0481

*Phone:* 1-888-205-8962
*E-mail:* contact@twinlesstwins.org
*Website:* http://www.twinlesstwins.org

**Wings of Light, Inc.**                               **National networks**
*3 support networks. Founded 1995.* Support and information network for individuals whose lives have been touched by aviation accidents. Separate networks for airplane accident survivors, families and friends of persons killed in airplane accidents, and persons involved in the rescue, recovery and investigation of crashes. Information and referrals, phone support.

Wings of Light, Inc.
16845 N. 29th Ave., PMB 448 #1
Phoenix, AZ 85053

*Phone:* 1-800-613-8531 or 623-516-1115
*Website:* http://www.wingsoflight.org

**Fiancées and Domestic Partners of 9/11**                      **Model**
*Various groups in NJ. Founded 2001.* Mutual support for those who lost loved ones in the September 11th tragedy. Open to common-law and same-sex partners.
*Phone:* Anthony (732)968-9838           *E-mail*: FianceesOf911@aol.com

**Griefnet**                                                    **Online**
E-mail discussion groups dealing with bereavement. Offers a variety of bereavement groups. Monthly charge of $5 per group. *Website*: http://www.griefnet.org

**Sibling Chat**                                                **Online**
Opportunity for adults and teens bereaving the loss of a sibling to share concerns and feelings. Live chat Thurs., 9pm (ET).     *Website:* http://www.compassionatefriends.org/
                                                        Chat/chat.htm

**Sibling Forum**                                               **Online**
Discussion board for siblings to share feelings and help each other cope with the grief of losing a sibling. Opportunity for siblings to ask questions, make a comment, or leave a thought for others to respond to.     *Website:* http://www.compassionatefriends.org
                                                        /forums/Siblings

# DEATH OF A CHILD / FETAL LOSS
*(Also see Bereavement General, Survivors of Suicide)*

**AGAST (Alliance of Grandparents, A Support in Tragedy)**            **International**
*3 groups. Founded 2001.* Dedicated to assisting grandparents in the loss of a grandchild.
Offers one-to-one peer support, literature and a bi-monthly newsletter.
AGAST                                 *Phone:* 1-888-774-7437 or 602-604-8462
P.O. Box 17281                        *E-mail:* reachout@agast.org
Phoenix, AZ 95011-0281                *Website:* http://www.agast.org

**AMEND (Aiding Mothers and Fathers**
**Experiencing Neonatal Death)**                                    **National network**
*Founded 1974.* Offers support and encouragement to parents having a normal grief reaction
to the loss of their baby. One-to-one peer counseling with trained volunteers.
AMEND                                 *Phone:* 314-487-7582
4324 Berrywick Terrace                *E-mail:* info@amendgroup.org
St. Louis, MO 63128                   *Website:* http://www.amendgroup.org

**Alive Alone, Inc.**                                               **National network**
*Founded 1988.* Self-help network of parents who have lost an only child or all of their
children. Provides education and publications to promote communication and healing, to
assist in resolving grief, and to develop the means to reinvest lives for a positive future.
Bi-monthly newsletter.                *Phone:* 419-238-7879
Alive Alone                           *E-mail:* KayBevington@alivealone.org
11115 Dull Robinson Rd.               *Website:* http://www.alivealone.org
Van Wert, OH 45891

**Bereaved Parents of the USA**                                     **National**
*50+ affiliated groups. Founded 1995.* Designed to aid and support bereaved parents and
their families who are struggling to survive their grief after the death of a child. Information
and referrals, newsletter, phone support, conferences, support group meetings. Assistance in
starting groups.
Bereaved Parents of the USA           *Phone:* 630-971-3490; *Fax:* 708-748-9184
P.O. Box 95                           *E-mail:* director1@bereavedparentsusa.org
Park Forest, IL 60466                 *Website:* http://www.bereavedparentsusa.org

**CLIMB, Inc. (Center for Loss In Multiple Birth)**                 **International network**
*Founded 1987.* Support by and for parents who have experienced the death of one or more
of their twins or higher multiples during pregnancy, birth, in infancy, or childhood.
Newsletter, information on specialized topics, pen pals, phone support. Materials for twins
clubs, professionals, and loss support groups.
CLIMB                                 *Phone:* 907-222-5321
P.O. Box 91377                        *E-mail:* climb@pobox.alaska.net
Anchorage AK 99509                    *Website:* http://www.climb-support.org

## Compassionate Friends, The                                    National

*600 chapters. Founded 1969.* Offers mutual assistance, friendship and understanding to families following the death of a child. Provides information on the grieving process, referrals to local chapter meetings, and publishes a quarterly magazine ($20/yr). Online chat, online forum, and pen pal program for those grieving the loss of a brother or sister.

The Compassionate Friends          *Phone:* 1-877-969-0010
P.O. Box 3696                       *Fax:* 630-990-0246
Oak Brook, IL 60522-3696           *Website:* http://www.compassionatefriends.org

## MISS (Mothers In Sympathy and Support)                        National

*20 chapters.* Provides emergency and on-going support to families grieving the death of their baby (stillbirth, neonatal death, premature birth, congenital anomalies, sudden death) or any child's death. Supports research, advocacy.

The M.I.S.S. Foundation             *E-mail:* info@misschildren.org
P.O. Box 5333                       *Website:* http://www.missfoundation.org
Peoria, AZ 85385

## National Organization of Parents of Murdered Children          National

*300 chapters and contact persons. Founded 1978.* Provides mutual support to persons who survived the violent death of someone close, as they seek to recover. Newsletter. Court accompaniment provided in many areas.

NOPMC                               *Phone:* 1-888-818-POMC or 513-721-5683
100 E. 8th St., B-41                *E-mail:* NatlPOMC@aol.com
Cincinnati, OH 45202               *Website:* http://www.pomc.com

## Open ARMS (Abortion Related Ministries)                        National

*Affiliated groups nationally. Founded 1986.* Christian post-abortion support group open to anyone suffering from abortion's emotional aftermath. Provides newsletters, phone support, conferences, information and referrals. Group development guidelines ($12).

Open ARMS                           *Phone:* 719-573-5790
c/o Patti Slauson
P.O. Box 9292
Colorado Springs, CO 80932

## SHARE: Pregnancy and Infant Loss Support, Inc.                 National

*130 chapters. Founded 1977.* Mutual support for bereaved parents and families who have suffered a loss due to miscarriage, stillbirth or neonatal death. Provides newsletter, pen pals, information on pastoral care. Chapter development guidelines. Online message board and weekly chat rooms.

National SHARE Office               *Phone:* 1-800-821-6819 or 636-947-6164
c/o St. Joseph Health Center        *Fax:* 636-947-7486
300 First Capital Dr.               *Website:* http://www.nationalshareoffice.com
St. Charles, MO 63301

**SIDS Alliance**                                                    **National**
*48 chapters. Founded 1987.* Provides emotional support for families of sudden infant death syndrome (SIDS) and other infant death victims. Supports research, educates the public and professionals. Newsletter, telephone support network, chapter development guidelines.
SIDS Alliance                              *Phone:* 1-800-221-7437 or 410-653-8226
1314 Bedford Ave., Suite 210               *E-mail:* info@sidsalliance.org
Baltimore, MD 21208                        *Website:* http://www.sidsalliance.org

**Tender Hearts**                                                   **International**
*Sponsored by Triplet Connection. Founded 1983.* Network of parents who have lost one or more children in multiple births. Information on selection reduction. Newsletter, information and referrals, phone support and pen pals.
Tender Hearts                              *Phone:* 209-474-0885
c/o Triplet Connection                     *Fax:* 209-474-9243
P.O. Box 99571                             *Website:* http://www.tripletconnection.org
Stockton, CA 95209

**Unite, Inc.**                                                     **National**
*14 groups. Founded 1975.* Support for parents grieving miscarriage, stillbirth and infant death. Also provides support for parents through subsequent pregnancies. Phone help, newsletter, conference. Offers group facilitator and grief counselor training programs. Professionals have advisory roles in groups.
Unite, Inc.                                *Phone:* 215-728-3777 (tape)
c/o Janis Keyser                           *E-mail:* uniteinc1975@aol.com
Jeanes Hospital                            *Website:* http://www.unite.freeservers.com
7600 Central Ave.
Philadelphia, PA 19111-2499

**Abortion Survivors Anonymous**                                    **Model**
*1 group in California. Founded 1988.* 12-step support for those affected by abortion loss. For persons seeking to recover from the impact of abortion on their lives and relationships. 12-Step Workbook/manual ($15).
Abortion Survivors Anonymous               *Phone:* Sara 760-741-7050
P.O. Box 161                               *Phone:* Mary 858-578-9079
Escondido, CA 92033

**Save Our Sons And Daughters (SOSAD)**                             **Model**
*1 group in Michigan. Founded 1987.* Crisis intervention and violence prevention program that provides support and advocacy for survivors of homicide or other traumatic loss. Weekly bereavement groups, professional grief counseling and training. Advocacy, public education, Newsletter, conferences, rallies and assistance in starting groups.
SOSAD                                      *Phone:* 313-361-5200
2441 W. Grand Blvd.                        *Fax:* 313-361-0055
Detroit, MI 48208-1210                     *E-mail:* sosadb@aol.com

# PET LOSS

⌨ **Delta Society Pet Bereavement Support Groups**                    Online
Maintains a database of pet bereavement support groups and resource persons.
Delta Society                         *Phone:* 425-226-7357 *Fax:* 425-235-1076
289 Perimeter Rd. East                *E-mail:* info@deltasociety.org
Renton, VA 98035-1329                 *Website:* http://www.deltasociety.org


⌨ **Pet Loss Grief Support Website**                               Online
(Multilingual) Moderated board and chat room offering support and understanding for persons grieving the loss of their pet, or who have a pet that is ill. Provides personal support and thoughtful advice. Offers "Monday Pet Loss Candle Ceremony," and other resources. Various languages available.     *Website:* http://www.petloss.com

# SUICIDE SURVIVORS

*(Also see Bereavement General, Death of a Child, Widows and Widowers)*


📖 **American Association of Suicidology**                          Resource
*350 affiliated groups.* Provides referrals to local self-help groups for survivors of suicide. National directory of groups ($15). Newsletter, pamphlets, etc. available for a fee. Manual on starting self-help groups ($30).
American Assn. of Suicidology         *Phone:* 202-237-2280; *Fax:* 202-237-2282
4201 Connecticut Ave. NW, #408        *E-mail*: info@suicidology.org
Washington, DC 20008                  *Website:* http://www.suicidology.org


📖 **American Foundation for Suicide Prevention**                  Resource
*18 chapters. Founded 1987.* Provides state-by-state directories of survivor support groups for families and friends of a suicide. Also provides information regarding suicide statistics and prevention.
American Suicide Fdn.                  *Phone:* 1-888-333-2377 or 212-363-3500
120 Wall St., 22nd fl.                 *E-mail:* inquiry@afsp.org
New York, NY 10005                     *Website:* http://www.afsp.org


**Ray of Hope, Inc.**                                           International
*10 affiliated groups. Founded 1977.* Provides mutual support for after suicide bereavement. Offers educational materials on suicide postvention and books on after suicide grief (call for price list). Also provides telephone counseling, workshops and seminars. Consultation for starting survivor support groups.
Ray of Hope                            *Phone:* 319-337 9890 (Voice/Fax)
P.O. Box 2323
Iowa City, IA 52244


*"Who then can so softly bind up the wound of another*
*as he who has felt the same would himself." — Thomas Jefferson*

**Heartbeat**                                                      **Model**
*26 chapters in Colorado. Founded 1980.* Mutual support for those who have lost a loved one through suicide. Information and referrals, phone support, chapter development guidelines ($10). Speaker's bureau.
Heartbeat                          *Phone:* 719-596-2575
2015 Devon St.                     *E-mail:* archlj@msn.com
Colorado Springs, CO 80909

**Suicide Anonymous**                                              **Model**
*3 groups in Tennessee. Founded 1996.* 12-step fellowship of men and women who share their experience, strength and hope with each other that they may solve their common problem of suicidal ideation and behavior. Provides a safe environment for people to share their struggles with suicide, to prevent suicides, and to develop strategies for support and healing from the devastating effects of suicidal preoccupation and behavior. Networking, literature, advocacy.
S.A.                               *Phone:* 901-763-3693; *Fax:* 901-767-4728
P.O. Box 341395                    *E-mail:* samemphis@hotmail.com
Memphis, TN 38119                  *Website:* http://www.geocities.com/samemphis

🖳   **SOLES (Survivors Of Law Enforcement Suicide)**              **Online**
*Founded 1995.* Provides emotional support to the families of police officers who died by suicide. Information and referrals on national and local resources including support groups, conferences, grief workshops. Online e-mail discussion list and weekly online chat. Quarterly newsletter.
SOLES                              *Phone:* 941-541-1151 (Voice/Fax)
2708 SW 48 Terrace                 *E-mail:* AskT8@aol.com
Cape Coral, FL 33914               *Website:* http://www.tearsofacop.com

🖳   **SOLOS (Survivors Of Loved One's Suicides)**                 **Online**
Offers various e-mail support groups for persons affected by suicide. Groups include survivors of a loved one's suicide, parents of attempters, medical/crisis response professionals, parents, spouses, siblings, gays/lesbians, men, grandparents, teens and children who have lost someone to suicide. Also groups for persons affected by murder-suicides, post-partum depression suicides, and facilitators of suicide support groups.
SOLOS, Inc.                        *E-mail:* solos@1000deaths.com
P.O. Box 592                       *Website:* http://www.1000deaths.com
Dumfries, CA 22026-0592

# WIDOWS / WIDOWERS
*(Also see Bereavement General, Single Parenting)*

**AARP Grief and Loss Programs**                               **National**
*240 groups. Founded 1973.* Offers a wide range of resources and information on grief and loss issues to adults who are bereaved and their families. Programs include one-to-one

outreach support (e.g. Widowed Persons Services), a grief course, support groups, interactive online support groups, and informational booklets and brochures. Works cooperatively with local organizations to develop community-based bereavement programs.

AARP Grief and Loss Program     *Phone:* 202-434-2260 *Fax:* 202-434-6474
601 E Street NW                 *E-mail:* griefandloss@aarp.org
Washington, DC 20049            *Website:* http://www.aarp.org/griefandloss

## Beginning Experience, The                                    International
*145 teams. Founded 1974.* Offers support programs for widowed, separated or divorced adults and their children enabling them to work through the grief of a lost marriage.

The Beginning Experience       *Phone:* 219-283-0279
c/o Int'l Ministry Ctr.        *Fax:* 219-283-0287
1657 Commerce Dr.              *Website:* http://www.beginningexperience.org
South Bend, IN 46628

## COPS (Concerns Of Police Survivors), Inc.                    National
*41 chapters. Founded 1984.* Provides resources for the surviving families of law enforcement officers killed in the line of duty according to federal criteria. Offers law enforcement training, newsletter, departmental guidelines, peer support, special hands-on programs for survivors. Summer camp for children and their parent/guardian, retreats for parents and spouses, spouse's get-aways, Outward Bound for young adults, sibling and adult children's retreats.

COPS                          *Phone:* 573-346-4911; *Fax:* 573-346-1414
P.O. Box 3199, S. Highway 5    *E-mail:* cops@nationalcops.org
Camdenton, MO 65020           *Website:* http://www.nationalcops.org

## North American Conference
## Of Separated and Divorced Catholics                          International
*3000+ groups. Founded 1972.* Religious, educational and emotional aspects of separation, divorce, remarriage and widowhood are addressed through self-help groups, conferences and training programs. Families of all faiths are welcome. Group development guidelines. Newsletter. Dues $30 (includes newsletter).

NACSDC                        *Phone:* 541-893-6089 (Voice/Fax #51)
P.O. Box 360                   *E-mail:* nacsdc@pinetel.com
Richland, OR 97870            *Website:* http://www.nacsdc.org

## Society of Military Widows                                   National
*27 chapters. Founded 1968.* Support and assistance for widows/widowers of members of all U.S. uniformed services. Offers help in coping with the adjustment to life on their own. Promotes public awareness. Bi-monthly magazine/journal. Dues $12. Chapter development guidelines.

Soc. of Military Widows        *Phone:* 703-750-1342; *Fax:* 703-354-4380
5535 Hempstead Way             *E-mail:* naus@ix.netcom.com
Springfield, VA 22151         *Website:* http://www.militarywidows.org

**To Live Again**                                                              **Model**
*19 chapters in Pennsylvania. Founded 1974.* Mutual help organization covering the greater Delaware Valley, for widowed women and men who support one another through the grief cycle. Monthly meetings, social programs, chapter development assistance, program for newly bereaved, conferences, newsletter. Dues $15.
TLA                                          *Phone:* 610-353-7740
P.O. Box 415                                 *Fax:* 215-634-2633
Springfield, PA 19064-0415

ርፄ ౭ට

*"Regardless of their backgrounds, ages, and circumstances, widows who joined support groups recovered much faster. After one year, members of support groups felt less depression and used less medication and alcohol to alter their feelings of sadness. The more deeply involved they became in the groups, the greater their signs of recovery. They became less anxious, had a greater sense of well-being, higher self-esteem, and rated themselves as much improved."* - Dr. Morton A. Lieberman, reporting upon his own research of 500 widows from his book, <u>Doors Close, Doors Open: Widows, Grieving and Growing</u> (Putnam's Sons, 1996).

ርፄ ౭ට

The following are excerpts from some of the presentations made at the Clearinghouse Conference, "Learning from 'Those Who Have Been There' - Gathering Comfort & Hope from Self-Help Support Groups" held 1/12/02 for 9/11 families, in Piscataway, NJ:

*"I have found that discussing the event with others, who understand your experience first-hand, is very beneficial. We have a bond with each other that defies description... We are all members of this horrendous club. It is not a club in which we welcome new members. But it is one where we reach out to our new members and say we understand your pain, we want to reach out to help, and we want to offer you hope."* - Diane Leonard, Oklahoma City Family Support Groups, who lost her husband in the bombing of the Oklahoma City Federal Building in 1995.

*"Bereaved parents are very powerful people... they can take that enormous love for their child and reinvest their energy to make this a better world in memory of their son or daughter."* - Ceil Buonocore, a Compassionate Friends chapter leader, who lost her son in the terrorist attack on Rome Airport in 1985.

*"A unique bond and genuine trust is established between someone who has traveled a similar journey years earlier, and one who is just beginning. Seeing that someone else survived through the years can be healing and reassuring."* - Heidi Snow, Founder of AirCraft Casualty Emotional Support Services (ACCESS), after losing her fiancé in the explosion of TWA Flight 800 in 1996, being helped by the Pan Am 103 Families group.

# DISABILITIES

*"If God had wanted me otherwise,*
*He would have created me otherwise."*
*- Johann von Goethe*

## AMPUTATION / LIMB DEFICIENCY
*(Also see Disabilities General)*

**American Amputee Foundation, Inc.**                                    **National**
*8 chapters. Founded 1975.* Information, referrals and peer support for amputees. Hospital visitation and counseling. Publishes group development guidelines, and national resource directory for patients, families and caregivers.
American Amputee Fdn.            *Phone:* 501-666-2523 (day)
P.O. Box 250218                     *Fax:* 501-666-8367
Little Rock, AR 72225-0218          *E-mail:* american_amputee_foundation
                                    @hotmail.com

**Amputee Coalition of America**                                         **National**
*200+ groups. Founded 1989.* Coalition of amputees, support groups, professionals and disability-related organizations established to provide outreach, education and empowerment for persons with limb loss. Referrals to support groups and peer contacts. How-to guide for starting a group. Information hotline, In Motion magazine.
Amputee Coalition of America        *Phone:* 1-888-267-5669
900 E. Hill Ave., Suite 285         *E-mail:* acainfo@amputee-coalition.org
Knoxville, TN 37915                 *Website:* http://www.amputee-coalition.org

**National Amputation Foundation, Inc.**                                 **National**
*Founded 1919.* Self-help for amputees of all ages. "Amp-to-Amp" program links individuals to others with similar amputations. Newsletter, library, information, advocacy, vocational guidance, information and referrals. Dues $25/yr.
Nat'l Amputation Fdn.               *Phone:* 516-887-3600; *Fax:* 516-887-3667
38-40 Church St.                    *E-mail:* amps76@aol.com
Malverne, NY 11565                  *Website:* http://www.nationalamputation.org

**▣ I-CAN (International Child Amputee Network)**                         **Online**
Mailing list for parents of children with either acquired or congenital limb loss. Opportunity to share experiences with other parents. *Website:* http://www.amp-info.net/childamp.htm

*"He has not learned the lesson of life who does not every day surmount a fear."*
*— Ralph Waldo Emerson*

# AUTISM / ASPERGER SYNDROME

**Autism Society of America**                                **National**
*200+ chapters. Founded 1965.* Organization of parents, professionals and citizens working together via education, advocacy and research for children and adults with autism. Newsletter, mail order bookstore, annual conference.
ASA                          *Phone:* 301-657-0881 or 1-800-3-AUTISM
7910 Woodmont Ave., #300     *Fax:* 301-657-0869
Bethesda, MD 20814           *Website:* http://www.autism-society.org/

**Autism Network International**                          **International**
*Founded 1992.* Organization run by and for autistic people. Provides peer support, tips for coping, and problem-solving. Offers information and referrals, advocacy, and education. Newsletter ($15). Retreats/conferences. Long distance phone calls will be returned collect. Online listserv discussion forum.
ANI                          *Phone:* 315-476-2462; *Fax:* 315-425-1978
P.O. Box 35448               *E-mail:* jisincla@mailbox.syr.edu
Syracuse, NY 13235-5488      *Website:* http://www.ani.ac

**Autism Network for Hearing and Visually Impaired Persons**     **International network**
*Founded 1991.* Provides communication, education, research and advocacy for persons with autism combined with a hearing or visual disability, their families, and professionals. Sharing of educational materials, phone help, support groups, referrals, and conferences.
Autism Network               *Phone:* 757-428-9036
7510 Ocean Front Ave.        *Fax:* 757-428-0019
Virginia Beach, CA 23451

**ParentLink**                                            **Model**
*1 group in New York. Founded 1996.* Support and education for parents of children with higher functioning autism, Asperger syndrome or other pervasive developmental disorder. Develops activities, educates professionals, information and referrals. Newsletter, literature. Assistance in starting groups.        *Phone:* Nina 914-591-0744
Parent Link                  *Phone:* Susan 914-763-0971
c/o Nina Spooner             *E-mail:* nina_spooner@yahoo.com
350 South Buckhout St.       *E-mail:* nspo@netzero.net
Irvington, NY 10533          *Website:* http://www.westchesterparentlink.org

**OASIS (Online Asperger Syndrome Information & Support)**     **Online**
Provides information and support for Asperger syndrome and related disorders. Includes research papers, descriptions, local, national and international support groups. Message boards and chat rooms, family stories, research projects, links to evaluators, and other online resources. Forums for families and professionals.
*E-mail:* bkirby@udel.edu    *Website:* http://www.aspergersyndrome.org

# BLIND / VISUALLY IMPAIRED
*(Also see specific disorder)*

**Achromatopsia Network**                                          **National network**
Information and support network for individuals and families concerned with the rare inherited vision disorder achromatopsia (aka achromatopia), including both rod monochromacy and blue cone monochromacy.

Achromatopsia Network                 *E-mail:* editor@achromat.org
P.O. Box 214                          *Website:* http://www.achromat.org
Berkeley, CA 94701-0214


**American Council of The Blind**                                        **National**
*70 affiliates. Founded 1961.* Aims to improve the well-being of all blind and visually impaired people and their families through education, support, and advocacy. National conference, information and referrals, phone support, state and special interest affiliates (e.g. guide dog users, blind lawyers, teachers and students, etc), monthly magazine (available in Braille, half-speed cassette, large print, diskette, online or via e-mail). Scholarships. Online job bank. Chapter development guidelines.

American Council of the Blind          *Phone:* 1-800-424-8666 or 202-467-5081
1155 15th St. NW, Suite 1004           *E-mail:* info@acb.org
Washington, DC 20005                   *Website:* http://www.acb.org


**Association for Macular Diseases, Inc.**                              **National**
*Local support groups. Founded 1978.* Support for persons suffering from macular diseases, and their families. Distributes information on vision equipment. Supports national eye donor projects for macular disease research. Quarterly newsletter, telephone support network, participates in seminars. Group development guidelines. Dues $20/year.

Assn. for Macular Diseases             *Phone:* 212-605-3719 (eve)
210 E. 64th St.                        *Fax:* 212-605-3795
New York, NY 10021                     *Website:* http://www.macula.org


**Autism Network for Hearing and Visually Impaired Persons**    **International network**
*Founded 1991.* Communication, education, research and advocacy network for persons with autism combined with a hearing or visual disability, their families, and professionals. Sharing of educational materials, phone help, information, referrals to groups, conferences.

Autism Network for Hearing and         *Phone:* 757-428-9036
   Visually Impaired Persons           *Fax:* 757-428-0019
7510 Ocean Front Ave.
Virginia Beach, VA 23451


**Blinded Veterans Association**                                        **National**
*52 regional groups. Founded 1945.* Information, support and outreach to blinded veterans. Assists in job searches, information on benefits and rehabilitation programs. Bimonthly

147

newsletter. Chapter development guidelines. Regional meetings.

BVA
477 H St., NW
Washington, DC 20001

*Phone:* 202-371-8880 or 1-800-669-7079
*E-mail:* bva@bva.org
*Website:* http://www.bva.org

### Council of Citizens with Low Vision International                    International

*(A special interest affiliate of the American Council of the Blind) Founded 1978.* Encourages low vision people to make full use of vision through use of equipment, technology and services. Education and advocacy. Newsletter, information and referrals, group development guidelines, scholarships, and conferences. Dues $10/yr.

CCLVI
c/o Amer. Council of the Blind
1155 15th St. NW
Washington, DC 20005

*Phone:* 1-800-733-2258 or 727-443-0350
*Website:* http://www.cclvi.org

### Deaf-Blind Division/National Federation of the Blind            National network

Support network for deaf-blind persons and their families. Annual conventions, networking, literature and advocacy. Dues $5/yr.

NFB/Deaf-Blind Div.
c/o Joseph B. Naulty, Pres.
11943 Suellen Circle
Wellington, FL 33414

*Phone:* 561-753-4700 (day/eve)
*Fax:* 561-793-1104
*Website:* http://www.nfb-db.org

### Foundation Fighting Blindness, The                                         National

*45 groups. Founded 1971.* Offers information and referral services for affected individuals and their families, as well as doctors and eye care professionals. Provides comprehensive information kits on retinitis pigmentosa, macular degeneration, Usher syndrome and Stargardt disease. Newsletter. Supports research into the causes, treatment and prevention of retinal degenerative diseases. National conferences.

Foundation Fighting Blindness
11435 Cronhill Dr.
Owings Mills, MD 21117-2220

*Phone:* 1-888-665-9010 or 1-800-683-5555
*TDD:* 1-800-683-5551 or 410-785-9687
*E-mail:* info@blindness.org
*Website:* http://www.blindness.org

### Lighthouse International                                                    National

Mission is to overcome vision impairment for people of all ages through rehabilitation services, education, research and advocacy. Free literature on eye diseases (macular degeneration, glaucoma, cataracts, diabetes, and more) and various resource lists (reading options, adaptive computer technology, financial aid, etc.) Referrals to support groups, low vision services, rehabilitation agencies, state agencies and advocacy groups. Free catalog of low vision aids.

Lighthouse Int'l
111 E. 59th St.
New York, NY 10022

*Phone:* 1-800-829-0500 or 212-821-9200
*TDD:* 212-821-9713
*E-mail:* info@lighthouse.org
*Website:* http://www.lighthouse.org

**Macular Degeneration International**                                    National network
*Founded 1991.* Helps those affected by juvenile macular dystrophies and age-related macular degeneration, their families and friends. Provides information on eye diseases related to macular disease. Conferences, phone support, information and referrals. Large print news journal. Also has Stargardt Self-Help Support Network.
Macular Degeneration Int'l                    *Phone:* 1-800-393-7634 or 520-797-2525
6700 N. Oracle Rd., Suite 505                *E-mail:* info@maculardegeneration.org
Tucson, AZ 85704                             *Website:* http://www.maculardegeneration.org

**National Association For Parents of Children**
**with Visual Impairments**                                                        National
*16 groups. Founded 1980.* Outreach and support for parents of visually impaired children. Promotes formation of local parent support groups. Increases public awareness. Newsletter. Dues $25/family. Group development guidelines.
NAPVI, Inc.                                   *Phone:* 1-800-562-6265
P.O. Box 317                                  *E-mail:* napvi@perkins.pvt.k12.ma.us
Watertown, MA 02471-0317                      *Website:* www.spedex.com/NAPVI/Index.htm

**National Association for Visually Handicapped**                                    National
*Offices in NY and CA. Founded 1954.* (Multilingual) Support groups for partially-seeing persons, some of which are professionally-run. Newsletter, phone support, information and referrals. Guide to starting groups for elders losing their sight. Free large print loan library by mail. Large print informational materials available in Russian and Spanish.
NAVH                                          *Phone:* 212-889-3141
Attn: E. Cohen                                *Fax:* 212-727-2931
22 W. 21st St.                                *E-mail:* staff@navh.org
New York, NY 10010                            *Website:* http://www.navh.org

**National Federation of the Blind**                                                National
*52 affiliates. Founded 1940.* Serves as both an advocacy and a public information vehicle. Contacts newly blind persons to help with adjustment. Provides information on services and applicable laws. Student scholarships. Assists blind persons who are victims of discrimination. Literature, monthly meetings and magazine. Assistance in starting groups.
National Federation of Blind                  *Phone:* 410-659-9314
1800 Johnson St.                              *E-mail:* nfb@nfb.org
Baltimore, MD 21230                           *Website:* http://www.nfb.org/nopc.htm

**National Keratoconus Foundation**                                        National network
*Founded 1986.* An information and support network for persons with keratoconus, an eye condition where the cornea progressively thins causing a cone-like bulge. Newsletter, phone support, information and referrals. Online support group. Encourages research into cause and treatment.

Nat'l Keratoconus Foundation       *Phone:* 1-800-521-2524
8733 Beverly Blvd., Suite 201      *E-mail:* warrenc@cshs.org
Los Angeles, CA 90049              *Website:* http://www.nkcf.org

**National Organization of Parents of Blind Children                National**
*23 divisions. Founded 1983.* Support for parents of blind children. Serves as both an advocacy and public information vehicle. Offers positive philosophy and insights to blindness and practical guidance in raising a blind child. Newsletter, parent seminars, free information packet, conventions. Dues $8.

NOPBC, Attn: Barbara Cheadle       *Phone:* 410-659-9314
c/o Nat'l Fed. of the Blind        *Fax:* 410-685-5653
1800 Johnson St.                   *E-mail:* bcheadle@nfb.org
Baltimore, MD 21230                *Website:* http://www.nfb.org

**Vision Community Services                                          National**
*(Division of Massachusetts Association for the Blind) 39 groups. Founded 1970.* Support network for persons coping with sight loss. Sponsors support groups for elders and mixed ages. Outreach services, phone support, community volunteers, Braille transcriptions, recording studio, large print literature and cassettes, newsletter. Assistive devices for a fee.

Vision Comm. Services              *Phone:* 617-926-4232
23A Elm St.                        *E-mail:* ir@mablind.org
Watertown, MA 02472.               *Website:* http://www.mablind.org

**Vision Northwest                                                   Model**
*50 groups in OR. Founded 1983.* Mission is to reach out with compassion, encouragement and understanding to those coping with vision loss, their families and friends. Helps persons with vision loss to become more independent through a network of peer support groups and individual peer counseling. Information and referral, membership newsletter, community newsletter. Loan-lending optical aids network.

Vision Northwest                   *Phone:* 503-684-8389; *Fax:* 503-684-9359
9225 SW Hall Blvd., Suite G        *E-mail:* kevin@visionnw.com
Tigard, OR 97223                   *Website:* http://www.visionnw.com

🖳 **Aniridia Network                                                Online**
International network that aims to bring people with aniridia (missing one or both irises) together for support. Provides practical information.

Aniridia Network                   *E-mail:* hannah@aniridia-network.net
P.O. Box 6444                      *Website:* http://www.aniridia.org
Colchester, CO4 3XU, UK

🖳 **Leber's Congenital Amaurosis eGroup                             Online**
Listserv for persons with Leber's congenital amaurosis, a genetic eye disorder, to share support and information.            *Website:* http://groups.yahoo.com/group/LCA

⌨ **Online ROP (Retinopathy Of Prematurity) Support Group**                    Online
Mailing list that provides information and support for persons with retinopathy of prematurity and their families. Opportunity to share feelings and experiences with those who have been through the same experiences.

Online ROP Support Group            *Website:* http://www.konnections.com/
c/o Country Hills Eye Ctr.            /eyedoc/ropsupp.html
875 E. Country Hills Dr.
Ogden, UT 84403

# BRAIN INJURY
*(Also see Accidents, Aphasia, Disabilities General, Brain Tumor, Trauma)*

**Brain Injury Association, Inc.**                              **National**
*47 state associations. 600 affiliated groups. Founded 1980.* Provides services to persons with brain injuries, their families and professionals. Increases public awareness through state associations, support groups, information and resource network, seminars, conferences, literature, advocacy and prevention programs.

Brain Injury Assn.                   *Phone:* 1-800-444-6443 or 703-236-6000
105 N. Alfred St.                    *Fax:* 703-236-6001
Alexandria, VA 22314                 *Website:* http://www.biausa.org

**Coma Recovery Association**                          **National network**
*Founded 1980.* Support and advocacy network for families of coma and traumatic brain injury survivors. Provides information and referrals. Survivor support group meetings for recovering coma victims. Case management. Quarterly newsletter.

Coma Recovery Assn.                  *Phone:* 516-997-1826 or 516-746-7706
807 Carman Ave.                      *Fax:* 516-997-1613
Westbury, NY 11590                   *E-mail:* office@comarecovery.org
                                     *Website:* http://comarecovery.org

⌨ **T.H.E. BRAIN TRUST (The Healing Exchange)**                    Online
*Founded 1993.* Mission is to create exchange of information and support among people affected by neurological disorders including patient-survivors, families, caregivers and health professionals. Online support groups cover a large range of brain tumors, focal brain disorders and injuries, and other special interests.

T.H.E. BRAIN TRUST                   *Phone:* 617-876-2002; *Fax:* 617-876-2332
186 Hampshire St.                    *E-mail:* info@braintrust.org
Cambridge, MA 02139-1320             *Website:* http://www.braintrust.org

*"While there's life, there's hope."*
*- Terence, comic dramatist*

151

# BURN SURVIVORS
*(Also see Facial Disfigurement)*

**Burns United Support Groups**                                      **National**
*4 affiliated groups. Founded 1986.* Support for children and adults who have survived being burned, regardless of the severity of the burn, and their families. Visitation, newsletter, pen pals, phone support, assistance in starting groups.

Burns United Support Groups        *Phone:* Donna Schneck 313-881-5577
P.O. Box 36416                     *Fax:* 313-417-8702
Grosse-Pointe, MI 48236            *E-mail:* burnsunited@hotmail.com

**National Burn Victim Foundation**                             **International**
*Founded 1974.* Advocacy and services for burn victims and their families. Provides burn-related information and referrals, support system for disaster response, evaluation services for burned children suspected of being abused, community education and burn prevention, and research into new treatments. Forensic Burn Unit reconstructs how burn injuries occur. Newsletter, brochures.   *Phone:* 908-953-9091
NBVF                               *Fax:* 908-953-9099
P.O. Box 409                       *E-mail:* natlbvf@aol.com
Basking Ridge, NJ 07920            *Website:* http://www.nbvf.org

**Phoenix Society for Burn Survivors, Inc., The**               **International**
*Founded 1977.* Opportunity for recovered burn survivors to work with other severely burned people and their families during and after hospitalization. Pen pals, newsletter, phone network, national and international conferences, books, and audio-visual materials. Referrals to camps for burned children. Online chats.
Phoenix Society                    *Phone:* 1-800-888-BURN or 616-458-2773
2153 Wealthy SE, Suite 215         *E-mail:* info@phoenix_society.org
Grand Rapids, MI 49506             *Website:* http://www.phoenix-society.org

**▣ Burn Survivors Online**                                          **Online**
Information and support for burn survivors and their families. Burn survivor profiles, burn statistics, scheduled peer support chats, outreach to newly burned patients and families. List of books, articles, question and answer forum.
                                   *Website:* http://www.burnsurvivoronline.com

# CEREBRAL PALSY
*(Also see Disabilities General)*

**United Cerebral Palsy Associations, Inc.**                        **National**
*140 affiliates. Founded 1949.* Supports local affiliates that run programs for individuals with cerebral palsy and other disabilities. Local programs include support groups for parents and adults with cerebral palsy. Information and referral, advocacy, and research reports.

UCP
1660 L St., NW, Suite 700
Washington, DC 20036-5603

*Phone:* 1-800-872-5827
*TTY:* 202-973-7197; *Fax:* 202-766-0414
*Website:* http://www.ucp.org

**Worster-Drought Syndrome Support Group**                                **Model**
Provides support and information for families of children with Worster-Drought syndrome (aka congenital suprabulbar paresis), a form of cerebral palsy. The main problems occur with the mouth, tongue and swallowing muscles. Offers phone support in the United Kingdom, pen pals, networking of families, literature, newsletter, and occasional national meetings.

Worster-Drought Synd. Group
c/o Contact-a-Family
170 Tottenham Court Rd.
London W1T 7HA UK

*Phone:* 020 7383 3555
*Fax:* 020 7383 0259.
*E-mail:* W.D.S.P.G@btinternet.com
*Website:* http://www.wdssg.org.uk/

## DEAF / HEARING DISORDERS

**American Society for Deaf Children**                                    **National**
*120 affiliates. Founded 1967.* Information and support for parents and families with children who are deaf or hard-of-hearing. Quarterly magazine, biennial conventions, information and referral. Dues $40.

Amer. Soc. for Deaf Children
P.O. Box 3355
Gettysburg, PA 17325

*Phone:* 1-800-942-2732
*TDD:* 717-334-7922
*E-mail:* asdc1@deafchildren.org
*Website:* http://www.deafchildren.org

**American Tinnitus Association**                                         **National**
*102 groups. Founded 1971.* Provides information and lists of service providers to persons affected by tinnitus. Publishes quarterly journal and bibliography. Funds research. Coordinates support groups.

American Tinnitus Assn.
P.O. Box 5
Portland, OR 97207

*Phone:* 1-800-634-8978 or 503-248-9985
*E-mail:* Tinnitus@ata.org
*Website:* http://www.ata.org

**Auditory-Verbal International, Inc.**                          **International network**
Aim is to provide the choice of listening and speaking as a way of life for children and adults who are deaf or hard-of-hearing. Newsletter, networking, literature, phone support, information and referrals. Networking opportunities and links for parents of deaf children. Conferences. Referrals to certified auditory-verbal therapists. Dues $50-$60.

Auditory-Verbal Int'l
2121 Eisenhower Ave., #402
Alexandria, VA 22314

*Phone:* 703-739-1049
*TDD:* 703-739-0874
*E-mail:* avi@auditory-verbal.org
*Website:* http:///www.auditory-verbal.org

**Autism Network for Hearing and Visually Impaired Persons     International network**
*Founded 1991.* Provides communication, education, research and advocacy for persons with autism combined with a hearing or visual disability, their families, and professionals. Sharing of educational materials, phone help, support groups, referrals, and conferences.
Autism Network for Hearing and          *Phone:* 757-428-9036
  Visually Impaired Persons              *Fax:* 757-428-0019
7510 Ocean Front Ave.
Virginia Beach, VA 23451

**Cochlear Implant Association                                       International**
*30 affiliated groups in U.S. and Canada. Founded 1981.* Support through fellowship for cochlear implant recipients and their families. Pre- and post-operation counseling, and information on new technology. Quarterly magazine. Chapter development guidelines.
Cochlear Implant Assn.                   *Phone:* Dr. Peg Williams 202-895-2781
5335 Wisconsin Ave. NW, #440            *E-mail:* pwms.cici@worldnet.att.net
Washington, DC 20015-2034               *Website:* http://www.cici.org

**CODA (Children Of Deaf Adults)                                     International**
*12 affiliated groups. Founded 1983.* Provides mutual support for hearing children of deaf parents. Promotes family awareness and individual growth through self-help groups, educational programs, advocacy and resource development. Newsletter, information and referral, assistance in starting groups. Dues $20/year.
CODA                                     *Phone:* 805-682-0997 (Voice/TTY)
Box 30715                                *Website:* http://www.coda-international.org
Santa Barbara, CA 93130

**Deaf-Blind Division/National Federation of the Blind          National network**
Support for deaf-blind persons and their families. Annual conventions, networking, literature and advocacy. Dues $5/yr.
NFB/Deaf-Blind Div.                      *Phone:* 561-753-4700 (day/eve)
c/o Joseph B. Naulty, Pres.             *Fax:* 561-793-1104
11943 Suellen Circle                     *Website:* http://www.NFB-DB.org
Wellington, FL 33414

**Meniere's Network                                                       National**
*35 groups. Founded 1987.* Support and information for persons with Meniere's disease. Education regarding the condition, treatment, and coping strategies. Newsletter. Group development guidelines, phone buddies, pen pals. Dues $25/yr.
Meniere's Network                        *Phone:* 1-800-545-4327
1817 Patterson St.                       *E-mail:* mn@earfoundation.org
Nashville, TN 37203                      *Website:* http://www.earfoundation.com

**National Association of the Deaf                                         National**
*51 chapters. Founded 1880.* Nation's largest constituency organization safeguarding the

154

accessibility and civil rights for 28 million deaf and hard-of-hearing Americans in education, employment, health care, and telecommunications. Provides grassroots advocacy and empowerment, captioned media, deafness-related information and publications, legal assistance, policy development and research, and youth leadership programs.

| | |
|---|---|
| Nat'l Assn. of the Deaf | *Phone:* 301-587-1788; *TTY:* 301-587-1789 |
| 814 Thayer Ave., Suite 250 | *E-mail:* nadinfo@nad.org |
| Silver Spring, MD 20910-4500 | *Website:* http://www.nad.org |

### National Fraternal Society of The Deaf                                National
*72 divisions. Founded 1901.* Self-help organization for deaf and hard-of-hearing persons, their families and concerned professionals. Provides low-cost life insurance, scholarships for students, information and referrals, fellowship and advocacy. Quarterly newsletter. Membership dues vary.

| | |
|---|---|
| | *Phone:* 217-789-7429 |
| Nat'l Fraternal Soc. of the Deaf | *Fax:* 217-789-7489; *TDD:* 217-789-7438 |
| 1118 S. Sixth St. | *E-mail:* thefrat@nfsd.com |
| Springfield, IL 62703 | *Website:* http://www.nfsd.com |

### Parent's Section, A.G. Bell Association for the Deaf                   International
*Founded 1958.* Network of parents who advocate independence through education, early diagnosis, and auditory, language and speech training for their children who are hard-of-hearing. Serves as a clearinghouse to dispense information and exchange ideas. Dues $40 (includes newsletter).

| | |
|---|---|
| | *Phone:* 202-337-5220; *Fax:* 202-337-8314 |
| Parent's Section, AG Bell Assn. | *TTY:* 202-337-5221 |
| 3417 Volta Pl., NW | *E-mail:* agbell2@aol.com |
| Washington, DC 20007 | *Website:* http://www.agbell.org |

### Rainbow Alliance of the Deaf                                          National
*23 affiliated groups. Founded 1977.* Promotes the educational, economical and social welfare of deaf and hard-of-hearing gay, lesbian, bisexual, and transgendered persons, and their friends. Discussions of practical problems and solutions. Advocacy, conferences, newsletter, assistance in starting groups.

| | |
|---|---|
| RAD | *E-mail:* president@rad.org |
| 9751 Good Luck Rd., Apt. 4 | *Website:* http://www.rad.org |
| Lanham, MD 20706 | |

### SHHH (Self Help for Hard of Hearing People, Inc.)                     International
*250 chapters and groups. Founded 1979.* Aim is to open the world of communication to people with hearing loss by providing information, education, support and advocacy. Bimonthly journal, local group and chapters, referrals.

| | |
|---|---|
| SHHH | *Phone:* 301-657-2248; *TTY:* 301-657-2249 |
| 7910 Woodmont Ave., #1200 | *E-mail:* bthomas@shhh.org |
| Bethesda, MD 20814 | *Website:* http://www.shhh.org |

# DISABILITIES (GENERAL)
*(Also see specific disability)*

**American Society of Handicapped Physicians**                              **National**
*Founded 1981.* Support and advocacy for handicapped persons who have chosen a career in medicine or health. Promotes unity, continuing education and increased employment opportunities. Encourages and enables networking. Phone support system. Quarterly newsletter.
Amer. Soc. of Handicapped Physicians   *Phone:* Jericho Peden  417-881-1570
3424 S. Culpepper Court                *Fax:* 417-887-9830
Springfield, MO 65804

**Barn Builders Peer Support Group**                              **National network**
*Founded 1979.* Provides peer support network through publications for farmers and ranchers with disabilities. Connects recently injured individuals with persons with a similar disability. Support through talking, correspondence and visitation.
BBPSG                              *Phone:* 765-494-5088 or 1-800-825-4264
c/o Breaking New Ground            *Fax:* 765-496-1356
Purdue University                  *E-mail:* bng@ecn.purdue.edu
1146 ABE Bldg.                     *Website:* http://pasture.ecn.purdue.edu/~bng/barn/
West Lafayette, IN 47907-1146

**Coalition for Disabled Musicians, Inc.**                              **National**
*Founded 1986.* Introduces disabled musicians to each other who have an understanding of disability-related problems. Assistance, education and workshops for disabled adults, whether beginners, amateurs or professional musicians, for in-studio and stage bands. National referral service, newsletter, group development guidelines. Specializes in adaptive equipment and techniques.
CDM                              *Phone:* 631-586-0366
P.O. Box 1002M                   *E-mail:* cdmnews@aol.com
Bay Shore, NY 11706              *Website:* http://www.disabled-musicians.org

**C.U.S.A.**                              **National**
*120 correspondence groups. Founded 1947.* Correspondence support groups for persons of all faiths with any type of disability or chronic illness. Catholic in founding, but open to all. Emphasis on spiritual values and mutual support. Through group letters members find close relationships, understanding and courage. Dues $10/yr. (can be waived).
C.U.S.A.                              *E-mail:* ams4@juno.com
176 W. 8th St.                        *Website:* http://www.Cusan.org
Bayonne, NJ 07002

*"The secret of life isn't in what happens to you,
but what you do with what happens to you."– Norman Vincent Peale*

**Disabled American Veterans**                                    **National**
*2221 chapters. Founded 1920.* Assists veterans in gaining benefits earned in military service. Sponsors self-help groups for all disabled veterans and their families. Supports legislation benefiting disabled vets. Magazine. Guidelines for developing chapters.
Disabled American Veterans          *Phone:* 859-441-7300; *Fax:* 959-442-2090
P.O. Box 14301                      *E-mail:* feedback@davmail.org
Cincinnati, OH 45259-0301           *Website:* http://www.dav.org

**Disabled Artists' Network**                              **National network**
*Founded 1985.* Mutual support and exchange of information for professional visual artists with physical or mental disabilities. Provides information and referrals, pen pals, and reports to active members. Include self-addressed stamped envelope when writing.
Disabled Artists' Network
P.O. Box 20781
New York, NY 10025

**National Council on Independent Living**                          **National**
*220 independent living centers. Founded 1982.* Advocates for the independent living movement and aims to strengthen independent living centers through technical assistance and other membership services. Information and referrals, conferences.
NCIL                               *Phone:* 703-525-3406; *Fax:* 703-525-3409
1916 Wilson Blvd., Suite 209       *TTY:* 703-525-4153; *E-mail:* ncil@ncil.org
Arlington, VA 22201                *Website:* http://www.ncil.org

**Project DOCC (Delivery Of Chronic Care)**                   **International**
*20 chapters. Founded 1994.* Provides education regarding the impact of chronic illness or disability on a family. Information, referrals, phone support, e-mail correspondence and how-to guides on developing a local group.
Project DOCC                       *Phone:* 1-877-773-8747; *Fax*: 516-498-1899
1 South Rd.                        *E-mail:* projdocc@aol.com
Oyster Bay, NY 11771              *Website:* http://projectdocc.org

**⌨ Ability Online Support Network**                                **Online**
An electronic mail system that enables children and adolescents with disabilities or chronic illness to share experiences, information, encouragement and hope through e-mail messages.
Ability Online Support Network     *Phone:* 416-650-6207; *Fax:* 416-650-5073
503 – 1120 Finch Ave. W.          *BBS:* 416-650-5411; *Telnet:* bbs.ablelink.org
Toronto, ON M3J 3H7 Canada        *E-mail:* system.manager@ablelink.org
                                  *Website:* www.ablelink.org/public/default.htm

**⌨ Family Village**                                                **Online**
A global community that integrates information, resources and communication opportunities for persons with cognitive and other disabilities, their families, and

professionals. Broad range of discussion boards.
Family Village                     *Website:* http://www.familyvillage.wisc.edu/
c/o Univ. of Wisconsin
Waisman Ctr.
1500 Highland Ave.
Madison, WA 53705-2280

## FAMILIES OF DISABLED
*(Also see specific disability)*

**Birth Defect Research for Children**                          **National network**
Provides information about birth defects, as well as services and resources that may be
helpful to families. Links parents of children with similar birth defects for mutual sharing
and support. Sponsors national birth defect registry. Maintains database on medical
literature and research. Electronic newsletter.
Birth Defect Res. for Children       *Phone:* 407-895-0802; *Fax:* 407-895-0824
930 Woodcock Rd., Suite 225          *E-mail:* staff@birthdefects.org
Orlando, FL 32803                    *Website:* http://www.birthdefects.org

**Family Voices**                                                        **National**
*50 affiliated groups. Founded 1995.* (Bilingual) Grassroots organization that speaks on
behalf of children with special health care needs at the national, state and local levels.
Encourages and supports families who want to play a role in their child's health care.
Advocacy. Literature (Spanish and English).
Family Voices                        *Phone:* 1-888-835-5669 or 505-872-4774
3411 Candelaria NW, Suite M          *E-mail:* kidshealth@familyvoices.org
Albuquerque, NM 87107                *Website:* http://www.familyvoices.org

**Meld...Parenting that Works**                                          **National**
*65+ affiliated programs. Founded 1973.* Provides education, training and resources.
Nurtures the crucial connections between parents and children by building skills,
knowledge, support systems, and confidence. Offers peer-led  education programs to
improve the capacity of families to support, nurture and guide their children. Trains
professionals, paraprofessionals and support in areas of program development, group
facilitation, and home visitations. Publications on parenting, health, child development, etc.
Meld...Parenting That Works          *Phone:* 612-332-7563; *Fax:* 612-344-1959
123 N. Third St., Suite 507          *E-mail:* tholgate@meld.org
Minneapolis, MN 55401                *Website:* http://www.meld.org

**Mothers From Hell 2**                                          **National network**
*Founded 1992.* Support and advocacy for families of children with any type of disability.
Mission is to improve the quality of the lives and education of persons with disabilities.
Seeks to promote understanding and acceptance of people with disabilities. Dues $10/yr.
Newsletter, referral network, training packets. Assistance in starting groups. E-mail groups.

Mothers From Hell 2                    *Phone:* 815-362-5303; *Fax:* 303-374-3151
P.O. Box 19                            *E-mail:* beth@mothersfromhell2.org
German Valley, IL 61039                *Website:* http://www.mothersfromhell2.org

**MUMS National Parent-to-Parent Network**                              **National**
*61 affiliated groups. Founded 1979.* Mutual support and networking for parents or care providers of children with any disability, rare disorder, chromosomal abnormality or health condition using a database of over 17,000 families from 52 countries, covering 2700 disorders, very rare syndromes or undiagnosed conditions. Referrals to support groups. Assistance in starting groups. Newsletter ($15/parents; $25/prof). Matching services $5. Other literature.                  *Phone:* 1-877-336-5333 (parents) or
MUMS                                   920-336-5333; *Fax:* 920-339-0995
150 Custer Crt.                        *E-mail:* mums@netnet.net
Green Bay, WI 54301-1243               *Website:* http://www.netnet.net/mums/

**NATHHAN (National Challenged Homeschoolers)**              **National network**
*Founded 1990.* Christian organization that offers encouragement to families with special needs, particularly those who home educate. Magazine, lending library, family phone book, phone support, information and referrals. Dues $25.
NATHHAN                                *Phone:* 208-267-6246
P.O. Box 39                            *Website:* http://www.nathhan.com
Porthill, ID 83853

**National Parent Network on Disabilities**                             **National**
*175 groups. Founded 1988.* Coalition of parent organizations and parents who advocate for parents of persons with disabilities. Provides referrals. Newsletter. Networks organizations to share expertise. Dues vary.
Nat' Parent Network on Dis.            *Phone:* 202-463-2299 (Voice/TDD)
1130 17th St. NW, #400                 *Fax:* 202-463-9405
Washington, DC 10036-4641             *Website:* http://www.npnd.org

**Parent Network for the Post-Institutionalized Child**       **National network**
*(U.S./Canada) Founded 1993.* Connects families who have children who came from maternity hospitals, orphanages, or institutions for the irrecuperable or "street children" of economically deprived countries. Helps parents deal with the variety of problems (such as aggressive or autistic-like behaviors, learning disabilities, attachment disorders, etc) that can be created by an infant history of deprivation. Newsletter, videotapes. Calls returned collect.
PNPIC                                  *Phone:* 724-222-1766; *Fax:* 770-979-3140
P.O. Box 613                           *E-mail:* info@pnpic.org
Meadow Lands, PA 15347                 *Website:* http://PNPIC.org

*"Every survival kit should include a sense of humor."*

**Parents Helping Parents**                                                **Model**
*45 groups. Founded 1976.* (Bilingual) Parent-directed family resource center serving children with special needs (due to illness, accident, conditions of birth, learning differences, or family stress), their families, and the professionals who serve them. Information and referral, specialty programs, rap groups, peer counseling, training, library. Newsletter, group development guidelines. National resource directory online. Outreach in several languages.

PHP                                     *Phone:* 408-727-5775; *Fax:* 408-727-0182
3041 Olcott St.                         *E-mail:* info@php.com
Santa Clara, CA 95054-3222              *Website:* http://www.php.com

**Sibling Support Project - Sibshops**                                      **National**
*200+ affiliated groups. Founded 1994.* Opportunity for school-age brothers and sisters of children with special health and developmental needs to obtain peer support and education within a recreational context. Groups are sponsored by local agencies and may vary. Assistance in starting groups.

Sibling Support Project                 *Phone:* Donald Meyer 206-527-5712
c/o Donald Meyer                        *Fax:* 206-527-5705
Children's Hosp. & Med. Ctr.            *Website:* http://www.seattlechildrens.org/sibsupp
P.O. Box 5371, CL-09
Seattle, WA 98105

**Siblings for Significant Change**                                   **National network**
*Founded 1981.* Mutual support for siblings of handicapped persons. Trains siblings to be advocates for themselves and their families. Networking for support and socializing. Quarterly meetings. Newsletter, phone network, speakers bureau, audio-visual material, chapter development guidelines.

Siblings for Significant Change         *Phone:* 212-643-2663 or 1-800-841-8251
350 Fifth Ave., Room 627                *Fax:* 212-643-1244
New York, NY 10118                      *Website:* http:/specialcitizens.com

**Washington PAVE (Parents Are Vital in Education)**                        **Model**
*1 group in Washington. Founded 1979.* Parent-directed organization to increase independence, empowerment and opportunities for special needs children and their families through training, information, referrals and support. Newsletter, phone support, conferences on special education issues.

Washington PAVE                         *Phone:* 253-565-2266 or 1-800-5-PARENT
6316 S. 12th                            *E-mail:* wapave9@washingtonpave.org
Tacoma, WA 98465                        *Website:* http://www.washingtonpave.org

**Washington State Fathers Network**                                        **Model**
*15 groups in Washington. Founded 1986.* Mutual support and resources for fathers and families raising children with special needs and developmental disabilities. Online newsletters, extensive links, photo album of men and children, articles by dads, and

materials for providers on family-centered, culturally competent care. Videos. Statewide and regional conferences.

Kindering Center
c/o James May/WSFN
16120 NE Eight St.
Bellevue, WA 98008-3937

*Phone:* 425-747-4004 ext. 218
*E-mail:* jmay@fathersnetwork.org
*Website:* http://www.fathersnetwork.org

# LEARNING DISABILITIES / ATTENTION DEFICIT DISORDER

**AD-IN (Attention Deficit Information Network), Inc.**                    **National**
*6 affiliated groups. Founded 1984.* Network of support groups that provide information and support to parents of children, and to adults with attention deficit disorder. Education, information and sharing of ideas for parents, adults, educators and medical personnel. Referrals to support groups. Conferences. Group starter kit ($50).

AD-IN
475 Hillside Ave.
Needham, MA 02494-1200

*Phone:* 781-455-9895; *Fax:* 781-444-5466
*E-mail:* adin@gis.net
*Website:* http://www.addinfonetwork.org

**CHADD (Children/Adults Having Attention Deficit Disorder)**         **International**
*350+ affiliated groups. Founded 1987.* Support for parents of children with attention deficit/hyperactivity disorder. Provides information for parents, adults, teachers and professionals. Some chapters open to adults with ADD. Newsletter, bi-monthly magazine, annual conference. Guidelines and assistance on starting self-help groups. Dues $45.

CHADD
8181 Professional Pl., Suite 201
Landover, MD 20785

*Phone:* 1-800-233-4050 or 301-306-7070
*E-mail:* national@chadd.org
*Website:* http://www.chadd.org/

**Feingold Associations of the U.S.**                                      **National**
*Founded 1976.* Help for families of children with learning or behavioral problems, including attention deficit disorder. Supports members in implementing the Feingold program. Generates public awareness on the role of food, diet and synthetic additives. Newsletter. Phone support network.

Feingold Assn. of the U.S.
Box 6550
Alexandria, VA 22306

*Phone:* 703-768-3287 or 1-800-321-FAUS
*Website:* http://feingold.org

**Gifted with Learning Disabilities Educational Network, Inc.**      **National network**
*Founded 1984.* Mutual support and information network for parents of gifted children who are also learning disabled. Open to students and educators. Newsletter, library, information and referrals, advocacy, literature, conferences, phone support, and local group meetings in Maryland. Dues $30.

Gifted with/LD Ed. Network        *Phone:* 301-986-1422
2420 Ecceleston St.               *Fax:* 301-681-4884
Silver Spring, MD 20902           *E-mail:* gldnews@hotmail.com

**Learning Disabilities Association of America**                **National**
*500 chapters. Founded 1963.* (Bilingual) Organization formed by concerned parents devoted to defining and finding solutions for the broad spectrum of learning problems. Information and referrals, advocacy. Newsletter, journal. Chapter development guidelines. Literature available in English and Spanish.
LDA of America                    *Phone:* 412-341-1515; *Fax:* 412-344-0224
4156 Library Rd.                  *E-mail:* info@ldaamerica.org
Pittsburgh, PA 15234              *Website:* http://www.ldaamerica.org

**National ADDA (Attention Deficit Disorder Association)**        **National network**
Dedicated to advocating for adults and children with attention deficit disorder through education to increase awareness and understanding of ADD. Newsletter, information, national conference, speakers bureau. Developed guidelines for diagnosis and treatment. Assistance in starting groups. Dues $45-$150.
ADDA                              *Phone:* 847-432-2332; *Fax:* 847-432-5874
1788 Second St., Suite 200        *E-mail:* mail@add.org
Highland Park, IL 60035           *Website:* http://www.add.org

🖳 **Conduct Disorders Parent Message Board**                   **Online**
Support for parents living with a child with one of the many defiant behavior disorders including attention deficit hyperactivity disorder.
                                  *Website:* http://www.conductdisorders.com

🖳 **NLDA/Share Support**                                        **Online**
Opportunity for parents of children with non-verbal learning disabilities (NLD), adults with NLD and interested professionals to come together to communicate. Provides support and information. Membership subject to approval.
*E-mail:* versakel@earthlink.net    *Website:* http://www.nldline.com/nld-in-c.htm

## MENTAL RETARDATION
*(Also see Disabilities General)*

**Arc, The**                                                     **National**
*1100 chapters. Founded 1950.* Provides support for people with mental retardation and their families. Advocacy groups and direct services. Quarterly newspaper. Chapter development guidelines.
The Arc                           *Phone:* 301-565-3842; *Fax:* 301-565-5342
1010 Wayne Ave., Suite 650        *E-mail:* info@thearc.org
Silver Spring, MD 20910           *Website:* http://thearc.org

## NADD Association for Persons with Developmental Disabilities and Mental Health Needs                      National

*5 affiliated groups. Founded 1983.* Promotes the development of resources for persons with both mental retardation and a mental illness through education, advocacy, research and exchange of information. Conferences, national resource database, audio tapes and books available. Directory of members.

NADD                                    *Phone:* 845-331-4336; *Fax:* 914-331-4569
132 Fair St.                            *E-mail:* thenadd@aol.com
Kingston, NY 12401                      *Website:* http://www.thenadd.org

## National Down Syndrome Congress                                        National

*400+ parent group networks. Founded 1974.* Support, information and advocacy for families affected by Down syndrome. Promotes research and public awareness. Serves as clearinghouse and network for parent groups. Newsletter ($25/yr). Annual convention, phone support, chapter development guidelines.

Nat'l Down Syndrome Congress            *Phone:* 1-800-232-NDSC or 770-604-9500
Bldg. 5, Suite 100                      *Fax:* 770-604-9898
7000 Peachtree-Dunwood Rd.              *E-mail:* NDSCcenter@aol.com
Atlanta, GA 30328                       *Website:* http://www.NDSCcenter.org

## Voice of the Retarded                                                  National

*120 affiliated groups. Founded 1983.* Works to empower families of persons with mental retardation through information and advocacy. Weekly e-mail updates and quarterly newsletter for members. Networking, information and referrals, advocacy, phone support and conferences. Dues $25.

VOR                                     *Phone:* 847-253-6020; *Fax:* 847-253-6054
5005 Newport Dr., Suite 108             *E-mail:* vor@compuserve.com
Rolling Meadows, IL 60008               *Website:* http://www.vor.net

## People First                                                             Model

*33 groups in Washington. Founded 1977.* Self-help advocacy organization created by and for people with developmental disabilities. Provides help in starting new chapters. Quarterly newsletter.

People First                            *Phone:* 509-758-1123 (Voice/Fax)
P.O. Box 648                            *Fax:* 509-758-1289
Clarkston, WA 99403                     *E-mail:* pfow@clarkston.com

## Speaking for Ourselves                                                   Model

*9 groups in Massachusetts. Founded 1982.* Self-help advocacy for people with developmental disabilities. Monthly chapter meetings. Members help each other resolve problems, gain self-confidence, and learn leadership skills. Chapter development guidelines. Newsletter.

Speaking for Ourselves
1 Plymouth Meeting, #630
Plymouth Meeting, PA 19462

*Phone:* 610-825-4592; *Fax:* 610-825-4595
*E-mail:* speakingfo@aol.com
*Website:* http://www.speaking.org

## SPINAL CORD INJURY / PARALYSIS
*(Also see Disabilities General, Accident, Trauma, specific illness)*

**National Spinal Cord Injury Association**                                    **National**
*42 chapters and support groups. Founded 1948.* Provides information and referrals on many topics to persons with spinal cord injuries and diseases, their families and interested professionals. Group development guidelines, quarterly newsletter, support groups, peer counseling.

NSCIA
6701 Democracy Blvd., #300-9
Bethesda, MD 20817

*Phone:* 1-800-962-9629 or 301-588-6959
*Fax:* 301-588-9414
*Website:* http://www.spinalcord.org

**Paralyzed Veterans of America**                                              **National**
*Chapters nationwide. Founded 1947.* To ensure that spinal cord injured or diseased veterans achieve the highest quality of life possible. Membership open to American citizens who suffer from spinal cord dysfunction as a result of trauma or disease. Must have served on active duty and had an other than dishonorable discharge. Information and referrals, magazine.

PVA
801 18th St., NW
Washington, DC 20006

*Phone:* 202-872-1300
*E-mail:* info@pva.org
*Website:* http://www.pva.org

**Spinal Cord Society**                                                  **International**
*200+ chapters. Founded 1978.* Advocacy organization for the spinal-injured, their families and friends, and the scientists and physicians working with them. Ultimate goal is to find a cure through improved treatment and research. Promotes public awareness. Monthly newsletter.

Spinal Cord Society
c/o Charles Carson
19051 County Highway 1
Fergus Falls, MN 56537

*Phone:* 218-739-5252
*Fax:* 218-739-5262
*Website:* http://users.aol.com/scsweb

**▣   QUAD-LIST Discussion Group**                                             **Online**
Unmoderated online discussion for quadriplegics and tetraplegics to communicate with others who share the same condition. For anyone who has suffered a partial or full loss of function in three or four body extremities. Families and caregivers welcome. Bulletin board.

*Website:* http://www.eskimo.com/~jlubin/
disabled/quadlist.htm

# FAMILY

*"Three grand essentials to happiness in this life are*
*something to do, something to love, and something to hope for."*
— Joseph Addison

## ADOPTION

**Adoptees In Search**                                              National network
*Founded 1975.* Mutual support for adult adoptees, adoptive parents, and birth relatives.
Professional search assistance in finding birth relatives for a fee. Post-adoption education,
advocacy, and counseling services. Maintains search registry. Dues $75. Send
self-addressed stamped long envelope when writing.
A.I.S.                                  *Phone:* 301-656-8555; *Fax:* 301-652-2106
P.O. Box 41016                          *E-mail:* AIS20824@aol.com
Bethesda, MD 20824                      *Website:* http://www.adopteesinsearch.org

**Adoption Crossroads**                                              International
*475 affiliated groups. Founded 1990.* Mutual support for persons separated by adoption.
Referrals to adoption search and support groups. Newsletter, phone support, conferences,
information and referrals. Assistance in starting groups. Dues $35/year.
Adoption Crossroads                     *Phone:* 212-988-0110 or 845-268-0283
444 E. 76th St.                         *Fax:* 212-988-0291; *E-mail:* cera@idt.net
New York, NY 10021                      *Website:* http://www.adoptioncrossroads.org

**Adoptive Families of America, Inc.**                                National
*275+ groups. Founded 1967.* Problem-solving assistance and information for adoptive and
prospective adoptive families. Creates opportunities for successful adoptive placement.
Bimonthly magazine, group development guidelines. Dues $25. Pen pals, phone network.
Adoptive Families of America           *Phone:* 212-366-0830
42 West 38th St., Suite 901            *Fax:* 212-366-0842
New York, NY 10018                     *Website:* http://www.adoptivefam.org

**ALMA Society, The (Adoptees' Liberty**
**Movement Association)**                                      International network
*Founded 1971.* Provides moral support and guidance for adopted children in finding their
birth parents and/or siblings. Also helps parents find the children they gave up for adoption.
Open to foster children (18+). International reunion registry. $50 one-time registration fee.
ALMA Society                           *Fax:* 973-586-1358
P.O. Box 85                            *Website:* http://almasociety.com
Denville, NJ 07834

**CUB (Concerned United Birthparents), Inc.** **National**
*11 branches. Founded 1976.* Support for adoption-affected people in coping with adoption. Aims to prevent unnecessary separations. Monthly newsletter. Dues $40/new members, $25/renewals. Pen pals, telephone network. Online chat room.
CUB                                    *Phone:* 1-800-822-2777
P.O. Box 230457                        *E-mail:* info@CUBirthparents.org
Encinitas, CA 92023                    *Website:* http://www.Cubirthparents.org

**Korean American Adoptee Adoptive Family Network** **National network**
*(U.S. and Canada)* Links individuals and organizations involved in Korean adoptions. Facilitates dialogue, promotes resource sharing, and disseminates information. Helps develop programs to benefit the Korean adoption community.
KAAN                                   *Phone*: 916-933-1447
P.O. Box 5585                          *E-mail*: KAANet@aol.com
El Dorado Hills, CA 95762              *Website*: http://www.kaanet.com

**National Council for Single Adoptive Parents** **National network**
*Founded 1973.* Provides information to assist unmarried people adopt children from the United States and abroad, and manage as single adoptive parents. Publishes Handbook For Single Adoptive Parents ($25). Referrals to local support groups.
NCSAP                                  *E-mail:* NCSAP@hotmail.com
P.O. Box 55
Wharton, NJ 07885

**North American Council on Adoptable Children** **International**
*(US/Canada). Founded 1974.* Focuses on special needs adoption. Provides referrals and maintains current listing of adoptive parent support groups which conduct a wide range of activities. Helps new groups get started, and sponsors an annual adoption conference which features workshops for adoptive parents, prospective parents, foster parents, child welfare professionals, and other child advocates. Newsletter. Membership $40/U.S. and $60/Canada. Parent group manual ($7).
No. Amer. Council on                   *Phone:* 651-644-3036 (day)
  Adoptable Children                   *Fax:* 651-644-9848
970 Raymond Ave., Suite 106            *E-mail:* info@nacac.org
St. Paul, MN 55114-1149                *Website:* http://www.nacac.org

**Parent Network for the**
**Post-Institutionalized Child** **International network**
*Founded 1993.* Connects families who have children who came from maternity hospitals, orphanages, or institutions for the irrecuperable or "street children" of economically deprived countries. Helps parents deal with the variety of problems (such as aggressive or autistic-like behaviors, learning disabilities, attachment disorders, etc) that can be created by an infant history of deprivation. Newsletter.

PNPIC
P.O. Box 613
Meadow Lands, PA 15347

*Phone:* 724-222-1766; *Fax:* 770-979-3140
*E-mail:* info@pnpic.org
*Website:* http://PNPIC.org

**Stars of David, Inc.**                                                    **International**
*32+ chapters.* Support and advocacy group for Jewish or interfaith adoptive families, extended families, interested clergy, social service agencies and adoption professionals. Socials, phone help, literature and education. Newsletter. Dues $35/family; $125/prof.

Stars of David
P.O.573
Woodbury, NJ 08096-0573

*Phone:* 800-STAR-349 *Fax:* 847-509-9545
*E-mail:* starsdavid@aol.com
*Website:* http://www.starsofdavid.org

## FOSTER FAMILIES
*(Also see Adoption)*

**National Foster Parent Association, Inc.**                                     **National**
*100+ affiliated groups. Founded 1972.* Support, education and advocacy for foster parents and their children. Resource center for foster care information. Newsletter. National conference, workshops. Chapter development guidelines.

Nat'l Foster Parent Assn.
7215 Stanich Ave., #6
Gig Harbor, WA 98335

*Phone:* 1-800-557-5238 or 253-853-4000
*Fax:* 253-853-4001
*Website:* http://www.nfpainc.org

**FACT (Fostered Abandoned Children Together)**                                     **Model**
*1 group in Michigan. Founded 1999.* Provides mutual support for former foster children. Literature. Provides assistance in starting similar groups.

FACT
226 S. Burkhart Rd.
Howell, MI 48843

*Phone:* 517-546-7818 (Voice/Fax)
*E-mail:* carolannlucas@hotmail.com
*Website:* http://www.factsupportgroup.com

## GRANDPARENTING
*(Also see Parenting, Separation/ Divorce)*

**Creative Grandparenting**                                                    **National network**
*Founded 1990.* Provides education to enable and empower grandparents and older adults to value and encourage the natural development of children as unique individuals. Helps persons become better grandparents. Newsletter. Assistance in starting new groups. Also has Creative Eldering, Creative Mentoring, Creative Youth Development and Creative Community Building.

Creative Grandparenting
100 W. 10th St., Suite 1007
Wilmington, DE 19801

*Phone:* 302-656-2122
*Fax:* 302-656-2123
*E-mail:* mainoffice@creativegrandparenting.org
*Website:* http://www.creativegrandparenting.org

## GAP (Grandparents As Parents)                                    National
*7 groups. Founded 1987.* Support network and sharing of experiences and feelings between grandparents who are raising their grandchildren for various reasons. Information and referrals, phone support network. Assistance in starting groups.

GAP                                    *Phone:* 562-421-7991
P.O. Box 964                           *Fax:* 714-828-1375
Lakewood, CA 90714                     *E-mail:* GLWasson@juno.com

## Grandparents Information Center                                    National
Provides information and referrals for grandparents raising their grandchildren. Referrals to support groups. Free publications on a variety of issues related to raising grandchildren, financial assistance, advocacy. Sponsored by AARP.

Grandparents Information Center        *Phone:* 202-434-2296; *Fax:* 202-434-6470
601 E St., NW                          *E-mail:* gic@aarp.org
Washington, DC 20049                   *Website:* http://www.aarp.org

## Young Grandparents' Club                                    National
*Founded 1989.* Promotes the understanding and education of grandparents to develop close relations between generations. Referrals to local groups, advocacy on grandparents' rights, information and referrals. Offers workshops, classes, seminars, conferences, and networking. Assistance in starting informal neighborhood groups.

Young Grandparents' Club               *Phone:* 913-642-8296
5217 Somerset Dr.
Prairie Village, KS 66207

# MARRIAGE

## ACME (Association of Couples for Marriage Enrichment)        National network
*Founded 1973.* Network of couples who want to enhance their own relationship as well as help strengthen marriages of other couples. Local chapters sponsor support groups, retreats, workshops. Newsletter. Leadership training, conferences.

ACME                                   *Phone:* 1-800-634-8325 or 336-724-1526
P.O. Box 10596                         *E-mail:* acme@marriageenrichment.com
Winston-Salem, NC 27108                *Website:* http://www.bettermarriages.org

## No Kidding!                                    International
*60+ chapters in four countries. Founded 1984.* Mutual support and social activities for married and single people who either have decided not to have children, are postponing parenthood, are undecided, or are unable to have children. Chapter development guidelines.

No Kidding!                            *Phone:* 604-538-7736 (24 hr)
Box 2802                               *E-mail:* info@nokidding.net
Vancouver, BC V6B 3X2 Canada          *Website:* http://www.nokidding.bc.ca

**Recovering Couples Anonymous**                                    **International**
12-step group to help couples find freedom from dysfunctional patterns in relationships.
Helps restore healthy communication, caring, and greater intimacy to relationships.
RCA                                    *Phone:* 510-663-2312
P.O. Box 11029                         *E-mail:* info@recovering-couples.org
Oakland, CA 94611                      *Website:* http://www.recovering-couples.org

**WESOM (We Saved Our Marriage)**                                      **National**
*3 affiliated groups. Founded 1986.* Self-help for spouses whose marriage is affected by
infidelity. Helps couples deal with adultery in order to save their marriage. Assistance
available for starting groups.
WESOM                                  *Phone:* 773-792-7034
P.O. Box 46312
Chicago, IL 60646

🖳  **After the Affair**                                                **Online**
Discussion forum to help persons recover after an extra-marital affair.
                                       *Website:* http://members3.boardhost.com/affair

## PARENTING (GENERAL)
*(Also see specific issue)*

**DAD-to-DAD**                                                        **National**
*Founded 1995.* Brings at-home fathers together through children's play groups, field trips,
and dad's night-out dinners. Information and referrals, phone support, literature. Assistance
in starting local chapters.
DAD-to-DAD                             *Phone:* Curtis Cooper 952-423-3705
13925 Duluth Dr                        *E-mail:* dadtodad@aol.com
Apple Valley, MN 55124.                *Website:* http://www.slowlane.com/dad/index.htm

**Family Pride Coalition**                                            **National**
*160+ local groups. Founded 1979.* Support, education and advocacy for gay and lesbian
parents and prospective parents, and their families. Information and referrals, phone support,
family events, literature. Newsletter. Assistance in starting groups.
Family Pride Coalition                 *Phone:* 202-331-5015; *Fax:* 202-331-0080
P.O. Box 5326                          *E-mail:* info@familypride.org
Washington, DC 20035-5327              *Website:* http://www.familypride.org

**MAD DADS, Inc. (Men Against Destruction**
**Defending Against Drugs and Social-disorder)**                      **National**
*57 affiliated groups in 15 states. Founded 1989.* Grassroots organization of fathers aimed at
fighting gang- and drug-related violence. Provides family activities, community education,
speaking engagements, and "surrogate fathers" who listen to, and care about, street teens.
Assistance in starting groups. Also groups for kids, mothers, grandparents.
MAD DADS, Inc.                         *Phone:* Eddie Staton 402-451-3500
3030 Sprague St.                       *Fax:* 402-451-3477
Omaha, NE 68111                        *Website:* http://maddadsnational.com

**Meld...Parenting that Works**                                    **National**
*65+ affiliated programs. Founded 1973.* Provides education, training and resources to parents. Nurtures the crucial connections between parents and children by building skills, knowledge, support systems, and confidence. Offers peer-led education programs to improve the capacity of families to support, nurture and guide their children. Trains professionals, paraprofessionals. Provides support in areas of program development, group facilitation, and home visitations. Publications on parenting, health, child development, etc.

Meld...Parenting That Works          *Phone:* 612-332-7563; *Fax:* 612-344-1959
123 N. Third St., Suite 507          *E-mail:* tholgate@meld.org
Minneapolis, MN 55401                *Website:* http://www.meld.org

**Mocha Moms, Inc.**                                               **National**
*18 affiliated groups. Founded 1997.* Provides support for at-home mothers of color. Provides weekly or bi-weekly play groups, monthly potluck meals, and on-going community service and volunteer services. Dues $12/year. Newsletter, information and referrals. Assistance in starting groups.

Mocha Moms, Inc.                     *E-mail:* Jolevelv@cs.com
7202 Quisinberry Way                 *Website:* http://mochamoms.org
Bowie, MD 20720

**MOMS Club**                                                    **International**
*1100+ affiliated groups. Founded 1983.* Mutual support for mothers-at-home. Groups provide at-home mothers of children of all ages emotional and moral support, as well as a wide variety of activities. Annual dues $15-25. Provides assistance in starting and maintaining chapters through local coordinators (enclose $2 to cover postage).

MOMS Club                            *Phone:* 805-526-2725
25371 Rye Canyon Rd.                 *E-mail:* momsclub@aol.com
Valencia, CA 91355                   *Website:* http://www.momsclub.org

**MOPS, International (Mothers Of Pre-Schoolers)**               **International**
*2400 affiliated groups. Founded 1973.* Non-denominational Christian support group designed for mothers with children under school age. MOPS groups meet in churches throughout the U.S., Canada, and 15 other countries. Help in starting groups.

MOPS, Int'l                          *Phone:* 1-800-929-1287 or 303-733-5353
P.O. Box 102200                      *Phone:* 1-888-910-6677 (to start a MOPS group)
Denver, CO 80250-2200                *E-mail:* info@mops.org
                                     *Website:* http://www.mops.org

**Mothers and More (the Network for Sequencing Women)**          **National**
*180 chapters. Founded 1987.* Support for women who have altered their career paths to care for their children at home. It is not about opposing mothers who work outside the home; rather it is about respecting, supporting and advocating for choice in how one combines working and parenting. Advocates for public and employment policies that accommodate stay-at-home mothers. Newsletter, chapter development guidelines.

170

Mothers and More
P.O. Box 31
Elmhurst, IL 60126

*Phone:* 630-941-3553
*Fax:* 630-941-3551
*Website:* http://www.mothersandmore.org

## NATHHAN (National Challenged Homeschoolers)                National network
*Founded 1990.* Christian organization encouraging families with specials needs children, particularly those who home educate. Online magazine, library, family phone book, phone support, information and referrals. Dues $25.

NATHHAN
P.O. Box 39
39 Porthill, ID 8385

*Phone:* 208-267-6246
*E-mail:* nathanews@aol.com
*Website:* http://www.nathhan.com

## National Association of Mothers' Centers                            National
*50 sites. Founded 1975.* Support system for those involved in parenting, pregnancy, childbirth and child-rearing. Non-hierarchal and non-judgmental. Literature, newsletter, conferences, research, advocacy. Referrals to local chapters. Helps women to start mother's centers. Starter's manual.

Nat'l Assn. of Mothers' Centers
64 Division Ave.
Levittown, NY 11756

*Phone:* 1-800-645-3828 or 516-520-2929
*Fax:* 516-520-1639
*E mail:* info@motherscenter.org
*Website:* http://www.motherscenter.org

## Resource Center for Fathers and Families                             National
*Founded 1991.* Provides resources for men so that they may become better parents and better parenting partners regardless of marital status. Aims to prevent violence and to provide the model that all children deserve. Newsletter, networking, literature, advocacy, group meetings, professional referrals, conferences. Donations accepted. Assistance in starting local chapters.

Res. Ctr. for Fathers & Families
1201 89th Ave., NE
Blaine, MN 55434

*Phone:* 763-783-4938 (day)
*Fax:* 763-783-4900
*E-mail:* aengelby@juno.com
*Website:* http://www.resourcesforfathers.org

## Able Parents                                                          Model
*1 group in Alabama. Founded 2002.* Support and advocacy for mental health consumers who are parents. Advocates for the parental rights of consumer parents as well as provides emotional peer support. Online message board.

Able Parents
c/o Michael J. Pitts
P.O. Box 37
Peterson, Al 35478-0037

*Phone*: 205-553-0609
*E-mail*: aporg@bellsouth.net
*Website*: http://www.ableparents.org

*"Laughing through the tears is my favorite emotion."*
*- Trudy in Steel Magnolias*

**Fathers' Network, The**                                                                     **Model**
*1 group in California. Founded 1979.* Aims to increase the involvement of fathers in parenting. Encourages mutually fulfilling relationships between fathers and their children. Challenges traditional "provider" role regardless of marital/custodial status. Lists national men's resources on website. Not a divorce resource.

The Father's Network                      *E-mail:* fathersnetwork@menstuff.org
P.O. Box 800-SH                           *Website:* http://www.menstuff.org
San Anselmo, CA 94979-0800

**Postpartum Education for Parents**                                                          **Model**
*1 group in California. Founded 1977.* Provides emotional support for parents by parent volunteers. Helps parents adjust to changes in their lives that a baby brings. Telephone help. Education on basic infant care and parent adjustment. Monthly newsletter. Group development guidelines.

PEP                                       *Phone:* 805-564-2595
P.O. Box 6154                             *Website:* http://www.sbpep.org
Santa Barbara, CA 93160

🖳 **Parent Empowerment Network**                                                             **Online**
*Founded 1996.* E-mail group for parents with disabilities, including potential parents, and partners of disabled parents.        *E-mail:* TrishDay@concentric.net
                                          *Website:* http://www.disabledparents.net

🖳 **Parent Soup Message Boards**                                                             **Online**
Offers a large variety of message boards that deal with parenting issues including parenting challenges, parents of disabled, newborns, toddlers, adoption, family issues, etc.
                                          *Website:* http:/www.parentsoup.com/boards/

## PARENTS OF UNCONTROLLABLE CHILDREN
*(Also see Addictions, specific issue)*

**Because I Love You: The Parent Support Group**                                             **National**
*45 affiliated groups. Founded 1982.* Self-help group for parents who have children of all ages with behavioral problems such as truancy, substance abuse, or other forms of defiance of authority. Focus is on parents getting back their self-esteem and control of their home.

Because I Love You                        *Phone:* 310-659-5289
P.O. Box 2062                             *E-mail:* BILY1982@aol.com
Winnetka, CA 91396-2062                   *Website:* http://www.becauseiloveyou.org

**Families Anonymous**                                                                    **International**
*500+ groups. Founded 1971.* 12-step fellowship for relatives and friends of persons with drug, alcohol, or behavioral problems. Members learn to achieve their own serenity in spite of the turmoil which surrounds them. Booklets, pamphlets, and bookmarks, daily thought book, and a bi-monthly newsletter.

F.A.                                    *Phone:* 1-800-736-9805
P.O. Box 3475                           *E-mail:* famanon@FamiliesAnonymous.org
Culver City, CA 90231-3475              *Website:* http://www.FamiliesAnonymous.org

**TOUGHLOVE International**                                        **International**
*200+ groups. Founded 1979.* Self-help program for parents, kids and communities in
dealing with the out-of-control behavior of a family member. Parent support groups help
parents take a firm stand to help kids take responsibility for their behavior. Newsletter.
Group development guidelines.
TOUGHLOVE Int'l                         *Phone:* 1-800-333-1069 or 215-348-7090
P.O. Box 1069                           *E-mail:* service@toughlove.org
Doylestown, PA 18901                    *Website:* http://www.toughlove.org

**Abused Parents of America**                                             **Model**
*1 group in Michigan. Founded 1990.* Mutual support and comfort for parents who are
abused by their adult children. Provides technical advice and assistance available for starting
similar groups.
APOA                                    *Phone:* Beulah Warner 616-349-6920
c/o Beulah Warner
2873 Roosevelt Ave.
Kalamazoo, MI 49004

## PREGNANCY / CHILDBIRTH
*(Also see Parenting General)*

**Abiding Hearts, Inc.**                                          **International**
*18 affiliated groups. Founded 1995.* Emotional support to parents, caregivers, and their
families who are continuing a pregnancy after an adverse prenatal diagnosis of a fatal or
non-fatal birth defect. Information and referrals, newsletter, phone support, advocacy and
literature. Networks parents and grandparents with volunteers who have experienced similar
situations.
Abiding Hearts                          *Phone:* 406-293-4416; *TDD:* 1-800-253-4091
P.O. Box 904                            *E-mail:* support@abidinghearts.com
Libby, MT 59923                         *Website:* http://www.abidinghearts.com

**Cesarean Support Education and Concern**                             **National**
*Founded 1972.* Support, information and referral regarding cesarean birth, cesarean
prevention, and vaginal delivery after cesarean. Listing of cesarean support groups
nationwide. Back issues of newsletter. Guidelines for starting groups ($2.25).
CSEC                                    *Phone:* 508-877-8266 (recorded message)
22 Forest Rd.
Framingham, MA 01701

**ICAN (International Cesarean Awareness Network), Inc.**                    **International**
*20 chapters. Founded 1982.* Support for women healing from cesarean birth. Encouragement and information for those wanting vaginal birth after a previous cesarean. Provides education with goal of lowering the high cesarean rate. Newsletter. Chapter development guidebook.

ICAN                                *Phone:* 310-542-6400; *Fax:* 310-542-5368
1304 Kingsdale Ave.                  *E-mail:* info@ICAN-online.org
Redondo Beach, CA 90278             *Website:* http://www.ICAN-online.org

**La Leche League**                                                  **International**
*3000 chapters. Founded 1956.* Support and education for breastfeeding mothers. Group discussions, personal help, classes and conferences. Publishes literature on breastfeeding and parenting. Bi-monthly newsletter, quarterly abstracts. Phone support network.

La Leche League                     *Phone:* 1-800-LA-LECHE or 847-519-7703
P.O. Box 4079                       *E-mail:* LLLHQ@llli.org
Schaumburg, Il 60168-4079           *Website:* http://www.lalecheleague.org

**Lamaze International**                                              **International**
*19 chapters. Founded 1960.* Dedicated to promoting normal, natural, healthy and fulfilling childbearing, breastfeeding and early parenting experiences through education, advocacy and reform. Newsletter, publications.

Lamaze Int'l                        *Phone:* 1-800-368-4404; *Fax:* 202-857-1102
2025 M St., NW, Suite 800           *E-mail:* lamaze@dc.sba.com
Washington, DC 20036-3309           *Website:* http://www.lamaze.org

**NAPSAC (National Association of Parents and**
**Professionals for Safe Alternatives in Childbirth)**                    **National**
*35 affiliated groups. Founded 1975.* Information and support regarding home birth, family centered maternity care and midwifery. Offers scientific research on safety or home birth vs. hospital. Directory of alternative birth practitioners. Childbirth activist handbook. How-to's on starting chapters. Newsletter.

NAPSAC                              *Phone:* 573-238-2010 (Voice/Fax)
Rt. 4, Box 646                      *E-mail:* napsac@clas.net
Marble Hill, MO 63764

**National Association of Mothers' Centers**                          **National**
*50 sites. Founded 1975.* Support system for those involved in parenting, pregnancy, childbirth and child-rearing. Non-hierarchal and non-judgmental. Literature, newsletter, conferences, research, advocacy. Referrals to local chapters. Helps start mother's centers.

Nat'l Assn. of Mothers' Centers     *Phone:* 1-800-645-3828 or 516-520-2929
64 Division Ave.                    *E-mail:* info@motherscenter.org
Levittown, NY 11756                 *Website:* http://www.motherscenter.org

**Sidelines National Support Network**                        **National network**
*Founded 1991.* Trained former high-risk pregnancy moms provide support to current high-risk patients and their families. Education, resources, advocacy and emotional support provided via telephone and e-mail.
Sidelines Nat'l Support Network        *Phone:* 949-497-2265; *Fax:* 949-497-5598
P.O. Box 1808                          *E-mail:* sidelines@sidelines.org
Laguna Beach, CA 92652                 *Website:* http://www.sidelines.org

**Confinement Line, The**                                                **Model**
*Covers greater Washington, DC area. Founded 1984.* Telephone support network for women confined to bed during a high-risk pregnancy. Information and referrals, guidelines and assistance available for starting networks.
Confinement Line                       *Phone:* 703-941-7183
P.O. Box 1609
Springfield, VA 22151

🖳 **Parent Soup Message Boards**                                       **Online**
Offers a large variety of message boards which deal with parenting issues including pregnancy, parenting challenges, parents of disabled, pregnancy loss, newborns, etc.
                                       *Website:* http://www.parentsoup.com/boards/

🖳 **Preemie-List**                                                      **Online**
Online group that provides mutual support for parents with children born six weeks or more before due date. Open to their families and friends.
                                       *Website:* http://groups.yahoo.com/group/
                                       preemie-list

## SEPARATION / DIVORCE
*(Also see Single Parenting)*

**Association for Children for Enforcement of Support**                **National**
*400 affiliated groups. Founded 1984.* Information and support for parents who have custody of their children and have difficulty collecting child support payments. Location service on non-payers. Newsletter, information and referrals, assistance in starting groups.
ACES                                   *Phone:* 1-800-738-ACES or 419-472-6609
c/o Geraldine Jensen                   *Fax:* 419-472-6295
2260 Upton Ave.                        *E-mail:* gjensen@aces.fm
Toledo, OH 43606                       *Website:* http://www.childsupport-aces.org

**Beginning Experience, The**                                     **International**
*140 teams. Founded 1974.* Support programs for divorced, widowed and separated adults and their children enabling them to work through the grief of a lost marriage.

The Beginning Experience
c/o St. John Bosco Parish Center
1247 171st Pl.
Hammond, IN 46324

*Phone:* 219-989-8915
*Fax:* 219-989-8916
*E-mail:* imc@beimc.attmail.com
*Website:* http://www.BEINFO.com

**Children's Rights Council**                            **International**
*Chapters in 32 states, Japan, Africa and England. Founded 1985.* Concerned parents provide education and advocacy for reform of the legal system regarding child custody. Offers help with visitation, mediation, custody and support groups. Newsletter, information and referrals, child transfer centers in various states, directory of parenting organizations, catalog of resources, conferences, group development guidelines.
CRC
c/o David L. Levy, Pres.
300 I St., NE, Suite 401
Washington, DC 20002

*Phone:* 202-547-6227; *Fax:* 202-546-4272
*E-mail:* crcdc@erols.com
*Website:* http://www.info4parents.com
*Website:* http://www.gocrc.com

**CODAS (Children Of Divorce And Separation)**            **National**
*50 states in service area. Founded 1980.* Purpose is to provide consultation in areas of child custody, visitation, child support, initial custody, joint custody, modification, interstate custody and guardianship services.
CODAS
c/o Dr. Ken Lewis
P.O. Box 202
Glenside, PA 19038

*Phone:* 215-576-0177
*Fax:* 215-576-9411
*E-mail:* DrKenLewis@snip.com
*Website:* http://www.codas.bigstep.com

**DivorceCare**                                           **International**
*8000 affiliated groups. Founded 1993.* Network of support groups to help people recover from separation or divorce. Information and referrals, support group meetings, literature. Assistance in starting new groups.
Divorce Care
220 S. White
P.O. Box 1739
Wake Forest, NC 27587

*Phone:* 919-562-2112
*Fax:* 919-562-2114
*E-mail:* info@divorcecare.org
*Website:* http://www.divorcecare.org

**EX-POSE (Ex-Partners Of Servicemembers for Equality)**   **National network**
*Founded 1981.* Lobbies for changes in military divorce laws. Disseminates information concerning military divorce. Lawyer referral. Quarterly newsletter. Publishes Guide for Military Separation and Divorce. Membership dues $15.
EX-POSE
P.O. Box 11191
Alexandria, VA 22312

*Phone:* 703-941-5844; *Fax:* 703-212-6951
*E-mail:* ex-pose@juno.com
*Website:* http://www.angelfire.com/va/EXPOSE

**Grandparents Rights Organization**                                              National
*Founded 1984.* Advocates and educates on behalf of grandparent-grandchild relationships primarily with respect to grandparent visits. Assists in the formation of local support groups dealing with the denial of grandparent visitation by custodial parent or guardian. Newsletter, information and referrals, conferences. Donations $40/yr.

Grandparents Rights Org.              *Phone:* 248-646-7191; *Fax:* 248-646-9722
100 W. Long Lake Rd., #250            *E-mail:* RSVlaw@aol.com
Bloomfield Hills, MI 48304            *Website:* http://www.grandparentsrights.org

**GRINS (Grandparent Rights In New Strength)**                                    National
*Founded 1992.* Aims to reunite family bonding and heritage, allowing the ancestry of children, grandparents and relatives to continue after divorce or extraction from parents by Family Social Services. Works with religious, local, state and federal officials to adopt uniform laws allowing visitation. Court and mediation support, phone help. Assistance in starting new groups.

GRINS                                 *Phone:* Ray & Kay Berryhill 260-281-2384
Box 0689 CR5                          *Fax:* 260-281-2384
Corunna, IN 46730

**Joint Custody Association**                                                  International
*250 affiliated groups. Founded 1979.* Assists divorcing parents and their families in achieving joint custody. Disseminates information concerning family law research and judicial decisions. Advocates for legislative improvement of family law in state capitols.

Joint Custody Assn.                   *Phone:* James A. Cook 310-475-5352
10606 Wilkins Ave.                    *Fax:* 310-475-6541
Los Angeles, CA 90024

**National Association for Fathers**                                          International
*50 affiliated groups. Founded 1991.* Provides mutual support and advocacy for fathers, second wives, grandparents or any paternal family member assert their lawful rights in divorce situations. Information and referrals, phone support, conferences, and literature. Dues $45/yr. Assistance in starting local groups.

Nat'l Assn. for Fathers              *Phone:* 1-800-HELP-DAD
2995 Van Buren Blvd., #A-13124        *Phone:* 909-776-9971
Riverside, CA 92503                   *Fax:* 909-780-4754

**National Organization For Men**                                                 National
*15 chapters. Founded 1983.* Seeks equal rights for men, uniform national divorce, custody, property and visitation law. Educational seminars. Lawyer referral. Quarterly newsletter.

Nat'l Org. for Men                    *Phone:* 212-686-MALE
11 Park Pl.                           *Phone:* 212-766-4030
New York, NY 10007-2801               *Website:* http://www.tnom.com

**North American Conference of Separated
and Divorced Catholics**                                                **International**
*3000+ groups. Founded 1972.* Religious, educational and emotional aspects of separation, divorce, remarriage and widowhood are addressed through self-help groups, conferences and training programs. Families of all faiths are welcome. Group development guidelines. Newsletter. Membership dues $30 (includes newsletter, discounts and resources).
NACSDC                              *Phone:* 541-893-6089
P.O. Box 360                        *E-mail:* nacsdc@pinetel.com
Richland, OR 97870                  *Website:* http://www.nacsdc.org

**RAINBOWS**                                                            **International**
*8500 affiliated groups. Founded 1983.* Establishes peer support groups in churches, schools or social agencies for children and adults who are grieving a death, divorce or other painful transition in their family. Groups are led by trained adults. Online newsletter, information and referrals.                       *Phone:* 1-800-266-3206 or 847-952-1770
RAINBOWS                            *Fax:* 847-952-1774
2100 Golf Rd., Suite 370            *E-mail:* info@rainbows.org
Rolling Meadows, IL 60008-4231      *Website:* http://www.rainbows.org

**New Beginnings, Inc.**                                                 **Model**
*1 group in Washington, DC area. Founded 1979.* Self-help group for separated and divorced men and women in the DC Metro area. Discussion meetings, speakers, social events, workshops. Newsletter. Assistance available for starting groups. Dues $45/yr.
New Beginnings. Inc.                 *Phone:* 301-924-4101 (Voice/Fax)
2711 Covered Wagon Way              *E-mail:* NewBCarol@aol.com
Olney, MD 20832                     *Website:* http://www.newbeginningsusa.org

## SINGLE PARENTING
*(Also see Parenting, Widows/Widowers, Separation/Divorce)*

**National Organization of Single Mothers**                             **National**
*3 affiliated groups. Founded 1991.* Networking system helping single mothers meet the challenges of daily life with wisdom, dignity, confidence and courage. Information and referrals. Dues $19. Assistance in starting new groups.
NOSM                                *Phone:* 704-888-KIDS; *Fax:* 704-888-1752
P.O. Box 68                         *E-mail:* solomother@aol.com
Midland, NC 28107                   *Website:* http://www.singlemothers.org

**Parents Without Partners**                                            **National**
*350+ chapters/5 affiliates. Founded 1957.* Educational organization of single parents (either divorced, separated, widowed or never married). Newsletter. Online chat room. Newsletter, chapter development guidelines. Dues $20-40.

PWP
1650 S. Dixie Hwy., Suite 510
Boca Raton, FL 33432

*Phone:* 1-800-637-7974 or 561-391-8833
*E-mail:* Fpf62930@aol.com
*Website:* http//www.parentswithoutpartners.org

### Single Mothers By Choice
**National**

*25 chapters. Founded 1981.* Support and information to mature, single women who have chosen, or who are considering, single motherhood. "Thinkers" workshops. Newsletter. Brochure and list of back issues of newsletter available.

SMC
P.O. Box 1642 Gracie Sq. Sta.
New York, NY 10028

*Phone:* 212-988-0993
*E-mail:* mattes@pipeline.com
*Website:* http://www.singlemothersbychoice.org

### Single Parent Resource Center
**International**

*7 affiliated groups. Founded 1975.* Network of single parent self-help groups. Information and referral, seminars, consultation, resource library. Separate group for men, homeless single parents and mothers coming out of prison. Also some coed groups. Newsletter. Guidelines and materials for starting parenting and teen groups.

Single Parent Resource Ctr.
31 E. 28th St.
New York, NY 10016

*Phone:* 212-951-7030; *Fax:* 212-951-7037
*E-mail:* SJones532@aol.com
*Website:* http://www.singleparentusa.com

### Unwed Parents Anonymous - The Whole Parent
**Model**

*1 group in Arizona. Founded 1979.* Offers support and parenting guidance to anyone affected by an out-of-wedlock pregnancy. Encourages pre-marital sexual abstinence. Literature, newsletter, group development guidelines $30.

Unwed Parents Anonymous
P.O. Box 15466
Phoenix, AZ 85060-5466

*Phone:* 480-421-2374; *Fax:* 480-421-2376
*E-mail:* upawhole@yahoo.com
*Website:* http://www.thewholeparent.org

## STEPPARENTING
*(Also see Separation/Divorce)*

### Stepfamily Association of America, Inc.
**National**

*47 support groups. Founded 1979.* Information and advocacy for stepfamilies. Educational resources. Semi-annual professional training. Online chat room. Bimonthly magazine.

Stepfamily Assn. of America
650 J St., Suite 205
Lincoln, NE 68508

*Phone:* 1-800-735-0329
*E-mail:* saa@saafamilies.org
*Website:* http://www.saafamilies.org

## TWINS / TRIPLETS / MULTIPLE BIRTHS
*(Also see Pregnancy/Childbirth)*

### Conjoined Twins International
**International network**

*Founded 1996.* Support for conjoined twins, their families, and professionals. Offers peer support, professional counseling, crisis intervention, telephone helpline, pen pal network, videos, information and referrals, peer counseling, and speakers bureau. Maintains registry of affected families. Newsletter.

Conjoined Twins Int'l            *Phone:* 520-445-2777
P.O. Box 10895                   *E-mail:* dwdegeraty@myexcel.com
Prescott, AZ 86304-0895

### MOST (Mothers Of SuperTwins)                                    National

*50+ affiliated groups. Founded 1987.* Support network of families who are expecting, or are already the parents of, triplets or more. Provides information, support, resources and empathy during pregnancy, infancy, toddlerhood and school age. Magazine, networking, phone and online support, catalogue. Specific resource persons for individual challenges. Help in starting groups.

MOST                             *Phone:* Maureen Boyle 631-859-1110
P.O. Box 951                     *E-mail:* info@MOSTonline.org
Brentwood, NY 11717-0627         *Website:* http://www.MOSTonline.org

### National Organization of Mothers of Twins Clubs                 National

*475 clubs. Founded 1960.* Opportunity for parents of multiple birth children (twins, triplets, quads) to share information, concerns and advice on dealing with their unique challenges. Literature, quarterly newspaper ($15/yr.), group development guidelines, educational materials, special needs and bereavement support, pen pals. Membership through local chapters or as individuals.            *Phone:* 1-877-540-2200 (referrals only)
NOMOTC                           or 615-595-0936
P.O. Box 438                     *E-mail:* nomotc@aol.com
Thompson Station, TN 37179       *Website:* http://www.nomotc.org/

### Triplet Connection                                    International network

*Founded 1982.* Caring and sharing network for families of multiple birth. Emphasis is on providing quality information regarding pregnancy management and preterm birth prevention for high-risk multiple pregnancies. Expectant parent's packet, quarterly newsletter, phone support and resources.

Triplet Connection               *Phone:* 209-474-0885; *Fax:* 209-474-9243
P.O. Box 99571                   *E-mail:* tc@tripletconnection.org
Stockton, CA 95209               *Website:* http://www.tripletconnection.org

*"There is great comfort and inspiration in the feeling of close human relationships, and its bearing on our mutual fortunes—a powerful force, to overcome the 'tough breaks' which are certain to come to most of us from time to time."*
*- Walt Disney*

# HEALTH

*"The art of living lies less in eliminating our troubles
than in growing with them."*
*- Bernard M. Baruch*

## 5P- SYNDROME / CRI DU CHAT

**5P- Society**                                      **International network**
*Founded 1986.* Support organization for families having a child with 5P- syndrome (aka cri du chat), genetic disorder characterized by a high-pitched cry. Dedicated to facilitating flow of information among affected families and medical professionals. Listing of families in U.S and Canada. Newsletter. Annual meeting. International chat room (Sun. and Thurs).
5P- Society                          *Phone:* 1-888-970-0777; *Fax:* 562-920-5240
P.O. Box 268                         *E-mail:* director@fivepminus.org
Lakewood, CA 90714-0268              *Website:* http://www.fivepminus.org

## 9P- DISORDERS
*(Also see Chromosome Disorders)*

**Chromosome 9P- Network**                            **International network**
*Founded 1983.* Provides information, parent-to-parent networking and technical support to parents of children with 9P- and other deletions of 9P, ring 9, mosaic, translocations, inverted 9P, etc. Facilitates research. Referrals, phone support and yearly conferences.
Chromosome 9P- Network               *Phone:* 435-574-1121
c/o Beverly Udell                    *Fax:* 435-574-2000
393 N. Grass Valley Rd..             *E-mail:* beverly.udell@9pminus.org
Pine Valley, UT 84781                *Website:* http://www.9pminus.org

## 11Q ABNORMALITIES
*(Also see Chromosome Disorders)*

⌨ **11q Research and Resource Group**                             **Online**
Mutual support for families of children with structural abnormalities of chromosome 11, including deletions, duplications and translocations. Networking of families, researchers and organizations. Newsletter, conferences, books, videos.
11q Research & Resource Group        *Website:* http://www.11q.net
c/o Univ. of Colorado
Campus Box 295
Boulder, CO 80309

# 49XXXXY
*(Also see Chromosome Disorders)*

**49XXXXY**                                                    **National network**
*Founded 1990.* Mutual support and networking for families affected by 49XXXXY disorder. Information, pen pals, phone support, newsletter.
49XXXXY                                        *Phone:* Elise Watzka 650-941-2408
870 Miranda Green                          *E-mail:* epwatzka@iname.com
Palo Alto, CA 94306

# AARSKOG SYNDROME

**Aarskog Syndrome Family Support Group**              **International network**
*Founded 1993.* Mutual support, networking and sharing of ideas for families of children and adults affected with Aarskog syndrome. Pen pals, telephone support, information and referrals, newsletter. Networking of parents.
Aarskog Synd. Family Support Group   *Phone:* Shannon Caranci 215-943-7131
62 Robin Hill Lane
Levittown, PA 19055-1411

# ABETALIPOPROTEINEMIA /
# BASSEN-KORNZWEIG SYNDROME

🖳 **Abetalipoproteinemia Discussion Board**                          **Online**
*Founded 2001.* Support and information for people with abetalipoproteinemia (aka Bassen-Kornzweig syndrome), a rare blood disease. Opportunity to exchange information and communicate with others.        *Website:* yahoo.com/group/Abetalipoproteinemia

# ACHALASIA
*(Also see Digestive Motility Disorders, specific disorder)*

🖳 **Achalasia eGroup**                                               **Online**
Opportunity to share information and support with others affected by achalasia, a condition in which a spasm of the lower esophagus prevents the normal passage of food from the esophagus to the stomach.        *Website:* http://groups.yahoo.com/group/achalasia

# ACHROMATOPSIA / ACHROMATOPIA
*(Also see Blind/Visually Impaired)*

**Achromatopsia Network**                                    **National network**
A support network for persons affected by the rare inherited vision disorder achromatopsia (aka achromatopia), including both rod monochromacy and blue cone monochromacy.

Achromatopsia Network                *E-mail:* editor@achromat.org
P.O. Box 214                         *Website:* http://www.achromat.org
Berkeley, CA 94701-0214

# ACID MALTASE DEFICIENCY / POMPE DISEASE

**Acid Maltase Deficiency Association**                **International network**
*Founded 1995.* Support and information for persons affected by Pompe disease (acid maltase deficiency). Newsletter, literature, information and referrals, and phone support. Supports research into the cause and cure.
AMDA                                 *Phone:* 210-494-6144; *Fax:* 210-490-7161
P.O. Box 700248                      *E-mail:* tianrama@aol.com
San Antonio, TX 78270                *Website:* http://www.amda-pompe.org

# ACNE SCAR
*(Also see Facial Disfigurement)*

**Acne Scar Support Group**                                        **Model**
*1 group in Maryland. Founded 2001.* Sharing of information on the results of scar-revision procedures with others. Offers phone support and e-mail pen pals.
Acne Scar                            *Phone:* 301-718-0952
5500 Friendship Blvd., Apt. 821      *Fax:* 301-718-0126
Chevy Chase, MD 20815-7258           *E-mail:* gregestrade@netzero.net

# ACOUSTIC NEUROMA
*(Also see Brain Tumors)*

**Acoustic Neuroma Association**                                **National**
*46 affiliated groups. Founded 1981.* Support and information for patients who have been diagnosed with, or experienced acoustic neuromas or other benign tumors affecting the cranial nerves. Quarterly newsletter ($30/yr), nationwide support group network, biennial national symposium, and patient information booklets.
ANA                                  *Phone:* 770-205-8211; *Fax:* 770-205-0239
600 Peachtree Parkway, #108          *E-mail:* ANAUSA@aol.com
Cumming, GA 30041-6899               *Website:* http://www.anausa.org

# ADRENAL DISORDERS / ADDISON'S DISEASE
*(Also see specific disorder)*

**Addison News**                                         **National network**
*Founded 1993.* Networks, educates and supports persons with Addison's disease through a newsletter that contains information, educational material, and personal stories. Referrals to support groups nationwide. Parents booklet. Voluntary donations.

Addison News                    *Phone:* Joan Hoffman 517-769-6891
6142 Territorial                *E-mail:* hoffmanrj@dmci.net
Pleasant Lake, MI 49272         *Website:* http://www2.dmci.net/users/hoffmanrj

**National Adrenal Diseases Foundation**                        **National**
*17 affiliated groups. Founded 1984.* Dedicated to serving the needs of those with adrenal diseases and their families, especially through education, support groups, where possible, and "buddies." Newsletter, pamphlets and group development guidelines.
NADF                            *Phone:* 516-487-4992
505 Northern Blvd.              *E-mail:* nadfmail@aol.com
Great Neck, NY 11021            *Website:* http://medhelp.org/www/nadf

## AGENESIS OF THE CORPUS CALLOSUM

**The ACC Network**                            **International network**
*Founded 1990.* Helps individuals with agenesis (or other anomaly) of the corpus callosum, their families and professionals. Sharing of similar issues for support. Phone support, information, newsletter and referrals. Coordinates online discussion group.
ACC Network                     *Phone:* 207-581-3119
University of Maine             *Fax:* 207-581-3120
5749 Merrill Hall, Rm. 118      *E-mail:* UM-ACC@maine.edu
Orono, ME 04469-5749

## AGNOSIA, PRIMARY VISUAL / PROSOPAGNOSIA
*(Also see Brain Injury)*

**International Agnosia Foundation**                    **International network**
*7 affiliated groups. Founded 1987.* Support, information and referrals for persons with primary visual agnosia (including prosopagnosia) and related traumatic brain injuries. Provides phone support, online support group, conferences and advocacy. Newsletter ($10).
Int'l Agnosia Fdn.              *Phone:* Michael Herman 818-996-6464
4774 Park Granada, Suite 2      *Fax:* 818-222-9124
Calabasas, CA 91302-1550        *E-mail:* tauntra@aol.com

## AICARDI SYNDROME

**Aicardi Syndrome Newsletter, Inc.**               **International network**
*Founded 1983.* Support for families with daughters with Aicardi syndrome, a rare seizure disorder characterized by retinal lesions. Information and referrals, resources, research projects. Phone support network, research group, newsletters. Dues $25/year.
Aicardi Syndrome Newsletter     *Phone:* Denise Parsons 502-244-9152 (Voice/Fax)
1510 Polo Fields Ct.            *E-mail:* aicnews@aol.com
Louisville,KY 40245             *Website:* http://www.aicardi.com

# AIDS

**National Association of People With AIDS**                              **National**
*Founded 1986.* Opportunity for persons with AIDS to share information. Acts as a collective voice for health, social and political concerns. Phone, mail and electronics network, speakers bureau, quarterly newsletter, free publications.
NAPWA                                   *Phone:* 202-898-0414; *Fax:* 202-898-0435
1413 K St., NW, 7th fl.                  *E-mail:* napwa@napwa.org
Washington, DC 20005-3442                *Website:* http://www.napwa.org

**Body Positive of New York**                                           **Model**
*1 group in New York. Founded 1987.* (Bilingual) Support and education for people affected by HIV. Information and referrals, public forums, support groups, social activities. Publishes monthly magazine, bi-monthly Spanish magazine.
Body Positive of NY                      *Phone:* 212-566-7333; *Fax:* 212-566-4539
19 Fulton St., #308B                     *E-mail:* bodypositive@bodypos.org
New York, NY 10038                       *Website:* http://www.thebody.com

**One Day At A Time**                                                    **Model**
*10 affiliated groups in Pennsylvania. Founded 1987.* Helps people with HIV infection become aware of and make use of services provided. Encourages self-empowerment through the support given by other HIV+ people. Newsletter, group development assistance.
One Day At A Time                        *Phone:* 215-545-6868; *Fax:* 215-545-8437
425 S. Broad St.                         *E-mail:* wtp@critpath.org
Philadelphia, PA 19147                   *Website:* http://www.peoplewithaids.org

**WORLD (Women Organized to Respond to Life-threatening Disorder)**      **Model**
*1 group in California.* Grassroots organization that provides support, information and referrals to women living with HIV, their families and friends. Peer advocacy, information and referrals, phone support. Various support group meetings. Offers a model program for women's education and empowerment. National retreats, direct services. Newsletter.
WORLD                                    *Phone:* 510-986-0340
414 13th St., 2nd fl.                    *Fax:* 510-986-0341
Oakland, CA 94612                        *Website:* http://www.womenhiv.org

# ALAGILLE SYNDROME
*(Also see Liver Disorders)*

**Alagille Syndrome Alliance**                                  **National network**
*Founded 1993.* Support network for anyone who cares about people with Alagille syndrome, a genetic liver disorder. Aims to increase awareness in health professionals. Newsletter, phone support, information and referrals, scientific advisory board.

Alagille Syndrome Alliance           *Phone:* Cindy Hahn 503-639-6217 (day/eve)
10630 S.W. Garden Park Pl.            *E-mail:* alagille@earthlink.net
Tigard, OR 97223                     *Website:* http://www.alagille.org

## ALBINISM / HYPOPIGMENTATION

**NOAH (National Organization for Albinism and Hypopigmentation)**        **National**
*14 chapters. Founded 1982.* Support and information for individuals, families, and
professionals about albinism (a lack of melanin pigment). Encourages research leading to
improved diagnosis and treatment. Newsletter, chapter development guidelines, national
conference. Dues $15 individual; $20 family.
NOAH                                 *Phone:* 1-800-473-2310 or 603-887-2310
P.O. Box 959                         *Fax:* 603-887-2310; *E-mail:* info@albinism.org
East Hempstead, NH 03826-0959        *Website:* http://www.albinism.org/

## ALLERGY
*(Also see specific disorder)*

**Asthma and Allergy Foundation of America**                              **National**
*100+ educational support groups and 11 chapters. Founded 1953.* Serves persons with
asthma and allergic diseases through the support of research, patient and public education,
and advocacy. Newsletter, support/education groups. Assistance in starting and maintaining
groups. Books, videos and other educational resources.
AAFA                                 *Phone:* 202-466-7643 or 1-800-7-ASTHMA
1233 20th St. NW, Suite 402          *Fax:* 202-466-8940; *E-mail:* info@aafa.org
Washington, DC 20036                 *Website:* http://www.aafa.org

**ELASTIC (Education for Latex Allergy Support
Team Information Coalition)**                                             **National**
*47 chapters. Founded 1995.* Information, support and networking for persons with latex
allergies, their families, and healthcare workers. Phone support, conferences, literature.
Membership package includes non-latex product samples, resource information, mailing list
for group meetings. Networking, message boards. Dues $25. Affiliated newsletter ($40/yr).
ELASTIC                              *Phone:* 610-436-4801; *Fax:* 610-436-1198
P.O. Box 2228                        *E-mail:* ELASTIC@latex-allergy.org
West Chester, PA 19380               *Website:* http://www.latex-allergy.org/

**Food Allergy and Anaphylaxis Network**                              **National network**
*Founded 1991.* Mission is to increase public awareness about food allergies and
anaphylaxis, provide education, and advance research. Information and referrals,
conferences, literature, phone support, booklets and newsletters.
Food Allergy Network                 *Phone:* 1-800-929-4040 or 703-691-3179
10400 Eaton Pl., Suite 107           *Fax:* 703-691-2713; *E-mail:* faan@foodallergy.org
Fairfax, VA 22030                    *Website:* http://www.foodallergy.org

# ALOPECIA

**National Alopecia Areata Foundation** **National**
*85 support groups. Founded 1981.* Support network for people with alopecia areata, totalis, and universalis. Aim is to set up support groups around the country, and to educate the public. Fund-raises for research. Newsletter, support group guidelines.
Nat'l Alopecia Areata Fdn.        *Phone:* 415-456-4644; *Fax:* 415-456-4274
P.O. Box 150760                        *E-mail:* info@naaf.org
San Rafael, CA 94901                *Website:* http://www.naaf.org

# ALPHA-1 ANTITRYPSIN DEFICIENCY
*(Also see Respiratory)*

**Alpha 1 Association** **International**
*70 affiliated groups. Founded 1988.* Support, advocacy and information for persons with alpha-1 antitrypsin deficiency and their families. Networking of members through newsletter and support groups across the country. Sharing of current information on treatments and research. Newsletter, group development guidelines, educational materials and advocacy information.
Alpha 1 Assn.                          *Phone:* 952-703-9979 or 1-800-521-3025
c/o Dennis Barbour                   *Fax:* 952-703-9977
8120 Penn Ave. South, Suite 549   *E-mail:* barbour@alpha1.org
Minneapolis, MN 55431-1326      *Website:* http://www.alpha1.org

# ALSTROM SYNDROME

**Alstrom Syndrome International** **International**
*2 affiliated groups (Canada and UK). Founded 1995.* Support and networking for families affected by Alstrom syndrome. Supports medical research initiatives to more fully understand the complexities of Alstrom syndrome and develop better therapies for Alstrom patients. Newsletter. Provides information and resources to families and physicians.
Alstrom Syndrome Int'l             *Phone:* 1-800-371-3628 or 207-288-6385
14 Whitney Farm Rd.                *E-mail:* jdm@jax.org
Mount Desert, ME 04660          *Website:* http://www.jax.org/alstrom

# ALVEOLAR CAPILLARY DYSPLASIA

**Alveolar Capillary Dysplasia Association** **International network**
*Founded 1996.* Mutual support for families who have lost a child to alveolar capillary dysplasia, a congenital lung disorder. Aim is to share information while offering supportive environment to share fears and concerns. Encourages research into cause and cure. Literature, networking, information and referrals.

ACDA                                    *Phone:* Madonna Myers 630-416-6776 (day/eve)
28 West 520 Douglas Rd.                 *E-mail:* mmyers531@earthlink.net
Naperville, IL 60564-9593               *Website:* http://www.acd-association.com

## ALZHEIMER'S DISEASE

**Alzheimer's Association**                                              **National**
*150 chapters. Founded 1980.* Provides information and assistance for caregivers of
Alzheimer's patients. Quarterly newsletter, literature.
ADRDA                                   *Phone:* 1-800-272-3900 or 312-335-8700
919 N. Michigan Ave., #1100             *TDD:* 312-335-8882; *E-mail:* info@alz.org
Chicago, IL 60611-1676                  *Website:* http://www.alz.org

## AMBIGUOUS GENITALIA
*(Also see Sexual Orientation)*

**Ambiguous Genitalia Support Network, The**                     **National network**
*Founded 1993.* Provides mutual support and information to those (mainly parents) affected
by ambiguous genitalia or intersex conditions caused by various genetic or endocrine
disorders. Information and referrals, pen pal networking, phone support, education and
advocacy. Newsletter. Donations accepted.
AGSN                                    *Phone:* 209-727-0313 (Voice/Fax)
P.O. Box 313                            *E-mail:* agsn@jps.net
Clements, CA 95227-0313                 *Website:* http://www.jps.net/agsn

## AMYLOIDOSIS
*(Also see Neurology)*

**Amyloidosis Network International, Inc.**                  **International network**
Information and support for persons affected by amyloidosis, an accumulation of abnormal
proteins. Networks individuals together for support. Provides education to the public and
professionals about the disease.
Amyloidosis Network Int'l, Inc.         *Phone:* 1-888-AMYLOID (269-5643)
7118 Cole Creek Dr.                     *Website:* http://www.amyloidosis.org/
Houston, TX 77092-1421

🖳  **The FAMYL Organization**                                           **Online**
Interactive support group for persons affected by familial amyloidosis polyneuropathy
disease, a liver protein disorder. Local meeting in Indiana.
*Phone:* 219-436-5476                   *E-mail:* Ekoenig@peoplepc.com
                                        *Website:* http://www.famyl.com

*"Hope is necessary in every condition."*
*– Samual Johnson, biographer and essayist*

---

# AMYOTROPHIC LATERAL SCLEROSIS / LOU GEHRIG'S DISEASE

**A.L.S. Association**                                              **National**
*75+ chapters and support groups. Founded 1984.* Dedicated to finding the cause, prevention and cure of amyotrophic lateral sclerosis, and to enhance quality of life for ALS patients and their families. Quarterly newspaper, chapter development guidelines.

A.L.S. Assn.                        *Phone:* 1-800-782-4747 or 818-880-9007
27001 Agoura Rd., #150              *Fax:* 818-880-9006; *Website:* www.alsa.org
Calabasas Hills, CA 91301          *E-mail:* alsinfo@alsa-national.org

# ANDROGEN INSENSITIVITY / TESTICULAR FEMINIZATION SYNDROME

**Androgen Insensitivity Syndrome Support Group**              **International**
*3 affiliated groups. Founded 1988.* Worldwide consortium of support groups. Provides information and support to adults and families affected by androgen insensitivity syndrome (aka testicular feminization syndrome) and similar conditions (e.g. XY gonadal dysgenesis, Swyer's syndrome, 5-alpha reductase deficiency, leydig cell hyoplasia, Mayer Rokitansky Kuster Hauser syndrome, Mullerian dysgenesis/aplasia and vaginal atresia). Offers referrals, support group meetings, literature, advocacy, conferences and newsletter.

AISSG                             *E-mail:* spaiscadet@yahoo.com (East Coast)
P.O. Box 750273                   *E-mail:* aissgusa@hotmail.com (Midwest)
Duncan, OK 73575-0273             *E-mail:* causavon@yahoo.com (West Coast)

# ANEMIA / BONE MARROW DISEASES / MYELODYSPLASTIC SYNDROMES

**Aplastic Anemia and MDS International Foundation, Inc.**     **International**
*25 chapters. Founded 1983.* Serves as a resource for patient assistance and emotional support for persons with bone marrow failure diseases. Provides educational materials and updated medical information. Financially supports research to find effective treatments for aplastic anemia, myelodysplastic syndromes and other related bone marrow failure diseases.

Aplastic Anemia/MDS Int'l Fdn.    *Phone:* 1-800-747-2820 or 410-867-0242
P.O. Box 613                      *Fax:* 410-867-0240; *E-mail:* help@aamds.org
Annapolis, MD 21404               *Website:* http://www.aamds.org

**Cooley's Anemia Foundation**                                 **National**
*18 chapters. Founded 1954.* Offers education and networking for families affected by Cooley's anemia (thalassemia). Fund-raising for research. Newsletter, annual seminars, research grants, young adult group, patient services, chapter development guidelines.

Cooley's Anemia Fdn.                *Phone:* 718-321-2873 or 1-800-522-7222 (NY)
129-09 26th Ave.                    *Fax:* 718-321-3340; *E-mail:* ncaf@aol.com
Flushing, NY 11354                  *Website:* http://www.thalassemia.org

**Fanconi Anemia Research Fund, Inc.**                    **International network**
*Founded 1989.* Provides support and exchange of information regarding medical advances in Fanconi anemia research. Phone support, semi-annual family newsletter, semi-annual science letter, annual family meetings, regional meetings, news bulletins, family directory, Fanconi anemia handbook, annual scientific symposium. Grants and fund-raising for scientific research. Networking opportunities for families and researchers.
Fanconi Anemia Research Fund        *Phone:* 1-800-828-4891 or 541-687-4658
1801 Willamette St., Suite 200      *Fax:* 541-687-0548; *E-mail:* info@fanconi.org
Eugene, OR 97401                    *Website:* http://www.fanconi.org

⌨ **Myelodysplastic Syndromes Foundation**                           **Online**
Forums for patients and professionals dealing with myelodysplastic syndromes, a group of bone marrow diseases. Also has referrals to treatment centers.
                                    *Website:* http://mds-foundation.org

## ANENCEPHALY

**Anencephaly Support Foundation**                        **International network**
*Founded 1992.* Provides support for parents who are continuing a pregnancy after being diagnosed with an anencephalic infant. Information and resources for parents and professionals. Phone support, pen pals, literature, pictures.
Anencephaly Support Fdn.            *Phone:* 1-888-206-7526
20311 Sienna Pines Court            *E-mail:* asf@asfhelp.com
Spring, TX 77379                    *Website:* http://www.asfhelp.com

## ANGELMAN SYNDROME

**Angelman Syndrome Foundation, Inc.**                            **International**
*19 affiliated chapters. Founded 1992.* Support and advocacy for persons with Angelman syndrome, their families and interested others. Education, information, referrals, literature, newsletter, conferences. Fund-raises. Promotes research. Dues $50.
Angelman Syndrome Fdn.              *Phone:* 1-800-432-6435 or 630-734-9267
414 Plaza Dr., Suite 209           *Fax:* 630-655-0391; *E-mail:* info@angelman.org
Westmont, IL 60559                 *Website:* http://www.angelman.org

⌨ **Angel Message Board, The**                                       **Online**
Private forum and message board for families of Angelman syndrome children. Opportunity to share experiences and coping skills. *Website:* http://www.ascelpius.com/angel/

## ANKYLOSING SPONDYLITIS
*(Also see Arthritis)*

**Spondylitis Association of America**            **International network**
*Founded 1983.* Dedicated to eradicating ankylosing and related disorders through education, awareness, advocacy and research. Includes Reiter's syndrome, reactive arthritis, psoriatic arthritis, and inflammatory bowel disease. Publications, videotapes, newsletter.
Spondylitis Assn. of Amer.          *Phone:* 1-800-777-8189 or 818-981-1616
14827 Ventura Blvd., Suite 222      *Fax:* 818-981-9826; *E-mail:* info@spondylitis.org
Sherman Oaks, CA 91413              *Website:* http://www.spondylitis.org

**KickAS.org**                                                      **Online**
Support and information for persons with ankylosing spondylitis and related disorders. Provides inspiration, friendship and humor. Message boards. Forums for affected persons, families and friends, and teens.          *Website:* http://www.kickas.org

## ANORCHIDISM

**Anorchidism Support Group**                    **International network**
*Founded 1995.* Information and support for families and persons affected by anorchidism (absence of the testes) whether congenital or acquired (testicular regression or vanishing testes syndrome, anorchia, or absent testes). Newsletter. Information. Support via phone, letter or e-mail. Will return calls outside of UK; allow for time difference when telephoning.
ASG                          *Phone:* 44(0)1708 372597
P.O. Box 3025                *Website:* http://freespace.virgin.net/asg.uk
Romford, Essex               *Website:* http://community.nj.com/cc/
RM3 8GX England              anorchidismsupportgroup

## ANORECTAL MALFORMATIONS
*(Also see VATER Association, specific disorder)*

**The Pull-Thru Network**                                          **National**
*2 affiliated groups. Founded 1988.* (A chapter of United Ostomy Assn.) Support, education and networking for families with children born with anorectal malformations (including cloaca, VATER, cloacal exstrophy or an imperforate anus and Hirschsprung's disease). Newsletter. Online discussion group. Phone support and literature. Dues $20-$31.
The Pull-Thru Network        *Phone:* 205-978-2930
2312 Savoy St.               *E-mail:* pullthru@bellsouth.net
Hanover, AL 35226-1582       *Website:* http://www.pullthrough.org

*"The firmest friendships have been formed in mutual adversity,*
*as iron is most strongly united by the fiercest flames." – C.C. Colton*

# ANOSMIA

🖥 **Anosmia Resource Center**                              **Online**
Mailing list and resources for people with anosmia (lacking the sense of smell).
*Website:* http://groups.yahoo.com/group/anosmia

# APERT SYNDROME

**Apert Syndrome Pen Pals**                         **National network**
*Founded 1992.* Group correspondence program for persons with Apert syndrome to share experiences. Information and referrals, pen pals, phone help.
Apert Syndrome Pen Pals              *Phone:* 401-421-9076 (after 4:30pm)
P.O. Box 115
Providence, RI 02901

# APHASIA
*(Also see Brain Injury)*

**National Aphasia Association**                             **National**
*Founded 1987.* Aim is to educate the public about aphasia. Provides information to patients and their families. Referrals to local groups. Young People's Network for people (13-30) with acquired aphasia. Networking of parents to share information. Newsletter. Manual available for starting community groups.
Nat'l Aphasia Assn.                    *Phone:* 1-800-922-4622; *Fax:* 212-989-7777
156 Fifth Ave., Suite 707              *E-mail:* naa@aphasia.org
New York, NY 10010                     *Website:* http://www.aphasia.org

# APNEA

**AWAKE Network Groups**                                    **National**
*200 affiliated groups. Founded 1990.* Education, support and social interaction for persons with sleep apnea, their families and friends. Dues $25. Guidelines for starting groups ($30).
A.W.A.K.E. ASAA                        *Phone:* 202-293-3650; *Fax:* 202-293-3656
1424 K St., NW, Suite 302             *E-mail:* awake@sleepapnea.org
Washington, DC 20005                   *Website:* http://www.sleepapnea.org

🖥 **A.P.N.E.A. Net**                                         **Online**
Support and information for persons affected by obstructive sleep apnea. Forum to exchange information and ideas.        *Website:* http://www.apneanet.org/

*"Our own rough edges become smooth as we help a friend smooth her edges."*
                              *- Sue Atchley Ebough*

# APRAXIA
*(Also see Speech)*

⌨ **Apraxia Kids**                                                              **Online**
Information and support for parents of children with apraxia of speech, a motor speech disorder. Education, listserv, referrals to self-help groups nationwide.
*Website:* http://www.apraxia.org          *Website:* http://www.apraxia.kids.org

# ARACHNOIDITIS
*(Also see Neurology, Pain)*

**ASAM (Arachnoid Sufferers, Action and Monitoring) Society**        **International**
*Founded 1996.* Provides mutual support and information to people who suffer from arachnoiditis, and their families and caregivers. Aim is to empower members by raising public awareness and understanding of arachnoiditis, and to reduce future occurrences of this condition. Online message board and patient stories.
ASAM Society                         *E-mail:* asams.newzealand@xtra.co.nz
39 Jackson St.                       *Website:* http://www.aboutarachnoiditis.com
Wanganui, New Zealand

# ARNOLD CHIARI MALFORMATION

⌨ **World Arnold Chiari Malformation Association**                              **Online**
*900+ members. Founded 1995.* Provides information, support and understanding to persons concerned with Arnold Chiari malformation. Adult and children's online support groups.
WACMA                                *Phone:* Bernice Meyer 610-353-4737
31 Newton Woods Rd.                  *E-mail:* chip@pressenter.com
Netown Square, PA 19073              *Website:* http://www.pressenter.com/~wacma

# ARTHRITIS
*(Also see specific disorder, Pain)*

**American Juvenile Arthritis Organization**                                    **National**
*Founded 1981.* (Council of the Arthritis Foundation) Devoted to serving the special needs of children, teens and young adults with childhood rheumatic diseases (including juvenile rheumatoid arthritis, systemic lupus erythematosus and ankylosing spondylitis) and their families. Provides support groups, information, advocacy, educational materials, programs, and conferences. Dues $20 (to join the Arthritis Foundation).
AJAO                                 *Phone:* 404-872-7100 ext. 7538
1330 West Peachtree St.              *Fax:* 404-872-9559
Atlanta, GA 30309                    *Website:* http://www.arthritis.org

**Arthritis Foundation**                                              **National**
*55 chapters. Founded 1948.* Mission is to improve the lives of persons with arthritis through the prevention, control and cure of arthritis and related diseases. Offers education, support and activities for people with arthritis, and their families and friends. Self-help instruction programs. Land and water exercises. Magazine. Dues $20.

Arthritis Fdn.                    *Phone:* 1-800-283-7800 (Option 5) or
1330 West Peachtree St            404-872-7100 ext. 1; *Fax:* 404-872-9559
Atlanta, GA 30309                 *E-mail:* help@arthritis.org
                                  *Website:* http://www.arthritis.org

## ARTHROGRYPOSIS

**Avenues: A National Support Group for Arthrogryposis**        **National network**
*Founded 1980.* Connects families affected by arthrogryposis with each other for mutual support and sharing of information. Educates medical and social service professionals. Occasional newsletter.

Avenues                           *Phone:* 209-928-3688
P.O. Box 5192                     *E-mail:* avenues@sonnet.com
Sonora, CA 95370                  *Website:* http://www.sonnet.com/avenues

## ASHERMANS SYNDROME / INTRAUTERINE SYNECHIAE

▣ **Ashermans Syndrome Online Community**                            **Online**
Community of women who have been diagnosed with Ashermans syndrome (aka intrauterine or uterine synechiae). Sharing of information and knowledge.
*E-mail:* ashermans2000@hotmail.com   *Website:* http://www.ashermans.freeservers.com/

## ASTHMA
*(Also see Respiratory)*

**Asthma and Allergy Foundation of America**                        **National**
*100+ educational support groups and 11 chapters. Founded 1953.* Serves persons with asthma and allergic diseases through the support of research, patient and public education, and advocacy. Newsletter, support/education groups. Assistance in starting and maintaining groups. Books, videos and other educational resources.

AAFA                              *Phone:* 202-466-7643 or 1-800-7-ASTHMA
1233 20th St. NW, Suite 402       *Fax:* 202-466-8940; *E-mail:* info@aafa.org
Washington, DC 20036              *Website:* http://www.aafa.org

**SAY (Support for Asthmatic Youth)**                               **National**
*30 affiliated groups. Founded 1989.* Provides an atmosphere of support, reassurance and fun for children (9-17) with asthma and allergies. Exchanging of personal experiences and concerns. Education, information and referrals, phone support, conferences, pen pals, newsletter, advocacy, literature. How-to on starting groups ($3).

SAY                                    *Phone:* Renee Theodorakis 516-625-5735 (day)
Asthma & Allergy Fdn. of Amer.         *Fax:* 516-625-2976
1080 Glen Cove Ave.                    *E-mail:* ReneeTheo1@aol.com
Glen Head, NY 11545                    *Website:* http://www.aafa.org

# ATAXIA

**National Ataxia Foundation**                                        **National**
*52 groups. Founded 1957.* Assists families with ataxia. Provides education for professionals and the public. Encourages prevention through genetic counseling. Promotes research into causes and treatment. Newsletter, information and referral, assistance in starting support groups. Group development guidelines.

Nat'l Ataxia Fdn.                      *Phone:* 763-553-0020
c/o Donna Gruetzmacher                 *Fax:* 763-553-0167
2600 Fernbrook Lane, Suite 119         *E-mail:* naf@mr.net
Minneapolis, MN 55447                  *Website:* http://www.ataxia.org

**▣ A-T Children's Project**                                          **Online**
(Bilingual) Enables families of children affected by ataxia telangiectasia to seek information and share thoughts with other families. Online forum. Listserv. Information, workshops.

A-T Children's Project                 *Phone:* (954)481-6611 or 1-800-5-HELP-AT
668 S. Military Trail                  *Fax:* 954-725-1153; *E-mail:* info@atcp.org
Seerfield Beach, FL 33442              *Website:* http://www.atcp.org

# ATRESIA / MICROTIA/
# CRANIOFACIAL MICROSOMIA

**EAR (Ear Anomalies Reconstructed):**
**Atresia/Microtia Support Group**                          **International network**
*Founded 1986.* Networking for families whose members have microtia, atresia, or craniofacial microsomia. Sharing of experiences and medical information. Phone support, visitation, conferences. Support group meets periodically in New York City.

EAR                                    *Phone:* Betsy Old 973-761-5438
c/o Jack Gross                         *Phone:* Jack Gross 212-620-4040 ext. 11
307 Seventh Ave.                       *E-mail:* grossinsco@aol.com
New York, NY 10001

# BATTEN DISEASE

**Batten Disease Support and Research Association**              **International**
*18 affiliated groups. Founded 1987.* Emotional support for persons with Batten disease. Information and referrals, support group meetings, phone support, conferences, newsletter. Assistance provided for starting new groups.

195

Batten Dis. Support & Res. Assn.        *Phone:* 1-800-448-4570
120 Humphries Dr., Suite 2              *E-mail:* bdsra1@bdsra.org
Reynoldsburg, OH 43068                  *Website:* http://bdsra.org

## BECKWITH-WIEDEMANN SYNDROME / ISOLATED HEMIHYPERTROPHY

**Beckwith-Wiedemann Support Network**              **International network**
*Founded 1989.* Support and information for parents of children with Beckwith-Wiedemann or isolated hemihypertrophy, and medical professionals. Phone support, newsletter, parent directory, information and referrals. Educates public. Encourages research.
Beckwith-Wiedemann Support Ntwrk    *Phone:* 734-973-0263; *Fax:* 734-973-9721
c/o Susan Fettes, President          *Phone:* 1-800-837-2976 (parents)
2711 Colony Rd.                      *E-mail:* a800bwsn@aol.com
Ann Arbor, MI 48104                  *Website:* http://www.beckwith-wiedemann.org

## BEHCET'S DISEASE

**American Behcet's Disease Association**                **National network**
*Founded 1978.* Mutual support and information for Behcet's patients, their families, and professionals. Newsletter (transcribed on tape for visually impaired), information and referrals, phone support, pen pals, conferences, medical advisory board. Pamphlets, literature, press kit.
ABDA                                *Phone:* 1-800-7-BEHCET or 618-343-9966
P.O. Box 15247                      *E-mail:* abdavplinda@aol.com
Chatanooga, TN 37415                *Website:* http://www.behcets.com

## BELL'S PALSY

**Bell's Palsy Research Foundation**                    **National network**
*Founded 1995.* Provides information and support to persons diagnosed with Bell's Palsy (facial paralysis). Referrals, phone support, advocacy, pen pals, and literature. For information packet, please send a donation to help cover costs.
Bell's Palsy Research Fdn.          *Phone:* 1-877-412-5335
9121 E. Tanque Verde, #105-286      *E -mail:* BellsPalsy@aol.com
Tucson, AZ 85749                    *Website:* http://www.bellspalsyresearch.com

## BENIGN ESSENTIAL BLEPHAROSPASM

**Benign Essential Blepharospasm Research Foundation, Inc.**            **National**
*170 groups. Founded 1981.* Information and emotional support to persons with benign essential blepharospasm. Networks people together with similar symptoms. Doctor referrals, education. Supports research. Newsletter. Group development guidelines.

B.E.B. Fdn.                    *Phone:* 409-832-0788; *Fax:* 409-832-0890
P.O. Box 12468                *E-mail:* bebrf@ih2000.net
Beaumont, TX 77726-2468       *Website:* http://www.blepharospasm.org

## BERYLLIUM POISONING

🖳 **Beryllium Support Group**                                    **Online**
Support and information for persons exposed to beryllium and who are now having adverse effects. Referrals to support groups.    *Website:* http://www.dimensional.com/~mhj/

## BIOTINIDASE DEFICIENCY /
## MULTIPLE CARBOXYLASE DEFICIENCY
*(Also see Neurological / Neurometabolic)*

🖳 **Biotinidase Deficiency Family Support Group**               **Online**
Listserv for persons with biotinidase deficiency (aka multiple carboxylase deficiency) and their families to share experiences in detecting, managing and living with this rare disorder.
                              *Website:* http://www.geocities.com/
                              biotinidasedeficiency/list_serve.htm

## BLADDER EXSTROPHY

**Association for Bladder Exstrophy Community**          **International network**
*Founded 1991.* Mutual support for persons affected by bladder exstrophy including parents of children with bladder exstrophy, adults, healthcare professionals and others interested in exstrophy. Newsletter, literature, information and referrals, informal pen pal program, conferences, advocacy. Informal kids e-mail exchange. Dues $25/yr.
ABC                           *Phone:* Karen Moseley 910-864-4308
P.O. Box 1472                 *E-mail:* admin@bladderexstrophy.com
Wake Forest, NC 27588-1472    *Website:* http://www.bladderexstrophy.com/

## BLEPHAROPHIMOSIS PTOSIS EPICANTHUS INVERSUS

**BPES Family Network**                                    **National network**
*Founded 1994.* Provides information and support to families affected by blepharophimosis, ptosis, epicanthus inversus. Phone support.
BPES Family Network           *Phone:* 509-332-6628
SE 820 Meadow Vale Dr.        *E-mail:* lschauble@gocougs.wsu.edu
Pullman, WA 99163-2423

*"Trouble shared is trouble halved."*
*- Dorothy L. Sayers*

197

# BONE MARROW / STEM CELL TRANSPLANT
*(Also see specific disorder)*

📑 **Blood and Marrow Transplant Information Network**                    **Resource**
Publishes a newsletter for bone marrow, peripheral stem cell, and cord blood transplant
patients. Also publishes a book on bone marrow and stem cell transplants guide. Has
information about 250+ transplant programs in U.S. and Canada, a resource directory,
attorney referral service, and a patient-to-survivor link service.

BMT Info Net                          *Phone:* 847-433-3313 or 1-888-597-7674
2900 Skokie Valley Rd., # B           *E-mail:* help@bmtinfonet.org
Highland Park, IL 60035               *Website:* http://www.bmtinfonet.org

# BRACHIAL PLEXUS INJURY / ERB'S PALSY

**Brachial Plexus Palsy Foundation, The**                               **International**
*4 affiliated groups. Founded 1994.* Education and support for families affected by brachial
plexus palsy, a condition caused by injury. Information on treatment. Newsletter, phone
support, information and referral. Fund-raising.

Brachial Plexus Palsy Fdn.            *Phone:* 610-792-0974; *Fax:* 610-948-0678
210 Springhaven Circle                *E-mail:* brachial@aol.com
Royersford, PA 19468                  *Website:* http://www.membrane.com/bpp

🖥 **Erb's Place**                                                          **Online**
Provides support, information and networking for persons affected by Erb's palsy (aka
brachial plexus injury). Live chat on Monday evenings. Message board, listserv.

Erb's Place                           *Website:* http://www.delphi.com/nationalbpi
P.O. Box 23
Larsen, WI 54947

# BRAIN TUMOR
*(Also see Cancer, specific disorder)*

**American Brain Tumor Association**                                     **National**
*Founded 1973.* Dedicated to eliminating brain tumors by funding and encouraging research.
Provides free patient education, materials and resource information. Pen pal program,
newsletter, publications, resource listings.

ABTA                                  *Phone:* 847-827-9910 or 1-800-886-2282
2720 River Rd., Suite 146             *Fax:* 847-827-9918; *E-mail:* info@abta.org
Des Plaines, IL 60018                 *Website:* http://www.abta.org

**Brain Tumor Society, The**                                            **National**
*5 affiliated groups. Founded 1989.* Committed to finding a cure for brain tumors through
fund-raising, professional education and patient/family support programs. Sponsors medical
seminars, and disseminates educational materials. Newsletter, resource guide.

Brain Tumor Society                     *Phone:* 1-800-770-8287 or 617-924-9997
124 Watertown St., Suite 3-H            *Fax:* 617-924-9998; *E-mail:* info@tbts.org
Watertown, MA 02472-2500                *Website:* http://www.tbts.org

### Children's Brain Tumor Foundation, Inc.                        National network
*Founded 1988.* Provides support services and educational materials for parents of children
with, and young survivors of, brain tumors. Conferences, literature, advocacy, phone
support, referrals to support groups. Assistance in starting similar support groups.
CBTF                                    *Phone:* 212-448-9494; *Fax:* 212-448-1022
274 Madison Ave., Suite 1301            *E-mail:* cbtf@aol.com
New York, NY 10016                      *Website:* http://www.cbtf.org

### National Brain Tumor Foundation                                       National
*150+ affiliated groups. Founded 1981.* Support and information for persons with brain
tumors. Provides funding for research and client services for patients. Newsletter,
information and referrals, conferences, literature. Assistance in starting and maintaining
support groups.
NBTF                                    *Phone:* 1-800-934-CURE or 510-839-9777
414 13th St., Suite 700                 *E-mail:* NBTF@braintumor.org
Oakland, CA 94612-2603                  *Website:* http://www.braintumor.org

### 🖥  Musella Foundation Virtualtrials                                    Online
Provides emotional support and exchange of information for persons affected by brain
tumors (patients, parents, families, caregivers and professionals). Offers mailing lists,
resources, referrals to support groups, live chats and forums. Newsletter and Daily Brain
Tumor News Blast. Information on clinical trials.
Brain Stem Glioma List                  *Phone:* 516-295-4740
Mesella Foundation                      *Fax:* 516-295-2870
1100 Peninsula Blvd.                     *E-mail:* mesella@aol.com
Hewlett, NY 11557                        *Website:* www.virtualtrials.com/btlinks/list.html

### 🖥  T.H.E. BRAIN TRUST (The Healing Exchange)                          Online
*Founded 1993.* Mission is to create exchange of information and support among people
affected by neurological disorders including patient-survivors, families, parents, teens,
caregivers and health professionals. Online support groups cover a large range of brain
tumors (including brain stem glioma, ependymomam craniopharyngioma, dysembryoplastic
neuro-ectodermal, juvenile pilocytic astrocytoma, meningioma, oligodendroglioma, sand
spinal tumors), focal brain disorders and injuries, and other special interests.
T.H.E. BRAIN TRUST                      *Phone:* 617-876-2002; *Fax:* 617-876-2332
186 Hampshire St.                       *E-mail:* info@braintrust.org
Cambridge, MA 02139-1320                *Website:* http://www.braintrust.org

*"Without a sense of caring, there can be no sense of community."*– Anthony J. D'Angelo

# BUNDLE BRANCH BLOCK
*(Also see Heart)*

**International Bundle Branch Block Association**                    **National network**
*Organized 1979.* Provides support and information to help bundle branch block persons and families cope. Educates the public. Periodic newsletter. Pen pals, informal phone support system. Guidelines and assistance for starting groups. Dues $10 (more for professionals).
Int'l Bundle Branch Block Assn.          *Phone:* R.K. Lewis 310-670-9132
6631 W. 83rd St.
Los Angeles, CA 90045-2875

# CANAVAN DISEASE
*(Also see Leukodystrophy, Tay-Sachs)*

**Canavan Foundation**                                              **International**
*Founded 1992.* Provides information on Canavan disease. Literature, phone support, education, and advocacy. Supports research. Conferences. Online support and chat rooms.
Canavan Foundation                *Phone:* 212-873-4640; *TTY:* 1-877-422-6283
110 Riverside Dr., 4F             *E-mail:* canavandisease@aol.com
New York, NY 10024                *Website:* http://www.canavanfoundation.org

# CANCER
*(Also see specific disorder)*

**Breast Cancer Support / Reach to Recovery Discussion Group**          **National**
Local outgrowth of Reach to Recovery Program which in most areas is a one-to-one visitation program but in some areas is a support group. Contact your chapter of American Cancer Society to determine availability of such groups and trained volunteers.
*Phone:* 1-800-227-2345                *Website:* http://www.cancer.org

**Cancer Care, Inc.**                                               **National**
Mutual support for cancer patients and their families. Financial assistance, information and referrals, community and professional education. On-going telephone and in-person support groups. Free counseling.
Cancer Care, Inc.                 *Phone:* 1-800-813-HOPE; *Fax:* 212-719-0263
275 Seventh Ave.                  *E-mail:* info@cancercare.org
New York, NY 10001                *Website:* http://www.cancercare.org

**Candlelighters Childhood Cancer Foundation**                         **International**
*300+ groups. Founded 1970.* Support for parents of children and adolescents with cancer, their families, adult survivors of childhood cancer, and the professionals working with them. Links parents, families and groups. Psychosocial support, educational materials and advocacy. Newsletter, youth newsletter, educational materials and publication list.

200

Candlelighters                          *Phone:* 1-800-336-2223 or 301-962-3520
P.O. Box 498                            *E-mail:* info@candlelighters.org
Kensington, MD 20895-0498               *Website:* http://www.candlelighters.org

**Colorectal Cancer Network**                                        **National**
*7 affiliated groups.* (Multilingual) Support and advocacy for colorectal cancer survivors, and their caregivers. Peer-to-peer support groups, library of online links and resources. Chat room for survivors and their caregivers, and online clubhouse that provides a peaceful place to spend time online. Website in English, French, German, Italian, Portuguese, and Spanish.
Colorectal Cancer Network               *Phone:* 301-879-1500
P.O. Box 182                            *E-mail:* ccnetwork@colorectal-cancer.net
Kensington, MD 20895-0182               *Website:* http://www.colorectal-cancer.net

**DES Cancer Network**                                               **National**
*Founded 1983.* Mutual support and education for DES-exposed women, with a special focus on DES cancer issues. Provides research, advocacy and medical/legal resources. Newsletter ($25). Annual conferences.
DES Cancer Network                      *Phone:* 1-800-DES-NET-4
P.O. Box 220465                         *E-mail:* desnetwrk@aol.com
Chantilly, VA 20153-0465                *Website:* http://www.descancer.org

**IMPACC (Intestinal Multiple Polyposis**
**And Colorectal Cancer)**                                    **National network**
*Founded 1986.* Support network to help patients and families dealing with familial polyposis and hereditary colon cancer. Information and referrals, encourages research, and educates professionals and public. Phone support, correspondence, and literature.
IMPACC                                  *Phone:* Ann Fagan 570-788-1818 (day) or
P.O. Box 11                             570-788-3712 (eve); *Fax:* 570-788-4046
Conyngham, PA 18219                     *E-mail:* impacc@epix.net

**Kids Konnected**                                                   **National**
*18 affiliated groups. Founded 1993.* Connects children who have a parent with cancer with other children in similar situations for support and understanding. Groups are headed by youth leaders and co-facilitated by professionals. Hotline, Youth Leadership program, monthly meetings, information and referrals, newsletter, summer camps.
Kids Konnected                          *Phone:* 1-800-899-2866 or 949-582-5443
27071 Cabot Rd., Suite 102              *E-mail:* info@kidskonnected.org
Laguna Hills, CA 92653                  *Website:* http://www.kidskonnected.org

**Kidney Cancer Association**                                        **National**
*Founded 1990.* Provides information about kidney cancer to patients and doctors. Sponsors research, and advocates on behalf of patients with government and insurance companies. Newsletter, information and referrals, literature, conferences.

Kidney Cancer Assn.                 *Phone:* 1-800-850-9132 or 847-332-1051
1234 Sherman, Suite 203             *Fax:* 847-332-2978; *E-mail:* office@nkca.org
Evanston, IL 60202                  *Website:* http://www.kidneycancerassociation.org

**Leukemia and Lymphoma Society**                                      **National**
*58 affiliated groups. Founded 1949.* Mutual support for patients, families and friends
coping with leukemia, lymphoma, multiple myeloma and Hodgkin's disease. Support group
meetings held monthly.              *Phone:* 1-800-955-4572 or 212-450-8834
LLS                                 *Fax:* 914-821-8834
1311 Mamoroneck Ave., 3rd fl.       *E-mail:* jacobic@leukemia-lymphoma.org
White Plains, NY 10605              *Website:* http://www.leukemia-lymphoma.org

**Lymphoma Research Foundation of America**                            **National**
*Founded 1991.* Provides emotional support for lymphoma patients and their families. Offers
educational materials, lymphoma helpline, national "Cell-Mates" buddy program linking
patients. Quarterly newsletter, support/networking groups, and annual patient educational
forum and local seminars. Fund-raises for research.
Lymphoma Research Fdn. of Amer.     *Phone:* 310-204-7040; *Fax:* 310-204-7043
8800 Venice Blvd., Suite 207        *E-mail:* LRFA@lymphoma.org
Los Angeles, CA 90034               *Website:* http://www.lymphoma.org

**Man To Man Program**                                                 **National**
*300 affiliated groups. Founded 1990.* Support and education for men with prostate cancer to
enable them to better understand their options and to make informed decisions. Phone
support, information and referrals, support group meetings, education and support visitation
program, newsletter. Some chapters invite wives and partners for some meetings. Assistance
available for starting new groups.  *Phone:* 1-800-ACS-2345
                                    *Website:* http://www.cancer.org

**National Carcinoid Support Group**                               **National network**
*Founded 1994.* Peer-to-peer support through networking with others who have carcinoid, a
rare form of cancer. Literature, quarterly newsletter. Monthly conference call between
interested members. Periodic national conferences.
Nat'l Carcinoid Support Group       *E-mail:* jean@mick.com
PMB 146, 6666 Odana Rd.             *Website:* http://members.aol.com/thencsg
Madison, WI 53719-1012

**National Coalition for Cancer Survivorship**                     **National network**
*Founded 1986.* Grassroots network that works on behalf of persons with any type of cancer.
Mission is to ensure quality cancer care for all Americans by leading and strengthening the
survivorship movement, empowering cancer survivors, and advocating for policy issues
affecting survivor's quality of life. Information on employment and insurance issues,
referrals, and publications. Newsletter.

NCCS                                      *Phone:* 1-877-NCCS-YES
1010 Wayne Ave., 7th floor                *Fax:* 301-565-9670; *E-mail:* info@cansearch.org
Silver Spring, MD 20910                   *Website:* http://www.cansearch.org

**National Ovarian Cancer Coalition**                                    **National**
*40 affiliated divisions. Founded 1995.* Promotes education and awareness re: ovarian cancer
for patients, families, and medical community. Information and referrals, networking,
conferences, literature, and phone support.
Nat'l Ovarian Cancer Coalition            *Phone:* 1-888-OVARIAN or 561-393-0005
500 NE Spanish River Blvd., #14           *Fax:* 561-393-7275; *E-mail:* nocc@ovarian.org
Boca Raton, FL 33431                      *Website:* http://www.ovarian.org

**PAACT (Patient Advocates for Advanced Cancer Treatment)**         **International**
*150 affiliated groups. Founded 1984.* Provides support and advocacy for prostate cancer
patients, their families and the general public at risk. Offers information relative to the
advancements in the detection, diagnosis, evaluation and treatment of prostate cancer.
Information, referrals, phone help, conferences, newsletters. Group development guidelines.
Legal action committee available to help patients with insurance problems.
PAACT                                     *Phone:* 616-453-1477; *Fax:* 616-453-1846
P.O. Box 141695                           *E-mail:* paact@paactusa.org
Grand Rapids, MI 49514-1695               *Website:* http://www.paactusa.org

**Side By Side**                                                          **National**
(Sponsored by the American Cancer Society) Mutual support for wives and partners of men
with prostate cancer. Information and referrals, support group meetings.
*Phone:* 1-800-ACS-2345                    *Website:* http://www.cancer.org

**Sisters Network Inc.**                                                  **National**
*35 affiliated chapters. Founded 1994.* An African-American breast cancer survivor
organization that offers support, education, advocacy, outreach, training and research.
Newsletter, information and referrals, groups, phone support, conferences. Assistance in
starting new groups.                      *Phone:* 1-866-781-1808 or 713-781-0255
SNI                                       *Fax:* 713-780-8998
8787 Woodway Dr., Suite 4206              *E-mail:* sistercentral@aol.com
Houston, TX 77063                         *Website:* http://www.sistersnetworkinc.org/

**SPOHNC (Support for People with Oral and Head and Neck Cancer)**     **National**
*13 affiliated groups. Founded 1991.* Patient-directed self-help program offering
encouragement, support, acceptance and self-expression for persons with oral and head and
neck cancer. Group meetings, phone support, education, newsletter, one-on-one support,
information and referrals. Assistance in starting groups. Dues $20 (includes newsletter).
SPOHNC                                    *Phone:* 1-800-377-0928
P.O. Box 53                               *E-mail:* NLeupold@spohnc.org
Locust Valley, NY 11560-0053             *Website:* http://www.spohnc.org

**US TOO International, Inc.**                                    **International**
*500+ affiliated groups. Founded 1990.* Mutual support, information and education for prostate cancer patients, their families and friends. Provides newsletter, information, phone support, assistance in starting new groups. Some groups have separate groups for partners of prostate cancer victims.

| | |
|---|---|
| US TOO! Int'l, Inc. | *Phone:* 1-800-80-US-TOO or 630-795-1002 |
| 5003 Fairview Ave. | *Fax:* 630-795-1602; *E-mail:* ustoo@ustoo.com |
| Downers Grove, IL 60515-5286 | *Website:* http://www.ustoo.com |

**Y-ME National Breast Cancer Organization**                      **National**
*Affiliates across the country. Founded 1978.* (Bilingual) Mission is to decrease the impact of breast cancer, create and increase breast cancer awareness, and ensure through information, empowerment and peer support that no one faces breast cancer alone. Information and peer support for breast cancer patients and their families during all stages of the disease. Offers 24-hour hotlines (English and Spanish), a Latino Outreach program, a Men's Match program for husbands and partners of women with breast cancer, support groups, a Teen Education program, and Advocacy Network promoting increases in funding for research, publications, wig and prosthesis bank and newsletter.

| | |
|---|---|
| Y-ME | *Phone:* 1-800-221-2141 |
| 212 W. Van Buren St. | *Spanish:* 1-800-986-9505; *Fax:* 312-294-8598 |
| Chicago, IL 60607-3908 | *Website:* http://www.y-me.org/ |

**African American Breast Cancer Alliance**                       **Model**
*1 group in Minnesota. Founded 1990.* Support and advocacy for Black women with breast cancer, and their families. Provides information and referrals, education, newsletter, and a forum for women to discuss issues and concerns.

| | |
|---|---|
| AABCA | *Phone:* 612-825-3675 |
| P.O. Box 8981 | *E-mail:* aabcainc@yahoo.com |
| Minneapolis, MN 55408 | *Website:* http://geocities.com/aabcainc/ |

**Mothers Supporting Daughters with Breast Cancer**              **Model**
*Founded 1995.* Offers emotional support to the mothers of daughters newly diagnosed with breast cancer to help them to be better "care partners" to their daughters. Helps mothers cope with stress, learn about breast cancer treatment, and promote breast cancer awareness. Literature, advocacy, phone support. Online message board.

| | |
|---|---|
| MSDBC | *Phone:* 410-778-1982; *Fax:* 410-778-1411 |
| c/o Charmayne Dierker | *E-mail:* msdbc@dmv.com |
| 21710 Bayshore Rd. | *E-mail:* lilliepie@aol.com |
| Chestertown, MD 21620 | *Website:* http://www.mothersdaughters.org |

**Mary-Helen Mautner Project for Lesbians with Cancer**          **Model**
*Several groups in Washington, DC. Founded 1990.* Mutual support for lesbians with cancer, their partners, and caregivers. Helps educate health professionals about working with lesbians with cancer. Educates the lesbian community about risks of cancer and prevention

issues. Information and referrals, phone support, literature, newsletter, advocacy. Guidelines for starting similar groups ($10).

| | |
|---|---|
| Mautner Project for Lesbians | *Phone:* 202-332-5536 (Voice/TDD) |
| with Cancer | *Fax:* 202-332-0662 |
| 1707 L St., Suite 500 | *E-mail:* mautner@mautnerproject.org |
| Washington, DC 20036 | *Website:* http://www.mautnerproject.org |

### People Living Through Cancer                                            Model
*35 groups in New Mexico. Founded 1983.* Helps cancer survivors and their loved ones make informed choices and improve the quality of life by sharing in a community of people who have "been there." Newsletter, information and referrals, support groups, advocacy. Dues $25/yr. Training for American Indians and Alaskan natives who are interested in developing cancer survivor programs based on a grassroots program serving Pueblo Indians.

| | |
|---|---|
| People Living Through Cancer | *Phone:* 505-242-3263; *Fax:* 505-242-6756 |
| 323 Eighth St. SW | *E-mail:* pltc@pltc.org |
| Albuquerque, NM 87102 | *Website:* http://www.pltc.org |

### SHARE: Self-Help for Women with Breast or Ovarian Cancer                Model
*18 sites in NY Metro Area. Founded 1976.* (Bilingual) Support for women faced with the emotional and social problems of breast or ovarian cancer, their families and friends. Groups led by trained leaders who have had breast or ovarian cancer. Educational programs, newsletter, and phone support.

| | |
|---|---|
| | *Phone:* 1-866-891-2392 or 212-719-0364 |
| SHARE | *Breast Hotline:* 212-382-2111 |
| 1501 Broadway, Suite 1720 | *Ovarian Hotline:* 212-719-1204 |
| New York, NY 10036 | *Spanish:* 212-719-4454 |
| | *Website:* http://www.sharecancersupport.org |

### 🖳 ACOR (Association of Cancer Online Resources)                        Online
Provides over 70 online discussion groups related to different cancers (e.g. adenocarcinoma, bladder, colon, esophageal, head/neck, hematological, liver, lung, lymphedema, melanoma, Peutz-Jeghers syndrome, neuroblastoma, lymphoma, pancreatic, pediatric, sarcomas, testicular, thyroid, etc). Also has contacts for persons with rare cancers, and for caregivers.

| | |
|---|---|
| ACOR | *Phone:* 212-226-5525 |
| 173 Duane St., 3rd fl. | *Fax:* 212-219-3109 |
| New York, NY 10013-3334 | *Website:* http://www.acor.org |

### 🖳 FORCE (Facing Our Risk of Cancer Empowered)                          Online
*Founded 1999.* Support and education for women whose family history and genetic status put them at high risk of getting ovarian or breast cancer, and their families. Provides resources for women to determine if they are at high risk. Forums, chats, bulletin boards, member profiles. Telephone support network.

| | |
|---|---|
| FORCE | *Phone:* Sue Friedman 954-255-8732 |
| 934 N. University Dr., PMB #213 | *-mail:* info@facingourrisk.org |
| Coral Springs, FL 33071 | *Website:* http://www.facingourrisk.org/ |

⬛ **Johns Hopkins Cancer Websites**                                        **Online**
Provides information and support to cancer patients and their families through disease-specific message boards. Cancers include: colon, pancreatic, ovarian, gallbladder and bile duct. Also has message board for Barrett's esophagus.

*Website:* http://www.path.jhu.edu

⬛ **MaleBC**                                                                **Online**
*Founded 1997.* Brings men together who have been diagnosed with male breast cancer so they can share experiences, gain information and support each other. Once on website, click on "Mailing List" and scroll down to "MaleBC")

*Website:* http://www.acor.org

⬛ **ThyCa Support**                                                         **Online**
Support for thyroid cancer survivors. Local group information. Offers mutual support and sharing of information. Provides assistance in starting local groups.

Website: http://www.thyca.org

⬛ **Warmnet**                                                              **Online**
Support and information discussion group for cancer patients, their families and friends. Initiated and run by cancer patients and caregivers. Provides an alternative for those who are unable to attend support groups, or who enjoy communicating at their convenience from home with other people "who have been there." To subscribe send an e-mail with "subscribe warmnet" in the body.          *E-mail:* warmnet-equest@maillist.mdacc.tmc.edu

## CARDIO-FACIO-CUTANEOUS SYNDROME

**CFC Family Network, Inc.**                                    **International network**
*Founded 1991.* Mutual support for parents of children with cardio-facio-cutaneous syndrome. Strives to find and disseminate information on CFC syndrome. Offers newsletter, information and referrals, phone support. Medical advisors. Conferences. Listserv.

CFC Family Network                  *Phone:* Brenda Conger 607-772-9666 (eve)
183 Brown Rd.                       *E-mail:* cliffordiv@juno.com
Vestal, NJ 13850                    *Website:* http://www.cfcsyndrome.org

## CARPAL TUNNEL SYNDROME /
## REPETITIVE MOTION INJURY
*(Also see Pain)*

**ARMS (Association for Repetitive Motion Syndromes)**             **National network**
*Founded 1990.* To support, educate, and protect persons with carpal tunnel syndrome and related repetitive motion injuries. Advocates for prevention of CTS for persons at risk. Newsletter, information. Dues $20-$150.

ARMS
P.O. Box 471973
Aurora, CO 80047

*Phone:* 303-369-0803 (day)
*Website:* http://www.certifiedpst.com/arms

## CELIAC SPRUE / GLUTEN INTOLERANCE
## DERMATITIS HERPETIFORMIS

**American Celiac Society / Dietary Support Coalition**                    National
*66 affiliated chapters. Founded 1976.* Mutual support and information for celiac-sprue patients, families and health care professionals. Buddy system, visitation, phone help system, participation in educational efforts. Also supports dermatitis herpetiformis and Crohn's disease. Newsletter.         *Phone:* Annette Bentley 973-325-8837
American Celiac Society                  *Fax:* 973-669-8808
59 Crystal Ave.                          *E-mail:* AmerCeliacSoc@netscape.net
W. Orange, NJ 07052

**Celiac Disease Foundation**                                              National
*10 affiliated groups. Founded 1990.* (Bilingual) Creates awareness and provides services and support for patients and professionals seeking information about celiac disease/dermatitis herpetiformis. Free information packets, some in Spanish. Quarterly newsletter included with annual membership.
Celiac Disease Foundation               *Phone:* 818-990-2354; *Fax:* 818-990-2379
13251 Ventura Blvd., Suite 1            *E-mail:* cdf@celiac.org
Studio City, CA 91604                   *Website:* http://celiac.org

**Celiac Sprue Association/United States of America, Inc.**                National
*85 chapters and 46 resource units. Founded 1969.* Provides educational materials on celiac sprue, dermatitis herpetiformis and basics for the gluten-free diet to patients, parents of children and professionals. Provides opportunities for support groups and networking with patients and professionals. Newsletter, annual conference. Group development guidelines.
Celiac Sprue Assn. USA                  *Phone:* (402)558-0600; *Fax:* (402)558-1347
P.O. Box 31700                          *E-mail:* dianecsa@aol.com; celiacs@csaceliacs.org
Omaha, NE 68131-0700                    *Website:* http://www.csaceliacs.org

**Gluten Intolerance Group of North America**                    National network
*Founded 1974.* Provides information and support to persons with gluten intolerance, celiac disease or dermatitis herpetiformis, their families and health care professionals. Newsletter ($30), information and referral, conferences, group development guidelines, cookbooks.
Gluten Intolerance Group                *Phone:* 206-246-6652
   of North America                     *Fax:* 206-246-6531
15110 10th Ave. SW, Suite A            *E-mail:* gig@gluten.net
Seattle, WA 98166-1820                 *Website:* http://www.gluten.net

**ROCK (Raising Our Celiac Kids)**                                    **National**
*23 affiliated chapters. Founded 1991.* Support for parents of children on a gluten-free diet. Pen pals, newsletter, phone support, information and referrals, literature, conferences. Assistance in starting local groups. Local parties for the kids. Listserv.

ROCK                                    *Phone:* 858-758-8144; *Fax:* 858-756-0431
3527 Fortuna Ranch Rd.                  *E-mail:* danna@celiackids.com
Encinitas, CA 92024                     *Website:* http://www.celiackids.com

## CEREBELLAR HYPOPLASIA

**⌨ Children with Cerebellar Hypoplasia**                              **Online**
Mutual support for parents, grandparents, siblings, etc. of children with cerebellar hypoplasia and other similar conditions. Helps families better understand the condition and battle for better health care. Member directory, message board.

*Website:* http://www0.delphi.com/cerebellar

## CEREBROCOSTOMANDIBULAR SYNDROME

**Cerebrocostomandibular Syndrome Support Group**          **National network**
*Founded 1998.* Provides support and guidance to families of children with cerebrocostomandibular syndrome (recessed lower mandible and rib anomalies). Exchange of messages through e-mail. Participates in research study. Newsletter.

Tara Montague                           *Phone:* 609-239-7831; *Fax:* 609-239-6916
63 Stirrup Way                          *E-mail:* tmontague@home.com
Burlington, NJ 08016                    *Website:* http://www.members.home.net/tmontague

## CHARGE SYNDROME

**CHARGE Syndrome Foundation, Inc.**                        **National network**
*Founded 1993.* Network of families affected by CHARGE syndrome (Coloboma of the eye; Heart malformations; Atresia of the nasal passages; Retardation of growth and/or development' Genital hypoplasia; Ear malformations). Offers organization manual for parents, newsletter, information, and parent-to-parent support. Biannual international conferences. Dues $15-30.

CHARGE Syndrome Fdn., Inc.              *Phone:* 573-499-4694
c/o Marion N. Norbury                   *Phone:* 1-800-442-7604 (families only)
2004 Parkade                            *E-mail:* marion@chargesyndrome.org
Columbia, MO 65202                      *Website:* http://www.chargesyndrome.org

*"It is one of the most beautiful compensations of this life
that no man can seriously help another without helping himself."– C.D. Warner*

# CHARCOT-MARIE-TOOTH DISEASE / PERONEAL MUSCULAR ATROPHY / HEREDITARY MOTOR SENSORY NEUROPATHY

**Charcot Marie Tooth Association**                         **National**
*25 affiliated groups. Founded 1983.* Information and support for patients and families affected by Charcot-Marie-Tooth disorders (also known as peroneal muscular atrophy or hereditary motor sensory neuropathy). Referrals, newsletter, phone help, VCR tapes, support groups, conferences.     *Phone:* Pat Dreibelbis 1-800-606-2682 or
CMT Assn.                            610-499-9264
2700 Chestnut Parkway                *Fax:* 610-499-9267
Chester, PA 19013                    *E-mail:* cmtassoc@aol.com

**C.M.T. International**                         **International network**
*2000+ members. Founded 1984.* Sharing and caring for those with Charcot-Marie-Tooth disease (also known as peroneal muscular atrophy or hereditary motor and sensory neuropathy). Information for patients and professionals. Newsletter, publications.
CMT Int'l                            *Phone:* 905-687-3630;
One Springbank Dr.                   *E-mail:* cmtint@vaxxine.com
St. Catharines, Ontario L2S 2K1      *Website:* http://www.cmtint.org
Canada                               *Website:* http://www.charcot-marie-tooth.org

## CHEMICAL SENSITIVITY
*(Also see Environmental Issues)*

**HEAL (Human Ecology Action League, Inc.)**                  **National**
*60+ chapters. Founded 1977.* Education and information for persons concerned about the health effects of environmental exposures. Newsletter. Other publications include information sheets, resource list, directories, and book Fragrance and Health. Referrals to local and regional chapters and support services. Dues $26 (US); $32 (Canada); $36 (Int'l).
HEAL                                 *Phone:* 404-248-1898
P.O. Box 29629                       *Website:* http://members.aol.com/HEALNatnl/
Atlanta, GA 30359                    index.com

**National Center for Environmental Health Strategies**        **National network**
*Founded 1986.* Fosters the development of creative solutions to environmental health problems with a focus on indoor air quality, chemical sensitivities and environmental disabilities. Clearinghouse and technical services, educational materials, workshops, community outreach, policy development, research, support and advocacy for persons injured by chemical/environmental exposures. Special projects on school-related exposures and Gulf War Veterans. Books and publications, newsletter. Focus on access and accommodation rights.

NCEHS                          *Phone:* Mary Lamielle 856-429-5358
1100 Rural Ave.                *E-mail:* mary@ncehs.org
Voorhees, NJ 08043             *Website:* http://www.ncehs.org

# CHROMOSOME 16 DISORDER
*(Also see Chromosome Disorders General)*

**Disorders of Chromosome 16 Foundation**          **International network**
*Founded 1998.* Provides support and information to families of children affected by any chromosome 16 disorder, including partial trisomy 16 and unbalanced translocations. Information and referrals, phone support, literature.
DOC16                          *Phone:* Karen Lange 847-816-0627
331 Haddon Circle              *Fax:* 847-367-4631; *E-mail:* kblange1@aol.com
Vernon Hills, IL 60061         *Website:* http://trisomy16.org

# CHROMOSOME 18 DISORDER
*(Also see Chromosome Disorders General)*

**Chromosome 18 Registry and Research Society**          **International network**
*Founded 1990.* Provides support and education concerning disorders of chromosome 18. Encourages and conducts research. Links affected families and their physicians to the research community. Newsletter, phone support, information and referrals, annual conference, listservs, and Parent Network. Dues $20/US; Int'l/$25.
Chromosome 18 Reg. & Res. Soc.    *Phone:* Jannine Cody 210-657-4968 (Voice/Fax)
6302 Fox Head                     *E-mail:* office@chromosome18.org
San Antonio, TX 78247             *Website:* http://www.chromosome18.org

# CHROMOSOME DISORDERS (GENERAL)
*(Also see specific disorder)*

**Chromosome 22 Central**          **International network**
*Founded 1996.* Networking and support for parents of children with any chromosome disorder. Supports research. Literature, phone support, newsletter and pen pals. Online bulletin boards.
Chromosome 22 Central          *Phone:* 705-268-3099 (Voice/Fax)
2327 Kent Ave.
Timmins, ON, Canada P4N 3C2

**Chromosome Deletion Outreach**          **National network**
*Founded 1992.* Provides support and information for families having a child diagnosed with any type of rare chromosome disorder.
CDO                            *Phone:* 1-888-CDO-6880 or 561-391-5098
P.O. Box 724                   *E-mail:* cdo@worldnet.att.net
Boca Raton, FL 33429-0724      *Website:* http://chromodisorder.org

**National Center for Chromosome Inversions**                    **National network**
Mutual support for families affected by chromosome inversions. Information and referrals,
phone support, pen pal program.
Nat'l Ctr .for Chromosome Inversions    *Phone:* 515-287-6798 (Voice/Fax)
1029 Johnson St.                        *E-mail:* ncfci@msn.com
Des Moines, IA 50315                    *Website:* http://www.barkersnet.com/NCFCI

## CHRONIC FATIGUE SYNDROME

**CFIDS Association, Inc.**                                            **National**
*Founded 1987.* Advocacy, information and encouragement for persons with chronic fatigue
immune dysfunction syndrome. Newsletter ($35/US; $45/Canada; $60/Overseas).
CFIDS Assn., Inc.                       *Phone:* 704-365-2343  or 1-800-442-3437
P.O. Box 220398                         *Fax:* 704-365-9755; *E-mail:* cfids@cfids.org
Tucson, AZ 28222-0398                   *Website:* http://www.cfids.org

**Fibromyalgia Network**                                              **National**
*Founded 1988.* Provides information on fibromyalgia and chronic fatigue syndrome.
Referrals to support groups, health care professionals, and other services. Newsletter, phone
support, information and referrals, conferences. Assistance in starting new groups.
Fibromyalgia Network                    *Phone:* 1-800-853-2929
P.O. Box 31750                          *E-mail:* fmnetter@msn.com
Tucson, AZ 85751-1750                   *Website:* http://www.fmnetnews.com

**National Chronic Fatigue Syndrome**
**and Fibromyalgia Association, Inc.**                            **International**
*2 affiliated groups and contacts worldwide. Founded 1985.* To educate patients, the public,
and the medical professional about chronic fatigue syndrome and fibromyalgia. Support
groups, periodic newsletter, funds research, conducts seminars. Literature available for
patients and physicians. Guidelines and assistance available for starting support groups.
Nat'l CFS & Fibromyalgia Assn.          *Phone:* (816)313-2000 (24 hr. hotline)
P.O. Box 18426                          *Fax:* 816-524-6782; *E-mail:* info@ncfsfa.org
Kansas City, MO 64133                   *Website:* http://www.ncfsfa.org

## CHURG-STRAUSS SYNDROME
*(Also see Immune Disorders)*

**Churg-Strauss Syndrome International Support Group**      **International network**
*Founded 1997.* Support and information for persons with Churg-Strauss syndrome, their
families, and health professionals. Information, referrals, phone support and pen pals.
Churg-Strauss Syndrome Int'l            *Phone:* 904-824-1083
2 St. Andrew's Court
St. Augustine, FL 32084

⌨ **A Savvy Vasculitis: the Med'zine for Contact, Information, Opinion**   **Online**
*Founded 1998.* Connects persons affected by Churg-Strauss, PAN, and other rare systemic autoimmune illnesses for support and exchange of information. Members exchange messages by a web-based mailing list.   *Website:* http://www.blackandwhite.org/savvy or http://groups.yahoo.com/group/savvy (to subscribe)

# CLEFT PALATE
*(Also see Facial Disfigurement)*

**Cleft Palate Foundation**                                          **National network**
*Founded 1973.* Information and referrals to individuals with cleft lip and palate or other craniofacial anomalies. Referrals to local cleft palate/craniofacial teams for treatment and parent support groups. Free information on clefting for parents and individuals.

Cleft Palate Fdn.                         *Phone:* 1-800-24-CLEFT or 919-933-9044
104 S. Estes Dr., Suite 204               *E-mail:* cleftline@aol.com
Chapel Hill, NC 27514                     *Website:* http://www.cleftline.org

**Prescription Parents, Inc.**                                            **Model**
*1 group in Massachusetts. Founded 1973.* Support group for families of children with cleft lip and palate. Education for parents of newborns, presentations by professionals. Family social events, phone support network, group development guidelines.

Prescription Parents, Inc.                *Phone:* Amy Kapinos 781-31-1398
45 Brentwood Cir.                         *Website:* http://www.samizdat.com/#cleft
Needham, MA 02492

⌨ **CLEFT-TALK**                                                          **Online**
Support, inspiration, information and networking for families dealing with the challenges associated with clefting. Sharing of struggles, joys and triumphs. Referrals to doctors.

Wide Smiles                               *Phone:* 209-942-2812
P.O. Box 5153                             *Fax:* 209-464-1497
Stockton, CA 95205-0153                   *Website:* http://www.widesmiles.org

# CLUBFOOT

⌨ **Clubfoot Mailing List**                                              **Online**
Support group for parents of children with clubfoot/feet, persons with clubfoot/feet, or any needing support on this topic. Operates through an e-mail mailing list.
                              *Website:* http://groups.yahoo.com/group/Clubfoot/

*"The only journey of knowledge is from the depth of one being to the heart of another."*
*— Norman Mailer*

## COBALAMIN METABOLISM, INBORN ERRORS OF
*(Also see Metabolic Disorders)*

**The Cobalamin Network**                                  **International network**
*Founded 1985.* Emotional support and information for families of children affected by inborn errors of cobalamin metabolism. Referrals to pediatric metabolic practitioners.

Cobalamin Network                              Cobalamin Network
P.O. Box 174                                   207 E. 14th Pl.
Thetford Center, VT 05075                      Cut Off, LA 70345
*Phone:* 802-785-4029; 802-785-3112    *Phone:* 504-798-5631 or 504-798-7928
*E-mail:* SueBee18@valley.net           *E-mail:* menta@cajunnet.com

## COCKAYNE SYNDROME / CACHECTIC DWARFISM
*(Also see Growth Disorders)*

**Share and Care Cockayne Syndrome Network**              **International network**
*Founded 1981.* (Bilingual)   Mutual support and networking for families affected by Cockayne syndrome (cachectic dwarfism). Sharing of information between families and professionals. Maintains registry of families. Information and referrals, newsletter, phone support. Pamphlet available in English, Spanish and Japanese.

Share and Care Cockayne Network     *Phone:* 1-866-262-2963 or 972-613-6273
P.O. Box 570618                     *E-mail:* J93082@aol.com
Dallas, TX 75357                    *Website:* http://www.cockayne-syndrome.com

## COFFIN-LOWRY SYNDROME

**The Coffin-Lowry Syndrome Foundation**                  **International network**
*Founded 1991.* Clearinghouse for information on Coffin-Lowry syndrome. Forum for exchanging experiences, advice and information with other CLS families. Seeks to become a visible group in the medical, scientific, educational, and professional communities in order to facilitate referrals of newly diagnosed individuals, and to encourage medical and behavioral research in order to improve methods of social integration of CLS individuals. Mailing list of families and professionals. Newsletter, family support, informational packet.

The CLS Fdn.                        *Phone:* Mary Hoffman 425-427-0939 (eve)
3045 255th Ave., S.E.               *E-mail:* clsfoundation@yahoo.com
Sammamish, WA 98075                 *Website:* http://www.clsfoundation.tripod.com/

## COGAN'S SYNDROME

**Cogan's Contact Network**                                        **National network**
*Founded 1989.* Support and sharing of experiences and strategies for persons with Cogan's syndrome. Helps people this rare disorder that affects hearing, eyes, balance, etc. Networking, pen pals, literature. Online dues $10/yr. Written membership $20/yr.

YUPPA/Cogan's Contact
P.O. Box 145
Freehold, NJ 07728-0145

*Phone:* Anthony 732-761-9809 (TDD/Fax)
*E-mail:* uscogans@juno.com

## COHEN SYNDROME / PEPPER SYNDROME

**Cohen Syndrome Support Group**      **International network**
*Founded 1996.* Information and support for families of children with Cohen syndrome (aka Pepper syndrome), a rare, genetic disorder. Parent-to-parent networking, information, newsletter and booklet.

Cohen Syndrome Support Group
7 Woods Court
Brackley, Northants
England NN13 6HP
*Phone:* (01280)704515

Cohen Syndrome Support Group
30 Stony Corners Rd.
East Montpelier, VT 05651
*Phone:* Mary Tousignant 802-223-7251
*E-mail:* granimp@sover.net

## CONGENITAL ADRENAL HYPERPLASIA
*(Also see Adrenal Disorders)*

**CARES Foundation**      **International**
*Founded 2001.* Aim is to educate the public and professionals about all types of congenital adrenal hyperplasia including symptoms, treatment, diagnosis, and early intervention through newborn screening. Offers information and support to affected individuals and their families.

CARES Fdn.
P.O. Box 264
Short Hills, NJ 07078

*Phone:* 1-866-227-3737 or 973-912-3895
*E-mail:* Kelly@caresfoundation.org
*Website:* http://www.caresfoundation.org

**Congenital Adrenal Hyperplasia**      **National network**
*Founded 1989.* (Division of MAGIC Foundation). Offers educational and emotional support to families of children with congenital adrenal hyperplasia. Provides information and referrals, kids program, phone support, annual convention, networking. Quarterly newsletter. Assistance in starting new groups.

CAH Div. of MAGIC Fdn.
c/o Mary Andrews
1327 N. Harlem Ave.
Oak Park, IL 60302

*Phone:* Mary Andrews 1-800-362-4423
*Fax:* 708-383-0899
*E-mail:* mary@magicfoundation.org
*Website:* http://www.magicfoundation.org

## CONGENITAL CENTRAL HYPOVENTILATION / ONDINE'S CURSE

**CCHS Network**      **International network**
*Founded 1990.* Mutual support for families caring for a child who has congenital central

hypoventilation syndrome (aka Ondine's curse). Provides family newsletter, physician directory, phone support, equipment information, information and referrals. Facilitates and supports CCHS research. Holds family educational conferences every three years.

CCHS Network
c/o Mary Vanderlaan
71 Maple St.
Oneonta, NY 13820

*Phone:* (607)432-8872
*Fax:* (607)431-4351
*E-mail:* vanderlaanm@hartwick.edu
*Website:* http://www.cchsnetwork.org

## CONGENITAL CYTOMEGALOVIRUS DISEASE

**National Congenital Cytomegalovirus Disease Registry**          **National network**
*Founded 1990.* Parent support network that provides support to families of children with congenital cytomegalovirus disease (CMV). Information and referrals, newsletter, literature.

Nat'l Congenital CMV Dis. Reg.
c/o Feigin Ctr.
Suite 1150, MC3-2371
Houston, TX 77030-2399

*Phone:* Carol Griesser, RN 832-824-4387
*Fax:* 832-825-4347
*E-mail:* cmv@bcm.tmc.edu
*Website:* http://www.bcm.tmc.edu/pedi/infect/cmv

## CONGENITAL DISORDERS OF GLYCOSYLATION
*(Also see Metabolic Disorders)*

**CDG Family Network Foundation**                           **International network**
*Founded 1996.* Support for parents of children diagnosed with congenital disorders of glycosylation, an inherited metabolic disease affecting all body parts, especially the central and peripheral nervous systems. Support is attained primarily online, but the group also provides information and referrals, bi-annual newsletter, phone support, and advocacy. Bulletin board for families to interact with questions, comments and updates.

CDG Family Network Fdn.
10238 N. Bellview Rd.
Orangeville, IL 61060

*Phone:* Debbie Hahn 815-789-4744
*E-mail:* tyland88@aeroinc.net
*Website:* http://www.cdgs.com

## CONGENITAL PULMONARY LYMPHANGIECTASIA

**National Congenital Pulmonary Lymphangiectasia Foundation**      **National network**
*Founded 1995.* Provides support and information for families and friends of persons with congenital pulmonary lymphangiectasia. Funds research projects. Information and referrals, phone support, pen pals, literature.

Nat'l CPL Fdn.
1202 S. Columbia Ave.
Somerset, PA 15501-9387

*Phone:* 814-445-3686

*"No one, professional or amateur, should underestimate the immense fund of goodness, knowledge and resourcefulness possessed by ordinary parents."*– Clara Clairborne Park

215

# CONJOINED TWINS

**Conjoined Twins International**                          **International network**
*Founded 1996.* Support for conjoined twins, their families, and professionals. Offers peer support, professional counseling, crisis intervention, telephone helpline, pen pal network, videos. Information and referrals. Peer counseling speakers bureau. Registry of affected families. Quarterly newsletter. Membership directory.
Conjoined Twins Int'l            *Phone:* (520)445-2777
P.O. Box 10895                   *E-mail:* dwdegeraty@myexcel.com
Prescott, AZ 86304-0895

# CORNELIA DE LANGE SYNDROME

**Cornelia de Lange Syndrome Foundation, Inc.**                          **National**
*2500+ member families. Founded 1981.* Provides support and education to families affected by Cornelia de Lange syndrome. Supports research. Newsletter. Family album available for networking and mutual support. Annual convention. Professional network. Assistance in starting groups.                    *Phone:* 1-800-223-8355 or 860-676-8166
Cornelia de Lange Syndrome Fdn.  *Fax:* 860-676-8337
302 West Main St., Suite 100     *E-mail:* info@cdlsusa.org
Avon, CT 06001                   *Website:* http://www.cdlsusa.org

# CORTICOBASAL GANGLIONIC DEGENERATION
*(Also see Neurological Disorders)*

**CBGD Support Network**                          **International network**
*Founded 1998.* Emotional support and networking for families and caregivers of persons with corticobasal ganglionic degeneration (a rare neurological disorder characterized by cell loss in the brain). Offers education, information and newsletter.
CBGD Support Network             *Phone:* 562-596-5181
c/o Theresa Roberts              *E-mail:* trobertsz@aol.com or to subscribe
1941 Stevely Ave.                cbdg_support-subscribe@yahoogroups.com
Long Beach, CA 90815             *Website:* groups.yahoo.com/group/cbdg_support

# COSTELLO SYNDROME

**International Costello Syndrome Support Group**                          **International network**
*Founded 1996.* Support for parents of children with Costello syndrome. Information and referrals, literature, phone support, pen pals, online chat room, newsletter.
Colin and Cath Stone             *Phone:* 44(0)161-682-2479
90 Parkfield Rd. North           *E-mail:* bigred@costellokids.co.uk
New Moston, Manchester           *Website:* http://costellokids.co.uk
M40 3RQ England

216

# CRANIOPHARYNGIOMA
*(Also see Brain Tumors)*

⌨ **Craniopharyngioma Internet Support Group**                    **Online**
*Founded 1996.* Private e-mail list which consists of over 250 craniopharyngioma brain tumor patients, their families, caregivers and professionals. Topics include medical, social and emotional issues for those who are affected by craniopharyngioma tumors.
*E-mail:* bphinney@goes.com          *Website:* http://www.braintrust.org/cranio

# CREUTZFELDT-JAKOB DISEASE

**Creutzfeldt-Jakob Disease Foundation, Inc.**        **International network**
*Founded 1993.* Seeks to promote research, education and awareness of Creutzfeldt-Jakob disease, as well as to reach out to people who have lost loved ones to this illness.
Creutzfeldt-Jakob Disease Fdn.      *E-mail:* crjakob@aol.com
P.O. Box 611625                      *Website:* http://CJDFoundation.org
North Miami, FL 33261-1625

⌨ **CJD Voice**                                                   **Online**
Provides emotional support to persons who have a loved one with, or lost someone to, Creutzfeldt-Jakob disease, a fatal brain-deteriorating disorder. Advocacy. E-mail discussion group, message board and scheduled chat.
*Website:* http://www.cjdvoice.org      *E-mail:* larmstr853@aol.com

# CROHN'S DISEASE / COLITIS

**American Celiac Society / Dietary Support Coalition**          **National**
*66 affiliated chapters. Founded 1976.* Mutual support and information for celiac-sprue patients, families and health care professionals. Buddy system, visitation, phone help system, participation in educational efforts. Also supports dermatitis herpetiformis and Crohn's disease. Newsletter.      *Phone:* Annette Bentley 973-325-8837
American Celiac Society               *Fax:* 973-669-8808
59 Crystal Ave.                       *E-mail:* AmerCeliacSoc@netscape.net
W. Orange, NJ 07052

**Crohn's and Colitis Foundation of America**                    **National**
*56 chapters. Founded 1967.* Educational programs and supportive services for people with Crohn's disease or ulcerative colitis, their family and friends. Funds research to find a cure. Membership includes a national magazine, and book discounts. Brochures. Dues $25/year.
CCFA                                 *Phone:* 1-800-932-2423; *Fax:* 212-779-4098
386 Park Ave. South, 17th Fl.        *E-mail:* info@ccfa.org
New York, NY 10016                   *Website:* http://www.ccfa.org

# CUSHING'S DISEASE
*(Also see Adrenal Disorders)*

**Cushing's Help and Support**                                        **International**
*4 affiliated groups.* Provides support and information for persons with Cushing's disease or syndrome. Family and friends welcome. Provides literature, pen pals, phone support network, hospital visitations, advocacy, website message boards and chat room.

Cushing's Help and Support          *Phone:* Mary O'Connor 517-796-4615
13222 Point Pleasant Dr.            *Phone:* Sue 1-877-825-0128
Fairfax, VA 22033-3515             *Website*: http://www.cusshings-help.com

**Cushing's Support and Research Foundation, Inc.**                   **International**
*5 regional sites. Founded 1995.* Provides support for persons with Cushing's disease through information and referrals, advocacy, scientific research and education. Publishes newsletter. Regional get-togethers, conferences, pen pals and phone support. Assistance in starting local groups. Maintains a national database of patients.

Cushing Support & Res. Fdn.        *Phone:* Louise Pace 617-723-3674
65 East India Row, 22B             *E-mail:* scrf@world.std.com
Boston, MA 02110                   *Website:* http://world.std.com/~csrf/

Cushing Support & Res. Fdn.        *Phone:* Mary Brim 303-554-6116
1078 Marble Court                  *E-mail:* cushbrim@aol.com
Boulder, CO 80303

# CUTIS LAXA

**Cutis Laxa Internationale**                                        **International**
*Founded 2001.* Provides emotional support and information to persons affected by cutis laxa, a rare, genetic, connective tissue disorder which causes the skin to lack elasticity. Aim is to ease the sufferer's loneliness, educate the medical world on cutis laxa, and to collect data on this disorder. Supports research. Newsletter. Dues $25.

Cutis Laxa Internationale          *Phone*: 33 (0)5 46 55 00 59
35, route des Chianges             *E-mail:* mcjlboiteux@aol.com
17740 Sainte Marie de Re           *Website*: http://www.orpha.net/associations/
France                             cutislaxainternationale

# CYSTIC FIBROSIS
(Also see Respiratory)

**International Association of Cystic Fibrosis Adults**          **International network**
*Founded 1983.* Aim is to improve the quality of life of adults with cystic fibrosis by identifying common problems, finding solutions, and enhancing the exchange of information between patients. Education and advocacy, information and referrals, newsletter, support group meetings, international conferences. Supports research.

IACFA
82 Ayer Rd.
Harvard, MA 01451

*Phone:* 978-456-8387; *Fax:* 978-456-8387
*E-mail:* fantognini@tinet.ch
*Website:* http://www.iacfa.org

**Cystic Fibrosis Foundation**                                    **National**
*80 affiliated groups. Founded 1955.* Provides information and referrals to individuals, families and professionals on cystic fibrosis. Supports over 110 care centers nationwide. Research grants, newsletter, literature, conferences.

Cystic Fibrosis Fdn.
6931 Arlington Rd.
Bethesda, MD 20814

*Phone:* 1-800-FIGHT-CF
*Fax:* 306-951-6378; *E-mail:* info@cff.org
*Website:* http://www.cff.org

## CYSTINOSIS

**Cystinosis Foundation, Inc.**                              **National network**
Dedicated to providing services for those suffering from cystinosis. Provides information and referrals, parent directory and national registry. Offers conferences, newsletter, public education and literature.

Cystinosis Fdn., Inc.
604 Vernon St.
Iakland, CA 94601

*Phone:* 1-800-392-8458
*E-mail:* Frank@cystinosis.com
*Website*: http://www.cystinosis.com
or http://www.medhelp.org/amshc/amshc324.htm

## CYSTINURIA
*(Also see Kidney Disorders)*

**Cystinuria Support Network**                          **International network**
*Founded 1994.* Support and an opportunity for sharing information for persons with cystinuria, a disorder that causes kidney stones. Information and referrals, newsletter.

Cystinuria Support Network
21001 NE 36th St.
Sammamsh, WA 98074

*Phone:* 425-868-2996 (eve)
*E-mail:* cystinuria@aol.com
*Website:* http://www.cystinuria.com

## DANCING EYE / KINSBOURNE SYNDROME / OPSOCLONUS MYOCLONUS / MYOCLONIC ENCEPHALOPATHY OF INFANTS

**Dancing Eye Syndrome**                                **International network**
*Founded 1988.* Support and information for families of children with dancing eye syndrome (aka Kinsbourne syndrome, opsoclonus myoclonus, or myoclonic encephalopathy of infants), a disorder consisting of loss of balance, irregular eye movements and muscle jerking. Newsletter, phone help.

219

Dancing Eye Syndrome
J. Stanton-Roberts
78 Quantock Rd.
W. Sussex BN13 2HQ England

*Phone:* 01903-532383 (Voice/Fax)
*E-mail:* support@dancingeyes.org.uk
*Website:* http://www.dancingeyes.org.uk

## DANDY-WALKER SYNDROME

**Dandy-Walker Syndrome Network**                    **International network**
*Founded 1993.* Provides mutual support, information and networking for families affected by Dandy-Walker syndrome. Phone support.
Dandy-Walker Synd. Network          *Phone:* 952-423-4008
5030 142nd Path
Apple Valley, MN 55124

## DeBARSY SYNDROME

**Family Ties of Nevada**                                   **National network**
*Founded 1997.* Support and information sharing for parents of children with DeBarsy syndrome, a rare disorder. Pen pals, phone support, peer support and counseling.
Family Ties of Nevada          *Phone:* 775-784-4921 ext. 2352
2695 Laguna Way          *Fax:* 775-784-4997
Sparks, NV 89434          *E-mail:* dcdinnell@mindspring.com

## DENTATORUBRAL PALLIDOLUYSIAN ATROPHY

**Dentatorubral Pallidoluysian Atrophy Network**          **International network**
*Founded 1999.* Support and information for persons affected by dentatorubral pallidoluysian atrophy, a rare genetic disorder that leads to physical and cognitive problems. Phone support, pen pals. Online and e-mail discussions.
DRPLA          *Phone:* 415-753-5695 (voice/TTY/Fax)
c/o Frank J. Marone, Ph.D.          *E-mail:* bmsca@juno.com
1426 46th Ave.
San Francisco, CA 94122-2903

## DERCUM'S DISEASE / ADIPOSIS DOLOROSA

🖳 **Dercum's Disease**                                              **Online**
*Founded 1998.* Support for persons with Dercum's disease (aka adiposis dolorosa), characterized by fatty lipomas (masses) under the skin that cause pain. Aim is to eradicate the pain and suffering of Dercum's disease through finding the cause and cure. Forum for personal stories, links to support groups, and medical articles.
*Phone:* 805-386-3125          *Website:* http://www.dercum.org

# DES-EXPOSURE
*(Also see Cancer)*

**DES-Action U.S.A.**                                                                            **National**
*22 groups. Founded 1977.* Support for women who took DES during pregnancy, and their children. Support groups, physician referrals, education for the public and health workers. Quarterly newsletter. Group development guidelines.
DES-Action U.S.A.                                     *Phone:* 510-465-4011; *Fax:* 510-465-4815
610 16th St., Suite 301                              *E-mail:* desaction@earthlink.net
Oakland, CA 94612                                   *Website:* http://www.desaction.org

**DES Cancer Network**                                                                          **National**
*Founded 1983.* Mutual support and education for DES-exposed women, with a special focus on DES cancer issues. Provides research, advocacy and medical/legal resources. Newsletter ($25). Annual conferences.
DES Cancer Network                                   *Phone:* 1-800-DES-NET-4
P.O. Box 220465                                      *E-mail:* desnetwrk@aol.com
Chantilly, VA 20153-0465                             *Website:* http://www.descancer.org

# DIABETES

**American Diabetes Association**                                                                **National**
*51 affiliates. Founded 1940.* Seeks to prevent and cure diabetes and to improve the lives of all people affected by diabetes. Fund-raising for research. Local offices and chapters provide many support services. Dues $28 (includes magazine).
Amer. Diabetes Assn.                                 *Phone:* 1-800-DIABETES (day/eve)
1701 N. Beauregard St.                               *Fax:* 703-549-6995
Alexandria, VA 22311                                 *Website:* http://www.diabetes.org

**Juvenile Diabetes Research Foundation**                                                     **International**
*110 chapters in North America; 11 international affiliates. Founded 1970.* Supports and funds research to find a cure for diabetes and its complications. Individual chapters offer support groups and other activities for families affected by diabetes. Awards research grants and sponsors career development and research training programs. International conferences and workshops for researchers. Chapter development guidelines.
JDF Int'l                                            *Phone:* 212-785-9500 or 1-800-533-CURE
120 Wall St.                                         *Fax:* 212-785-9595; *E-mail:* info@jdrf.org
New York, NY 10005-4001                              *Website:* http://www.jdrf.org

**Diabetics Anonymous**                                                                           **Model**
*Founded 1990.* Fellowship of men and women with diabetes who share their experience, strength, hope and recovery with each other. Primary purpose is the management of diabetes. Phone support, assistance in starting new groups.

D.A.                                    *Phone:* Jim 408-746-2022
P.O. Box 60905                          *E-mail:* da@jawisa.vip.best.com
Sunnyvale, CA 94088-0905                *Website:* http://www.DiabeticsAnonymous.org

💻 **Diabetic Mommies**                                              **Online**
Support for women who are pregnant and diabetic. Help for dealing with complications of pregnancy and child birth. Offers information, message boards, online magazine and newsletter.                          *Website:* http://www.diabeticmommy.com

## DIABETES INSIPIDUS

**Diabetes Insipidus Foundation, Inc.**                  **International network**
*Founded 1996.* (Multilingual) Support for families and professionals coping with neurogenic/central, nephrogenic, gestagenic and dipsogenic/polydipsic diabetes insipidus. Information and referrals, phone support, and advocacy. Website includes articles (English, French and Spanish). 24-hour chat room, message board. Newsletter.
D.I. Foundation                         *Phone:* Mary Evans-Lee 706-323-7576
4533 Ridge Dr.                          *E-mail:* diabetesinsipidus@maxinter.net
Baltimore, MD 21229                     *Website:* http://diabetesinsipidus.maxinter.net

## DIGESTIVE MOTILITY DISORDERS
*(Also see specific disorder)*

**Association of Gastrointestinal
Motility Disorders, Inc.**                               **International network**
*Founded 1991.* Support and education for persons affected by digestive motility disorders. Serves as educational resource and information base for medical professionals. Physician referrals, video tapes, educational materials, networking support, symposiums, and many educational publications. Dues $35-$52 (can be waived).
AGMD Int'l Corp. Headquarters           *Phone:* 781-861-3874; *Fax:* 781-861-7834
11 North St.                            *E-mail:* AGMDinc@aol.com
Lexington, MA 02420                     *Website:* http://www.digestivemotility.org

**Guardian Society Inc.**                                **International network**
Dedicated to serving the needs of parents and adults who suffer motility disorders such as Hirschsprung disease, GERD, short bowel, and many other diseases that affect a person's motility. Offers newsletter, provides online chat sessions and hold local, regional meetings and activities. Online listserv.            *Phone:* 573-406-1412 (US)
*Phone:* +44 (0)1908-560519 (UK)        *Website:* http://theguardiansociety.org

**Intestinal Disease Foundation, Inc.**                              **Model**
*1 group in Pittsburgh. Founded 1987.* Provides information and support to persons with inflammatory bowel disease, irritable bowel syndrome, diverticular disease and short bowel syndrome, and their families. Literature, newsletter, referrals, and phone support.
222

Intestinal Disease Fdn.              *Phone:* 412-261-5888
1323 Forbes Ave., Suite 200          *Fax:* 412-471-2722
Pittsburgh, PA 15219

## DUBOWITZ SYNDROME

**Dubowitz Syndrome Information and Parent Support**          **National network**
*Founded 1998.* Provides support, understanding and information to families affected by Dubowitz syndrome, a rare, genetic disorder defined by growth retardation, microcephaly, and a characteristic facial appearance. Literature, information and referrals, telephone support network, pen pal program. Family listserv.
*E-mail:* bobbie@dubowitz.org          *E-mail:* kim@dubowitz.org
                                       *Website:* http://www.dubowitz.org

**NE Dubowitz Syndrome Support**                                    **Model**
*1 group in Rhode Island. Founded 1997.* Information, education, support and networking for parents of children with Dubowitz syndrome, and concerned professionals. Information on assistive technology and educational issues. Information and referrals, pen pals, advocacy, information on geneticists and other professionals.
NE Dubowitz Syndrome Support         *Phone:* Sharon Terzian 401-737-3138
106 Verndale St.                     *E-mail:* flamingo@ids.net
Warwick, RI 02889

## DYSAUTONOMIA

**The Dysautonomia Foundation, Inc.**                          **International**
*16 chapters. Founded 1997.* Peer support, information and referrals for families affected by familial dysautonomia. Fundraises for research and clinic maintenance. Newsletter.
Dysautonomia Foundation              *Phone:* 212-949-6644
633 Third Ave., 12th fl.             *Fax:* 212-682-7625
New York, NY 10017                   *Website:* http://www.familialdysautonomia.org

**National Dysautonomia Research Foundation**              **National network**
*Founded 1996.* Provides emotional support, educational materials and medical referrals for persons who have dysautonomia (a disorder of the autonomic nervous system). Offers support group meetings, networking, literature, advocacy, phone support, and conferences. Newsletter. Encourages research. Online email and discussion support forum, groups.
NDRF                                 *Phone:* 651-267-0525; Fax: 651-267-0524
1407 West 4th St., Suite 160         *E-mail:* ndrf@ndrf.org
Red Wing, MN 85069                   *Website:* http://www.ndrf.org

*"Shared pain decreases; shared joy increases."*- Anonymous

**National Society for MVP & Dysautonomia**                        **National**
*59 affiliated groups. Founded 1987.* Assists individuals suffering from mitral valve prolapse syndrome and dysautonomia to find support and understanding. Education on symptoms and treatment. Newsletter, literature.    *Phone:* 205-592-5765 (day)
Nat'l Soc. for MVP/Dysautonomia    *Phone:* 1-800-541-8602 *Fax:* 205-592-5707
880 Montclare Rd., #370             *E-mail:* staff@MVProlapse.com
Birmingham, AL 35213                *Website:* http://www.mvprolapse.com

## DYSTONIA

**Dystonia Medical Research Foundation**                       **International**
*200 chapters. Founded 1976.* Education and support groups for persons with dystonia. Fundraises for research. Newsletter, information and referrals, conferences.
Dystonia Med. Research Fdn.        *Phone:* 312-755-0198; *Fax:* 312-803-0138
1 E. Wacker Dr., Suite 2430        *E-mail:* dystonia@dystonia-foundation.org
Chicago, IL 60601-1905             *Website:* http://www.dystonia-foundation.org/

## DYSTROPHIC EPIDERMOLYSIS BULLOSA

**DEBRA of America (Dystrophic Epidermolysis**
**Bullosa Research Association)**                            **National network**
*National. 7 chapters. Founded 1980.* Support and information for families affected by dystrophic epidermolysis bullosa. Promotes research, provides education for patients, families, and professionals, pen pals, phone network, referrals, newsletter, conferences.
DEBRA of America                   *Phone:* 1-877-88-DEBRA (medical help)
40 Rector St.                      *Phone:* 212-513-4090; *Fax:* 212-513-4099
New York, NY 10006                 *E-mail:* mrivera.debra@exario.net
                                   *Website:* http://www.debra.org

## EATING DISORDERS
## (ANOREXIA / BULIMIA / OVEREATING)
*(Also see Overeating, Overweight)*

**Eating Addictions Anonymous - SANE Fellowship**                   **National**
*6 affiliated chapters.* 12-step recovery for men and women recovering from all forms of eating and body image addictions. Includes anorexia, bulimia, binge eating, overeating, exercise addiction, etc. Focuses on internal growth and reclaiming bodies rather than weight or appearance.                      *Phone:* (202)882-6528
*E-mail:* 12n12@tidalwave.net       *Website:* http://dcregistry.com/users/
                                    eatingaddictions/main.html

*"Help your sister's boat across the water, and yours too will reach the other side."*
*- Anonymous*

**Eating Disorders Anonymous**                                    **International**
*Founded 2000.* Fellowship of men and women who share their experience, strength and hope with each other that they may solve their common problems and help others to recover from their eating disorders. Focuses on the solution, not the problem. EDA endorses sound nutrition. Literature, information and referrals, pen pals, phone support. Assistance in starting groups.                    *Phone:* 602-788-4990
EDA                                         *E-mail:* EDAEmail@EatingDisorders
18233 N. 16th Way                           Anonymous.org
Phoenix, AZ 85022                           *Website:* EatingDisordersAnonymous.org

**National Association of Anorexia Nervosa
and Associated Disorders, Inc.**                                 **International**
*300+ affiliated groups. Founded 1976.* Provides information on self-help groups, therapy, and referrals to professionals. Newsletter. Group development guidelines.
ANAD                                        *Phone:* 847-831-3438; *Fax:* 847-433-4632
P.O. Box 7                                  *E-mail:* anad20@anad.org
Highland Park, IL 60035                      *Website:* http://www.anad.org

## ECTODERMAL DYSPLASIAS

**National Foundation for Ectodermal Dysplasias**            **National network**
*Founded 1981.* Distributes information on ectodermal dysplasias syndrome and treatments. Provides support programs for families and cooperates with research projects. Bi-monthly newsletter. Annual family conference and regional conferences, dental implant program and scholarship opportunities. Directory of members for informal contacts among families.
Nat'l Fdn. for Ectodermal Dysplasias        *Phone:* 618-566-2020; *Fax:* 618-566-4718
410 E. Main St., Box 114                     *E-mail:* maryk@nfed.org
Mascoutah, IL 62258-0114                     *Website:* http://www.nfed.org

## ECZEMA

**National Eczema Association for Science and Education**      **National network**
*Founded 1988.* Support for persons with atopic dermatitis (a common, chronic, non-contagious, inflammatory skin condition), and other forms of constitutional eczema. Information, referrals, networking, and newsletter.
Nat'l Eczema Assn.                          *Phone:* 503-228-4430 or 1-800-818-7546
  For Science & Education                   *Fax:* 503-224-3363
6600 SW 92nd Ave., #230                     *E-mail:* info@nationaleczema.org
Portland, OR 97223-7195                      *Website:* http://www.nationaleczema.org

*"He stands erect by bending over the fallen. He rises by lifting others."*
*– Robert Green Ingersoll*

225

## EHLERS-DANLOS SYNDROME

**Ehlers-Danlos National Foundation**                                    **National**
*25 branches. Founded 1985.* Emotional support and updated information to persons with Ehlers-Danlos syndrome. Serves as a vital informational link to and from the medical community. Provides computerized database to network members. Conducts periodic learning conferences.                    *Phone:* 323-651-3038
Ehlers-Danlos Nat'l Fdn.                    *Fax:* 323-651-1366
6399 Wilshire Blvd., Suite 203         *E-mail:* EDNFBoard@aol.com
Los Angeles, CA 90048                   *Website:* http://www.ednf.org

## ELLIS VAN CREVELD SYNDROME/
## CHONDROECTODERMAL DYSPLASIA
*(Also see Growth Disorders)*

**Ellis Van Creveld Support Group**                          **International network**
*Founded 1997.* Provides support, information and networking for families affected by Ellis Van Creveld syndrome (aka chondroectodermal dysplasia), an extremely rare form of dwarfism. Literature, advocacy, information and referrals, phone support. Connects with medical community to find ways to save the lives of affected infants.
Ellis Van Creveld Support Group      *Phone:* 716-624-8277 (day/eve)
17 Bridlewood Trail
Honeoye Falls, NY 14472

## ENCEPHALITIS

**Encephalitis Support Group**                              **International network**
*Founded 1994.* Provides support and information for persons affected by encephalitis (inflammation of the brain usually caused by a viral infection) and their families. Links individuals together for mutual support (in UK only). Aims to educate public and professionals about the condition, especially the long-term problems. Web-based information, computer networking. Fund-raises.
Encephalitis Support Group            *Phone:* Elaine Dowell 01-653 699 599 (Voice/Fax)
44A Market Pl.                              *E-mail:* info@esg.org.uk
Malton, North Yorkshire               *Website:* http://www.esg.org.uk
Y017 7LW UK

🖥 **Encephalitis Global**                                              **Online**
Provides support and information for persons affected by encephalitis, and their families. Live chats and e-mail discussions.        *Web:* communities.msn.com/EncephalitisGlobal

# ENCHONDROMAS

**Ollier's/Maffucci's Self-Help Group**                    **National network**
*Founded 1985.* Mutual support and exchange of ideas for persons with enchondromas, especially Ollier's, Maffucci's or MHE disease, their families and physicians. Aims to prevent these diseases, find a cure, and reduce the resulting disabilities. Literature, newsletter, conferences.

Ollier's/Maffucci's SH Group          *E-mail:* hschmid@stny.rr.com
c/o Hermann Schmid                    *Website:* http://www.olliers-maffucci.org
74 Aitchison Rd.
Binghamton, NY 13905

# ENDOMETRIOSIS
*(Also see Women's Health)*

**Endometriosis Association**                                    **International**
*300 support groups and chapters. Founded 1980.* (Multilingual) Offers group support to those affected by endometriosis. Educates the public and medical community about the disease. Funds and promotes research. Newsletters, literature, data for researchers, support groups, special teen program, and networks are some of the benefits for members. Brochures in 28 languages. Dues $35/year. Gift memberships are available. Chapter development guidelines. Online support group, and e-mail support.

Endometriosis Assn.                   *Phone:* 1-800-992-3636 or 414-355-2200
8585 N. 76th Pl.                      *E-mail:* endo@endometriosisassn.org
Milwaukee, WI 53223                   *Website:* http://www.endometriosisAssn.org
                                      *Website:* http://www.KillerCramps.org

🖳 **Endometriosis Research Center**                               **Online**
Listserv for women to communicate, share experiences and learn about endometriosis along with topics related to this chronic gynecological disorder. Online fact sheets, newsletters, and articles.          *Website:* http://groups.yahoo.com/group/erc

# EOSINOPHILIA MYALGIA SYNDROME

**National Eosinophilia Myalgia Syndrome Network**          **National network**
*1000 members.Founded 1993.* Mutual support for persons with eosinophilia myalgia syndrome (EMS) caused by using L-tryptophan, and their families. Information and support through online support groups, phone contacts and newsletter. Medical and legal information, advocacy, literature, and conferences.

Nat'l EMS Network                     *Phone:* Sharon Lobaugh 907-789-5028
c/o Sharon Lobaugh                    *Fax:* 907-789-9114
3340 Fritz Cove                       *E-mail:* JHayes@dnet.net or Lobaugh@gci.net
Juneau, AK 99801                      *Website:* http://www.nemsn.org

## EPILEPSY / SEIZURE DISORDERS
*(Also see specific disorder)*

**Epilepsy Foundation**                                    **National**
*60+ affiliates. Founded 1967.* (English/Spanish) Information and support for people with epilepsy, their families and friends. Pharmaceutical program. Newsletter. Affiliates' development kit. Referrals to local affiliates (many of which have employment related programs). Information and referrals.     *Phone:* 301-459-3700; *Fax:* 301-577-4941
Epilepsy Fdn.                                *Consumer Infoline:* 1-800-332-1000
4351 Garden City Dr.                         *E-mail:* postmaster@efa.org
Landover, MD 20785                           *Website:* http://www.epilepsyfoundation.org

## ERYTHROMELALGIA
*(Also see Neurology)*

**TEA (The Erythromelalgia Association)**              **National network**
*Founded 1999.* Provides emotional support and information for persons with erythromelalgia, their families and friends. Aim is to foster communication between members by sharing personal experiences, work with medical community to help find treatments and cures, and increase public awareness of this rare disorder.
TEA                                          *Phone:* 206-632-0894; *Fax:* 206-632-1894
4343 Roosevelt Way, NE, #305                 *E-mail:* jeanmilt@prodigy.net
Seattle, WA 98105                            *Website:* http://www.erythromelalgia.org

## ESSENTIAL TREMOR

**International Tremor Foundation**                        **International**
*52 affiliated groups. Founded 1989.* Provides information and support for persons affected by essential tremor. Information and referrals, literature, research updates. Quarterly newsletter. Dues $25.
Int'l Tremor Fdn.                            *Phone:* 1-888-387-3667 or 913-341-3880
7046 W. 105th St.                            *E-mail:* staff@essentialtremor.org
Overland Park, KS 66212                      *Website:* http://www.essentialtremor.org/

## EXTRACORPOREAL MEMBRANE OXYGENATION
*(Also see specific disorder)*

**ECMO Moms and Dads**                                **International network**
*Many regional groups. Founded 1987.* Mutual support for parents who have agreed to extracorporeal membrane oxygenation procedure on their infant or child as a last resort to attempt to save the life. Telephone support, newsletter, pen pal, conferences, information and referrals, help in starting groups.

ECMO Moms and Dads
Rt. 1, Box 176AA
Idalou, TX 79329

*Phone:* Gayle Willson 806-892-3348
*Fax:* 806-792-1289
*E-mail:* bgw@odyssey.net

### 🖳 Ecmo Support                                               Online
Support and information for families of children, or individuals, who need or have been on ecmo (extracorporeal membrane oxygenation) for severe meconium aspiration, chronic diaphragmatic hernia or strep b sepsis. Chat room, message boards, e-mail list.
*Phone:* Connie Umstead 609-893-6457  *Fax:* 609-893-1310
*Website:* http://www.geocities.com/Athens/4069

## FABRY SYNDROME

### Fabry Support and Information Group                    National network
*Founded 1996.* Dedicated to dispensing information and encouraging mutual self-help as a means of emotional support to Fabry patients and family members. Information and referrals, newsletters, networking of members, discussion page.
FSIG
P.O. Box 510
Concordia, MO 64020

*Phone:* 660-463-1355; *Fax:* 660-463-1356
*E-mail:* JJohnson@fabry.org
*Website:* http://www.fabry.org

## FACIAL DISFIGUREMENT
*(Also see specific disorder)*

### AboutFace USA                                                National
*24 chapters. Founded 1991.* Provides emotional support and information to persons with facial differences and their families. Networks families who have similar concerns. Promotes public education and awareness. Newsletter, information and referrals, assistance in starting local chapters.
AboutFace USA
P.O. Box 969
Batavia, IL 60510-0969

*Phone:* 1-888-486-1209
*E-mail:* AboutFace2000@aol.com
*Website:* http://www.aboutfaceusa.org

### Let's Face It                                                National
*US Branch of Int'l. Founded 1987.* Networking of people with facial disfigurement. Links people to information and to each other. Annual 40-page resource list with over 200 resources available by sending 9" x 12" $3.50 stamped self-addressed envelope with interest (child or adult) or information can be downloaded.
Let's Face It
P.O. 29972
Bellingham, WA 98228-1972

*Phone:* Betsy Wilson 360-676-7325
*E-mail:* letsfaceit@faceit.org
*Website:* http://www.faceit.org

*"My lifetime listens to yours."*– Muriel Rukeyser

**Forward Face**                                                          **Model**
*Founded 1978.* Mutual support for people with craniofacial disfigurement and their families. Strongly advocates educating members and the public in the quest for understanding and acceptance. Liaison with medical personnel. Newsletter. Videotapes. Dues $20. Teen/young adult support group: The Inner Faces.

Forward Face                              *Phone:* 1-800-393-3223 or 212-684-5860
317 E 34th St., 9th Fl., Rm. 901A         *Fax:* 212-684-5864
New York, NY 10016                        *E-mail:* Admin@forwardface.org
                                          *Website:* http://www.forwardface.org

## FACIOSCAPULOHUMERAL DISEASE/
## LANDOUZY-DEJERINE MUSCULAR DYSTROPHY
*(Also see Muscular Dystrophy)*

**FSH Society, Inc.**                                           **National network**
*Founded 1992.* Support, information, education, networking and advocacy for individuals with facioscapulohumeral disease (aka Landouzy-Dejerine muscular dystrophy). Funds research. Newsletter, support group meetings, conferences, literature. Assistance in starting chapters.

FSH Society                               *Phone:* Carol Perez 781-860-0501 (day)
3 Westwood Rd.                            *Fax:* 781-860-0599
Lexington, MA 02420                       *E-mail:* info@fshsociety.org
                                          *Website:* http://www.fshsociety.org

## FACTOR V LEIDEN / THROMBOPHILIA

🖵 **Factor V Leiden Mailing List and Digest**                          **Online**
Mailing list that offers support and information for persons affected by Factor V Leiden (thrombophilia), a hereditary blood coagulation disorder. Daily digest (condensed version of the mailing list) also available.          *Website:* http://www.fvleiden.org/mail_list.htm

## FATTY OXIDATION DISORDERS
*(Also see Metabolic Disorders)*

**FOD Family Support Group**                               **International network**
*Founded 1991.* Opportunity for families dealing with fatty oxidation disorders (i.e. MCAD, LCHAD, LCAD, SCAD) to network with others dealing with these rare, genetic metabolic disorders. Printed newsletter, information and referrals, phone support, pen pals.

FOD Family Support Group                  *Phone:* Deb & Dan Gould 336-547-8682
805 Montrose Dr.                          *E-mail:* fodgroup@hotmail.com
Greensboro, NC 27410                      *Website:* http://www.fodsupport.org

## FENPHEN

⌨ **Fenphen 2**                                                    Online
*Founded 1997.* Support and information for persons who have suffered damages as a result of using the diet pills fenphen/redux.   *Website:* http://www.onelist.com/community/
2Bfriends

## FETAL ALCOHOL SYNDROME

**Family Empowerment Network**                          National network
*Founded 1982.* Support, education and training for families of children with fetal alcohol syndrome or fetal alcohol effects, and interested professionals. Annual family retreats, conferences, newsletter. Networks families together for support. Membership is free. Assistance in starting support groups.
FEN                                  *Phone:* 651-267-0525;  *Fax:* 651-267-0524
610 Langdon St.,  Room 517           *E-mail:* fen@dcs.wisc.edu
Madison, WI 53703                    *Website:* http://www.dcs.wisc.edu/pda/hhi/fen

**Fetal Alcohol Network**                                    International
*Founded 1990.* Mutual support for parents of children with fetal alcohol syndrome. Offers advocacy, educational issues, behavioral problems and accessing community services.
Fetal Alcohol Network                *Phone:* 610-384-1133
158 Rosemont Ave.                    *E-mail:* 72157.564@compuserve.com
Coatesville, PA 19320

**Fetal Alcohol Syndrome Family Resource Institute**          International
*Founded 1990.* Grassroots coalition of families and professionals concerned with fetal alcohol syndrome/effects. Educational programs, brochures, information packets. Regional representatives being identified. Support group meetings. Advocacy, information and referrals, phone support, conferences.
FAS Family Resource Inst.            *Phone:* 1-800-999-3429 (in WA) or 253-531-2878
P.O. Box 2525                        *E-mail:* vicfas@hotmail.com
Lynnwood, WA 98070                   *Website:* http://fetalalcoholsyndrome.org

## FETAL ANTICONVULSANT SYNDROME

**Fetal Anticonvulsant Syndrome Association**           International network
*16 affiliated groups. Founded 1996.* Emotional support for families affected by fetal anticonvulsant syndrome (a condition caused by commonly prescribed medicines given to mothers during pregnancy.) Works toward public and professional awareness. Promotes research. Networks families together for support. Newsletter, literature, information and referrals, buddy system.

FACS                                    *Phone:* (01)97 55 71340 (day)
Newton of Brux                          *E-mail:* facsline@aol.com
Gelnkindle, By Alford
Aberdeenshire, AB33 8RX Scotland

## FG SYNDROME

💻 **FG Syndrome Homepage**                                               **Online**
Support network and listserv for persons interested in FG Syndrome, a multiple congenital
anomaly/mental retardation syndrome. Newsletter, conferences, fundraising.
*Website:* www.geocities.com/HotSprings/Spa/3687

## FIBRODYSPLASIA OSSIFICANS PROGRESSIVA

**International Fibrodysplasia**
**Ossificans Progressiva Association**                        **International network**
*Founded 1988.* Serves as a support network for families dealing with fibrodysplasia
ossificans progressiva (FOP). Supports education and medical research. Newsletter.
Int'l FOP Assn.                         *Phone:* 407-365-4194
Box 196217                              *E-mail:* together@ifopa.org
Winter Springs, FL 32719-6217           *Website:* http:/www.ifopa.org

## FIBROMYALGIA

**Fibromyalgia Network**                                                  **National**
*Founded 1988.* Provides information on fibromyalgia syndrome and chronic fatigue
syndrome. Referrals to support groups, health care professionals, and other services.
Newsletter, phone support, information and referrals, conferences, and guidelines and
assistance in helping new groups.
Fibromyalgia Network                    *Phone:* 1-800-853-2929 *Fax:* 520-90-5550
P.O. Box 31750                          *E-mail:* fmnetter@msn.com
Tucson, AZ 85751-1750                   *Website:* http://www.fmnetnews.com

**National Chronic Fatigue Syndrome and**
**Fibromyalgia Association, Inc.**                                    **International**
*2 affiliated groups and contacts worldwide. Founded 1985.* To educate patients, the public,
and the medical profession about chronic fatigue syndrome and fibromyalgia. Support
groups, quarterly newsletter, funds research, conducts seminars. Literature available for
patients and physicians. Guidelines and assistance available for starting support groups.
Nat'l CFS & Fibromyalgia Assn.          *Phone:* 816-313-2000 (24 hr. hotline)
P.O. Box 18426                          *Fax:* 816-524-6782
Kansas City, MO 64133                   *E-mail:* ncfsfa@aol.com

◧ **National Fibromyalgia Partnership, Inc.**                          **Resource**
*Founded 1992.* (Bilingual) Mission is to distribute current resource information on fibromyalgia. Networking, phone support, conferences, literature. Referrals to self-help groups, and legal and financial assistance nationwide. Advocacy. Assistance in starting groups ($3). Dues $25 (US); $30 (Int'l)
Nat'l Fibromyalgia Partnership *Phone:* 866-725-4404; *Fax:* 540-622-2998
140 Zinn Way                           *E-mail:* mail@fmpartnership.org
Linden, VA 22642-5609                  *Website:* http://www.fmpartnership.org


▣ **Hypermobility and Fibromyalgia Site**                              **Online**
Provides information and support for people with both joint hypermobility and fibromyalgia. Members exchange information, coping skills, and support.
*E-mail:* hm-ed-fm@onebox.com        *Web:* http://anaiis.tripod.com/hmedfm/index.html

## FIBROUS DYSPLASIA
*(Also see McCune-Albright Syndrome, Growth Disorders)*

▣ **Fibrous Dysplasia Support Online**                                 **Online**
Support for persons affected by fibrous dysplasia, a chronic disorder of the skeleton, including McCune-Albright syndrome and cherubism.
*E-mail:* fdsupport@aol.com          *Website:* members.aol.com/fdsupport/index.html

## FLOATING HARBOR SYNDROME

**Floating Harbor Syndrome Support Group of North America**      **National network**
*Founded 1999.* Provides mutual support and networking for parents of children with Floating Harbor syndrome. Newsletter, literature, phone support.
Floating Harbor Synd. Support Grp.   *Phone:* Deana Swanson 616-447-9175
160 Guild NE                         *E-mail:* JDSwanson@aol.com
Grand Rapids, MI 49505               *Website:* http://hometown.aol.com/jdswanson

## FRAGILE X SYNDROME
*(Also see Mental Retardation)*

**National Fragile X Foundation, The**                              **International**
*50 groups. Founded 1984.* Promotes education and research regarding fragile x syndrome, a hereditary condition which is the most common familial cause of mental impairment. Phone support, information packet, medical and genetic services referrals, advocacy, phone consultation, newsletter, family assistance and research grants, local, national and international conferences. Quarterly newsletter and educational resources (books, audiotapes, videotapes) for a fee. Information and referrals.

Nat'l Fragile X Fdn.                    *Phone:* 1-800-688-8765 or 510-763-6030
P.O. Box 190488                         *Fax:* 510-763-6223
San Francisco, CA 94119-0488            *E-mail:* NATLFX@sprintmail.com
                                        *Website:* http://www.FragileX.org

**FRAXA Research Foundation**                                      **International**
*30 affiliated groups. Founded 1994.* Information and support on fragile x syndrome. Funds medical research investigator-initiated grants and postdoctoral fellowships. Newsletter, literature. Some chapters have support group meetings.
FRAXA Research Fdn.                     *Phone:* 978-462-1866; *Fax:* 978-463-9985
45 Pleasant St.                         *E-mail:* info@fraxa.org
Newburyport, MA 01950                   *Website:* http://www.fraxa.org

## FREEMAN-SHELDON SYNDROME

**Freeman-Sheldon Parent Support Group**                    **International network**
*Founded 1982.* Provides emotional support for parents of children with Freeman-Sheldon syndrome, and for adults with this syndrome. Sharing of helpful medical literature. Provides information on growth and development of individuals affected. Participates in research projects. Members network by phone and mail. Newsletter.
Freeman-Sheldon Parent Support Grp     *Phone:* 801-364-7060
509 E. Northmont Way                    *E-mail:* fspsg@aol.com
Salt Lake City, UT 84103                *Website:* http://www.fspsg.org

## GALACTOSEMIA
*(Also see Neurological / Neurometabolic)*

**Parents of Galactosemic Children, Inc.**                     **National network**
*Founded 1985.* Mutual support for parents of galactosemic children. Newsletter, literature, pen pals, conferences, and phone support.
Parents of Galactosemic Children       *Phone:* Evelyn Rice 775-626-0885
885 Del Sol St.                         *E-mail:* mesameadow@aol.com
Sparks, NV 89436

## GASTROESOPHAGEAL REFLUX DISORDER
*(Also see Digestive Motility Disorders)*

**PAGER (Pediatric/Adolescent**
**Gastroesophageal Reflux Association)**                       **National network**
*Founded 1992.* Offers support and information for parents whose children suffer from gastroesophageal reflux (GER), an inappropriate backwash of stomach contents into the esophagus that affects 10 million children and 50 million adults. Educates the public on this disorder. Newsletter, literature, telephone support network. Helps new chapters start. Dues $25/yr.                              *Phone:* 301-601-9541 (Maryland)

PAGER                               *Phone:* or 760-747-5001 (San Diego)
P.O. Box 1153                       *E-mail:* gergroup@aol.com
Germantown, MD 20875-1153           *Website:* http://www.reflux.org

## GASTROINTESTINAL DISORDERS
*(Also see specific disorder)*

**International Foundation for Functional
Gaucher Gastrointestinal Disorders**                              **International**
*Founded 1990.* Educational and research organization that provides information, assistance
and support for people affected by functional gastrointestinal disorders, irritable bowel
syndrome, gastroesophageal reflux disorder, and bowel incontinence. Publishes three
quarterly newsletters (one for lower GI problems, one for upper GI problems, and one for
pediatric digestive problems). Many other fact sheets and educational publications available.
IFFGD                               *Phone:* 1-888-964-2001 or 414-964-1799
P.O. Box 170864                     *Fax:* 414-964-7176; *E-mail:* iffgd@iffgd.org
Milwaukee, WI 53217-8076            *Website:* http://www.iffgd.org

**Intestinal Disease Foundation, Inc.**                            **Model**
*1 group in Pittsburgh. Founded 1987.* Information and support to persons with
inflammatory bowel disease, irritable bowel syndrome, diverticular disease and short bowel
syndrome, and their families. Literature, newsletter, referrals, and phone support.
Intestinal Disease Fdn.             *Phone:* 412-261-5888
1323 Forbes Ave., Suite 200         *Fax:* 412-471-2722
Pittsburgh, PA 15219

## GAUCHER DISEASE

**National Gaucher Foundation**                                    **National**
*2 chapters. Founded 1984.* Provides information and assistance for those affected by
Gaucher disease. Provides education and outreach to increase public awareness. Operates
the Family Support Network. Quarterly newsletter, telephone support, medical board.
Nat'l Gaucher Fdn.                  *Phone:* 1-800-428-2437; *Fax:* 301-816-1516
5410 Edson Lane #260                *E-mail:* ngf@gaucherdisease.org
Rockville, MD 20852-3130            *Website:* http://www.gaucherdisease.org

## GENETIC DISORDERS
*(Also see Rare Disorders, specific disorder)*

**The Genetic Alliance**                                 **International network**
*350 affiliated groups. Founded 1986.* Consortium of support groups, professional
organizations, industry, and governmental agencies dedicated to helping persons affected by
genetic disorders. Information and referrals to support groups and genetic services.

Genetic Alliance
4301 Connecticut Ave. NW #404
Washington, DC 20008

*Phone:* 1-800-336-4363 or 202-966-5557
*E-mail:* info@geneticalliance.org
*Website:* http://geneticalliance.org

## GERSTMANN SYNDROME

**Gerstmann Syndrome Support Network**                                National network
*Founded 1997.* Mutual support and education for persons with Gerstmann syndrome, which causes an inability to do math, express thoughts in writing, distinguish between right and left, and distinguish one's own finger from another's. Provides education about the disorder to professionals. Pen pals, advocacy, phone support, information and referrals, newsletter.
Gerald Olseski, Jr.                          *Phone:* 734-479-1517 (day)
14246 Heritage Dr.                           *Website:* http://www.iser.com/gerstmann.html
Riverview, MI 48192

## GLYCOGEN STORAGE DISEASE

**Association For Glycogen Storage Disease**                           International network
*U.S and Canadian network. 3 affiliated groups. Founded 1979.* Mutual support and information sharing among parents of children with glycogen storage disease. Fosters communication between parents and professionals, creates public awareness, and encourages research. Newsletter, phone support, conference.
Assn. for Glycogen Storage Disease          *Phone:* 563-785-6038
P.O. Box 896                                *Fax:* 563-785-6038
Durant, IA 52747                            *Website:* http://www.agsdus.org

## GOLDENHAR SYNDROME / HEMIFACIAL MICROSOMIA

**Goldenhar Syndrome Support Network**                                International network
*Founded 1998.* Support and information for families affected by Goldenhar syndrome (aka hemifacial microsomia). Information and referrals, newsletter, literature, pen pals, and advocacy. Online mailing list.          *Website:* http://goldenharsyndrome.org
Barb Miles
9325 163 Street
Edmonton, AB T5R 2P4, Canada

## GORLIN SYNDROME / NEVOID BASAL CELL CARCINOMA

**The Gorlin Syndrome Group**                                         International network
*3 affiliated groups. Founded 1992.* Provides support and information for individuals with Gorlin (aka nevoid basal cell carcinoma) and their families. Information on coping skills, treatments, and current research. Helpline, newsletter, meetings, networking.

Gorlin Syndrome Group
11 Blackberry Way
Penwortham, Preston
Lancashire PR1 9LQ England

*Phone:* Jim Costello (0177)2-496849 (day/eve)
*E-mail:* gorlin-group@blueyonder.co.uk
*Website:* gorlin-group.pwp.blueyonder.co.uk

## GRAVES' DISEASE
*(Also see Thyroid)*

**National Graves' Disease Foundation**                              **National**
*25 affiliated groups in 18 states. Founded 1990.* Aims is to establish patient-based Graves' exclusive support groups to provide better treatment and to increase public awareness. Participates in research. Newsletter, information and referrals, phone support, national conferences, internet bulletin board, and weekly online chat room. Medical resources.
Nat'l Graves' Disease Fdn.           *Phone:* Dr. Nancy Patterson 828-877-5251
P.O. Box 1969                        *Fax:* 828-877-5250; *E-mail:* ngdf@citcom.net
Brevard, NC 28712                    *Website:* http://www.ngdf.org

▣ **Grave's Disease and Thyroid Discussion**                          **Online**
Offers a large variety of topics for persons concerned about Grave's disease and other thyroid disorders. Online chats.          *Website:* http://www.mediboard.com

## GRANULOMATOUS DISEASE, CHRONIC

**Chronic Granulomatous Disease Association, Inc.**          **International network**
*Founded 1982.* Support and information for persons with chronic granulomatous disease, their families and physicians. Networks patients with similar CGD-related illnesses. Support through correspondence and telephone. Newsletter publishes medical and research articles. International registry of patients. Referrals to physicians.
CGD Assn.                            *Phone:* 626-441-4118
2616 Monterey Rd.                    *E-mail:* cgda@socal.rr.com
San Marino, CA 91108                 *Website:* http://www.cgdassociation.org

## GROWTH DISORDERS
*(Also see specific disorder, Height Issues)*

**Growth Hormone Deficiency Support Network**          **National network**
(Division of MAGIC Foundation). *Founded 1989.* Network and exchange of information for families of children with growth hormone deficiency disorders. Information and referrals, phone support, pen pals, conferences, literature. Newsletter. Dues $25.
Growth Hormone Def. Network          *Phone:* 1-800-3-MAGIC-3
c/o MAGIC Foundation                 or 708-383-0808
1327 N. Harlem                       *E-mail:* pam@magicfoundation.org
Oak Park, IL 60302                   *Website:* http://www.magicfoundation.org

**Human Growth Foundation**                                         **National**
*48 chapters. Founded 1965.* Local chapters provide members the opportunity to meet other parents of children with growth-related disorders. Mutual sharing of problems, research and public education. Monthly and quarterly newsletter. Parent-to-parent support and networking program. Conferences. Chapter development guidelines.

Human Growth Fdn.                    *Phone:* 516-671-4041 or 1-800-451-6434
997 Glen Cove Ave.                   *Fax:* 516-671-4055; *E-mail:* hgf1@hgfound.org
Glen Head, NY 11545-1564             *Website:* http://www.hgfound.org

**MAGIC Foundation for Children's Growth**                  **National network**
*Founded 1989.* Provides education and networking for families of children with growth-related disorders. Divisions include: growth hormone deficiency, congenital adrenal hyperplasia, Turner's syndrome, precocious puberty, McCune Albright syndrome, panhypopituitarism, genital/reproductive anomalies in children, and rare disorders including hypophosphatasia, Russell Silver syndrome, hypothyroidism, and septo optic dysplasia. Information and referrals, phone support, pen pals, annual convention and conferences. Newsletters for children and adults. Dues $25.

The MAGIC Foundation                 *Phone:* 1-800-3-MAGIC-3
1327 N. Harlem                       *E-mail:* mary@magicfoundation.org
Oak Park, IL 60302                   *Website:* http://www.magicfoundation.org

## GUILLAIN-BARRE SYNDROME

**Guillain-Barre Syndrome Foundation, International**          **International**
*160 chapters. Founded 1981.* Emotional support, visitation and education for people affected by Guillain-Barre syndrome. Promotes support, education and research. Newsletter, pen pals, phone network, online chat rooms, newsletters. Group development guidelines, international symposium.

Guillain-Barre Syndrome Fdn.         *Phone:* 610-667-0131; *Fax:* 610-667-7036
P.O. Box 262                         *E-mail:* gbint@ix.netcom.com
Wynnewood, PA 19096                  *Website:* http://www.webmast.com/gbs

## HALLERVORDEN-SPATZ SYNDROME

**Hallervorden-Spatz Syndrome Association**              **International network**
*Founded 1996.* Provides emotional support to families affected by Hallervorden-Spatz syndrome, a rare, progressive neurological disorder resulting in iron deposits in the brain that causes loss of muscle control. Educates public on HSS, and supports and monitors research. Newsletter, literature, phone support network, pen pals, advocacy.

HSS Assn.                            *Phone:* 619-588-2315; *Fax:* 619-588-4093
2082 Monaco Ct.                      *E-mail:* hssakwpac@msn.com
El Cajon, CA 92019-4235              *Website:* http://www.hssa.org

# HEADACHE
*(Also see Pain)*

**ACHE (American Council for Headache
Education) Support Group**                                          **National**
*50+ affiliated groups. Founded 1990.* Opportunity for headache sufferers to decrease their feeling of isolation, learn more about headaches, and enhance coping skills. Newsletter, information and referrals, group meetings. Assistance in starting groups. Dues $20.

ACHE                                    *Phone:* 1-800-255-2243 or 856-423-0258
19 Mantua Rd.                           *Fax:* 856-423-0082; *E-mail:* achehq@talley.com
Mt. Royal, NJ 08061                     *Website:* http://www.achenet.org

**National Headache Foundation**                                    **National**
*35+ affiliated groups. Founded 1970.* Mutual support for chronic headache sufferers and their families. Education on how to deal with chronic head pain. Group meetings, phone support, e-mail pen pals. Public awareness seminars, funds research. Newsletter. Information on diets and brochures.

Nat'l Headache Fdn.                     *Phone:* 1-888-NHF-5552; *Fax:* 773-525-7357
428 W. St. James Pl., 2nd fl.           *E-mail:* sbarron@headaches.org
Chicago, IL 60614-2750                  *Website:* http://www.headaches.org

**⌨ Cluster Headaches Message Board**                               **Online**
Message board and live chats for persons who suffer from cluster headaches. Resource information and other links.          *Website:* http://www.clusterheadaches.com

**⌨ OUCH (Organization for Understanding Cluster Headaches**        **Online**
Provides information and emotional support for cluster headache sufferers through message boards. Supports and participates in research to improve treatment. Annual conference.

OUCH                                    *Website:* http://www.clusterheadaches.org
807 E. Broadway
Gladewater, TX 75647

# HEART DISORDERS
*(Also see specific disorder)*

**CHASER (Congenital Heart Anomalies -
Support, Education, Resources)**                            **National network**
*Founded 1992.* Opportunity for parents of children born with heart defects to network with other parents. Education on hospitalization, surgeries, medical treatments, etc. Newsletter, information and referral, phone support. Directory of heart surgeons and facilities.

CHASER                                  *Phone:* Jim & Anita Myers 419-825-5575
2112 N. Wilkins Rd.                      *E-mail:* chaser@compuserve.com
Swanton, OH 43558                       *Website:* http://www.csun.edu/~hfmth006/chaser/

**Kids With Heart**                                              **National**
*3 affiliated groups. Founded 1985.* Mutual support for families and adults affected by
congenital or acquired heart defects. Matches persons together for support. Referrals to local
support groups nationwide. Books. Assistance in starting groups.

Kids With Heart                      *Phone:* 1-800-538-5390
c/o NACHD, Inc.                      or 920-498-0058 (Voice/Fax)
1578 Careful Dr.                     *E-mail:* kdswhrt@execpc.com
Green Bay, WI 54304                  *Website:* http://www.kidswithheart.org

**Mended Hearts**                                               **National**
*277 chapters. Founded 1951.* Support for persons who have heart disease, their families,
friends, and other interested persons. Quarterly magazine. Chapter development kit.

Mended Hearts                        *Phone:* (214)706-1442 or 1-800-AHA-USA1
7272 Greenville Ave.                 *E-mail:* cathy.clapp@heart.org
Dallas, TX 75231                     *Website:* http://www.mendedhearts.org

▣ **Adult Congenital Heart Association, Inc.**                   **Online**
*Founded 1998.* Education and support for adults with congenital heart defects, their families
and health care professionals. Newsletter, conferences. Message board. Dues $5/individual;
$10/professional.

ACHA                                 *Phone:* 617-325-1191
273 Perham St.                       *E-mail:* info@achaheart.org
West Roxbury, MA 02132               *Website:* http://www.achaheart.org

## HELLP SYNDROME
*(Also see Pre-eclampsia)*

**The HELLP Syndrome Society**                          **International network**
*Founded 1996.* Support, networking, and information for persons affected by HELLP
syndrome (Hemolysis, Elevated Liver enzymes and Low Platelet count) which can affect
pregnant mothers, and is usually in tandem with pre-eclampsia. Brochure, newsletter.

The HELLP Syndrome Society           *Website:* http://hometown.aol.com/
P.O. Box 44                          HELLP1995/hellp.html
Bethany, WV 26032

## HEMANGIOMA

**Hemangioma Support System**                            **National network**
*Founded 1990.* Provides parent-to-parent support for families with children affected by
hemangiomas.

Hemangioma Support System            *Phone:* Cynthia Schumerth 920-336-9399 (eve)
1484 Sand Acres Dr.
DePere, WI 54115

# HEMIFACIAL SPASM

**Hemifacial Spasm Support Group**                              **National network**
*Founded 1991.* Provides information and referrals regarding treatments and doctors for
people with hemifacial spasms. Phone support, pen pal program.
Hemifacial Spasm Support Group      *Phone:* 703-242-3056
9928 Clearfield Ave.                *E-mail:* nimbus1@erols.com
Vienna, VA 22181

🖳 **Hemifacial Spasm Association**                                 **Online**
*Founded 2001.* A support community of individuals who have, or are presently, suffering
from hemifacial spasm (HFS) and are eager to provide information, understanding and
support to other individuals and their families when coping with this disorder.
                              *Website:* http://www.hfs-assn.org/

# HEMIHYPERTROPHY

🖳 **Hemihypertrophy Support and Information Page**                 **Online**
Support and information for persons with hemihypertrophy, a rare condition in which one
side of the body grows faster than the other. Mailing list, chat room.
*E-mail:* Onionhead2@aol.com        *Website:* www.geocities.com/HotSprings/Spa/6112

# HEMIMEGALENCEPHALY

**HME Contact Group**                                       **International network**
*Founded 1991.* (Bilingual) Network provides mutual support for parents of children with
hemimegalencephaly through shared experiences, phone support and newsletter. Offers
literature on diagnostic tests and medication. Information, networking of families. Materials
in English and German.
HME Contact Group                   *Phone:* (GB) 0141 633 2617
c/o Dagmar and David Kerr           *E-mail:* hmecontactgroup@tinyworld.co.uk
3 Linn Dr.                          *Website:* www.cv.quik.com.au/hmegroup
Netherlee, Glasgow, G44 3PT Scotland

# HEMIPLEGIA / HEMIPARESIS / PEDIATRIC STROKE
*(Also see Stroke)*

**CHASA (Children's Hemiplegia And Stroke Association)**          **International**
*40 affilated groups. Founded 1996.* Offers support and information for families of children
who have hemiplegia, hemiparesis and/or pediatric stroke. Literature, information and
referrals, phone support, pen pals, advocacy. Annual retreats. Referrals to local support
groups. Newsletter ($15/year). E-mail list.

CHASA
c/o Nancy Atwood PMB149
4101 W. Green Oaks, Suite 305
Arlington, TX 76016

*Phone:* 817-492-4325 (day/eve)
*E-mail:* info@chasa.org
*Website:* http://www.hemikids.org/

## HEMOCHROMATOSIS / IRON OVERLOAD

**Hemochromatosis Foundation, Inc.**                                    **International**
*Founded 1972.* Mutual support for hemochromatosis families and interested professionals. Promotes general awareness, encourages screenings to identify families. Offers videotape, educational materials, genetic counseling, referrals, newsletters, videotape of Cleveland Clinic Conference, conferences and periodic teleconferences. Send self-addressed stamped envelope when writing.

Hemochromatosis Fdn.
P.O. Box 8569
Albany, NY 12208

*Phone:* 518-489-0972
*Fax:* 518-489-0227
*Website:* http://www.hemochromatosis.org

**Iron Overload Diseases Association, Inc.**                       **International network**
*Founded 1981.* A clearinghouse of support and information for hemochromatosis and other iron overload disease patients, their families, and physicians. Encourages research and public awareness. Bi-monthly newsletter "Ironic Blood." Membership dues $50/yr.

Iron Overload Diseases Assn.
433 Westwind Dr.
N. Palm Beach, FL 33408

*Phone:* 561-840-8512 or 561-840-8513
*Fax:* 561-842-9881; *E-mail:* iod@ironoverload.org
*Website:* http://www.ironoverload.org

## HEMOPHILIA / BLEEDING DISORDERS

**National Hemophilia Foundation**                                        **National**
*39 chapters. Founded 1948.* Provides service to persons with hemophilia and other bleeding disorders. Promotes research to find cures for bleeding disorders. Monthly newsletter, bimonthly magazine, annual meeting for patients and professionals.

Nat'l Hemophilia Fdn.
116 W 32nd St.
New York, NY 10001

*Phone:* 1-800-42-HANDI
*E-mail:* info@hemophilia.org
*Website:* http://www.hemophilia.org

## HEPATITIS
*(Also see Liver disease)*

**Hepatitis B Foundation**                                         **International network**
*Founded 1991.* Mutual support and information for persons affected by hepatitis B. Dedicated to finding a cure for hepatitis B. Supports research. Advocacy, information and referrals, educational literature, conferences, confidential phone and e-mail support, free quarterly newsletter. Referrals to liver specialists. Suggested donation $40.

Hepatitis B Fdn.                          *Phone:* 215-489-4900; *Fax:* 215-489-4920
700 E. Butler Ave.                        *E-mail:* info@hepb.org
Doylestown, PA 18901                      *Website:* http://www.hepb.org

**Hepatitis Foundation International**                    **International network**
*Founded 1995.* (Multilingual) Grassroots support network for persons with viral hepatitis.
Provides education about the prevention, diagnosis and treatment of viral hepatitis. Phone
support network and literature. Referrals to local support groups. Quarterly newsletter.
Information available in Spanish, French, Portuguese, Italian, Mandarin and Vietnamese.
Hepatitis Fdn. Int'l                      *Phone:* Thelma King Thiel 973-239-1035
30 Sunrise Terrace                        or 1-800-891-0707 (day); *Fax:* 973-857-5044
Cedar Grove, NJ 07009                     *Website:* http://www.hepfi.org

**HCV Anonymous**                                                          **Model**
*1 group in California. Founded 2000.* 12-step group that assists hepatitis C patients and
their loved ones in taking control of their spiritual, physical, mental and emotional health.
Provides current, comprehensive information.
HCV Anonymous                             *Phone:* 949-492-6255
129 W. Canada                             *Website*: http://www.hcvanonymous.com
San Clemente, CA 92672

💻 **South Carolina HCV Network**                                         **Online**
Support and exchange of information and coping strategies for persons with Hepatitis C.
Chat room open every night.               *Website:* http://gmwebs.bet/schepc

## HEREDITARY HEMORRHAGIC TELANGIECTASIA / OSLER-WEBER SYNDROME

**HHT Foundation International, Inc.**                              **International**
*Founded 1991.* Mutual support and education for persons interested in hereditary
hemorrhagic telangiectasia (aka Osler-Weber syndrome). Supports clinical and genetic
research. Counseling and advice for patients. Referrals to appropriate treatment centers.
Annual patient/doctor conference. Quarterly newsletter. Dues $45/yr.
HHT Foundation Int'l                      *Phone:* 1-800-448-6389 (US);
P.O. Box 8087                             604-596-3418 (Canada); 410-357-9932 (Int'l)
New Haven, CT 06530                       *E-mail:* hhtinfo@hht.org; *Website:* www.hht.org

## HERMANSKY-PUDLAK / CHEDIAK HIGASHI SYNDROME

**Hermansky-Pudlak Syndrome Network**                      **International network**
*2 affiliated groups. Founded 1992.* Mutual support and education for families affected by
Hermansky-Pudlak Syndrome and Chediak Higashi Syndrome. Networks families together
for support. Newsletter, annual conference. Supports research.

Hermansky-Pudlak Syndrome
  Network
c/o Donna Jean Appell
1 South Rd.
Oyster Bay, NY 11771-1905

*Phone:* 1-800-789-9HPS (voice/Fax)
  or 516-922-3440; *Fax:* 516-922-4022
*E-mail:* hpsnet@worldnet.att.net
*Website:* http://www.medhelp.org/web/hpsn.htm
*Website:* http://www.hpsnetwork.org

# HERNIA, CONGENITAL DIAPHRAGMATIC

**CHERUBS Association for Congenital
Diaphragmatic Hernia Research Advocacy, and Support**          **International network**
*Founded 1995.* Support and information to families of children born with congenital
diaphragmatic hernias. Phone support, online services, on-call volunteers, state and country
representatives, pen pals, medical research, information and referrals, newsletter. Online
chats, bulletin boards, and library.

CHERUBS
P.O. Box 1150
Creedmoor, NC 27565

*Phone:* 1-888-834-8158 or 919-693-8158
*E-mail:* info@cherubs-cdh.org
*Website:* http://www.cherubs-cdh.org

# HERPES

**Herpes Resource Center**                                        **National network**
*75+ groups. Founded 1914.* Emotional support and education for persons with herpes.
Referrals to support groups which provide a safe, confidential environment in which to
obtain accurate information and share experiences with others. Information and referrals,
pamphlets (send self-addressed stamped envelope). Quarterly journal ($25).

Herpes Resource Center
P.O. Box 13827
Research Triangle Park, NC 27709

*Phone:* 919-361-8488 (hotline)
*Phone:* 919-361-8486 (to start group)
*Fax:* 919-361-8425; *E-mail:* bonrei@ashastd.org
*Website:* http://www.ashastd.org

# HIDRADENITIS SUPPURATIVA

⌨ **Hidradenitis Suppurativa Webring**                              **Online**
Chat room and message board for persons affected by hidradenitis suppurativa, a disease of
the sweat glands that causes painful, boil-type lesions.

*Website:* http://clubs.yahoo.com/clubs/hidradenitis

# HISTIOCYTOSIS

**Histiocytosis Association of America**                       **International network**
*Founded 1985.* (Bilingual) Mutual support and information for parents and patients with
this group of rare disorders including hemophagocytic lymphohistiocytosis, pulmonary
eosinophilic granuloma and familial erythrophagocytic lymphohistiocytosis. Publishes

parent-patient directory to facilitate networking and communication. Funds research. Literature and pamphlets (some available in Spanish), newsletter.

Histiocytosis Assn. of America  *Phone:* Jeff/Sally Toughill 856-589-6606
302 N. Broadway  or 1-800-548-2758; *Fax:* 856-589-6614
Pitman, NJ 08071  *E-mail:* histiocyte@aol.com
  *Website:* http://www.histio.org

## HOLOPROSENCEPHALY

⌨ **The Independent Holoprosencephaly Support Site**                    **Online**
Emotional support and information for parents of HPE-affected children. Nurturing forum for people to discuss day-to-day concerns, share information, alleviate fears and vent frustrations. E-mail list.   *Website:* http://www.hpe.freeservers.com
  or www.team17.com/~tsmith/HPE/index.html

## HUMAN PAPILLOMA VIRUS / GENITAL WARTS

**HPV Support Program**                                                **National**
*15 affiliated groups. Founded 1999.* Support and education for persons with human papilloma virus (e.g., genital warts) and cervical cancer prevention. Referrals to HPV groups which provide a safe, confidential environment in which to share support and experiences with others with HPV. Information and referrals, quarterly news journal ($25) pamphlets. Assistance in starting new groups. How-to materials.

ASHA/HPV Program Coord.  *Phone*: 919-361-8486 (to start group)
Attn: Joanne, HPV Group  *Phone:* 919-361-4848 (hotline)
P.O. Box 13827  *E-mail:* bonrei@ashastd.org
Research Triangle Park, NC 27709  *Website:* http://www.ashastd.org
  *Website:* http://www.iwannknow.org (teens)

⌨ **Club HPV**                                                          **Online**
Opportunity for people with human papilloma virus (genital warts) to share experiences and information with others.   *Web:* http://clubs.yahoo.com/clubs/hpv

## HUNTINGTON'S DISEASE

**Huntington's Disease Society of America**                             **National**
*31 chapters/3 affiliates. Founded 1967.* Provides information and referrals to local chapters, support groups, and social workers, as well as referrals to local health care professionals and other resources. Supports and funds research for treatment and cure of Huntington's disease. Literature, audiovisual materials, and publishes three newsletters.

Huntington's Dis. Soc. of Amer.  *Phone:* 1-800-345-4372 or 212-242-1968
158 West 29th St., 7th Fl.  *Fax:* 212-239-3430; *E-mail:* hdsainfo@hdsa.org
New York, NY 10001-5300  *Website:* http://hdsa.org

# HYDROCEPHALUS

**Guardians of Hydrocephalus Research Foundation**          **National network**
*Founded 1977.* (Bilingual) Information and referral service to persons affected by hydrocephalus. Phone networking for parents of children with hydrocephalus. Referrals to doctors, newsletter, literature and book for children and adults with hydrocephalus.
Guardians of Hydrocephalus          *Phone:* Kathy Soriano 718-743-4473
  Research Fdn.                             or 1-800-458-8655; *Fax:* 718-743-1171
2618 Ave. Z                                *E-mail:* ghrf2618@aol.com
Brooklyn, NY 11235

**Hydrocephalus Association**                                **National network**
*Founded 1984.* Provides support, education and advocacy for people with hydrocephalus and their families. Provides a wealth of resource materials on hydrocephalus for all age groups, quarterly newsletter, directory of neurosurgeons, bi-annual national conference, and scholarships for young adults.          *Phone:* 1-888-598-3789 or 415-732-7040
Hydrocephalus Assn.                        *Fax:* 415-732-7044
870 Market St., Suite 705                  *E-mail:* info@hydroassoc.org
San Francisco, CA 94102                    *Website:* http://www.hydroassoc.org

**National Hydrocephalus Foundation**                        **National network**
*Founded 1979.* Mission is to establish and facilitate a communication network, provide informational and educational assistance for individuals and families affected by hydrocephalus, and their families, increase public awareness, and promote and support research on the cause, prevention and treatment of hydrocephalus.
Nat'l Hydrocephalus Fdn.                   *Phone:* 1-888-857-3434 (message center)
12413 Centralia Rd.                        or 562-402-3523; *Fax:* 562-924-6666
Lakewood, CA 90715-1623                    *E-mail:* hydrobrat@Earthlink.net
                                           *Website:* http://nhfonline.org

# HYPERACUSIS

**The Hyperacusis Network**                                  **International network**
*Founded 1991.* Mutual support and sharing of information, and education for individuals and their families with hyperacusis and recruitment (hypersensitive hearing). Promotes research into cause and cure. Newsletter, information and referrals, phone support, pen pals.
Hyperacusis Network                        *Phone:* 920-468-4663 (eve); *Fax:* 920-468-0168
444 Edgewood Dr.                           *E-mail:* hyperacusis@hotmail.com
Green Bay, WI 54302                        *Website:* http://www.hyperacusis.net

# HYPEREXPLEXIA

**Hyperexplexia Contact Group**                              **International network**
*Founded 1997.* Provides understanding and support to families dealing with hyperexplexia

(a rare neurological disorder characterized by an excessive startle reaction including muscle stiffness and apnea in response to sudden noise, movement or touch). Educates professionals. Information and referrals, phone support and literature.

Hyperexplexia Contact Group
c/o Steph Samson
216 Westcott Crescent
Hanwell, London W7 INU England

## HYPERLEXIA

**American Hyperlexia Association**                          **National network**
*20 contacts nationwide.* Provides information and support re: hyperlexia, a disorder characterized by a precocious reading ability, difficulty in understanding verbal language, and abnormal social skills. Newsletter, conferences, literature, phone support, listserv information and referrals. National membership directory.

Amer. Hyperlexia Assn.            *Phone:* 630-415-2212; *Fax:* 630-530-5909
195 W. Spangler, Suite B          *E-mail:* info@hyperlexia.org
Elmhurst, IL 60126                *Website:* http://www.hyperlexia.org/

## HYPOGLYCEMIA

**HELP, The Institute for Body Chemistry**                   **National network**
*Founded 1979.* Support and information for persons interested in body chemistry, especially hypoglycemia (low blood sugar) but also includes celiac disease, pre-menstrual syndrome, and cholesterol management. Promotes research. Phone support, referrals to support groups. Assistance in starting groups.

HELP                              *Phone:* 610-525-1225
P.O. Box 1338                     *E-mail:* ekrimmel12@earthlink.net
Bryn Mawr, PA 19010

## HYPOPARATHYROIDISM

**Hypoparathyroidism Association**                           **National network**
*Founded 1994.* Dedicated to improving the lives of people with all forms of hypoparathyroidism, a rare medical disorder. Maintains a worldwide network of families for support. Quarterly newsletter. Online newsletter, member gallery.

Hypoparathyroidism Assn., Inc.    *Phone:* 208-524-3857; *Fax:* 208-524-2619
c/o James E. Sanders              *E-mail:* hpth@hypoparathyroidism.org
2835 Salmon                       *Website:* http://www.hypoparathyroidism.org
Idaho Falls, ID 83406

*"Man is a special being and, if left to himself in an isolated condition, would be one of the weakest creatures; but associated with his kind, he works wonders." — Daniel Webster*

247

# HYPOPHOSPHATASIA

**Hypophosphatasia Division**                    **International network**
*Founded 1990.* Provides support for families affected by hypophosphatasia. Newsletters, updated medical information, phone support, annual conventions. Dues $25/yr.
Hypophosphatasia Div.              *Phone:* 1-800-3MAGIC3 (800-362-4423)
MAGIC Fdn.                         *Fax:* 708-383-0899
1327 North Harlem Ave.             *E-mail:* mary@magicfoundation.org
Oak Park, IL 60302                 *Website:* http://www.magicfoundation.org

# HYSTERECTOMY
*(Also see Infertility)*

**HERS Foundation (Hysterectomy Educational Resources and Service)**          **National**
*Founded 1982.* Provides information about the alternatives to, and consequences of, hysterectomy. Free packet of information, doctor referral, advocacy, medical journal articles.                          *Phone:* 610-667-7757 or 1-888-750-4377
HERS Fdn.                          *Fax:* 610-667-8096
422 Bryn Mawr Ave.                 *E-mail:* info@hersfoundation.com
Bala Cynwyd, PA 19004              *Website:* http://www.hersfoundation.com

🖳 **Sans Uteri**                                                **Online**
*Founded 1996.* A structured online forum for people to discuss the impact of hysterectomy on their lives. Internet mailing list.
Sans Uteri                         *Phone:* 310-399-4849
1621 Glyndon Ave.                  *E-mail:* findings@findings.net
Venice, CA 90291-2923              *Website:* http://www.findings.net/sans-uteri.html

# ICHTHYOSIS

**FIRST (Foundation for Ichthyosis and Related Skin Types)**          **National network**
*Founded 1981.* Provides support for people with ichthyosis through networking with others. Public and professional education. Supports research on treatment and cure, and advocacy issues. Quarterly newsletter, publications, bi-annual conference. Dues $35.
FIRST                              *Phone:* 215-631-1411 or 1-800-545-3286
650 N. Cannon Ave., Suite 17       *Fax:* 215-631-1413; *E-mail:* info@scalyskin.org
Lansdale, PA 19446                 *Website:* http://www.scalyskin.org

# IDIOPATHIC THROMBOCYTOPENIC PURPURA

**Platelet Disorder Support Association**                        **Online**
Provides information and support to persons who have ITP (idiopathic thrombocytopenic purpura) and related blood disorders. Members regularly exchange messages. Support

meetings, convention, advocacy, newsletter, and written material. Online support for women with ITP who are, or thinking about becoming, pregnant.

PDSA                                          *Phone:* 1-87-PLATELET (voice/fax)
Box 61533                                     *E-mail:* pdsa@pdsa.org
Potomac, MD 20859                             *Website:* http://www.pdsa.org
                                              *Website:* http://www.itppeople.com

## IgA NEPHROPATHY
*(Also see Kidney)*

**IgA Nephropathy Support Network**                          **National network**
*Founded 1992.* Acts as a clearinghouse of information for persons with IgA nephropathy. Forum in which patients can express their concerns. Promotes research into the causes and cures. Information, phone support, network of patients. Newsletter.

IgA Nephropathy Support Network              *Phone:* Dale Hellegers, Pres. 413-863-8663
9 G Street, #B                               *E-mail:* igan@gis.net
Turner Falls, MA 01376

## IMMUNE DEFICIENCY
*(Also see specific disorder)*

**American Autoimmune Related Diseases Assn., Inc.**              **International**
*2 affiliated groups. Founded 1991.* Mutual support and education for patients with any type of autoimmune disease. Advocacy, referrals to support groups, literature, conferences. Newsletter. Supports research. Assistance in starting groups. Dues $24.

Amer. Autoimmune Rel. Dis. Assn.             *Phone:* 586-776-3900; *Fax:* 586-776-3903
22100 Gratiot Ave.                           *E-mail:* aarda@aol.com
East Detroit, MI 48021-2227                  *Website:* http://www.aarda.org

**Immune Deficiency Foundation**                                    **National**
*Chapters in 22 states. Founded 1980.* Provides support and education for families affected by primary immune deficiency diseases. Newsletter, handbook, videotape and educational materials for public and medical professionals. Scholarships and fellowship program. Group development guidelines.

Immune Deficiency Fdn.                        *Phone:* 1-800-296-4433; *Fax:* 410-321-9165
40 W. Chesapeake Ave., #308                  *E-mail:* idf@primaryimmune.org
Towson, MD 21204                             *Website:* http://www.primaryimmune.org /

**⌨ Primary Immune Deficiencies Online Group**                        **Online**
Email group for adults with primary immune deficiencies, and their families and friends. Dedicated to exchanging information, sharing experiences, and getting support for primary immune deficiencies and their treatments. List is restricted in order to protect the privacy of members.                                    *Web:* www.yahoo.com/group/Immune_Deficiency

⬛ **SCID Mailing Group**                                            **Online**
*Founded 1997.* Online self-help group for families afflicted with severe combined immune deficiency or who have lost a child to this very rare genetic disorder which results in severe infections. Opportunity for families to share information and resources with one another.
*E-mail:* SCIDemail@scid.net          *Website:* http://www.scid.net

# INCONTINENCE
*(Also see specific disorder)*

**Continence Restored Inc.**                                 **International**
*8 affiliated groups. Founded 1984.* Forum where persons with incontinence, their families and friends can express concerns and receive assistance. Information on bladder control. Phone support. Assistance in starting groups.
Continence Restored Inc.          *Phone:* 203-348-0601
407 Strawberry Hill Ave.          *Fax*: 203-348-0601
Stamford, CT 06902                *E-mail*: smith_younganne@hotmail.com

**Pull-Thru Network, The**                                 **National network**
*Founded 1988.* (A chapter of United Ostomy Assn.) Support and education for families with children born with anorectal malformations (including cloaca, VATER, cloacal exstrophy, imperforate anus and/or Hirschsprung's disease). Maintains a database for networking. Quarterly newsletter. Online discussion group. Phone support and literature. Dues $31 (UOA/PTN); $20 (PTN only).
The Pull-Thru Network           *Phone:* 205-978-2930
2312 Savoy St.                  *E-mail:* pullthru@bellsouth.net
Hoover, AL 35226-1528           *Website:* http://www.pullthrough.org

**Simon Foundation for Continence**                               **National**
*500+ affiliated groups. Founded 1983.* Support and advocacy for people suffering from incontinence. Newsletter, pen pals, books, videos, group development guidelines.
Simon Fdn. for Continence       *Phone:* 847-864-3913 or 1-800-23-SIMON
P.O. Box 835                    *Fax:* 847-864-9758
Wilmette, IL 60091              *Website:* http://www.simonfoundation.org

# INCONTINENTIA PIGMENTI

**Incontinentia Pigmenti International Foundation**     **International network**
*Founded 1995.* Dedicated to research, family support and physician awareness on incontinentia pigmenti. Maintains national database of patients.
IPIF                            *Phone:* 212-452-1231; *Fax:* 212-452-1406
30 East 72nd St., 16th Fl.      *E-mail:* ipif@ipif.org
New York, NY 10021              *Website:* http://imgen.bcm.tmc.edu/ipif

## INFANTILE SPASMS / WEST SYNDROME
*(Also see Epilepsy)*

### 🖳 Infantile Spasms List                                           Online
Support and information for parents and caregivers of children with infantile spasms. Opportunity to discuss their children and treatment options. Professionals welcomed.
*Website:* groups.yahoo.com/group/infantilespasms

## INFECTIOUS DISEASES
*(Also see specific disorder)*

### PKIDs (Parents of Kids with Infectious Diseases)        National network
*Founded 1986.* Provides informational and educational support for parents of children with chronic viral infectious diseases, with an emphasis on HIV, and hepatitis B and C. Opportunity for persons to share information and experiences. Newsletter, literature, advocacy, pen pals, phone support. Supports research. Email list, support group.
PKIDS                                    *Phone:* 360-695-0293 or 1-877-55-PKIDS
P.O. Box 5666                            *E-mail:* pkids@pkids.org
Vancouver, WA 98668                      *Website:* http://www.pkids.org

## INFERTILITY
*(Also see Hysterectomy, Adoption, specific disorder)*

### NINE (National Infertility Network Exchange)                    National
*Founded 1988.* Support for persons with impaired fertility to understand and cope. Educational meetings, newsletter, talk line, library, advocacy, and referral. Dues $35/yr.
NINE                                     *Phone:* 516-794-5772; *Fax:* 516-794-0008
P.O. Box 204                             *E-mail:* GeneralMail@Nine-infertility.org
East Meadow, NY 11554                    *Website:* http://www.nine-infertility.org

### No Kidding!                                                   International
*76 chapters in four countries. Founded 1984.* Mutual support and social activities for married and single people who either have decided not to have children, are postponing parenthood, are undecided, or are unable to have children. Chapter development guidelines.
No Kidding!                              *Phone:* 604-538-7736 (24 hr)
Box 2802                                 *E-mail:* info@nokidding.net
Vancouver, BC Canada V6B 3X2             *Website:* http://www.nokidding.net

### Organization of Parents Through Surrogacy                       National
*Founded 1988.* Educational, support and advocacy organization for families built through surrogate parenting. Members work together to address legislative bills on surrogacy. Online newsletter, information, networking, referrals, e-mail chat room, phone support, literature, meetings. Dues $150/parents; $100/surrogates.

OPTS                                    *Phone:* 847-782-0224
P.O. Box 611                            *E-mail:* bzager@msn.com
Gurnee, IL 60031                        *Website:* http://www.opts.com

**RESOLVE, the National Infertility Association**                    **National**
*50+ chapters. Founded 1974.* Emotional support and medical referrals for infertile couples. Support groups, education for members and public. Quarterly newsletter, publications. Chapter development guidelines.    *Phone:* 617-623-0744 (helpline)
RESOLVE                                 *Phone:* 617-623-1156 (office)
1310 Broadway                           *Fax:* 617-623-0252; *E-mail:* Info@Resolve.com
Somerville, MA 02144-1779               *Website:* http://www.resolve.org

**⌨ INCIID (International Council on Infertility Information Dissemination)**                                         **Online**
Website offers message boards on a variety of issues including fertility after forty, men, emotional issues, legal and insurance, grief, alternative therapies, polycystic ovarian syndrome, immune disorders, among others.
INCIID                                  *Phone:* Nancy Hemenway 703-379-9178
P.O. Box 6836                           *E-mail:* INCIIDinfo@inciid.org
Arlington, VA 22206                     *Website:* http://www.inciid.org

**⌨ Fertile Thoughts**                                                **Online**
Provides support for infertile couples through chat rooms and forums. Topics include: general issues, primary and secondary infertility, over 35, overweight, grief, polycystic ovarian syndrome, male infertility, adoption, and parenting.
                              *Website:* http://www.fertilethoughts.net

**⌨ TASC (The American Surrogacy Center)**                             **Online**
Support for persons dealing with surrogacy issues. Various email discussions and bulletin boards, live chats and virtual seminars. Topics include egg donation, multiple miscarriages, DES, and Mayer-Rokitansky-Kustur-Hauser syndrome.
*E-mail*: TASC@surrogacy.com       *Website:* http://www.surrogacy.com

# INFLAMMATORY BOWEL DISEASE
*(Also see specific disorder)*

**American Celiac Society / Dietary Support Coalition**              **National**
*66 affiliated chapters. Founded 1976.* Mutual support and information for celiac-sprue patients, families and health care professionals. Buddy system, visitation, phone help system, participation in educational efforts. Also supports dermatitis herpetiformis and Crohn's disease. Newsletter.    *Phone:* Annette Bentley 973-325-8837
American Celiac Society                  *Fax:* 973-669-8808
59 Crystal Ave.                          *E-mail:* AmerCeliacSoc@netscape.net
W. Orange, NJ 07052

**Crohn's and Colitis Foundation of America**                    **National**
*56 chapters. Founded 1967.* Offers educational programs and supportive services for people
with Crohn's disease or ulcerative colitis, as well as their family and friends. Funds research
that seeks the cure for these illnesses. Membership includes a national magazine, and
discounts on books. Brochures available free of charge. Dues $25/year.
CCFA                               *Phone:* 1-800-932-2423; *Fax:* 212-779-4098
386 Park Ave. South, 17th Fl.      *E-mail:* info@ccfa.org
New York, NY 10016                 *Website:* http://www.ccfa.org

**Intestinal Disease Foundation, Inc.**                          **Model**
*1 group in Pittsburgh. Founded 1987.* Provides information, support and guidance to
persons with inflammatory bowel disease, irritable bowel syndrome, diverticular disease
and short bowel syndrome, and their families. Literature, newsletter, information and
referral, and phone support.
Intestinal Disease Fdn.            *Phone:* 412-261-5888
1323 Forbes Ave., Suite 200        *Fax:* 412-471-2722
Pittsburgh, PA 15219

## INTERSTITIAL CYSTITIS

**Interstitial Cystitis Association**                            **National**
*85 groups. Founded 1984.* Provides education, information and support for persons with
interstitial cystitis and their spouses and families. Newsletter ($40/yr).
ICA                                *Phone:* 1-800-HELP-ICA or 301-610-5300
51 Monroe St.                      *Fax:* 301-610-5308; *E-mail:* icamail@ichelp.org
Rockville, MD 20850                *Website:* http://www.ichelp.org

## INTESTINAL MULTIPLE POLYPOSIS / COLORECTAL CANCER

**IMPACC (Intestinal Multiple Polyposis And Colorectal Cancer)**     **National network**
*Founded 1986.* Support network to help patients and families dealing with familial
polyposis and hereditary colon cancer. Information and referrals, encourages research, and
educates professionals and public. Phone support network, correspondence, and literature.
IMPACC                             *Phone:* Ann Fagan 570-788-1818 (day)
P.O. Box11                         or 570-788-3712 (eve); *Fax:* 570-788-4046
Conyngham, PA 18219                *E-mail:* impacc@epix.net

## INVERTED DUPLICATED 15

**IDEAS (IsoDicentric 15 Exchange, Advocacy and Support)**          **National network**
*Founded 1994.* Support and advocacy for people affected by inverted duplication 15.
Information and referrals, phone support, literature, newsletter.

IDEAS                                  *Phone:* Donna Bennet 717-225-5229 (day)
416 Big Mount Rd.                       *E-mail:* info@idic15.org
Thomasville, PA 17364-9431             *Website:* http://www.idic15.org

## IRRITABLE BOWEL SYNDROME
*(Also see Digestive Motility Disorders, Incontinence)*

**International Foundation for Functional**
**Gastrointestinal Disorders**                                    **International**
*Founded 1990.* Educational and research organization that provides information, assistance and support for people affected by functional gastrointestinal disorders, irritable bowel syndrome, gastroesophageal reflux disorder, and bowel incontinence. Publishes three quarterly newsletters (one for lower GI problems, one for upper GI problems, and one for pediatric digestive problems). Many other fact sheets and educational publications available.
IFFGD                                  *Phone:* 1-888-964-2001 or 414-964-1799
P.O. Box 170864                        *Fax:* 414-964-7176; *E-mail:* iffgd@iffgd.org
Milwaukee, WI 53217-8076               *Website:* http://www.iffgd.org

**Irritable Bowel Syndrome Self-Help Group**                     **International**
*6 groups in USA; 4 groups in Canada. Founded 1987.* Mutual support for persons with irritable bowel syndrome, their families, and health care professionals. Literature, phone support, advocacy, assistance in starting similar groups.
IBS Self-Help Group                    *Phone:* Jeffrey Roberts 416-932-3311
3324 Yonge St.                         *Fax:* 416-932-8909
P.O. Box 94074                         *E-mail:* ibs@ibsgroup.org
Toronto, Ontario M4N 3R1 Canada        *Website:* http://www.ibsgroup.org

**Intestinal Disease Foundation, Inc.**                                  **Model**
*1 group in Pittsburgh. Founded 1987.* Provides information, support and guidance to persons with inflammatory bowel disease, irritable bowel syndrome, diverticular disease and short bowel syndrome, and their families. Literature, newsletter, information and referral, and phone support.
Intestinal Disease Fdn.                *Phone:* 412-261-5888
1323 Forbes Ave., Suite 200            *Fax:* 412-471-2722
Pittsburgh, PA 15219

## JEUNE'S SYNDROME / ASPHYXIATING THORACIC / THORACIC-PELVIC-PHALANGEAL DYSTROPHY

**Jeune's Syndrome Support and Information Network**        **National network**
*Founded 1997.* Mutual support and sharing of information for parents of children with Jeune's Syndrome (aka asphyxiating thoracic dystrophy or thoracic-pelvic-phalangeal dystrophy). Information and referrals, newsletter, literature, phone support, pen pals.

Juene's Synd. Support & Info Network   *Phone:* Kurt Hernon 440 0246-1578
1400 S. Lakeview Blvd.                 *E-mail:* kurage@adelphia.net
Lorain, OH 44052

## JOSEPH DISEASE

**International Joseph Disease Foundation, Inc.**            **International network**
*Founded 1977.* Support network for patients, families and health care professionals concerned about Joseph disease. Information and referrals to services.
Int'l Joseph Disease Fdn.        *Fax:* 9250371-1288
P.O. Box 2550                    *E-mail:* bashor@ijdf.net
Livermore, CA 94551-2550         *Website:* http://www.ijdf.net

## JOUBERT SYNDROME

**Joubert Syndrome Foundation**                            **International network**
*7 chapters. Founded 1992.* (Multilingual) Mutual support and sharing of knowledge for parents of children with Joubert syndrome. Aims to educate physicians and support team. Information, family registry, quarterly newsletter, family networking, research registry, and biennial conference. Some materials in Spanish and French.
Joubert Syndrome Fdn.        *Phone:* 410-997-8084 or 410-992-9184
6931 S. Carlinda Ave.        *E-mail:* joubertfoundation@joubertfoundation.com
Columbia, MD 21046           *Website:* http://www.joubertfoundation.com

## KABUKI SYNDROME / NIIKAWAKUROKI SYNDROME

**Kabuki Syndrome Network**                                **International network**
*Founded 1997.* Provides mutual support and information for families affected by Kabuki syndrome (aka Niikawakuroki syndrome). Coordinates family directory. Literature, phone support, pen pals, newsletter.
Kabuki Syndrome Network        *Phone:* Margot & Dean Schmiedge 306-543-8715
8060 Struthers Cr.             *E-mail:* kabuki@sasktel.net
Regina, SK S4Y 1J3 Canada      *Website:* http://www.kabukisyndrome.com

## KIDNEY DISEASE
*(Also see specific disorder)*

**American Association of Kidney Patients**                        **National**
*17 chapters. Founded 1969.* Information, education and support for kidney dialysis and transplant patients, their families and friends. Educational materials, bi-monthly magazine, annual convention. Chapter development guidelines.
AAKP                       *Phone:* 1-800-749-2257 or 813-636-8100
3505 E. Frontage Rd. #315  *Fax:* 813-636-8122; *E-mail:* info@aakp.org
Tampa, FL 33607            *Website:* http://www.aakp.org

255

**PKD Foundation for Research in Polycystic Kidney Disease**      **International**
*47 volunteer chapters. Founded 1982.* Funds research and provides emotional support and education for persons with polycystic kidney disease and their families. Promotes public awareness. Holds medical seminars and fund-raisers. Conferences, phone support, newsletter, assistance in starting new groups.

PKR Fdn.                              *Phone:* 1-800-753-2873 or 816-931-2600
4901 Main St., Suite 200              *E-mail:* pkdcure@pkdcure.org
Kansas City, MO 64112                 *Website:* http://www.pkdcure.org

## KLINEFELTER SYNDROME

**Klinefelter Syndrome and Associates**                          **National network**
*4 affiliated groups. Founded 1990.* Mission is to educate, encourage research and foster treatment and cures for symptoms of sex chromosome variations. These include, but are not limited to, XXY, XXX, XYY, XXXY, XXXXXY, XXYY, etc. Offers brochures that describe basic symptoms, diagnoses and treatments. Newsletter. Dues $25-$30.

Klinefelter Syndrome and Assoc.       *Phone:* 1-888-999-9428 or 916-773-2999
P.O. Box 2119                         *Fax:* 916-660-1899; *E-mail:* ksinfo@genetic.org
Loomis, CA 95650                      *Website:* http://www.genetic.org/ks

**▣ Klinefelter Syndrome Support Group**                         **Online**
Online support and information for persons affected by Klinefelter syndrome. E-mail list enables members to chat with others. Offers information on the variations of the disorder. Conferences. Referrals to local groups.  *Website:* http://klinefeltersyndrome.org

## KLIPPEL-FEIL SYNDROME

**The KFS Circle of Friends**                                    **International network**
*Founded 1996.* Information on Klippel-Feil syndrome, a rare, congenital disorder primarily comprised of cervical-spine fusion, renal abnormalities and scoliosis. Networks families together for emotional support. Support and information provided mainly on-line, but literature and pen pals are available.

The KFS Circle of Friends             *E-mail:* 5492674@pager.mirabilis.com
877 Charlotte St.                     *Website:* http://www.fortunecity.com/
Fredericton, NB E3B 1M7               millennium/bigears/99/kfs.html
Canada

## KLIPPEL-TRENAUNAY SYNDROME

**Klippel-Trenaunay Support Group**                              **National network**
*Founded 1986.* Provides mutual support and sharing of experiences among families of children with KT, and adults with KT. Newsletter, phone support, meetings every two years. Chat room and online mailing list.

KT Support Group
5404 Dundee Rd.
Edina, MN 55436

*Phone:* 952-925-2596
*E-mail:* contactkt@hotmail.com
*Website:* http://www.k-t.org

## LANGER-GIEDION SYNDROME / TRICHORHINOPHALANGEAL SYNDROME TYPE II

**Langer-Giedion Syndrome Association**                    **International network**
*Founded 1997.* Mutual support for families affected by Langer-Giedion Syndrome (aka trichorhinophalangeal syndrome Type II) and TRPS Type I. Promotes research. Matches families together for support. Newsletter, phone support, advocacy. Dues $20.
Langer-Giedion Syndrome Assn.          *Phone:* Louise Kinross 416-465-3029
89 Intham Ave.
Toronto, ON M4K 2W8 Canada

## LARYNGECTOMY

**International Association of Laryngectomees**                          **International**
*285 chapters. Founded 1952.* Provides practical and emotional support to persons before laryngectomy surgery and continuing through rehabilitation and beyond. Newsletter. Chapter development guidelines.
Int'l Assn. of Laryngectomees          *Phone:* 1-866-425-3678
8900 Thorton Rd., Box 99311            *Fax:* 209-472-0516
Stockton, CA 95209

## LEAD POISONING

**Coalition to End Childhood Lead Poisoning**                          **National**
*15 affiliated groups. Founded 1986.* Dedicated to preventing childhood lead poisoning through advocacy, outreach and education. Committed to ensuring that all children grow up in affordable, lead-safe housing. Advocates for community-based solutions which will result in healthier children and communities. Services include monthly partnership meetings, early intervention/public health, legal rights education, lead-safe housing, lead hazard reduction and technical assistance.
Coal. to End Chldhd Lead Poison.       *Phone:* 410-534-6447 or 1-800-370-5323
2714 Hudson St.                        *E-mail:* ranorton@leadsafe.org
Baltimore, MD 21224                    *Website:* http://www.leadsafe.org

## LENNOX-GASTAUT SYNDROME

**LGS Group**                                            **International network**
*Founded 1995.* Mutual support and sharing of experiences for families dealing with Lennox-Gastaut syndrome. Provides phone support, literature.

LGS Group
901 Chantilly Rd.
Los Angeles, CA 90077

*Phone:* Candace Lovrich  310-440-2948
*Fax:* 310-440-3441
*E-mail:* Andydow@aol.com

## LEUKODYSTROPHY
*(Also see specific disorder)*

**United Leukodystrophy Foundation, Inc.**                    **National network**
*Founded 1982.* Provides information and resources for leukodystrophy patients and their families. Communication network among families. Promotes research, public and professional awareness. Newsletter. National conference. Dues $25-$50.

United Leukodystrophy Fdn.
2304 Highland Dr.
Sycamore, IL 60178

*Phone:* 815-895-3211 or 1-800-728-5483
*Fax:* 815-895-2432; *E-mail:* ulfoff@tbcnet.com
*Website:* http://www.ulf.org

## LEWY BODY DISEASE /
## DEMENTIA WITH LEWY BODIES
*(Also see Neurology)*

💻 **Lewy Body Disease Association**                                    **Online**
*Founded 2000.* Provides mutual support and exchange of information about Lewy Body Disease, a disorder that causes fluctuations in cognition and hallucinations. Also provides support for care partners of affected persons. Regularly scheduled online chat meetings, message boards and mailing list.

Lewy Body Disease Assn.
50 Malew St.
Castletown, Isle of Man
1M9 1AF, British Isles

*Phone*: +44 1624 823065
*E-mail*: drown@mcb.net
*Website:* http://www.lewybodydisease.org

## LIFE-THREATENING / CHRONIC ILLNESS
*(Also see specific disorder)*

**Center for Attitudinal Healing**                                    **National**
*130+ affiliates. Founded 1975.* Emotional and spiritual support for children, youth and adults facing their own, or a family member's life-threatening illness, long-term diagnosis, or bereavement. Also open to anyone wishing to change their perception of their lives. Workshops and bi-annual newsletter.

Center for Attitudinal Healing
33 Buchanan Dr.
Sausalito, CA 94965

*Phone:* 415-31-6161; *Fax*: 415-331-4545
*E-mail:* home123@aol.com
*Website:* http://www.healingcenter.org

**HopeKeepers**                                                  **International**
*150 affiliated groups. Founded 1997.* Christian ministry for people who live with chronic pain or illness, and their families. Provides emotional, spiritual and practical support.
258

Newsletter, pen pals, information and referrals, literature. Daily devotionals, share and prayer e-mail support mailing list, chat, couple's retreats, conferences. Manual for starting groups ($15) or complete kit available. Helps churches in setting up support groups, teaches church awareness and leadership on how to outreach to the chronically ill effectively.

| | |
|---|---|
| HopeKeepers | *Phone:* 1-888-751-REST or 858-486-4685 |
| c/o Rest Ministries, Inc. | *Fax:* 1-800-933-1078 |
| P.O. Box 502928 | *E-mail:* rest@restministries.org |
| San Diego, CA 92150 | *Website:* http://www.hopekeepers.org |

### 💻 Ability Online Support Network        Online

Opportunity for children and adolescents with disabilities or a chronic illness to share experiences, information, encouragement and hope through e-mail messages.

| | |
|---|---|
| Ability Online Support Network | *Phone:* 416-650-6207; *Telnet:* bbs.ablelink.org |
| 503 - 1120 Finch Ave. W. | *E-mail:* system.manager@ablelink.org |
| Toronto ON M3J 3H7 Canada | *Website:* www.ablelink.org/public/default.htm |

### 💻 Compassion in Dying Federation        Online

*Founded 1993.* Provides advocacy and education to improve pain care and expand choices at the end of life. Information and referrals, newsletter, literature. Moderated online support group for patients and family members facing end-of-life decisions.

| | |
|---|---|
| Compassion in Dying Federation | *Phone:* 503-221-9556; *Fax:* 503-228-9160 |
| 6312 SW Capitol Hwy., #415 | *E-mail:* info@compassionindying.org |
| Portland, OR 97201 | *Website:* http://www.compassionindying.org |

### 💻 Hospice Cares Discussion Board        Online

Provides three discussion forums focusing on consumers, clinical issues and volunteers dealing with life-threatening illnesses. Also has a 24-hour chatroom .

*Website:* http://hospice-cares.com

## LISSENCEPHALY / NEURONAL MIGRATION DISORDERS

### The Lissencephaly Network        International network

*Founded 1982.* Support for families affected by lissencephaly or other neuronal migration disorders, and their families. Helps relieve the stress of caring for an ill child. Research updates, newsletter, database of affected children. Networking of parents.

| | |
|---|---|
| Lissencephaly Network | *Phone:* 260-432-4310 |
| c/o Dianna Fitzgerald | *Fax:* 260-432-4310 |
| 10408 Bitterroot Ct. | *Email:* vlf@tbcnet.com |
| Ft. Wayne, IN 46804 | *Website:* http://www.lissencephaly.org |

*"Never criticize a man until you've walked a mile in his shoes."*
*- American Indian Proverb*

# LIVER DISEASE
*(Also see specific disorder)*

**American Liver Foundation**                                        **National**
*28 chapters. Founded 1976.* Dedicated to the prevention, treatment and cure of hepatitis and other liver diseases through research, education, and advocacy. Members include patients, families, professionals and supporters. Chapters operated by lay volunteers and staff. Information on liver disease.

American Liver Fdn.                    *Phone:* 1-800-465-4837
75 Maiden Lane, Suite 603              *E-mail:* webmail@liverfoundation.org
New York, NY 10038-4810                *Website:* http://www.liverfoundation.org

**CLASS (Children's Liver Association for Support Services)**        **Model**
*1 group in California. Founded 1995.* Dedicated to addressing the emotional, educational, and financial needs of families of children with liver disease or a liver transplantation. Phone hotline, newsletter, parent matching, literature and financial assistance. Supports research. Educates public about organ donations.

CLASS                                  *Phone:* 1-877-679-8256 or 661-255-0353
26444 Emerald Dove Dr.                 *E-mail:* info@classkids.org
Valencia, CA 91355                     *Website:* http://www.classkids.org

# LOIN PAIN HEMATURIA

**Hearts and Hands**                                                 **Model**
*1 group in NC. Founded 1993.* Emotional, spiritual, and educational support registry for persons with loin pain hematuria syndrome, and their families.

Hearts and Hands                       *Phone:* 336-788-1433
c/o Winoka Plummer                     *E-mail:* nursenokie@aol.com
4115 Thomasville Rd.                   *Website:* http://www.geocities.com/
Winston-Salem, NC 27107                hotsprings/spa/2464/index.html

# LOWE SYNDROME

**Lowe Syndrome Association**                            **International network**
*Founded 1983.* Fosters communication among families with Lowe syndrome. Provides medical and educational information. Supports medical research. Offers booklet, newsletter. International conference. Dues $15 (can be waived).

Lowe Syndrome Assn.                    *Phone:* 765-743-3634
222 Lincoln St.                        *E-mail:* info@lowesyndrome.org
W. Lafayette, IN 47906                 *Website:* http://www.lowesyndrome.org

*"The quality of caring for others is healing in the deepest and most accurate sense."*
*— M.C. Richards*

# LUPRON DRUG

**National Lupron Victims Network**                                    **National**
A grassroots organization comprised of men and women who have taken Lupron and are
now experiencing medical problems after stopping the drug. Information, literature,
advocacy.                             *Phone:* Dr. Linda Abend 856-858-2131
Nat'l Lupron Victims Network          *Fax:* 856-858-0550
P.O. Box 193                          *E-mail:* nlvn@lupronvictims.com
Collingswood, NJ 08108                *Website:* http://www.lupronvictims.com

# LUPUS

**Lupus Foundation of America, Inc., The**                             **National**
*61 chapters. Founded 1977.* Provides information and materials about lupus, and services to
people with lupus and their families. Conducts education and supports research programs.
Newsletter available through local chapters.
Lupus Fdn. of America                 *Phone:* 1-800-558-0121 or 301-670-9292
1300 Piccard Dr., Suite 200           *Fax:* 301-670-9486; *E-mail:* info@lupus.org
Rockville, MD 20850-4303              *Website:* http://www.lupus.org

# LYME DISEASE

**Lyme Disease Network**                                        **National network**
*Founded 1991.* Support, information, and referrals for victims of Lyme disease and their
families. Maintains computer information system.
Lyme Disease Network                  *E-mail:* carol@lymenet.org
43 Winton Rd.                         *Website:* http://www.lymenet.org
E. Brunswick, NJ 08816

# LYMPHANGIOLEIOMYOMATOSIS

**The LAM Foundation**                                        **International network**
*Founded 1995.* Provides support and hope for women and their families who have LAM
(lymphangioleiomyomatosis), a rare lung disorder affecting young women, where smooth
muscle cells grow throughout the lungs. Fund-raising activities to fund clinical and basic
research, and education through conferences. One newsletter for general distribution and
one solely for LAM patients, Patient directory. Listserv. Advocacy.
The LAM Fdn.                          *Phone:* Sue Byrnes 513-777-6889
10105 Beacon Hills Dr.                *Fax:* 513-777-4109; *E-mail:* lam@one.net
Cincinnati, OH 45241                  *Website:* http://lam.uc.edu/

# LYMPHEDEMA

**National Lymphedema Network Inc.**                                    **National**
*Founded 1988.* Provides support groups and information re: primary and secondary lymphedema for patients and professionals. Newsletter, telephone infoline, conferences, pen pal program, referrals to treatment centers and physicians. Assistance in starting new groups. Dues $35.·

Nat'l Lymphedema Network           *Phone:* 1-800-541-3259 (recording)
1611 Telegraph Ave., Suite 111     or 510-208-3200; *Fax:* 510-208-3110
Oakland, CA 94612                  *E-mail:* nln@lymphnet.org
                                   *Website:* http://www.lymphnet.org

# MALIGNANT HYPERTHERMIA

**Malignant Hyperthermia Association of the U.S.**              **National network**
*Founded 1981.* Education and support for malignant hyperthermia susceptible patients and their physicians. Information for health care professionals. Conducts limited research. Newsletter, literature, regional conferences.

MHAUS                              *Phone:* 1-800-98-MHAUS
39 E. State St.                    *Fax:* 607-674-7910
P.O. Box 1069                      *E-mail:* mhaus@norwich.net
Sherburne, NY 13460                *Website:* http://www.mhaus.org

# MANNOSIDOSIS /
# OLIGOSACCHARIDE DISORDER OF LYSOMAL STORAGE

**Int'l Society for Mannosidosis and Related Diseases, Inc.**    **International network**
*Founded 1999.* Provides emotional support for families affected by any oligosaccharide disorders of lysosomal storage. Educational resources for medical community. Promotes research to develop treatments. Phone support, literature, pen pals, information and referrals, newsletter, advocacy. Online message boards, chat rooms and e-mail discussions.

Int'l Soc. for Mannosidosis       *Phone:* 410-254-4903
3210 Batania Ave.                 *E-mail:* info@mannosidosis.org
Baltimore, MD 21214               *Website:* http://www.mannosidosis.org

# MAPLE SYRUP URINE DISEASE
*(Also see Neurological / Neurometabolic)*

**Maple Syrup Urine Disease Family Support Group**              **National network**
*Founded 1982.* Opportunity for support and personal contact for those with maple syrup urine disease and their families. Provides information on MSUD. Aims to strengthen the liaison between families and professionals. Encourages research and newborn screening for MSUD. Newsletter ($10/yr), phone support, conferences, advocacy.

MSUD Family Support Group          *Phone:* Sandra Bulcher 740-548-4475
82 Ravine Rd.                      *Website:* http://www.msud-support.org/
Powell, OH 43065

## MARDEN-WALKER SYNDROME

**The Marden-Walker Syndrome Organization**                **National network**
*Founded 1998.* Mutual support and education for families affected by Marden-Walker syndrome. Provides parent-to-parent network, and physician-to-physician dialogue. Information referrals, newsletter, phone support, pen pals, literature, and advocacy.
Marden-Walker Family Support Grp   *Phone:* Ann Marie Stearns 502-549-3028
P.O. Box 239                       *E-mail:* steansky@yahoo.com
New Haven, KY 40051                *Website:* http://www.mardenwalker.org

## MARFAN SYNDROME

**National Marfan Foundation**                             **National network**
*100+ chapters, support groups and telephone contact persons. Founded 1981.* Provides information on Marfan syndrome and related connective tissue disorders to patients, families and physicians. Provides a means for patients and relatives to share experiences and support one another. Supports and fosters research. Conference, newsletter, publications.
Nat'l Marfan Fdn.                  *Phone:* 1-800-8-MARFAN or 516-883-8712
382 Main St.                       *Fax:* 516-883-8040; *E-mail:* staff@marfan.org
Port Washington, NY 11050          *Website:* http://www.marfan.org

## MARINESCO-SJOGREN SYNDROME

**Marinesco-Sjogren Syndrome Support Group**               **National network**
*Founded 2000.* Support for families affected by Marinesco-Sjogren syndrome, a rare, genetic disorder characterized by ataxia, cataracts, small stature, and retardation. Encourages research. Information and referrals.
MSS Support Group                  *Phone:* 805-499-7410
1640 Crystal View Circle           *E-mail:* marinesco-sjogren@pacbell.net
Newbury Park, CA 91320             *Website:* http://www.marinesco-sjogren.org

## MASTOCYTOSIS

**The Mastocytosis Society**                              **International network**
*Founded 1994.* Support through a newsletter for persons with mastocytosis (a proliferation of mast cells), their families, friends, and professionals working with them. A separate newsletter is published for childhood-onset mastocytosis patients and their parents. Chat room, e-mail discussion group for patients and researchers. Pen pals, advocacy, fundraising for research, phone support. Section devoted to raising children with mastocytosis.

TMS
433 East 300 South
Spanish Fork, UT 84660

*Phone:* 801-798-2032; *Fax:* 801-794-2980
*E-mail:* cybermom@uswest.net
*Website:* http://www.mastocytosis.com

TMS
145 Waterloo St.
Warner, NH 03278

*Phone:* Nancie Salem 603-456-2236
*E-mail:* Nancie@mastokids.org
*Website:* http://www.mastokids.org

## McCUNE-ALBRIGHT SYNDROME
*(Also see Fibrous Dysplasia)*

**McCune-Albright Syndrome/Fibrous Dysplasia Division          International network**
*Founded 1990.* Provides support for families of McCune-Albright syndrome and fibrous dysplasia patients. Newsletters, medical information, phone support, annual conventions. Dues $25/yr.

McCune-Albright Synd. Div.
MAGIC Foundation
1327 North Harlem Ave.
Oak Park, IL 60302

*Phone:* 1-800-3MAGIC3 (1-800-362-4423)
*Fax:* 708-383-0899
*E-mail:* mary@magicfondation.org
*Website:* http://www.magicfoundation.org

## MEMBRANOPROLIFERATIVE GLOMERULONEPHRITIS/ DENSE DEPOSIT DISEASE
*(Also see Kidney)*

**Kidneeds                                                              National network**
*Founded 1997.* Grassroots support network for parents of children with membranoproliferative glomerulonephritis (MPGN) type II (aka dense deposit disease), a rare kidney disorder. Provides money for research on MPGN type 2. Phone support, newsletter, advocacy.

Kidneeds
11 Cherry Lane NE
Iowa City, IA 52240

*Phone:* 319-338-6404 (Voice/Fax)
*E-mail:* llanning@blue.weeg.uiowa.edu
*E-mail:* Kidneeds@usa.net
*Website:* http://www.medicine.uiowa.edu/kidneeds

## MENOPAUSE
*(Also see Premature Ovarian Failure, Women's Health)*

⌨ **Power Surge**                                                              **Online**
Provides support and information for women going through menopause. Online interactive chats, message boards, information, newsletters, weekly gab sessions.
*Website:* http://power-surge.com

## METABOLIC DISORDERS
*(Also see specific disorder)*

**CLIMB (Children Living with Inherited Metabolic Disease)**          **National network**
*20 affiliated groups. Founded 1981.* Networks parents of children with any type of metabolic disorder for mutual support. Encourages research into the cure and prenatal diagnosis of such disorders. Provides grants for treatment and cure. Information, referrals to support groups, newsletter, phone support, pen pals.

| | |
|---|---|
| CLIMB | *Phone:* 01270-250221 (day) |
| The Quadrangle | *Fax:* 0044-1270-250244 |
| Crewe Hall | *E-mail:* info@climb.org.uk |
| Weston Rd. | *Website:* http://www.climb.org.uk |
| Crewe, Cheshire CW1 6UR England | |

**Purine Research Society**                                                   **Model**
*Founded 1986.* Support for persons affected by purine metabolic disorders caused by a defective gene resulting in the production of an enzyme with too little to too much catalytic activity. Includes gout, purine autism, Lesch-Nyhan syndrome, ADA deficiency, and others. Funds research on purine autism. Information on diagnosis, purine restricted diet, referrals.

| | |
|---|---|
| Purine Research Soc. | *Phone:* Tahma Metz 301-530-0354 |
| 5424 Beech Ave. | *Fax:* 301-564-9597 |
| Bethesda, MD 20814 | *E-mail:* purine@erols.com |

## METATROPIC DWARFISM
*(Also see Growth Disorders)*

**Metatropic Dysplasia Dwarf Registry**                              **National network**
*Founded 1980.* Support and information for persons affected by metatropic dwarfism. Networks families and shares information. Phone support, information and referrals, limited literature.

| | |
|---|---|
| | *Phone:* 408-244-6354; *Fax:* 408-296-6317 |
| Metatropic Dysplasia Dwarf Reg. | *E-mail:* figone@netgate.net |
| 3393 Geneva Dr. | *Web:* http://u2.netgate.net/cfigone/mdr/Index.htm |
| Santa Clara, CA 95051 | |

## MILLER SYNDROME

**Foundation for Nager and Miller Syndromes**                        **International**
*Founded 1989.* Networking for families that are affected by Nager or Miller syndrome. Provides referrals, library of information, phone support, newsletter, brochures, scholarships for Camp About Face.

| | |
|---|---|
| FNMS | *Phone:* 1-800-507-3667 or 847-724-6449 |
| c/o Margaret Ieronimo | *Fax:* 847-724-6449 |
| 1827 Grove St., Suite 2 | *E-mail:* fnms@ameritech.net |
| Glenview, IL 60025-2913 | *Website:* http://www.nagerormillersyund.com/new |

265

# MITOCHONDRIAL DISEASE

**United Mitochondrial Disease Foundation**                        **National**
*8 chapters and 15 support groups. Founded 1995.* (Multilingual) Mutual support and networking for families affected by mitochondrial disease, a genetic, degenerative disease. Newsletter, information and referrals, library of medical publications, patient registry, support groups, phone help, and annual symposium. Awards research grants. Some literature in Spanish.           *Phone:* 412-793-8077; *Fax:* 412-793-6477
United Mitochondrial Dis. Fdn.     *Website:* http://www.umdf.org or
8085 Saltsburg Rd., Suite 201      http://thequestnet.com/DelValUMDF/dvumdf.htm
Pittsburgh, PA 15239

# MITRAL VALVE PROLAPSE SYNDROME
*(Also see Dysautonomia)*

**National Society for MVP & Dysautonomia**                        **National**
*59 affiliated groups. Founded 1987.* Assists individuals suffering from mitral valve prolapse syndrome and dysautonomia to find support and understanding. Education on symptoms and treatment. Newsletter, literature.    *Phone:* 205-592-5765 (day)
Nat'l Soc. for MVP/Dysautonomia    *Phone:* 1-800-541-8602 *Fax:* 205-592-5707
880 Montclare Rd., #370            *E-mail:* staff@MVProlapse.com
Birmingham, AL 35213               *Website:* http://www.mvprolapse.com

**Society for Mitral Valve Prolapse Syndrome**                   **International**
*23 affiliated groups. Founded 1991.* Provides support and education to patients, families and friends about mitral valve prolapse syndrome. Newsletter, phone support, literature, conferences, support group meetings.
Soc. for MVP Syndrome              *Phone:* 630-250-9327; *Fax:* 630-773-0478
P.O. Box 431                       *E-mail:* bonnie0107@aol.com
Itasca, IL 60143-0431              *Website:* http://www.mitralvalveprolapse.com

**Mitral Valve Prolapse Program of Cincinnati Support Group**        **Model**
*1 group in Ohio. Founded 1988.* Brings together persons frightened by their symptoms in order to learn to better cope with mitral valve prolapse. Fosters use of non-drug therapies. Supervised exercise sessions, diagnostic evaluations and specialized testing. Information and referrals, conferences, literature, newsletter ($20/yr), group meetings, MVP hotline. Assistance in starting groups.
MVP Prog. of Cincinnati            *Phone:* 513-745-9911
P.O. Box 626                       *E-mail:* kscordo@wright.edu
Loveland, OH 45140                 *Website:* http://www.nursing.wright.edu/

# MOEBIUS SYNDROME

**Moebius Syndrome Foundation**                                **International network**
*Founded 1994.* Communication and support network for persons with Moebius syndrome (a paralysis of the 6th and 7th cranial nerves), and their families. Information, education. Fund-raising for research. Newsletter, phone support, informal meetings, national conference. Help in starting groups.

Moebius Syndrome Fdn.              *Phone:* Vicki McCarrell 660-834-3406
P.O. Box 147                       *Fax:* 660-834-3407
Pilot Grove, MO 65276              *Website:* http://www.ciaccess.com/moebius

# MORQUIO TYPE A

**The Carol Ann Foundation**                                  **International network**
*Founded 1999.* Dedicated to providing mutual support to people who have Morquio Type A. Acts as an advocate between patients, physicians and scientists. Compiles medical information. Pursues funding for education, families and research. Pen pals, phone support, conferences, newsletter.

The Carol Ann Foundation          *Phone:* 520-44-2531; *Fax:* 775-255-1150
P.O. Box 64184                     *E-mail:* mbs85705@yahoo.com
Tucson, AZ 85728-4184             *Website:* http://www.morquio.com

# MUCOLIPIDOSIS TYPE 4

**ML4 Foundation**                                            **National network**
*Founded 1983.* Support network for families of children diagnosed with mucolipidosis type 4, a genetic disorder characterized by variable psychomotor retardation that primarily affects Ashkenazi Jews. Supports fund-raising for research. Information and referrals, phone support.

ML4 Foundation                    *Phone:* 718-434-5067; *Fax:* 718-59-7371
719 E. 17th St.                    *E-mail:* ml4www@aol.com
Brooklyn, NY 11230                *Website:* http://www.lumiarte.com/morquio
                                   *Website:* http://www.ml4.org

# MUCOPOLYSACCHARIDOSES

**National MPS Society**                                      **National**
*9 regional contacts. Founded 1974.* Support for families with mucopolysaccharidoses and related disorders. Support groups, public education, fund-raising for research, parent referral service for networking. Newsletter. Telephone support network.

Nat'l MPS Society                 *Phone:* 610-942-0100; *Fax:* 610-942-7188
102 Aspen Dr.                     *E-mail:* PresMPS@aol.com
Downingtown, PA 19335            *Website:* http://www.mpssociety.org

## MULTIPLE ENDOCRINE NEOPLASM TYPE I / WERMER / ADENOMATOSIS

**Canadian Multiple Endocrine**
**Neoplasm Type 1 Society, Inc.**                                    **National network**
*Founded 1995.* Mutual support to persons afflicted with familial multiple endocrine neoplasia type 1 (aka Wermer syndrome or adenomatosis), and their families. FMEN1 affects the endocrine glands. Literature, information and referrals, phone support and pen pals. Access to doctors and current research. Dues $10/yr.

Canadian MEN1 Soc.          *Phone:* 306-892-2080 (Voice/Fax)
Box 100                     *Fax:* 306-892-2587
Meota, SK, Canada S0M 1X0   *E-mail:* Hockey-Freak99@hotmail.com

## MULTIPLE HEREDITARY EXOSTOSIS

**MHE Family Support Group**                                    **International network**
*Founded 1993.* Provides mutual support and information about multiple hereditary exostosis, characterized by bony bumps on bones which can vary in size, location and number. Information and referrals, phone support.

MHE Family Support          *Phone:* Chele Zelina 440-235-6325
8838 Holly Lane             *E-mail:* CheleZ1@aol.com
Olmsted Falls, OH 44138

**MHE and Me: A Support Group for Kids with MHE**                          **Online**
*Founded 1999.* Provides peers and a supportive community to children suffering from multiple hereditary exostosis (bony bumps). Develops information and literature to assist children and their families in dealing with the disease. Advocacy, information and referrals, phone support.

MHE and Me                  *Phone:* Susan Wynn 845-258-6058
14 Stony Brook Dr.          *E-mail:* mheandme@yahoo.com
Pine Island, NY 10969       *Website:* http://www.geocities.com/mheandme

**The MHE Coalition**                                                        **Online**
*4 affiliated groups. Founded 2000.* Support and information for persons and their families affected by multiple hereditary exostosis, a skeletal disorder characterized by the formation of abnormal bony growths. Promotes and encourages research to find the cause, treatment and cure. Newsletter, networking, literature, advocacy, online groups, information and referrals, phone support, pen pals.

MHE Coalition               *Phone:* Susan Wynn 440-235-6325
8838 Holly Lane             *Website:* http://www.geocities.com/mhecoalition
Olmsted Falls, OH 44138

## MULTIPLE MYELOMA

**International Myeloma Foundation**                          **International network**
Mission is to improve the quality of life of myeloma patients while working toward a cure. Educational and supportive programs, information packets, phone support, newsletter. Networks patients together for mutual support. Referrals to self-help groups nationwide. Conferences.

Int'l Myeloma Fdn.                          *Phone:* 818-487-7455 or 1-800-452-CURE
12650 Riverside Dr., Suite 206          *E-mail:* TheIMF@aol.com
North Hollywood, CA 91607               *Website:* http://www.myeloma.org

## MULTIPLE SCLEROSIS

**Multiple Sclerosis Association of America**                          **International**
*4 regional U.S. offices/1 Canadian affiliated group. Founded 1970.* Mutual support and education for persons with multiple sclerosis. Offers phone support, information and referrals, networking program, support group meetings, lending library, home modification program, equipment distribution program, and more.

MSAA                          *Phone:* 1-800-532-7667; *Fax:* 856-488-8257
706 Haddonfield Rd.          *E-mail:* msaa@msaa.com
Cherry Hill, NJ 08002       *Website:* http://www.msaa.com

**National Multiple Sclerosis Society**                          **National**
*1700 self-help groups. Founded 1946.* Funds research in multiple sclerosis, provides information and referrals, support groups for patients and families. Professional education. Newsletter.

Nat'l MS Society                          *Phone:* 1-800-344-4867 (choose option #1)
700 Broadway, Suite 810          *E-mail:* Kristine.Beisel@nmss.org
Denver, CO 80203                 *Website:* http://www.nationalmssociety.org

## MULTIPLE SYMMETRICAL LIPOMATOSIS / BENIGN SYMMETRIC LIPOMATOSIS / MADELUNG'S / LANOIS-BENSAUDE SYNDROME
*(Also see Metabolic)*

**MSL Help**                          **National network**
*Founded 1996.* Support and networking for persons affected by multiple symmetrical lipomatosis (aka benign symmetric lipomatosis, Madelung's disease, or Lanois-Bensaude syndrome). MSL is a metabolic condition characterized by the growth of fatty masses symmetrically placed around the body. Provides encouragement, education and a sharing of resources for mutual support.

MSL Help                          *Phone:* 860-32-3834
27 Park Rd.                       *E-mail:* mslline@aol.com
W. Hartford, CT 06119            *Web*: home.earthlink.net/~REILLY65/MSL.html

# MUSCULAR DYSTROPHY
*(Also see specific disorder)*

**Parent Project for Muscular Dystrophy Research, Inc.**      **International network**
Support for parents of children with Duchenne and Becker muscular dystrophy. Supports research into the cause and cure. Conferences, newsletter, fund-raising for research. Duchenne muscular dystrophy online forum.

Parent Project for MD Research    *Phone:* 1-800-714-5437 or 513-424-0696
4785 Emerald Way                  *Fax:* 513-425-9907
Middletown, OH 45044             *Website:* http://www.parentproject.org
                                  *Website:* http://www.parentdmd.org

**Society for Muscular Dystrophy Information, Int'l**         **International network**
*Founded 1983.* Purpose is to share and encourage the exchange of non-technical, neuromuscular disorder and disability related information. Referrals to support groups, networking newsletter, pen pals, publication exchange. Dues $25-35.

SMDI, Int'l                       *Phone:* 902-685-3961; *Fax:* 902-685-3962
P.O. Box 479                      *E-mail:* smdi@auracom.com
Bridgewater, NS                   *Website:* www.auracom.com/~smdi/index.html
Canada B4V 2X6

**Muscular Dystrophy Association**                                    **National**
*156 chapters. Founded 1950.* Fights neuromuscular diseases through worldwide research, nationwide network of clinics, and through professional and public education. Some local chapters schedule support groups based upon interest and needs. National magazine and local newsletters.

MDA                               *Phone:* 520-529-2000; *Fax:* 520-529-5300
3300 E. Sunrise Dr.               *E-mail:* mda@mdausa.org
Tucson, AZ 85718                  *Website:* http://www.mdausa.org

# MYASTHENIA GRAVIS

**Myasthenia Gravis Foundation**                                     **National**
*35 chapters. Founded 1952.* Promotes research and education into myasthenia gravis, a chronic neuromuscular disease. Provides supportive services for patients and families. Information and referral. Newsletter, support groups, various web-based services, annual and scientific meetings.

Myasthenia Gravis Fdn.            *Phone:* 1-800-541-5454; *Fax:* 952-545-6073
5841 Cedar Lake Rd., Suite 204    *E-mail:* myastheniagravis@msn.com
Minneapolis, MN 55416            *Website:* http://www.myasthenia.org

# MYELIN DISORDERS

**Organization for Myelin Disorders Research and Support**        **International network**
*Founded 1996.* Provides a communication network among families affected by hypomyelination and myelin deficient disorders, and professionals. Aims to increase awareness, find causes and treatment, and fund research. Information and referrals, phone support, parent link, advocacy, newsletter.
Org. for Myelin Dis. Research Support  *Phone:* 513-734-6338
P.O. Box 54759                                    *Fax:* 513-734-6378
Cincinnati, OH 45254-0759                  *E-mail:* myelinrs@dot-net.net

# MYELOMA
*(Also see Cancer)*

**International Myeloma Foundation**                          **International network**
(Multilingual) Mission is to improve the quality of life of myeloma patients while working toward a cure. Educational programs, information packets, phone support, newsletter. Networks patients together for mutual support. Referrals to self-help groups. Conferences.
Int'l Myeloma Fdn.                             *Phone:* 818-487-7455 or 1-800-452-CURE
12650 Riverside Dr., Suite 206         *Fax:* 818-487-7454; *E-mail:* TheIMF@aol.com
North Hollywood, CA 91607              *Website:* http://www.myeloma.org

# MYELOPROLIFERATIVE DISEASE

**MPD Research Center, Inc.**                                **International network**
*9 affiliated groups. Founded 1989.* Support network enabling persons with myeloproliferative disease to share their experiences and problems. Supports research. Publishes materials. Newsletter, phone support, conferences, information and referrals. Online email listserve with 1800 members with MPD.
MPD Research Center, Inc.               *Phone:* 1-800-HELP-MPD or 212-535-8181
c/o Harriet S. Gilbert, MD               *Fax:* 212-535-7744
115 E. 72nd St.                                  *E-mail:* hgilbert@nyc.rr.com
New York, NY 10021                         *Website:* http://www.acor.org/mpd

🖳 **MPD-SUPPORT-L**                                                        **Online**
Medical mailing list for myeloproliferative disorders concentrating on essential thrombocythemia, polycythemia vera, agnogenic myeloid metaplasia and myelofibrosis. Patients, family members and health professionals are welcome to join.
*E-mail:* mensabrain@aol.com          *Website:* http://members.aol.com/mpdsupport

*"The difference between stumbling blocks and stepping stones is how you use them."*
*- Source Unknown*

# MYOCLONUS

**Moving Forward**                                              International network
*Founded 1995.* Disseminates information on myoclonus, a movement disorder of the sensory nervous system. Resource letter and brochures available.

Moving Forward                              *Phone:* 937-293-0409
2934 Glenmore Ave.
Kettering, OH 45409

# MYOSITIS

**Myositis Association of America**                              National network
*Founded 1993.* Dedicated to serving those with polymyositis, dermatomyositis, juvenile myositis, and inclusion body myositis. Provides education and support. Also serves as a clearinghouse between patients and scientists. Newsletter, research reviews, literature and telephone support. Area meetings available as well as annual conference. Fund-raising for research. Dues: $50.

Myositis Assn. of America          *Phone:* 540-433-7686 (day)
c/o Nancy Armentrout               *Fax:* 540-432-0206
755 Cantrell Ave., Suite C         *E-mail:* maa@myositis.org
Harrisonburg, VA 22801             *Website:* http://www.myositis.org

# MYOTUBULAR MYOPATHY

**Myotubular Myopathy Resource Group**                          International network
*Founded 1993.* Information for patients, parents and doctors regarding myotubular myopathy, a family of three rare muscle disorders usually causing low muscle tone and diminished respiratory capacity. Exchanging of successes with other affected families. Phone support, information and referrals, newsletter, literature.

Myotubular Myopathy Res. Group     *Phone:* Pam Scoggin 409-945-8569
2602 Quaker Dr.                    *E-mail:* gscoggin@aol.com
Texas City, TX 77590              *Website:* http://www.mtmrg.org

# NAGER SYNDROME

**Foundation for Nager and Miller Syndromes**                   International
*Founded 1989.* Networking for families that are affected by Nager or Miller syndromes. Provides referrals, library of information, phone support, newsletter, brochures, and scholarships for Camp About Face.

FNMS                               *Phone:* 1-800-507-3667
c/o Margaret Ieronimo              *Fax:* 847-724-6449
1827 Grove St., Suite 2            *E-mail:* fnms@ameritech.net
Glenview, IL 60025-2913            *Website:* http://www.fnms.net

# NAIL PATELLA SYNDROME

**Nail Patella Syndrome Networking/Support Group**          International network
*Founded 1996.* Support network for persons with nail patella syndrome to exchange information. Links to a research study and other NPS-related sites. Provides information and a place where people with NPS can communicate with each other via the internet.
NPS Networking/Support Group          *E-mail:* PACALI@aol.com
67 Woodlake Dr.                                *Website:* http://www.members.aol.com/
Holland, PA 18966                           PACALI/npspage.html

# NARCOLEPSY

**Narcolepsy Network**                                                              National
*100 affiliated groups. Founded 1986.* Support and education for persons with narcolepsy and other sleep disorders, their families and interested others. Helps with coping skills, family and community problems. Provides advocacy, education, supports research, newsletter, conferences, phone support and group development guidelines.
Narcolepsy Network                        *Phone:* 513-891-3522; *Fax:* 513-891-3836
10921 Reed Hartman Hwy., #119      *E-mail:* narnet@aol.com
Cincinnati, OH 45242                      *Website:* http://www.narcolepsynetwork.org

# NECROTIZING FASCIITIS / FLESH-EATING BACTERIA

**National Necrotizing Fasciitis Foundation**          International network
*2 affiliated groups. Founded 1997.* Provides education and support for persons affected by necrotizing fasciitis (aka flesh-eating bacteria). Aim is to educate public and advocate for research. Provides literature, phone support, newsletter, pen pals, conferences, and information and referrals. Publishes book on surviving the flesh-eating bacteria.
Nat'l Necrotizing Fasciitis Fdn.          *Phone:* Jacqueline Roemmele 860-739-3474
25 Prostpect Ave.                           *E-mail:* jroemmele@nnff.org
Niantic, CT 06357                          *Website:* http://www.nnff.com

# NEMALINE MYOPATHY

**Nemaline Myopathy Newsletter**                                          National network
*Founded 1991.* Grassroots group that offers newsletter that networks families affected by pediatric/adolescent nemaline myopathy for support and information. Pen pals, literature, phone support, information and referrals.
NMN                                            *Phone:* 913-814-0901
c/o Krystyn Orlicki                         *E-mail:* kmorlicki@hotmail.om
11991 Long St., Suite 2413              *Website:* http://www.davidmcd.freeuk.com
Overland Park, KS 66213

# NEPHROTIC SYNDROME
*(Also see Kidney)*

⌨ **Nephrotic Syndrome Parent's Place**                          **Online**
Forum for parents of children with nephrotic syndrome, a set of symptoms caused by various renal diseases in different stages of severity. Offers e-mail mailing lists.
*Website:* http://privat.schlund.de/k/kidney-children

# NEUROCARDIOGENIC SYNCOPE

⌨ **NCS Support Board**                                          **Online**
Provides support for persons affected by neurocardiogenic syncope. Offers general chats, personal stories, and exchange of information on medications and doctors.
*Website:* http://ncssupport.com

⌨ **Neurocardiogenic Syncope - Fainting List**                   **Online**
Support and understanding for those suffering from neurocardiogenic syncope, dysautonomia, orthostatic hypotension, neurally mediated hypotension, low blood pressure and other diseases that can cause fainting, heat sensitivity, nausea or dizziness. Open to families and friends. Sharing of stories, struggles, triumphs and information.
*Website:* http://groups.yahoo.com/group/
NeurocardiogenicSyncope-Fainting

# NEUROFIBROMATOSIS

**National Neurofibromatosis Fdn., Inc.**                        **National**
*30 chapters. Founded 1978.* For patients with neurofibromatosis and their families. Promotes and supports research on the causes of, and cure for neurofibromatosis. Provides information, assistance and education. Dues $35/ind; $50/family. Quarterly newsletter. Professional grants awarded for research.
Nat'l Neurofibromatosis Fdn.        *Phone:* 1-800-323-7938 or 212-344-6633
95 Pine St., 16th Fl.                *Fax:* 212-747-0004; *E-mail:* nnff@nf.org
New York, NY 10005                   *Website:* http://www.nf.org

**Neurofibromatosis, Inc.**                                      **National**
*8 groups. Founded 1988.* (Bilingual) Dedicated to individuals and families affected by the neurofibromatoses (NF-1 and NF-2) through educational, support, clinical and research programs. Newsletter, networking, video, printed materials, information and referrals, phone support. Assistance in starting groups. Some literature in Spanish.
Neurofibromatosis, Inc.             *Phone:* 301-918-4600 or 1-800-942-6825
8855 Annapolis Rd., Suite 110       *Fax:* 301-918-0009; *E-mail:* nfinc1@aol.com
Lanham, MD 20706-2924               *Website:* http://www.nfinc.org

## NEUROLOGICAL DISORDERS
*(Also see specific disorder)*

🖳 **MGH Neurology WebForums**                                    **Online**
Provides both unmoderated message boards and chat rooms for specific neurological disorders including: amyloidosis, arachnoiditis, cerebellar ataxia, congenital fiber type disproportion, CFS leak, DeMorsiers syndrome, erythromelalgia, Lewy body disease, meningitis, meralgia paresthetic, Norrie disease, periodic paralysis, phantom limb pain, Romberg disorder, Syndenhams chorea, tethered cord syndrome, and thoracic outlet syndrome, plus over a hundred more conditions and disorders.
*Website:* http://www.braintalk.org    *Website:* http://neuro-mancer.mgh.harvard.edu
                                       /cgi-bin/Ultimate.cgi

## NEUROMETABOLIC DISORDERS
*(Also see specific disorder)*

**Association for Neuro-Metabolic Disorders**          **National network**
*Founded 1981.* Education and support for families of children with four kinds of neurometabolic disorders (phenylketonuria, maple syrup urine disease, galactosemia and biotinidase deficiency). Parent support between families. Promotes research. Newsletter. Dues $5/yr. Telephone network, correspondence.
Assn. for Neuro-Metabolic Dis        *Phone:* Cheryl Volk (419)885-1497
5223 Brookfield Lane
Sylvania, OH 43560-1809

## NEUTROPENIA

**National Neutropenia Network, Inc.**                  **National network**
*Founded 1994.* Serves as a link for sharing information and support for persons affected by neutropenia and their families. Coordinates efforts nationwide to promote awareness, education and the development of a support system for affected persons. Offers newsletter, networking, literature, advocacy, phone support, conferences, information and referrals.
Nat'l Neutropenia Network, Inc.      *Phone:* 1-800-638-8768 (day/eve)
4547 Tillman Bluff Rd.               *E-mail:* sedpjd3@msn.com
Valdosta, GA 31602                   *Website:* http://www.neutropenia.org

**Neutropenia Support Association, Inc.**              **International**
*Serves 30 countries. Founded 1989.* Information and support for persons with neutropenia, their families and the medical community. Aims to increase awareness, support research, and disseminate literature. Support group meetings.
Neutropenia Support Assoc., Inc.     *Phone:* 204-489-8454 or 1-800-663-8876
P.O. Box 243-905 Corydon Ave.        *E-mail:* stevensl@neutropenia.ca
Winnipeg, MB R3M 3S7 Canada          *Website:* http://www.neutropenia.ca

275

# NEVUS / NEUROCUTANEOUS MELANOSIS

**Nevus Network**                                                **National network**
*Founded 1983.* (Multilingual) To provide a network of support and information for people with large congenital nevi and/or neurocutaneous melanosis. Some materials in French, Spanish and German.

| | |
|---|---|
| Nevus Network | *Phone:* 419-853-4525 or 405-377-3403 |
| P.O. Box 1981 | *E-mail:* info@nevusnetwork.org |
| Woodbridge, VA 22195 | *Website:* http://www.nevusnetwork.org |

**Nevus Outreach, Inc.**                                      **International network**
*Founded 1997.* Provides mutual support, information and interaction for persons affected by large congenital melanocytic nevi or neurocutaneous melanosis. Newsletter, literature, information and referrals, telephone support network, national conferences. Group meetings, e-mail pen pals.

| | |
|---|---|
| | *Phone:* 1-877-4-A-NEVUS |
| Nevus Outreach, Inc. | *Listserv:* support@nevus.org |
| 1601 Madison Blvd. | *E-mail:* info@nevus.org |
| Bartlesville, OK 74006 | *Website:* http://www.nevus.org |

# NIEMANN-PICK DISEASE

**National Niemann-Pick Disease Foundation, Inc.**          **International network**
*Founded 1992.* Provides support for families affected by Niemann-Pick disease. Promotes and supports research. Newsletter, family directory, networking, family conference, phone support, information and referrals. Dues $20.

| | |
|---|---|
| Nat'l Niemann-Pick Dis Fdn. | *Phone:* 920-563-8677; *Fax:* 920-563-5246 |
| P.O. Box 49 415 Madison Ave. | *E-mail:* nnpdf@idcnet.com |
| Fort Atkinson, WI 53538 | *Website:* http://www.nnpdf.org |

# NONKETOTIC HYPERGLYCEMIA
*(Also see metabolic Disorders)*

**NKH International Family Network**                          **International network**
*Founded 1995.* Support and networking for parents of children with nonketotic hyperglycinemia (NKH), an inherited metabolic disorder. Newsletter, online network, discussion board, information and referrals, phone support. Dues $25.

| | |
|---|---|
| NKH Int'l Family Network | *Phone:* 727-799-4977 (day/eve) |
| 2236 Birchbark Trail | *E-mail:* ketchcar@aol.com |
| Clearwater, FL 33763 | *Website:* http://www.NKH-Network.org |

# NOONAN SYNDROME

**Noonan Syndrome Support Group**                            **International network**
*Founded 1996.* Provides information for persons with Noonan syndrome, their families, and

276

interested others. Networks individuals together for peer support. Information and referrals, speakers bureau, telephone helpline.

Noonan Synd. Support Group          *Phone:* 1-888-686-2224 or 410-374-5245
P.O. Box 145                         *E-mail:* Wandar@bellatlantic.net
Upperco, MD 21155                    *Website:* http://www.noonansyndrome.org

# NYSTAGMUS

**American Nystagmus Network**                                      National
*Founded 1999.* Network of persons affected by nystagmus, an involuntary, rapid movement of the eyeball. Open to parents of affected children, adults with nystagmus, and interested professionals. Information. Promotes research. E-mail discussion group, biographies.
ANN, Inc.                            *E-mail:* webmaster@nystagmus.org
303 D Beltline Place #32             *Website:* http://www.nystagmus.org
DeCatur, AL 35603

# OCULOPHARYNGEAL MUSCULAR DYSTROPHY
*(Also see Muscular Dystrophy)*

🖳 **OPMD Support Group for News and Research**                     Online
E-mail discussion groups for persons with oculopharyngeal muscular dystrophy, their families and friends. Provides message exchange, support, and information on latest research.                        *Website:* http://groups.yahoo.com/group/opmd

# ODOROUS CONDITION

**NARA (Not A Rose Association)**                                    Model
*2 groups in GA. Founded 1998.* Mutual support for persons suffering from "odorous" conditions of the body, breath or unknown sources. Offers coping skills.
NARA                                 *Phone:* Bobbie 770-879-5922
5227 Selene Dr.                      *E-mail:* annhenry99@yahoo.com
Stone Mountain, GA 30088             *E-mail:* trimeth411@aol.com

# OPITZ-G / BBB SYNDROME

**Opitz G/BBB Family Network**                                International
*Founded 1994.* Support, encouragement, education, and sharing of successes and ideas for families affected by Opitz-G/BBB syndrome. Maintains database of members, literature, information, e-group, phone support, and newsletter. Family conferences.
Opitz Family Network                 *Phone:* 970-627-3466; *Fax:* 970-627-3476
P.O. Box 515                         *E-mail:* darcee@cubs.egbd.k12.co.us
Grand Lake, CO 80447                 *Website:* http://www.gle.egsd.k12.co.us/
                                     opitz/index.html

## OPSOCLONUS-MYOCLONUS SYNDROME

**Opsoclonus-Myoclonus Support Network**                    **National network**
*Founded 1994.* Networking for parents of children with opsoclonus-myoclonus syndrome through phone and online messages. Doctor referrals, consultation. Literature, current research information. Mutual support and exchange of coping strategies.
Opsoclonus-Myoclonus Sprt Ntwrk    *Phone:* Connie Quinn (717)325-3302
725 North St.                      *E-mail:* clquinn@ptd.net
Jim Thorpe, PA 18229

Opsoclonus-Myoclonus Sprt Ntwrk    *Phone:* Sandra Greenberg (626)339-7949 (day/eve)
420 Montezuma Way                  *E-mail:* Sandranembhard@hotmail.com
W. Covina, CA 91791                *Website:* www.geocities.com/hotsprings/spa/2190

## ORGANIC ACIDEMIA

**Organic Acidemia Association, Inc.**                              **International**
*Founded 1982.* Support, information and networking for families affected by organic acidemia and related disorders. Dues $18/yr. Telephone network. Newsletter.
Organic Acidemia Assn.             *Phone:* Kathy Stagni 763-559-1797
13210 35th Ave. North              *Fax:* 763-694-0017; *E-mail:* oaanews@aol.com
Plymouth, MN 55441                 *Website:* http://www.oaanews.org

## ORTHOPEDIC / JOINT REPLACEMENT

🖥 **Totally Hip**                                                   **Online**
Support to help relieve the fear of total hip replacement surgery, share experiences, and offer moral as well as spiritual support to patients. Helps answer questions on hip replacement. E-mail newsletter. Click on bulletin board for message exchange.
*E-mail:* Linda@totallyhip.org        *Website:* http://www.totallyhip.org

🖥 **Southern California Orthopedic Institute Bulletin Board**        **Online**
Opportunity for persons to share their orthopedic experiences with others. Topics include knee injuries, repairs and treatments, rotator cuff injuries and treatments, spine/back problems, and joint replacement.    *Website:* http://www.scoi.com/bbhome.htm

## OSTEOGENESIS IMPERFECTA

**Osteogenesis Imperfecta Foundation**                               **National**
*21 affiliated support groups. Founded 1970.* Support and resources for families dealing with osteogenesis imperfecta. Provides information for medical professionals. Supports research. Literature, newsletter. Phone support network.

O.I. Fdn.                          *Phone:* 1-800-981-2663 or 301-947-0083
804 W. Diamond Ave., #2101        *Fax:* 301-947-0456; *TDD:* 202-466-4315
Gaithersburg, MD 20878            *E-mail:* bonelink@oif.org
                                  *Website:* http://www.oif.org

## OSTEONECROSIS / AVASCULAR NECROSIS

💻 **Osteonecrosis/Avascular Necrosis Support Group Int'l**          **Online**
Support for persons who suffer from osteonecrosis or avascular necrosis. Goal is to educate and offer emotional support. Also has special section for youth with ON/AVN. Open to other chronic bone, joint or muscular conditions and persons with joint replacements.
                          *Website:* members.aol.com/MarieS1520/2bkn.html

## OSTEOPOROSIS

**National Osteoporosis Foundation**                                **National**
*104 affiliated support groups. Founded 1986.* Dedicated to reducing the widespread prevalence of osteoporosis through programs of research, education and advocacy. Provides referrals to existing support groups, as well as free resources, and materials to assist people to start groups. Newsletter, information and referrals, conferences.
NOF                               *Phone:* Laura Davis 202-721-6342
1232 22nd St., NW                 or NOF 202-223-2226
Washington, DC 20037-1292         *Website:* http://www.nof.org

## OSTOMY
*(Also see specific disorder)*

**Pull-Thru Network, The**                                **National network**
*Founded 1988. (* A chapter of United Ostomy Assn). Support and education for families with children born with anorectal malformations (including cloaca, VATER, cloacal exstrophy, imperforate anus and/or Hirschsprung's disease). Maintains a database for personal networking. Newsletter. Online discussion group. Phone support, literature. Dues $20-$31.
The Pull-Thru Network             *Phone:* 205-978-2930
2312 Savoy St.                    *E-mail:* pullthru@bellsouth.net
Hoover, AL 35226                  *Website:* http://www.pullthrough.org

**United Ostomy Association**                                        **National**
*450+ chapters. Founded 1962.* Dedicated to helping every person with an ostomy and related surgeries return to normal living. Also has support groups for parents of children with ostomies. Provides education, support to local chapters, and national identity. Chapter development assistance. Visitation program, magazine.

United Ostomy Assn.                  *Phone:* 1-800-826-0826 or 949-660-8624
19772 MacArthur Blvd., #200          *Fax:* 949-660-9262; *E-mail:* info@uoa.org
Irvine, CA 92612-2405                *Website:* http://www.uoa.org

## OVERWEIGHT / DIET
*(Also see Eating Disorders, Overeating)*

**National Association to Advance Fat Acceptance (NAAFA)**                **National**
*50 chapters. Founded 1969.* Fights size discrimination and provides fat people with the tools for self-empowerment. Public education regarding obesity. Provides a forum for peer support and activism. Dues $40 (includes newsletter), educational materials, pen pals, and annual convention. Special interest groups include: youth, families, gays, diabetics, men, women, sleep apnea, military, mental health professionals, and couples.
NAAFA                                *Phone:* 1-800-442-1214; *Fax:* 916-558-6881
P.O. Box 188620                      *E-mail:* mabnaafa@aol.com
Sacramento, CA 95818                 *Website:* http://www.naafa.org

**TOPS (Take Off Pounds Sensibly)**                                 **International**
*10493 chapters. Founded 1948.* A self-help support group helping overweight persons attain and maintain their goal weights. Promotes a sensible approach to weight control. Chapters meet weekly for discussion and programs to provide support and motivation. Newsletter. Chapter development guidelines. Dues $20/USA; $25/Canada.
TOPS                                 *Phone:* 1-800-932-8677
P.O. Box 070360                      *E-mail:* RuthGielow@aol.com
Milwaukee, WI 53207                  *Website:* http://www.tops.org

## OXALOSIS / HYPEROXALURIA

**Oxalosis and Hyperoxaluria Foundation**                          **National network**
*Founded 1989.* Provides support and current information for patients, families, and medical professionals. Educates the public, supports research. Newsletter, information and referrals, phone support, pen pals, conferences and funds research. Yearly dues $25/ind.; $50/prof.; $100/business.
OHF                                  *Phone:* 1-888-721-2432 (Pin# 5392)
5718 Holly Hills                     or 314-351-2177; *Fax:* 314-481-6368
St. Louis, MO 63109                  *E-mail:* exec-dir@ohforg
                                     *Website:* http://www.ohf.org

OHF Midwest Office                   *Phone:* 314-846-3645
5727 Westcliffe Dr.                  *Fax:* 314-846-6779
St. Louis, MO 63129-4265             *E-mail:* secy@ohf.org

*"Friendship of a kind that cannot easily be reversed tomorrow must have it's roots in common interests and shared beliefs."– Barbara W. Tuckman*

## PAGET'S DISEASE

**National Association for the Relief of Paget's Disease**                    **Model**
*5 regional groups in UK. Founded 1973.* Offers support to persons with Paget's disease. Aims to raise awareness of this disorder through newsletter and publications. Sponsors research. Information and referrals, phone support, literature.

Nat'l Assn. for the                    *Phone:* 0161-799-4646
  Relief of Paget's Disease            *Fax:* 44-161-799-6511
323 Manchester Rd.                     *E-mail:* 106064.2032@compuserve.com
Walkden, Worsley
Manchester M28 3HH, UK

## PAIN, CHRONIC
*(Also see specific disorder)*

**American Chronic Pain Association, Inc.**                                **National**
*400+ affiliated chapters. Founded 1980.* Offers help for people suffering from chronic pain. Provides support, understanding and sharing of skills to maintain wellness. Workbooks for self-help recovery. Newsletter. Group development guidelines. Phone network. Outreach to clinics.

American Chronic Pain Assn.            *Phone:* 916-632-0922; *Fax:* 916-632-3208
P.O. Box 850                           *E-mail:* ACPA@pacbell.net
Rocklin, CA 95677                      *Website:* http://www.theacpa.org

**HopeKeepers**                                                        **International**
*175 affiliated groups. Founded 1997.* Christian ministry for people who live with chronic pain or illness and their families. Provides emotional, relational, spiritual and practical support. Newsletter, pen pals, information and referrals, literature. Daily devotionals, share and prayer e-mail support mailing list, chat, conferences. Manual for starting groups ($15) or complete kit available. Helps churches set up support groups, teaches church awareness, and trains church leadership on how to outreach to the chronically ill effectively.

HopeKeepers                            *Phone:* 1-888-751-REST or 858-486-4685
c/o Rest Ministries, Inc.              *Fax:* 1-800-933-1078
P.O. Box 502928                        *E-mail:* rest@restministries.org
San Diego, CA 92150                    *Website:* http://www.hopekeepers.org

**National Chronic Pain Outreach Association, Inc.**                **National network**
*Founded 1980.* Clearinghouse for information about chronic pain, and pain management. Aims at increasing public awareness and decreasing the stigma of chronic pain. Provides kit to develop local support groups, national physician referral service and support group listings, quarterly magazine and other materials. Dues $25/yr.

Nat'l Chronic Pain Outreach Assn.      *Phone:* 540-862-9437
P.O. Box 274                           *Fax:* 540-862-9485
Millboro, VA 24460                     *E-mail:* ncpoa@cfw.com

281

🖳 **Back Pain Support Group**                                    **Online**
Online support group that operates through a message board. Started by a former back pain sufferer.                     *Website:* http://www.backpainsupportgroup.com

🖳 **Compassion in Dying Federation**                              **Online**
*Founded 1993.* Provides advocacy and education to improve pain care and expand choices at the end of life. Information and referrals, newsletter, literature. Moderated online support group for patients and family members facing end-of-life decisions.
Compassion in Dying Federation      *Phone:* 503-221-9556; *Fax:* 503-228-9160
6312 SW Capitol Hwy., #415          *E-mail:* info@compassionindying.org
Portland, OR 97201                  *Website:* http://www.compassionindying.org

🖳 **WebMD Back Pain Message Board**                               **Online**
Opportunity for persons with back pain to share their experiences and information. A physician is also available to answer questions. Registration required.
                        *Web:* http://boards.webmd.com/roundtale_topic/42

## PANHYPOPITUITARISM

**Panhypopituitarism Division of MAGIC**              **International network**
*Founded 1990.* Provides support for families affected by panhypopituitarism. Newsletters, medical information, phone support, annual conventions. Dues $25/yr.
Panhypopituitarism Div.             *Phone:* 1-800-3MAGIC3 (1-800-362-4423)
MAGIC Foundation                    *Fax:* 708-383-0899
1327 North Harlem Ave.              *E-mail:* mary@magicfoundation.org
Oak Park, IL 60302                  *Website:* http://www.magicfoundation.org

## PANNICULITIS DISORDERS

🖳 **Panniculitis eGroup**                                         **Online**
Support and information for persons affected by any panniculitis disorder (including: Weber Christian, erythema nodosum, mesenteric panniculitis, erythema induratum, lupus panniculitis, subcutaneous sarcoid, etc.) Members exchange information, resources and mutual support.           *Web:* http://groups.yahoo.com/group/panniculitis

## PAPILLOMATOSIS

**American Laryngeal Papilloma Foundation**              **National network**
*Founded 1991.* Assists those afflicted with laryngeal papillomatosis. Sharing of experiences and information through networking. Seeks to provide financial aid to needy families and affected persons. Vitamin supplement program. National registry. Newsletter, phone support, information and referrals, exhibits and conferences.

A.L.P.F.                          *Phone:* 352-684-7191 or 352-686-8583
P.O. Box 6108                     *Fax:* 352-684-7191
Spring Hill, FL 34611-6108.       *E-mail:* carrie@atlantic.net
                                  *Website:* http://www.alpf.org

**Recurrent Respiratory Papillomatosis Foundation**          **National network**
*Founded 1992.* Networking for families affected by recurrent respiratory papillomatosis (RRP) and interested professionals. Newsletter, phone support.
RRPF                              *Phone:* Bill Stern 609-530-1443
P.O. Box 6643                     *Fax:* 609-530-1912
Lawrenceville, NJ 08648-0643      *E-mail:* bills@rrpf.org
                                  *Website:* http://www.rrpf.org

## PARKINSON'S DISEASE

**American Parkinson Disease Association, Inc.**                  **National**
*65 chapters. Founded 1961.* Network of 800 support groups for patients and families. Chapter development guidelines. Quarterly newsletter. Promotes research. Fifty-four information and referral centers nationwide.
Amer. Parkinson Disease Assn.     *Phone:* 1-888-400-2732 or 718-981-8001
1250 Hyland Blvd., Suite B4       *Phone:* 1-800-223-2732; *Fax:* 718-981-4399
Staten Island, NY 10305           *Website:* http://www.apdaparkinson.org

**Parkinson's Disease Foundation, Inc.**                      **International**
*Founded 1957.* Aims to provide Parkinson patients a better quality of life through funding of research in the hopes of finding the cause and, ultimately, the cure. Provides referrals to support groups, newsletter, information and phone support. Assistance in developing new groups.
Parkinson's Disease Fdn.          *Phone:* 212-923-4700 or 1-800-457-6676
710 W. 168th St.                  *Fax:* 212-923-4778; *E-mail:* info@pdf.org
New York, NY 10032                *Website:* http://www.pdf.org

## PARRY-ROMBERG SYNDROME /
## PROGRESSIVE FACIAL HEMIATROPHY
*(Also see Neurology)*

⌨ **The Romberg's Connection**                                      **Online**
*Founded 1997.* Mutual support for persons affected by Parry-Romberg's Syndrome (aka progressive facial hemiatrophy or Romberg's Syndrome), a rare, genetic disorder, their families and friends. Aim is to locate affected persons and offer strength, hope, courage and friendship. Pen pal program online and via mail. Some face-to-face meetings. Phone support network in U.S.          *E-mail:* Rombergs@hotmail.com
                                  *Website:* www.geocities.com/HotSprings/1018/

# PEMPHIGUS

**National Pemphigus Foundation**                           **International network**
*5 affiliated groups. Founded 1994.* Provides support and information on pemphigus for patients, families, friends, and the medical community. Computer listserv. Literature, newsletter, information, referrals, advocacy and phone support. Online support group.
Nat'l Pemphigus Fdn.                    *Phone:* 510-527-4970; *Fax:* 510-527-8497
P.O. Box 9606                           *E-mail:* pemphigus@pemphigus.org
Berkeley, CA 94709-0606                 *Website:* http://www.pemphigus.org

# PERIPHERAL NEUROPATHY

**Neuropathy Association**                                        **International**
*190 affiliated groups. Founded 1995.* Provides support, education and advocacy for persons with peripheral neuropathy. Promotes and funds research into the cause and cure. Newsletter, literature, information and referrals, and phone support. Online bulletin board, referrals to support groups and doctors. Medical surveys.
Neuropathy Assn.                        *Phone:* 1-800-247-6968 or 212-692-0662
60 E. 42nd St., Room 942                *E-mail:* info@neuropathy.org
New York, NY 10165                      *Website:* http://www.neuropathy.org

# PERIODIC PARALYSIS /
# NON-DYSTROPHIC MYOTONIAS
*(Also see Neurology)*

🖳 **Periodic Paralysis Association**                                    **Online**
Provides information and support to individuals with periodic paralysis and non-dystrophic myotonias (disorders characterized by episodic paralysis and weakness), their families and health care professionals. Offers links to online specialist referrals, private e-mail list serve, and "Ask the Experts." Online newsletter. Patient advocacy.
Periodic Paralysis Resource Ctr.        *Phone:* 626-303-3244; *Fax:* 626-337-1966
1024 Royal Oak Dr., Suite 620           *E-mail:* info@periodicparalysis.org
Monrovia, CA 91016                      *Website:* http://www.periodicparalysis.org

🖳 **Periodic Paralysis International**                                   **Online**
Support and education for patients with periodic paralysis, and the medical community. Provides information, listservs (e-mail discussion groups), and medical databases. Online newsletter.                *Website:* www.calexplorer.com/list/ppsite.htm

*"We all have enough strength to bear the misfortunes of others."*
*- L Rochefoucauld*

## PERTHES / LEGG-CALVE-PERTHES DISEASE / COXA PLANA / OSTEOCHONDRITIS OF UPPER FEMORAL EPIPHYSIS

🖳 **Perthes Association Message Board**                                    **Online**
Opportunity for parents of children with Perthes disease (aka Legg-Calve-Perthes disease, Calve-Perthes disease, coxa plana, or osteochondritis of the upper femoral epiphysis) to exchange messages. Online newsletter. *Website:* http://www.clubs.yahoo.com/
clubs/perthesassociationuk

## PERIVENTRICULAR LEUKOMALACIA

🖳 **PVL Resource Center**                                                **Online**
Dedicated to bringing together parents, caregivers and friends of children with periventricular leukomalacia. Information and support. Email listserv, online chats.
PVL Resource Center               *E-mail:* reenie@computer-connection.net
c/o Maureen Schneeberger          *Website:* www.computer-connection.net/~reenie/
1195 Penfield Center Rd.
Penfield, NY 14526

## PETER'S ANOMALY

**Peters' Partners**                                        **International network**
*Founded 1997.* Support network for persons affected by Peter's anomaly, their families, friends and interested professionals. Opportunity to exchange personal and medical information. Provides newsletter, pen pals, phone support and information and referrals.
Peters' Partners                  *Phone:* 615-383-2514 (eve)
2011 Richard Jones Rd., E-23      or 615-401-5077 (day); *Fax:* 615-401-5086
Nashville, TN 37215-2837          *E-mail:* planetmccall@aol.com

🖳 **Peter's Anomaly Support Group**                                         **Online**
Support for families of children with Peter's anomaly. Message board.
*E-mail:* rmcginn66@yahoo.com        *Website:* http://rob66.freeyellow.com/

## PEUTZ JEGHERS SYNDROME

🖳 **Peutz Jeghers Syndrome Online Support Group**                           **Online**
*Founded 2000.* Provides information for individuals with Peutz Zeghers syndrome and their families. Peer support, networking. Medical referrals.
*E-mail:* pj4steph@aol.com              *Website:* http://listserv.acor.org/archives/pjs.html

## PHEOCHROMOCYTOMA / ADRENAL TUMOR / CHORMAFFIN CELL TUMOR

🖥 **Pheochromocytoma Group Site**                              **Online**
Offers support through information and awareness for persons affected by pheochromocytoma, a rare, neoplastic disorder (aka adrenal tumor or chormaffin cell tumor).                    *Website:* http://www.members.aol.com/
                                           threepeb/ indexpheo1.html

## PHENYLKETONURIA
*(Also see Metabolic)*

**Children's PKU Network**                            **National network**
*Founded 1991.* Provides support and services to families with phenylketonuria (PKU) and other metabolic disorders. Phone support, crisis intervention, information and referrals.
Children's PKU Network           *Phone:* 1-800-377-6677 or 858-509-0767
3790 Via De La Valle, Suite 120  *Fax:* 858-509-0768
Del Mar, CA 92014                *E-mail:* pkunetwork@aol.com

## PICK'S DISEASE / FRONTAL LOBE DEMENTIA

🖥 **Pick's Disease Network**                                  **Online**
Network of families of persons with Pick's disease or other forms of frontal lobe dementia. Also contact list for early/young onset dementia, and a chat group for families of Alzheimer's patients.          *Website:* http://www.bhoffcomp.com/coping/

🖥 **Pick's Disease Support Group**                            **Online**
Support for caregivers of persons with Pick's disease or other frontal lobe dementias. Mailing list forum where caregivers can discuss their problems and concerns. Newsletter, contact e-mail and phone directories.    *Website:* http://www.pdsg.org.uk

## PIERRE ROBIN SYNDROME

**Pierre Robin Network**                             **National network**
*Founded 1999.* Support and education for individuals, parents, caregivers and professionals dealing with Pierre Robin syndrome or sequence. Literature, newsletter, information, advocacy. Online e-mail group and bulletin board. Outreach network of families worldwide available to correspond via mail, phone, in person or e-mail.
Pierre Robin Network             *Phone:* 217-224-7480
c/o Nancy Barry                  *Fax:* 217-224-0292
P.O. Box 3274                    *E-mail:* help@pierrerobin.org
Quincy, IL 62305                 *Website:* http://www.pierrerobin.org

## PINK DISEASE / MERCURY TOXICITY

**Pink Disease Support Group**                           **International network**
*Founded 1989.* Support group for people who had Pink disease (babyhood mercury toxicity) and their relatives. Provides information, support and newsletters by mail and email. Online chat group. Dues $10 yr. (Australia); or $25 (int'l).
Pink Disease Support Group          *E-mail:* difarnsworth@bigpond.com
P.O. Box 134                        *Website:* www.users.bigpond.com/difarnsworth/
Gilgandra NSW Australia 2827

## PITUITARY DISORDERS
*(Also see specific disorder)*

**Pituitary Network Association**                          **International network**
*Founded 1992.* Mutual support for persons with all types of pituitary disorders and diseases. Promotes early diagnosis, medical and public awareness, and continued research to find a cure. Newsletter, information, referrals, phone support, resource guide, patient conferences.
PNA                                 *Phone:* 805-496-4932; *Fax:* 805-499-1523
P.O. Box 1958                       *E-mail:* ptna@pituitary.org
Thousand Oaks, CA 91358             *Website:* http://www.pituitary.org

## PITYRIASIS RUBRA PILARIS

⌨ **Pityriasis Rubra Pilaris Online Support Group**                      **Online**
Dedicated to providing information, resources, and online networking opportunities to individuals with pityriasis rubra pilaris. PRP is a rare, chronic inflammatory skin disorder. Website links to additional sources of information. Chat room, mailing list.
*Website:* http://personal.nbnet.nb.ca/mdetjld/Webpage/index.html

## POLIO

**Gazette International Networking Institute**             **International Network**
*Founded 1987.* Information for individuals with post-polio and users of home mechanical ventilation. Provides newsletter, networking, advocacy, literature, phone support, referrals, conferences, and information on starting groups.
G.I.N.I.                            *Phone:* 314-534-0475
4207 Lindell Blvd., Suite 110       *Fax:* 314-534-5070; *E-mail:* gini_intl@msn.com
St. Louis, MO 63118                 *Website:* http://www.post-polio.org

**International Polio Network**                              **National network**
*Founded 1958.* Information on late effects of polio for survivors and physicians. International conferences and proceedings. Quarterly newsletter ($22), annual directory ($8). Guidelines and workshops for support groups. Handbook on late effects ($11.50).

Int'l Polio Network                    *Phone:* 314-534-0475; *Fax:* 314-534-5070
4207 Lindell Blvd., Suite 110          *E-mail:* gini_intl@msn.com
St. Louis, MO 63108                    *Website:* http://www.post-polio.org

## POLYCYSTIC OVARIAN SYNDROME

**Polycystic Ovarian Syndrome Association**                        **International**
*70 affiliated groups. Founded 1997.* Emotional support and information for women with
polycystic ovarian syndrome. Provides information on various treatments and diagnosis.
Newsletter, phone support, literature, conferences, regional symposiums, and advocacy.
Online chats and e-mail lists. Assistance in starting local groups. Dues $40.
PCOSA                                  *Phone:* 1-877-775-PCOS
P.O. Box 80517                         *E-mail:* info@pcosupport.org
Portland, OR 97280                     *Website:* http://www.pcosupport.org

## PORPHYRIA
*(Also see Metabolic)*

**American Porphyria Foundation**                                **National network**
*40 groups. Founded 1982.* Supports research, provides education and information to the
public, patients and physicians, networks porphyria patients and support groups. Newsletter,
pen pals, telephone network. Donation $35/yr.
Amer. Porphyria Fdn.                   *Phone:* 713-266-9617; *Fax:* 713-871-1788
P.O. Box 22712                         *E-mail:* porphyrus@aol.com
Houston, TX 77227                      *Website:* http://www.porphyriafoundation.com

**Canadian Porphyria Foundation, Inc.**                          **National network**
*Founded 1988.* Dedicated to improving the quality of life for people affected by porphyria,
a group of rare genetic disorders characterized by disturbances of porphyria metabolism.
Offers education, service, advocacy and support. Promotes awareness of porphyria through
literature, fact sheets, newsletter, information and referrals. Support groups, advocacy,
registry. Encourages and supports research. Assistance in starting groups.
Canadian Porphyria Fdn., Inc.          *Phone:* 204-476-2800
P.O. Box 1206                          *E-mail:* porphyria@cpf-inc.ca
Neepawa, MB Canada R0J 1H0             *Website:* http://www.cpf-inc.ca

## POTTER SYNDROME

**National Potter Syndrome Support Group** ·                     **National network**
*Founded 1995.* Support group and information network for families that have babies
affected by Potter syndrome. Newsletter, information and referrals, phone support.
Nat'l Potter Synd. Support Group       *Phone:* Evy Wright 915-692-0831
541-B Bitteroot Circle
Anchorage, AK 99504

# PRADER-WILLI SYNDROME

**Prader-Willi Syndrome Association**                                    **National**
*38 chapters. Founded 1975.* Support and education for anyone impacted by Prader-Willi syndrome. Bi-monthly newsletter. Membership dues $35. Many publications available. Chapter development kits available.    *Phone:* 1-800-926-4797 or 941-312-0400
Prader-Willi Syndrome Assn.           *Fax:* 941-312-0142
5700 Midnight Pass Rd., Suite 6       *E-mail:* maaemba@bellatlantic.net
Sarasota, FL 34242                    *Website:* http://www.pwsausa.org

# PRECOCIOUS PUBERTY

**Precocious Puberty Support Network**                          **National network**
*Founded 1989.* Network and exchange of information for children who are experiencing precocious puberty, and their families. Information and referrals, phone support, pen pals, annual convention, conferences, literature. Newsletter ($25/yr).
Precocious Puberty Network           *Phone:* 1-800-3-MAGIC-3 or 708-383-0808
c/o MAGIC Foundation                 *Fax:* 708-383-0899
1327 N. Harlem                       *E-mail:* mary@magicfoundation.org
Oak Park, IL 60312                   *Website:* http://www.magicfoundation.org

# PRE-ECLAMPSIA
*(Also see Women's Health, HELLP Syndrome)*

🖳 **Action on Pre-Eclampsia**                                          **Online**
Provides information and support for individuals and families affected by pre-eclampsia, a life-threatening condition that only occurs in pregnancy. Hypertension and protein in the urine are two common symptoms. Provides information packets, newsletter, networking of members, and a staffed helpline.    *Phone:* 0208 427 4217 or 0208 863 3271
Action on Pre-Eclampsia              *Fax:* 0208 424 0653
84-88 Pinner Rd.                     *E-mail:* info@apec.org.uk
Harrow, Middx HA1 4HZ UK             *Website:* http://www.apec.org.uk

# PREMATURE OVARIAN FAILURE
*(Also see Menopause, Women's Health)*

**Premature Ovarian Failure Support Group**                    **National network**
*8 affiliated groups. Founded 1995.* Mutual support for women who have prematurely entered menopause. Members network by phone, letter or online. Information and referrals, phone support, literature. Conferences. Online chat room. Assistance in starting groups.
POF Support Group                    *Phone:* Catherine Corp 703-913-4787
P.O. Box 23643                       *E-mail:* info@POFSsupport.org
Alexandria, VA 22304                 *Website:* http://www.pofsupport.org

## PRIMARY LATERAL SCLEROSIS

🖳 **PLS Friends**                                                      **Online**
Opportunity for persons with primary lateral sclerosis, a progressive neuromuscular disease, to share information and support via an online mailing list. Fosters exchange of ideas among PLS patients, their relatives, caregivers, and health care professionals.
*Website:* www.onelist.com/subscribe/PLS-Friends

## PROGERIA

**Sunshine Foundation**                                       **International**
*25 chapters. Founded 1981.* Annual reunion for children from around the world with progeria and their families. Opportunity for children to meet other children with this life threatening, rare aging disorder. Network for parents for support between reunions.
Sunshine Foundation                    *Phone:* 215-396-4770; *Fax:* 215-396-4774
1041 Mill Creek Dr.                     *E-mail:* kim@sunshinefoundation.org
Feasterville, PA 19053                  *Website:* http://www.sunshinefoundation.org

## PROGRESSIVE OSSEOUS HETEROPLASIA

**Progressive Osseous Heteroplasia Association**              **National network**
*Founded 1995.* Support network for patients and families affected by progressive osseous heteroplasia. Fund-raising for research.
POH Assn.                               *Phone:* 708-246-9410; *Fax:* 708-246-9410
33 Stonehearth Square                   *E-mail:* poha@worldnet.att.net
Indian Head Park, IL 60525

## PROGRESSIVE SUPRANUCLEAR PALSY

**Society for Progressive Supranuclear Palsy, Inc.**         **International network**
*75 support groups. Founded 1990.* Provides support for patients with progressive supranuclear palsy, and their families. Advocacy. Offers newsletter, information and referrals, phone support, conferences, pen pals, assistance in starting support groups.
SPSP, Inc.                              *Phone:* 1-800-457-4777; *Fax:* 410-486-4283
1838 Greene Tree Rd.                    *E-mail:* spsp@psp.org
Baltimore, MD 21208                     *Website:* http://www.psp.org

## PROSTATE PROBLEMS

🖳 **Chronic Prostatitis/CPPS Discussion Forum**                        **Online**
Support and information for persons affected by chronic prostatitis and chronic pelvic pain syndrome. Exchange of information.     *Website:* http://www.chronicprostatitis.com

💻 **Prostatitis Chat Room**                                                    Online
Support and information for men concerned with prostate problems including prostatitis, benign prostatic hyperplasia or cancer. Open to men of all ages.
Prostatitis Foundation                    *Phone:* 1-888-891-4200
1063 30th St.,Box 8                        *Fax:* 309-325-7184
Smithshire, IL 61478                       *Website:* http://www.prostate.org

## PROTEUS SYNDROME

**Proteus Syndrome Foundation**                          International network
*Founded 1996.* Provides education and support for families or children with Proteus syndrome. Supports research into cause and cure of this disorder. Newsletter, pen pals, literature, and database of families. Fund-raising.
Proteus Syndrome Fdn.              *Phone:* Kim Hoag 719-264-8445 (day)
6235 Whetstone Dr.                 *Phone:* Barbara King 901-756-9375 (day)
Colorado Springs, CO 80918         *E-mail:* proteusorg@aol.com
                                   *Website:* http://www.proteus-syndrome.org

## PROXIMAL FEMORAL FOCAL DEFICIENCY

💻 **Proximal Femoral Focal Deficiency Virtual Support Group**          Online
Information and support for parents of children with proximal femoral focal deficiency, a rare birth defect where the end of the thigh bone closest to the hip is too short or not developed. Sharing of information, treatment and support.
                                   *Website:* http://www.nls.net/mplpffdvsg

## PROXIMALMYOTONICMYOPATHY / MYOTONIC DYSTROPHY TYPE 2
*(Also see Muscular Dystrophy)*

💻 **PROMM Discussion List Group**                                      Online
*Founded 2001.* Mutual support and sharing of information for persons with PROMM (proximalmyotonicmyopathy, aka myotonic dystrophy type 2). Opportunity for members to share tips on alleviating symptoms, and research developments. Real-time online chats and newsletter planned.
PROMM Discussion List Group        *Phone:* Barbara Rahn 215-428-2399
668 Stoneyhill Rd., #274           *E-mail:* kili1247@yahoo.com
Yardley, PA 19067                  *Website:* http://groups.yahoo.com/group/PROMM/

*"Community is no longer something that we are born into;*
*it is now something that we must choose."*
*- Robert Wuthnow, Sharing the Journey*

# PROZAC SURVIVORS
*(Also see Depression)*

**Prozac Survivors Support Group**                                    **National**
*34 chapters. Founded 1991.* Support and sharing of information for people who have been adversely affected by the antidepressant medication Prozac. Group development guidelines.

Bonnie Leitsch                          Rosellen Meysenburg
2212 Woodbourne Ave.                     11028 Creekmere Dr.
Louisville, KY 40205                     Dallas, TX 75218
*Phone:* 502-459-2086                    *Phone:* 214-328-1984

# PSEUDOTUMOR CEREBRI

**Pseudotumor Cerebri Society**                              **National network**
*Founded 1992.* Brings together individuals living with pseudotumor cerebri to share common experiences. Provides education about the disease, treatment, research advances, and ways to a better life. Conducts research. Information and referrals, literature, advocacy, conferences. Assistance in starting groups.

Pseudotumor Cerebri Society            *Phone:* Debra Friedman 315-464-3937
Health Care Center                     *E-mail:* friedman@mail.upstate.edu
90 Presidential Plaza
Syracuse, NY 13210

**Pseudotumor Cerebri Support Network**              **International network**
*Founded 1995.* Mutual support and education for persons with pseudotumor cerebri. Newsletter, information and referrals, phone support. PTC Primer: Living With Pseudotumor Cerebri ($5).

PSC Support Network                    *Phone:* 614-794-0442; *Fax:* 614-794-1403
4916 St. Andrews Circle                *E-mail:* sondra@sprynet.com
Westerville, OH 43082                  *Website:* http://www.pseudotumorcerebri.com

# PSEUDOXANTHOMA ELASTICUM

**National Association for Pseudoxanthoma Elasticum**        **National network**
*Founded 1988.* Support, education, research and advocacy for persons with pseudoxanthoma elasticum (PXE), their families, interested others, and professionals. Newsletter, information and referrals, phone support. Donations appreciated.

NAPE                                   *Phone:* 303-355-3866; *Fax:* 303-355-3859
c/o Joyce Kohn                         *E-mail:* derckd@ttuhsc.edu
3500 E. 12 Ave.                        *E-mail:*pxenape@estreet.com
Denver, CO 80206                       *Website:* http://www.pxenape.org

**PXE International, Inc.**                                    **International**
*50 affiliated groups. Founded 1995.* Support for persons affected by pseudoxanthoma elasticum (PXE), their families and friends. Peer support for physicians. Offers support groups, phone and mail contacts, literature, and quarterly newsletter.

PXE Int'l, Inc.                        *Phone:* 202-362-9599; *Fax:* 202-966-8553
4301 Connecticut Ave. NW, #404         *E-mail:* pxe@pxe.org
Washington, DC 20008-2304              *Website:* http://www.pxe.org

## PSORIASIS

**National Psoriasis Foundation**                            **National**
*Founded 1968.* (Bilingual) Support and information for people who have psoriasis and psoriatic arthritis, their families and friends. Education to increase public awareness of these disorders. Fund-raising for research. Bi-monthly newsletter. Pen pals, educational booklets, and physician directory. Support group development handbook. Literature in Spanish.

Nat'l Psoriasis Fdn.                   *Phone:* 503-244-7404 or 1-800-723-9166
6600 SW 92nd Ave., Suite 300           *E-mail:* getinfo@npfusa.org
Portland, OR 97223                     *Website:* http://www.psoriasis.org

## PULMONARY FIBROSIS / INTERSTITIAL LUNG DISEASE
*(Also see Respiratory)*

**Pulmonary Fibrosis Association**                           **National**
*Founded 1999.* (Bilingual) Provides information and mutual support to people with pulmonary fibrosis and interstitial lung disease, and their families. Networking, support groups, literature (also available in Spanish), phone support. Membership $35 (includes newsletter and network roster). Conferences. Assistance in starting new groups.

Pulmonary Fibrosis Assn.               *Phone:* 253-630-5179
P.O. Box 7148                          *E-mail:* breathing@pulmonaryfibrosisassn.com
Covington, WA 98042-0041               *Website:* http://www.pulmonaryfibrosisassn.com

## PULMONARY HYPERTENSION
*(Also see Heart)*

**Pulmonary Hypertension Association**                        **National network**
*Founded 1990.* Support and information for patients with pulmonary hypertension (a cardio-vascular disease), their families and physicians. Encourages research, promotes awareness. Resource references. Networking, phone help, pen pals, assistance in starting groups. Newsletter ($15).

Pulmonary Hypertension Assn.           *Phone:* 301-565-3004; *Fax:* 301-565-8994
817 Silver Spring Ave., Suite 303      *E-mail:* pha@phassociation.org
Silver Spring, MD 20910                *Website:* http://www.phassociation.org

⌨ **PHCentral**                                                    Online
*Founded 1999.* Provides support and information for persons with pulmonary hypertension, and their caregivers. Moderated listservs, message boards, patient and caregiver diaries. Chat rooms (general, night-owl, expert chat with guest speaker). Links to other resources.
PHCentral, Inc.                        *Phone:* 215-362-1180 (Voice/Fax)
P.O. Box 1155                          *E-mail:* info@phcentral.org
North Wales, PA 19454                  *Website:* http://www.phcentral.org

## PYRIDOXINE DEPENDENT

⌨ **Pyridoxine Dependent Kids**                                    Online
Support group for parents of children with pyridoxine dependency, or parents who are using B6 as an anticonvulsant.                  *Web:* http://groups.yahoo.com/group/b6children

## RARE DISORDERS GENERAL
*(Also see specific disorder)*

**National Organization for Rare Disorders**              National network
*Founded 1983.* Information and networking for persons with any type of rare disorder. Literature, information and referrals. Advocacy for orphan diseases. Networks persons or families with the same disorder for support.
NORD                                   *Phone:* 1-800-999-6673 or 203-746-6518
55 Kenosia Ave.                        *E-mail:* orphan@rarediseases.org
Danbury, CT 06812                      *Website:* http://www.rarediseases.org

**Hearts and Hands**                                              Model
*1 group in NC. Founded 1993.* Emotional, spiritual and educational support for persons with either rare or undiagnosed illnesses, and their families.
Hearts and Hands                       *Phone:* Winoka Plummer 336-788-1433
4115 Thomasville Rd.                   *Website:* http://www.geocities.com/
Winston-Salem, NJ 27107               hotsprings/spa/2464/index.html

## RAYNAUD'S PHENOMENON

**Raynaud's Association, Inc.**                                   Model
*1 group in NY. Founded 1992.* Mutual support to help sufferers cope with day-to-day activities to maintain or improve their quality of life. Aims to increase awareness of the disease among public and medical communities. Raises funds and supports research efforts. Newsletter, information and referrals, support group meetings, literature, assistance in starting groups. Optional dues $15.
Raynaud's Assn.                        *Phone:* Lynn Wunderman 914-682-8341
94 Mercer Ave.                         *E-mail:* Lwunderman@aol.com
Hartsdale, NY 10530                    *Website:* http://www.raynauds.org

## REFLEX ANOXIC SEIZURE / SYNCOPE / STEPHENSON'S SEIZURE / WHITE BREATH HOLDING / PALLID INFANTILE SYNCOPE

**STARS (Syncope Trust And Reflex Anoxic Seizures)**            International network
*Founded 1993.* Network of parents and sufferers of syncope and reflex anoxic seizure (characterized by temporary heart stoppage and a seizure-like response to any unexpected stimuli), also known as Stephenson's seizure, white breath holding or pallid infantile syncope. Information, education, video. Supports research.
STARS                              *Phone:* 843-671-4641
P.O. Box 6902
Hilton Head Island, SC 29938


STARS                              *Phone:* 011-44 1789 450564
c/o T.C.A. Lobban                  *E-mail:* trudi@stars.org.uk
P.O. Box 175                       *Website:* http://www.stars.org.uk
Stratford-Upon-Avon, Warwickshire
CV37 84D, UK

## REFLEX SYMPATHETIC DYSTROPHY/ CHRONIC REGIONAL PAIN SYNDROME
*(Also see Pain)*

**Reflex Sympathetic Dystrophy Syndrome Association**            National
*100 independent groups. Founded 1984.* Aims to meet the practical and emotional needs of reflex sympathetic dystrophy syndrome (aka chronic regional pain syndrome) patients and their families. RSDS is a disabling disease involving nerve, skin, muscle, blood vessels and bones. Promotes research, educates public and professionals. Newsletter. Group development guidelines.
RSDS Assoc.                        *Phone:* 203-877-3790
P.O. Box 502                       *E-mail:* jwbroatch@aol.com
New Milford, CT 06460              *Website:* http://www.rsds.org


⌨ **RSD Hope Teen Corner**                                      Online
Opportunity for teens with reflex sympathetic dystrophy (aka chronic regional pain syndrome) to express their feelings and give and receive support. Provides a listserv, message board, chat room, writer's corner, and e-mail address list.
                              *Website:* www.angelfire.com/wi/rsdhopeteens/


*"The deepest need of man is the need to overcome his separateness,*
*to leave the prison of his aloneness."– Erich Fromm, PhD*

# RESPIRATORY DISORDERS
*(Also see specific disorder)*

**American Lung Association**                                                    **National**
*Founded 1904.* Refers callers to regional resources for information on lung health, smoking and environment. Local chapters can refer to support groups for persons with chronic lung disorders (emphysema, chronic bronchitis, asthma, pulmonary problems, etc.) if available. These groups use names such as "Easy Breathers," or "Family Asthma Support Group."
Amer. Lung Assn.                            *Phone:* 1-800-586-4872 or 212-315-8700
1740 Broadway                               *Website:* http://www.lungusa.org
New York, NY 10019

🖥 **EFFORTS (Emphysema Foundation for Our Rights to Survive)**          **Online**
Works to promote research for more effective treatments, and hopefully a cure for emphysema and related lung disease. Support mailing list, educational resources. Referrals to local support groups.
EFFORTS                                     *Fax:* 816-413-0176
Claycomo Plaza                              *Website:* http://www.emphysema.net
411 NE US Highway 69
Claycomo, MO 64119

🖥 **Family of COPD Support Programs**                                    **Online**
As support and education forum for sharing ideas and solutions in dealing with chronic obstructive pulmonary disorders. Established to bring together people with COPD in order to communicate with one another, share ideas and knowledge, to support one another, and to live longer, better quality lives.
COPD-Support, Inc.                          *Website:* http://www.copd-support.com/
P.O. Box 490714
Ft. Lauderdale, FL 33349

# RESTLESS LEGS SYNDROME

**Restless Legs Syndrome Foundation**                              **National network**
*Founded 1993.* Provides information about restless legs syndrome, develops support groups, and supports research into causes and treatment of RLS. Membership includes quarterly newsletter which covers current research and treatment, information and booklet. Referrals to self-help groups.            *Phone:* 507-287-6465 or 1-877-463-6757
RLS Fdn.                                     *Fax:* 507-287-6312
819 Second St. SW                            *E-mail:* RLSFoundation@rls.org
Rochester, MN 55902-2985                     *Website:* http://www.rls.org

# RETINOBLASTOMA
*(Also see Blind/Visually-Impaired, Cancer)*

**New England Retinoblastoma Parents Support Group**          **National network**
Provides emotional support and resources for families stricken with retinoblastoma. Information and referral, phone support, conferences, literature, advocacy.
New England Retinoblastoma          *Phone:* 1-800-562-6265
  Parents Support Group          *Fax:* 617-972-7444 or 603-232-1352
P.O. Box 317          *E-mail:* napvi@perkins.pvt.k12.ma.us
Watertown, MA 02472

# RETT SYNDROME

**International Rett Syndrome Association**          **International**
*17 affiliated groups. Founded 1985.* For parents, interested professionals and others concerned with Rett syndrome. Provides information and referral, peer support among parents, and funds research. Quarterly newsletter. Dues $25-$35
IRSA          *Phone:* 1-800-818-7388 or 301-856-3334
9121 Piscataway Rd., Suite 2B          *E-mail:* irsa@rettsyndrome.org
Clinton, MD 20735-2561          *Website:* http://rettsyndrome.org

# REYE'S SYNDROME

**National Reye's Syndrome Foundation**          **National**
*Founded 1974.* Devoted to conquering Reye's syndrome, primarily a children's disease affecting the liver and brain, but can affect all ages. Provides support, information and referrals. Encourages research. Local chapters usually formed by parents. $25 dues includes newsletter.
Nat'l Reye's Syndrome Fdn.          *Phone:* 1-800-233-7393; *Fax:* 419-636-9897
P.O. Box 829          *E-mail:* nrsf@reyessyndrome.org
Bryan, OH 43506          *Website:* http://www.reyessyndrome.org

# ROBINOW SYNDROME /
# FETAL FACE SYNDROME
*(Also see Growth Disorders)*

**Robinow Syndrome Foundation**          **National network**
*Founded 1994.* Aim is to locate, educate and support persons affected by Robinow syndrome, (also known as fetal face syndrome) a very rare dwarfing syndrome.
Karla Kruger          *Phone:* 763-434-1152; *Fax:* 763-434-3691
P.O. Box 1072          *E-mail:* KMKruger@qwest.net
Anoka, MN 55303          *Website:* http://www.robinow.org

## RUBINSTEIN-TAYBI SYNDROME

**Rubinstein-Taybi Parent Group**                                   **National network**
*380 member families. Founded 1984.* (Multilingual) Mutual support, information and sharing for parents of children with Rubinstein-Taybi syndrome. Information, phone contact, parent contact list. Online information available in several languages.

Rubinstein-Taybi Parent Group          *Phone:* 1-888-447-2989 or 785-697-2989
c/o Garry and Lorrie Baxter            *E-mail:* lbaxter@ruraltel.net
P.O. Box 146                           *Website:* http://www.rubinstein-taybi.org
Smith Center, KS 66967                 *Website:* http://www.rubinsteintaybi.com

## RUSSELL-SILVER SYNDROME
*(Also see Growth Disorders)*

**Russell-Silver Syndrome Support Network**                         **National network**
*Founded 1989.* Network and exchange of information for parents of children with Russell-Silver syndrome. Information and referrals, phone support, pen pals, conferences, annual convention, literature. Newsletter ($25/year).

Russell-Silver Synd. Network           *Phone:* 1-800-3-MAGIC-3 or 708-383-0808
c/o MAGIC Foundation                   *Fax:* 708-383-0899
1327 N. Harlem                         *E-mail:* mary@magicfoundation.org
Oak Park, IL 60312                     *Website:* http://www.magicfoundation.org

## SARCOIDOSIS

**National Sarcoidosis Resource Center**                         **International network**
*2 affiliated groups. Founded 1992.* Mutual support for sarcoid patients and their families. Provides telephone support, networking, workshops and lectures, literature and education. Maintains national database, encourages research, provides support and physician referrals, resource guide. Dues $25/yr.

Nat'l Sarcoidosis Resource Ctr.        *Phone:* 732-699-0733; *Fax:* 732-699-0882
P.O. Box 1593                          *E-mail:* nsrc@nsrc-global.net
Piscataway, NJ 08855-1593             *Website:* http://www.nsrc-global.net

**Sarcoid Networking Association**                                 **National network**
*5 chapters. Founded 1992.* Provides support and education for sarcoidosis patients, their families and friends through newsletter, correspondence, phone, and e-mail. Seminars, conferences, research, advocacy, and meetings. Help with starting new groups.
*Phone:* (253)891-6886                 *E-mail:* sarcoidosis_networkprodigy.net

# SCHIZENCEPHALY

**Schiz Kidz Buddies**                                                    **Online**
E-mail list for persons with schizencephaly (a rare, developmental disorder characterized by abnormal clefts in the cerebral hemispheres) their families and professionals. Opportunity to ask questions and share experiences.    *Website:* http://www.geocities.com/Heartland/
Meadows/7384/

# SCLERODERMA

**Scleroderma Foundation, Inc.**                                        **National**
*25 affiliated groups. Founded 1970.* (Multilingual) Dedicated to providing emotional support to people with scleroderma and their families. Provides scleroderma education and public awareness and funds research. Referrals to local support groups and physicians. Advocacy. Conferences. Brochures in Spanish & Portuguese. Dues $25.
Scleroderma Fdn.                         *Phone:* 1-800-722-4673 or 978-463-5843
12 Kent Way, Suite 101                   *Fax:* 978-463-5809
Byfield, MA 01922                        *E-mail:* sfinfo@scleroderma.org
                                         *Website:* http://www.scleroderma.org

# SCOLIOSIS

**National Scoliosis Foundation**                                  **International**
*17 affiliated groups. Founded 1976.* Dedicated to helping children, parents, adults and health care providers deal with the complexities of spinal deformities such as scoliosis. Whether the issue is early detection and screening programs, treatment methods, pain management or patient care, NSF strives to promote public awareness, provide reliable information, encourage on-going research and educate and support the scoliosis community. Bi-annual newsletter, information packets, pen pals, conferences, and phone support. Assistance in starting local groups.    *Phone:* 1-800-673-6922 or 781-341-6333
Nat'l Scoliosis Fdn.                     *Fax:* 781-341-8333
5 Cabot Pl.                              *E-mail:* nsf@scoliosis.org or  scoliosis@aol.com
Stoughton, MA 02072                      *Website:* http://www.scoliosis.org

**Scoliosis Association, Inc.**                                          **National**
*28 chapters. Founded 1974.* Information and support network. Organization of scoliosis patients and parents of children with scoliosis. Establishes local patient and parent self-help groups. Encourages school screening programs. Supports research. Newsletter. Membership contribution $20. Guidelines for starting chapters.
Scoliosis Assn.Inc.                      *Phone:* 1-800-800-0669; *Fax:* 212-866-5797
c/o Stanley Sacks, Pres.                 *E-mail:* scolioassn@aol.com
P.O. Box 8117051                         *Website:* http://scoliosis-assoc.org
Boca Raton, FL 33481-1705                *Website:* http://www.scoliosis.org

# SELECTIVE DORSAL RHIZOTOMY
*(Also see Cerebral Palsy)*

💻 **SDR Parents**                                                          Online
Mutual support for parents of children that have had, or may have, selective dorsal rhizotomy (SDR), a procedure performed on children born with cerebral palsy to relieve tone in extremities to allow them to walk or function better. Sharing of physical therapy suggestions, insurance problems, coping skills, resources. Message exchange listserv.
SDR Parents                           *Phone:* Ann Harrell 219-342-0618
506 N. Washington St.                 *E-mail:* ann@hoosierlink.net
Bourbon, IN 46504                     *Website:* http://www.bourbon.org/dylanshaw

# SEMANTIC-PRAGMATIC DISORDER

💻 **Semantic-Pragmatic Disorder Forum**                                    Online
Opportunity for persons affected by semantic-pragmatic disorder, a communication disorder characterized by problems in processing the meaning of language. Open to families.
                          *Website*: http://members2.boardhost.com/pragma

# SEPTO OPTIC DYSPLASIA / OPTIC NERVE HYPOPLASIA / de MORSIER SYNDROME

**Septo Optic Dysplasia Division**                                  National network
*Founded 1989.* Provides public education and networking for families of children with septo optic dysplasia. Information and referrals, phone support, pen pals, annual convention and conferences.
Septo Optic Dysplasia Div.            *Phone:* 1-800-3-MAGIC-3
The MAGIC Fdn.                        *Fax:* 708-383-0899
1327 N. Harlem                        *E-mail:* mary@magicfoundation.org
Oak Park, IL 60302                    *Website:* http://www.magicfoundation.org

**SOD-I**                                                                   Online
Email support group for parents of children with septo-optic dysplasia and optic nerve hypoplasia (aka deMorsier syndrome). Opportunity to share experiences. Newsletter.
*E-mail:* Support@focusfamilies.org     *Website:* http://www.focusfamilies.org/focus/

# SHWACHMAN-DIAMOND SYNDROME / JOHANSEN-BLIZZARD SYNDROME

**Shwachman-Diamond Syndrome**                                  International network
*Founded 1994.* Mutual support and information for families affected by Shwachman-Diamond syndrome, which is characterized by pancreatic insufficiency, retarded bone growth and hematological abnormalities. Includes Johansen-Blizzard syndrome,

300

cartilage-hair and any unusual neutropenia. Advocates for research. Networking, literature, information and referrals, conferences, phone support. Newsletter.

| | |
|---|---|
| Shwachman Synd. Support Int'l | *Phone:* 1-877-737-4685 |
| 5195 Hampsted Village Ctr. Way | *Fax:* 614-939-0752 |
| PMB #162 | *E-mail:* 4sskids@shwachman-diamond.org |
| New Albany, OH 43054 | *Website:* http://www.shwachman-diamond.org |

💻 **Shwachman-Diamond America**                                   Online

Mutual support and education for families and professionals concerned with Shwachman-Diamond syndrome. Supports research. Opportunity for families to exchange information and ideas for living daily with SDS.     *Website:* www.shwachmandiamondamerica.org

## SICKLE CELL DISEASE

**Sickle Cell Parent and Family Network**                          National

*7 affiliated groups. Founded 1970.* Support and education for families affected by sickle cell disease, and interested professionals. Networking, literature, phone support, conferences, pen pals, advocacy. Assistance in starting local groups.

| | |
|---|---|
| Sickle Cell Parent/Family Ntwrk | *Phone:* 513-641-LOVE |
| P.O. Box 19854 | *Fax:* 513-929-0561 or 513-721-8229 |
| Cincinnati, OH 45219 | |

**Sickle Cell Disease Association of America, Inc.**               National

*90 chapters. Founded 1971.* Education for the public and professionals about sickle cell disease. Support and information for persons affected by the disease. Supports research. Quarterly newsletter, chapter development guidelines, phone network, videos.

| | |
|---|---|
| Sickle Cell Dis. Assn. of Amer. | *Phone:* 310-216-6363 or 1-800-421-8453 |
| 200 Corporate Pointe, Suite 495 | *Fax:* 310-215-3722 |
| Culver City, CA 90230-8727 | *Website:* http://www.sicklecelldisease.org |

## SILICONE / SALINE IMPLANTS

💻 **Silicone and Saline Implant Survivors**                        Online

Message board for persons adversely affected by silicone or saline implants. Offers live chat rooms on various evenings. Opportunity to exchange information, experiences and support.
                                       *Website:* www.geocities.com/HotSpirngs/8689/

## SJOGREN'S SYNDROME

**Sjogren's Syndrome Foundation Inc.**                             National

*98 groups/225 resource volunteers. Founded 1983.* Information and education for Sjogren's syndrome patients, families, health professionals and the public. Opportunities for patients to share ways of coping. Stimulates research for treatments and cures. Newsletter, chapter development assistance, video tapes, annual symposium, Sjogren's handbook.

Sjogren's Syndrome Fdn.            *Phone:* 516-933-6365; 1-800-4-SJOGRENS
366 N. Broadway, Suite PH-W2       *Fax:* 516-933-6368; *E-mail:* ssf@sjogrens.org
Jericho, NY 11753                  *Website:* http://www.sjogrens.org

## SMITH-LEMLI-OPITZ SYNDROME

**Smith-Lemli-Opitz Advocacy and Exchange**                **International network**
*Founded 1988.* Network of families with children with Smith-Lemli-Opitz (RSH) syndrome. Exchange of information, sharing of similar experiences, and correspondence between families. Provides education to medical community, new parents, and others. Phone support. Newsletter twice per year. Dues $10/year.
Smith-Lemli-Opitz Advocacy         *Phone:* 610-485-9663
  and Exchange                     *E-mail:* bhook@erols.com
2650 Valley Forge Dr.              *Web:* http://members.aol.com/SLO97/index.html
Boothwyn, PA 19061

## SMITH-MAGENIS SYNDROME

**PRISMS (Parents and Researchers**
**Interested in Smith-Magenis)**                            **International network**
*Founded 1992.* Parent-to-parent program offering support, advocacy and education for families affected by Smith-Magenis syndrome. Information and referrals, literature, phone support, newsletter, international conferences. Dues $25.
PRISMS                             *Phone:* 603-5547-8384; *Fax:* 603-547-3043
76 S. New Boston Rd.               *E-mail:* cbessette@monad.net
Francestown, NH 03043-3511         *Website:* http://www.smithmagenis.org

## SOTOS SYNDROME

**Sotos Syndrome Support Association**                      **International network**
*Founded 1984.* Provides information and mutual support for families of children with Sotos syndrome. Newsletter, information and referrals, phone support, pen pals, annual conferences.
SSSA                               *Phone:* 402-556-2445 or 1-888-246-SSSA
3 Danada Square                    *E-mail:* sssa@well.com
1E. PMB Suite 235                  *Website:* http://www.well.com/user/sssa
Wheaton, Il 60187

## SPASMODIC DYSPHONIA

**National Spasmodic Dysphonia Association**                            **National**
*36 affiliated support groups. Founded 1990.* Promotes the care and welfare of those with spasmodic dysphonia and their families. Goals include: advancing medical research into the

cause and treatment of spasmodic dysphonia; promoting physician and public awareness of the disorder; and sponsoring support groups for patients and their families. Newsletter.

Nat'l Spasmodic Dysphonia Assn.     *Phone:* 1-800-795-6732; *Fax:* 312-803-0138
1 E. Wacker Dr., Suite 2430             *E-mail:* NSDA@dysphonia.org
Chicago, IL 60601-1905                   *Website:* http://www.dystonia.org

**Spasmodic Dysphonia Support Group of New York**                              **Model**
*Founded 1987.* Provides members with the latest information regarding spasmodic dysphonia, and well as emotional and practical support. Offers workshops and discussions. Encourages education for the public and physicians. Guest speakers, information and referrals.

Spasmodic Dysphonia                   *Phone:* A. Simons 718-793-2442
    Support Group of NY
67-33 152 St.
Flushing, NY 11367

## SPASMODIC TORTICOLLIS

**National Spasmodic Torticollis Association**                              **National**
*75 chapters. Founded 1983.* Support group for spasmodic torticollis victims and their families. Interest in research, public education and establishment of support groups Newsletter, list of neurologists, pen pals, phone network, chapter development guidelines.

Nat'l S.T. Assn.                         *Phone:* 1-800-487-8385 or 714-378-7837
9920 Talbert Ave., Suite 233       *Fax:* 714-378-7830; *E-mail:* NSTAmail@aol.com
Fountain Valley, CA 92708          *Website:* http://www.torticollis.org

## SPASTIC PARAPARESIS

⌨ **HSP/FSP and Disability Links**                                            **Online**
Support and education for persons concerned about hereditary or familial spastic paraparesis. Discussion group, bulletin board, related links, research studies, pen pals, children's e-mail group. Conferences.     *Website:* http://hspinfo.org

## SPINA BIFIDA

**Spina Bifida Association of America**                                     **National**
*75 chapters. Founded 1972.* Encourages educational and vocational development of patients. Promotes public awareness, advocacy and research. Newsletter, chapter development guidelines, national resource center, scholarships, film/videotapes.

Spina Bifida Assn. of America       *Phone:* 1-800-621-3141 or 202-944-3285
4590 MacArthur Blvd. NW, #250   *Fax:* 202-944-3295; *E-mail:* sbaa@sbaa.org
Washington, DC 20007                  *Website:* http://www.sbaa.org

## SPINAL MUSCULAR ATROPHY / KENNEDY'S

**Families of S.M.A.**                                                           **International**
*20 chapters. Founded 1984.* Funding of research, support and networking for families affected by spinal muscular atrophy types I, II, III, adult onset and Kennedy's. Educational resources, group development guidelines, quarterly newsletter, pen pals, phone support and videotapes.                        *Phone:* 1-800-886-1762 or 847-367-7620
Families of SMA                     *Fax:* 847-367-7623 *E-mail:* sma@fsma.org
P.O. Box 196                        *Website:* http://www.fsma.org
Libertyville, IL 60048-0196         *Website:* http://www.curesma.com

**Kennedy's Disease Association, Inc.**                                          **National network**
*National network. Founded 1998.* Mutual support and information for persons with Kennedy's disease (aka spinal and bulbar muscular atrophy), and their families and caregivers. Opportunity to share personal experiences to help alleviate the feeling of aloneness and to engender hope and a positive attitude. Sharing of information regarding diagnosis, treatment and current research. Online chat room every two weeks.
KDA, Inc.                           *Phone:* 805-577-9591
P.O. Box 2050                       *E-mail:* tswaite@pacbell.net
Simi Valley, CA 93062-2050

## SPONTANEOUS PNEUMOTHORAX

🖥 **Pneumoworld**                                                               **Online**
*Founded 2002.* Support and resources for persons affected by spontaneous pneumothorax (aka lung collapse without apparent cause). Offers current medical information, chat room, forum and email correspondence.        *Website:* http://www.pneumoworld.org

## STEVENS JOHNSON SYNDROME /
## TOXIC EPIDERMAL NECROLYSIS

**Stevens Johnson Syndrome Foundation**                                          **International network**
*Founded 1995.* Provides the public and medical communities with information on adverse allergic drug reactions. Aim is to quicken diagnoses to avoid permanent damage. Literature, phone support, information and referrals. Meets on AOL, 2nd Thurs., 7pm, MT.
Stevens Johnson Syndrome Fdn.       *Phone:* 303-635-1241; *Fax:* 303-469-2528
P.O. Box 350333                     *E-mail:* sjsupport@aol.com
Westminster, CO 80035-0333          *Website:* http://www.sjsupport.org

**Stevens Johnson Syndrome Support Network**                                     **International network**
*Founded 1995.* Provides information to persons who are affected by Stevens Johnson or toxic epidermal necrolysis syndromes, disorders usually caused by adverse reactions to either a drug, chemical or virus. Aim is to build a support network to link persons together

for support. Newsletter, literature, phone support network.

SJS Support Network         *Phone:* Robertson Arbuckle 416-266-8910
5 Penetang Cr.              *E-mail:* sjssupport@interlog.org
Toronto, ON Canada M1K 4Y4  *Website:* http://www.interlog.com/~zzzz/

## STICKLER SYNDROME

**Stickler Involved People**                            **International network**
*Founded 1995.* Network that offers support and education for persons affected by Stickler syndrome. This genetic disorder affects connective tissues, including the joints, eyes, palate, heart and hearing. Phone support, information and referrals, annual conference, literature, pen pals, newsletter.

SIP                         *Phone:* 316-775-2993
15 Angelina Dr.             *E-mail:* sip@sticklers.org
Augusta, KS 67010           *Website:* http://www.sticklers.org

## STREPTOCOCCAL INFECTION, GROUP B

**Group B Strep Association**                          **International network**
*Founded 1990.* Educates the public about group b streptococcal infections during pregnancy. Information and referrals, advocacy, phone support, newsletter and assistance in developing state networks.

Group B Strep Assn.         *Phone:* 919-932-5344
P.O. Box 16515              *Fax:* 919-932-3657
Chapel Hill, NC 27516       *Website:* http://www.groupbstrep.org

## STROKE

**American Stroke Association**
**Division of American Heart Association**                          **National**
*1800 groups. Founded 1979.* Maintains a listing of support groups for stroke survivors, their families, friends and interested professionals. Publishes Stroke Connection magazine, a forum for stroke survivors and their families to share information about coping with strokes. Information and referrals. Stroke-related books, videos and literature available for purchase.

Stroke Connection           *Phone:* 1-800-553-6321
7272 Greenville Ave.        *E-mail:* garzav@heart.org
Dallas, TX 75231-4596       *Website:* http://www.strokeassociation.org

**CHASA (Children's Hemiplegia And Stroke Association)**            **International**
*40 affiliated groups. Founded 1996.* Support and information for families of children who have hemiplegia, hemiparesis and/or pediatric stroke. Literature, information and referrals, phone support, pen pals, advocacy. Annual retreats. Referrals to local support groups. Newsletter ($15/year). E-mail list.

CHASA
c/o Nancy Atwood PMB149
4101 W. Green Oaks, Suite 305
Arlington, TX 76016

*Phone:* 817-492-4325 (day/eve)
*E-mail:* info@chasa.org
*Website:* http://www.hemikids.org/

**National Stroke Association**                          **National**
*16 chapters. Founded 1984.* (Multilingual) Dedicated to reducing the incidence and impact of stroke through prevention, medical treatment, rehabilitation, family support and research. Research fellowships in cerebrovascular disease. Magazine, professional publications, information, and referrals to local support groups. Guidance for starting stroke clubs and groups. Website in English, Spanish and French.

Nat'l Stroke Assn.
9707 E. Easter Lane
Englewood, CO 80112-3747

*Phone:* 303-649-9299 or 1-800-STROKES
*Fax:* 303-649-1328; *E-mail:* jmccarty@stroke.org
*Website:* http://www.stroke.org

**Stroke Clubs International**                           **International**
*1000+ clubs. Founded 1968.* Organization of persons who have experienced strokes, their families and friends for the purpose of mutual support, education, social and recreational activities. Provides information and assistance to Stroke Clubs (which are usually sponsored by local organizations). Newsletter, videotapes, group development guidelines.

Stroke Clubs, Int'l
805 12th St.
Galveston, TX 77550

*Phone:* Ellis Williamson 409-762-1022
*E-mail:* strokeclub@aol.com

## STURGE-WEBER SYNDROME / PORT WINE STAIN / KLIPPEL-TRENAUNEY SYNDROME

**The Sturge-Weber Foundation**                         **International network**
*Area reps. in 34+ states/countries. Founded 1987.* Mutual support network for families affected by Sturge-Weber syndrome, port wine stain or Klippel-Trenauney syndrome. Disseminates information, funds and facilitates research. Newsletter, phone support, pen pals, active e-mail support group, bulletin board and private chat room. Group development guidelines. Annual conference. Dues $30/US; $40/int'l (includes newsletter and website membership).

Sturge-Weber Fdn.
P.O. Box 418
Mt. Freedom, NJ 07970

*Phone:* 1-800-627-5482 or 973-895-4445
*Fax:* 973-895-4846
*E-mail:* SWfoffice@aol.com
*Website:* http://www.sturge-weber.com

## SYRINGOMYELIA / CHIARI

**American Syringomyelia Alliance Project**             **International network**
*Founded 1988.* Support, networking and information for people affected by syringomyelia and chiari, and their families and friends. Newsletter, phone support, pen pals, conferences.

American Syringomyelia
Alliance Project
P.O. Box 1586
Longview, TX 75606-1586

*Phone:* 903-236-7079 or 1-800-272-7282
*Fax:* 903-757-7456
*E-mail:* info@asap4sm.org
*Website:* http://www.asap4sm.org

## SUDDEN ARRHYTHMIA DEATH SYNDROME
*(Also see Heart)*

**SADS (Sudden Arrhythmia Death Syndromes) Foundation**               National
*3 affiliated groups. Founded 1992.* Mutual support for young people who are predisposed
to sudden death due to cardiac arrhythmias. Dedicated to saving lives. Networking,
literature, advocacy, phone support, conferences, information and referrals. Online support.
SADS Foundation                     *Phone:* 1-800-786-7723
508 E. South Turnpike               *Website:* http://www.sads.org
Salt Lake City, UT 84902

## TAKAYASU'S ARTERITIS

**Takayasu's Arteritis Association**                                    Model
*Founded 1995.* Education and support for persons with Takayasu's arteritis (an
inflammation of the large elastic arteries and aorta), their families and health professionals.
Networking, phone and on-line support, literature, newsletters, and conferences.
Takayasu's Arteritis Assn.          *Phone:* Mary Patsos 603-641-2774
16 Rose Lane                        *E-mail:* dpatsos@taa.mv.com
Bedford, NH 03110                   *Website:* http://www.takayasus.com

## TAY-SACH'S
*(Also see Canavan)*

**Late Onset Tay-Sachs Foundation**                            National network
*Founded 1994.* Support and education for persons dealing with late onset Tay-Sachs. Aims
to educate medical and community at large. Advocacy, newsletter, information and
referrals, phone support, conferences, fundraising for research, and literature.
Late Onset Tay-Sachs Fdn.           *Phone:* 1-800-672-2022; *Fax:* 215-836-5438
1303 Paper Mill Rd.                 *E-mail:* mpf@bellatlantic.net
Erdenheim, PA 19038                 *Website:* http://www.lotsf.org

**National Tay-Sachs and Allied Diseases Association**                National
*5 affiliated groups. Founded 1957.* Dedicated to the treatment and prevention of Tay-Sachs,
Canavan, and related genetic diseases. Provides information and support services to
individuals and families affected by these disorders as well as the public at large. The
strategies for achieving these goals include public and professional education, research,
genetic screening, family services, and advocacy.

NTSAD                                    *Phone:* 1-800-906-8723 or 617-277-4463
2001 Beacon St., Suite 204               *E-mail:* ntsad-boston@att.net
Boston, MA 02135                         *Website:* http://www.ntsad.org

## TEMPOROMANDIBULAR JOINT DYSFUNCTION

**TMJ Association**                                          **International**
*14 affiliated groups. Founded 1986.* Developed by two patients suffering from TMJ (diseases and disorders that cause pain and dysfunction in and around the temporomandibular or jaw joint). Currently is a leading resource and advocacy organization for TMJ sufferers and their families, as well as a resource for researchers and health professionals. Provides informational services which include a newsletter, scientific journal and other publications.

TMJ Assn.                                *Phone:* 414-259-3223; *Fax:* 414-259-8112
P.O. Box 26770                           *E-mail:* info@tmj.org
Milwaukee, WI 53226-0770                 *Website:* http://www.tmj.org

## TETHERED SPINAL CORD SYNDROME
*(Also see Neurology)*

💻 **Tethered Spinal Cord Syndrome Support Network**                 **Online**
*Founded 2000.* Provides online support and education to persons affected by tethered spinal cord syndrome which is caused when the spinal cord becomes tethered by a lipoma tumor, scar tissue or other narrowing of the spinal canal, and other spinal anomalies. Some members exchange support via telephone. Open to interested professionals.

TSC Synd. Support Network                *Website:* http://www.tsc-support.org
121 Long Lane                            *E-mail:* tetheredspinalcord-owner
Bellefonte, PA 16823                     @yahoogroups.com

## THROMBOCYTOPENIA ABSENT RADIUS SYNDROME

**Thrombocytopenia Absent Radius Syndrome Association**       **International network**
*Founded 1981.* Information, networking and support for families children with thrombocytopenia absent radius syndrome (a shortening of the arms), and for affected adults. (Does not include ITP). Newsletter, pen pal program, phone network.

TARSA                                    *Phone:* 609-927-0418; *Fax:* 609-653-8639
212 Sherwood Dr.                         *E-mail:* spp212@aol
Egg Harbor Twp., NJ 08234-7658

## THROMBOTIC THROMBOCYTOPENIC PURPURA

**TTP Support Group**                                        **International network**
*Founded 1993.* Mutual support, information and advocacy for persons affected by

thrombotic thrombocytopenic purpura, a blood disorder dealing with platelets. Physician referrals. Newsletter, information and referrals, literature, support group meetings.

TTP Support Group
P.O. Box 10259
Baltimore, MD 21234

*Phone:* 800-765-5170
*Fax:* 410-383-0938

# THYROID DISORDERS
*(Also see specific disorder)*

### American Foundation of Thryoid Patients                    National
*6 affiliated chapters. Founded 1993.* Offers information, education and referrals to low-cost screening. Also provides newsletter, pen pals, phone support, advocacy and networking. Dues 30; $15/seniors/students; $50/professionals. Assistance offered in starting local groups. Online mailing lists and bulletin boards.

Amer. Fdn. of Thyroid Patients
18534 N. Lyford
Katy, TX 77449

*Phone:* 281-855-6608
*E-mail:* thyroid@flash.net

### Thyroid Foundation of America                    National
*10 affiliated groups. Founded 1985.* Information and support for persons concerned with any type of thyroid problem, including Hashimoto's disease, Grave's disease, goiter, thyroid lumps or nodules, hyperthyroidism, postpartum thyroiditis and cancer. Information, literature, referrals to specialists, and local support groups where available. Dues $25 (includes newsletter).

TFA
Ruth Sleeper Hall RSL 350
40 Parkman St.
Boston, MA 02114-2698

*Phone:* 1-800-832-8321
*Fax:* 617-726-4136
*E-mail:* info@allthyroid.org
*Website:* http://www.allthyroid.org

### The Thyroid Eye Disease Association                    International
*15 area helpline organizers/50 helplines nationwide. Founded 1989.* Provides information, care and support to persons affected by thyroid eye disease (aka thyroid associated ophthalmopathy or Graves' eye disease). Information and referral, literature, phone support, conferences, newsletter. Annual dues 5£.

TED
"Solstice"
Sea Rd.
Winchelsea Beach, East Sussex
TN36 4LH, England

*Phone:* (01797) 222338 (Voice/Fax)
*E-mail:* tedassn@eclipse.co.uk

### 🖳 Grave's Disease and Thyroid Discussion                    Online
Offers a large variety of topics for persons concerned about Grave's disease and other thyroid disorders. Online chats.          *Website:* http://www.mediboard.com

# TOURETTE SYNDROME

**Tourette Syndrome Association**                                      **National**
*50 chapters. Founded 1972.* Dedicated to identifying the cause, finding the cure, and controlling the effects of Tourette syndrome through education, research and service. Provides support services to families and professionals to enable patients to achieve optimum development. Chapter development guidelines, newsletter. Dues $45.

Tourette Syndrome Assn.              *Phone:* 718-224-2999 or 1-888-4-TOURETT
42-40 Bell Blvd., Suite 205          *Fax:* 718-279-9596; *E-mail:* ts@tsa-usa.org
Bayside, NY 11361-2820               *Website:* http://tsa-usa/org

# TRACHEOESOPHAGEAL FISTULA / ESOPHAGEAL ATRESIA

**EA/TEF Child and Family Support Connection, Inc.**                 **International**
*11+ chapters.* Dedicated to providing educational resources and emotional and practical support for families of children with esophageal atresia and tracheoesophageal fistula. Offers newsletter, family directory for telephone networking, information, lending library, educational brochures, and literature. Sunshine program sends birthday greetings and gifts to hospitalized children.

EA/TEF Child/Family                  *Phone:* 312-987-9085
  Support Connection                 *Fax:* 312-987-9086
111 West Jackson Blvd., #1145        *E-mail:* eatef2@aol.com
Chicago, IL 60604-3502               *Website:* http://eatef.org

**TEF/VATER Support Network**                                        **International**
*6 groups. Founded 1992.* Offers support and encouragement for parents of children with tracheo esophageal fistula, esophageal atresia and VATER. Aims to bring current information to parents and the medical community. Newsletter, information and referrals, phone support.

TEF/VATER Support Network            *Phone:* 301-952-6837
c/o Greg and Terri Burke             *Fax:* 301-952-9152
15301 Grey Fox Rd.                   *E-mail:* tefvater@ix.netcom.com
Upper Marlboro, MD 20772             *Website:* http://www.tefvater.org

# TRACHEOSTOMY
*(Also see specific disorder)*

▣ **Trachties**                                                       **Online**
*Founded 1998.* Mutual support and information sharing for persons who have, or anticipate having, a tracheostomy. Open to patients, families, caregivers and professionals. Through a listserv, members are given a chance to support each other, and offer coping tips.

Trachties
102 Morene Ave.
Waxahachie, TX 75165

*E-mail:* Kekillough@aol.com
*Website:* http://www.twinenterprises.com/
trach/misc/trachtie.htm

## TRANSPLANT, ORGAN
*(Also see specific disorder)*

**Second Wind Lung Transplant Association, Inc.**          **International network**
Developed by transplant patients. Opportunity for persons who have undergone, or who will undergo, lung transplants to share their stories on a web page. Newsletter available.
Second Wind
S. Duncan Ave., Suite 227
Clearwater, FL 33755

*Phone:* 1-888-855-9463 or 727-442-0892
*E-mail:* heering@2ndwind.org
*Website:* http://www.2ndwind.org

**Transplant Recipients International Organization**                    **International**
*43 chapters. Founded 1983.* Works to improve the quality of life of transplant candidates, recipients, donors, and their families. TRIO serves its members in the areas of donor awareness, support, education, and advocacy. Annual conference, newsletter, monthly membership update, support network, chapter development assistance.
*Phone:* 1-800-TRIO-386

*E-mail:* trio@primenet.com
*Website:* http://www.trioweb.org

## TRANSVERSE MYELITIS

**Transverse Myelitis Association**                                **National network**
Offers support and educational information to persons who have been diagnosed with transverse myelitis (an inflammation of the spinal cord), and their families. Networks families together for support. Provides educational information, articles and research literature. Investigates, advocates for and supports research and innovative treatment efforts. Online forum for people to communicate with others about transverse myelitis.
Transverse Myelitis Assn.
1787 Sutter Parkway
Powell, OH 43065

*Phone:* Sandy Siegel 614-766-1806
*E-mail:* ssiegel@myelitis.org
*Website:* http://www.myelitis.org

## TREACHER COLLINS SYNDROME

**Treacher Collins Foundation**                                  **National network**
*Founded 1988.* Support for families, individuals and professionals re: Treacher Collins syndrome and related disorders. Provides networking, educational materials, newsletter, information and referrals, phone support, resource list, and library, videos and booklets.
Treacher Collins Fdn.
P.O. Box156
Boston, MA 02131

*Phone:* 704-545-1921 or 1-800-TCF-2055
*E-mail*: judy@tcconnection.org
*Website:* treachercollinsfnd.org/

## TRIGEMINAL NEURALGIA / TIC DOULOUREUX

**Trigeminal Neuralgia Association**                                    **National**
*50 groups. Founded 1990.* Provides information, mutual support and encouragement to persons with trigeminal neuralgia (aka tic douloureux), and their families. Helps to reduce the isolation of those affected. Aims to increase public/professional awareness, and promote research into cause and cure. Quarterly newsletter. Phone support, pen pals, educational information.                          *Phone:* 352-376-9955 (national office)
TNA                                         or Cindy 904-779-0333 (patient info)
2801 SW Archer Rd., Suite C                 *Fax:* 352-8688; *E-mail:* tnainfo@aol.com
Gainsville, FL 32608                        *Website:* http://www.tna-support.org

## TRIPLE X SYNDROME
*(Also see Trisomy)*

**Triple X Support Group**                           **International network**
*Founded 1997.* Provides support, resources and informational materials to parents of children with triple x syndrome (aka trisomy x or 47,XXX syndrome). Aims to educate professionals and the public on this syndrome. Networks parents together for support. Literature, referrals, phone support.
Triple X Support Group                      *Phone:* Helen Clements (020)86909445
32 Francemary Rd.                           *E-mail:* helenclements@hotmail.com
Brockley, London, England SE4 1JS

## TRISOMY 9 DISORDER
*(Also see Chromosome Disorders)*

**9-TIPS (Trisomy International Parent Support)**          **International network**
*Founded 1992.* Support for families of children with Trisomy 9. Provides parental network system. Updates on medical resources. Packets of letters from trisomy 9 families for new parents available. Ongoing study of trisomy 9 children.
9-TIPS                                      *Phone:* 909-862-4470 (for parents)
c/o Bill and Alice Todd                     *E-mail:* atoddna@sprynet.com
4027 E. Piedmont Dr.                        *Website:* http://www.geocities.com/Heartland/
Highland, CA 92346                          Acres/5287/

9-TIPS                                      *Phone:* 313-745-4513 (day)
c/o Children's Hosp. of Michigan            *Listserv:* bltr@mindspring.com
3901 Beaubien Blvd.                         *Website:* http://www.multiline.com.au/softwa
Detroit, MI 48201-2196

## TRISOMY 18 DISORDER
*(Also see Chromosome Disorders)*

**SOFT (Support Organization For Trisomy)**                     **National**
*50 chapters. Founded 1979.* Support and education for families of children with trisomy 18 and 13 and related genetic disorders. Education for professionals. Bi-monthly newsletter. Pen pal program, phone network. Regional gatherings. Annual international conference, booklets. Dues $25.

SOFT                                 *Phone:* 716-594-4621
c/o Barbara Van Herreweghe           or 1-800-716-SOFT (for families)
2982 S. Union St.                    *Fax:* 716-594-1957; *E-mail* barbsoft@aol.com
Rochester, NY 14624                  *Website:* http://www.trisomy.org

## TUBE FEEDING
*(Also see specific disorder)*

**Oley Foundation, Inc.**                                       **National**
*60 affiliated groups. Founded 1983.* Provides information and psychosocial support for home nutrition support patients, their families, caregivers and professionals. Programs include bi-monthly newsletter, national network of volunteers providing patient support, annual summer conference, regional meetings, and patient-to-patient networking.

Oley Fdn.                            *Phone:* 1-800-776-6539 or 518-262-5079
Albany Medical Center                *Fax:* 518-262-5528
214 HUN Memorial, MC28               *E-mail:* BishopJ@mail.amc.edu
Albany, NY 12208                     *Website:* http://www.oley.org

## TUBEROUS SCLEROSIS

**Tuberous Sclerosis Alliance**                                 **National**
*Staff/Volunteer Area Representatives. Founded 1974.* Dedicated to finding a cure for tuberous sclerosis while improving the lives of those affected. Provides research, support and education among individuals, families and the helping professions. Newsletter, peer networking programs, conferences, information, audio tapes available.

Tuberous Sclerosis Alliance          *Phone:* 301-562-9890 or 1-800-225-6872
801 Roeder Rd., Suite 750            *E-mail:* linda.creighton@tsalliance.org
Silver Spring, MD 20910-4467         *Website:* http://www.tsalliance.org

## TURNER'S SYNDROME

**Turner's Syndrome Society**                                   **National**
*18 chapters. Founded 1981.* Provides support and education to Turner's syndrome patients and their families. Tapes, publications, referral to U.S. and Canada groups. Newsletter. Pen pal program, chapter development guidelines, annual conference.

Turner's Syndrome Society
c/o Sandi Hofbauer, Exec. Dir.
814 Glencairn Ave.
Toronto, ON M6B 2A3 Canada

*Phone:* 1-800-465-6744 or 416-781-2086
*Fax:* 416-781-7245
*E-mail:* tssincan@web.net
*Website:* http://www.turnersyndrome.ca

**Turner Syndrome Society of the U.S.**                                **National**
*38 chapters and 18 support groups. Founded 1988.* Offers support, educational forums,
social activities, advocacy and public awareness for individuals with Turner syndrome, and
their families.                         *Phone:* 1-800-365-99442 or 832-249-9988
Turner Syndrome Soc. of the U.S.        *Fax:* 832-249-9987
14450 TC Jester, Suite 260              *E-mail:* tsus@turner-syndrome-us.org
Houston, TX 77014                       *Website:* http://www.turner-syndrome-us.org/

**Turner Syndrome Support Network**                                **National network**
*Founded 1989.* Network and exchange of information for parents of children with Turner's
syndrome. Information and referrals, phone support, pen pals, conferences, literature.
Annual convention. Newsletter ($25/year).
Turner Synd. Support Network            *Phone:* 1-800-3-MAGIC-3 or 708-383-0808
c/o MAGIC Foundation                    *Fax:* 709-383-0899
1327 N. Harlem                          *E-mail:* pam@magicfoundation.org
Oak Park, IL 60302                      *Website:* http://www.magicfoundation.org

## TWIN-TO-TWIN TRANSFUSION SYNDROME

**Twin-to-Twin Transfusion Syndrome Foundation**                        **International**
*Founded 1992.* Dedicated to providing immediate and life-saving educational, emotional
and financial support for families, medical professionals, and caregivers before, during and
after pregnancy with twin-to-twin transfusion syndrome. Dedicated to saving the babies,
improving their future health and care, furthering medical research, providing neonatal
intensive care, special needs and bereavement support. Pen pals, newsletter, literature,
phone support, visitation, conferences. Guidelines for professionals on multiple birth loss
during pregnancy. Help in starting new chapters. International registry.
TTTS                                    *Phone:* 440-899-8887
411 Longbeach Parkway                   *E-mail:* tttsfound@aol.com
Bay Village, OH 44140                   *Website:* http://www.tttsfoundation.org

**Twin Hope**                                                   **International network**
*3 affiliated groups. Founded 1994.* Dedicated to serving the needs of families affected by
twin-to-twin transfusion syndrome and other twin-related diseases. Support group meetings,
phone support. Information and referrals, conferences, fund-raising, current treatment
options, bi-annual newsletter, library. Educates public. Assistance in starting new groups.
Twin Hope                               *Phone:* 502-243-2110 or 440-327-8335
2592 W. 14th St.                        *E-mail:* twinhope@twinhope.com
Cleveland, OH 44113                     *Website:* http://www.twinhope.com

# TYROSINEMIA TYPE I

**Groupe Aide Aux Enfants Tyrosinemiques du Quebec**                **Model**
*One group in Quebec. Founded 1989.* (Bilingual) Provides support and information for parents of children with tyrosinemia type I (aka alpha foetoprotein or hepatorenal type hereditary tyrosinemia). Pamphlets and diet book available in French; literature available in French and English. Networks on computer, and face-to-face meetings.

Gerard Tremblay                          *Phone:* 418-548-1580
3162, rue Granville                       *E-mail:* gerard.tremblay@sympatico.ca
Jonquiere, Quebec, G7S 2B9                *Website*: http://www.cegep-chicoutimi.qc.ca/gaetq
Canada

# UNDIAGNOSED ILLNESS
*(Also see Rare Disorders, Networking)*

**Hearts and Hands**                                              **Model**
*1 group in NC. Founded 1993.* Emotional, spiritual and educational support for persons with either rare or undiagnosed illnesses, and their families.

Hearts and Hands                         *Phone:* Winoka Plummer 336-788-1433
4115 Thomasville Rd.                      *E-mail:* nursenokie@aol.com
Winston-Salem, NC 27107                   *Website:* http://www.geocities.com/hotsprings/
                                          spa/2464/index.html

# UREA CYCLE DISORDERS

**National Urea Cycle Disorders Foundation**                **National network**
*Founded 1989.* Links families, friends and professionals who are dedicated to the identification, treatment and cure of urea cycle disorders, a genetic disorder causing an enzyme deficiency in the urea cycle. Networks families for support, educates professionals and public, and supports research. Phone support, literature, newsletter. Dues $35.

Nat'l Urea Cycle Dis. Fdn.               *Phone:* 1-800-386-8233; *Fax:* 818-248-9770
4841 Hill St.                            *E-mail:* info@nucdf.org
La Canada, CA 91011                      *Website:* http://www.nucdf.org

🖳 **ASA Kids**                                                   **Online**
Opportunity for parents of children with the urea cycle disorder argininosuccinic aciduria to come together for support and information. Discussion board, stories on affected children, and links.                            *Website:* www.geocities.com/oliphint4/index.html

🖳 **TRUE (Transplanted to Resolve Urea-cycle Enzyme-deficient) Kids**      **Online**
Mutual support and information for families of transplanted children with urea cycle disorder.                           *Website:* http://www.geocities.com/paulajoe123/

⌨ **Urea Cycle Disorder Discussion Board**                                    Online
Opportunity for parents caring for a child with a urea cycle disorder to discuss concerns and
ideas. Goal is to increase awareness of urea cycle disorders in order to improve diagnosis.
*Website:* http://www.2endure.com

## VACCINE INJURY

**National Vaccine Information Center**                                      National
*20 affiliated groups. Founded 1982.* Support, information and advocacy group for parents
whose children were adversely affected by vaccines. Advocates for safety reforms in the
mass vaccination system and safer vaccines. Promotes education for parents and
professionals. Various literature ($5-13); newsletter with dues ($25/yr.)
NVIC                                      *Phone:* 703-938-DPT3 or 1-800-909-SHOT
421 E. Church St.                         *E-mail*: Nat-Kathi@909shot.com
Vienna, VA 22180                          *Website:* http://www.909shot.com

## VATER ASSOCIATION

**The VATER Connection, Inc.**                              International network
*Founded 1996.* Information and support to families whose children have VATER
Association (Vertebrae problems, Anal anomalies, Trachea problems, Esophagus problems,
Radius and/or Renal problems). Newsletter. Online bulletin board.
The VATER Connection, Inc.                *Phone:* 316-342-6954 (day/eve)
1722 Yucca Lane                           *Website:* http://www.vaterconnection.org
Emporia, KS 66801

## VELO-CARDIO-FACIAL / SHPRINTZEN SYNDROME

**Northeast VCFS Support Group**                                 National network
*25 affiliated groups. Founded 1996.* Support and resource network for families coping with
velo-cardio-facial syndrome (aka Shprintzen syndrome). Provides information and referrals,
pen pals, literature, conferences, and assistance in starting local groups. Uses a listserv.
Northeast VCFS Support Group              *Phone:* Maureen Anderson 603-898-6332
2 Lansing Dr.                             *E-mail:* mladja@aol.com
Salem, NH 03079

## VENTILATOR-ASSISTED
*(Also see specific disorder)*

**Gazette International Networking Institute**               International Network
*Founded 1987.* Information for individuals with post-polio and users of home mechanical
ventilation. Provides newsletter, networking, advocacy, literature, phone support, referrals,
conferences, and information on starting groups.

G.I.N.I.                                    *Phone:* 314-534-0475; *Fax:* 314-534-5070
4207 Lindell Blvd., Suite 110               *E-mail:* gini_intl@msn.com
St. Louis, MO 63118                         *Website:* http://www.post-polio.org

**International Ventilator Users Network**                        **International network**
*Founded 1987.* Information sharing between ventilator users and health care professionals
experienced in home mechanical ventilation. Annual directory ($8). Quarterly newsletter
($18/US; $28/Overseas).
Int'l Ventilator Users Network              *Phone:* 314-534-0475; *Fax:* 314-534-5070
4207 Lindell Blvd., Suite 110               *E-mail:* gini_intl@msn.com
St. Louis, MO 63108                         *Website:* http://www.post-polio.org/ivun

## VESTIBULAR DISORDERS

**Vestibular Disorders Association**                                   **International**
*125 independent groups. Founded 1983.* Information, referrals and support for people
affected by disorders caused by inner ear problems. Public education, group development
assistance, quarterly newsletter, library of resources, support network. Distributes several
videotapes and publishes 70 documents, including full-length books on Meniere's disease
and benign paroxysmal positional vertigo (BPPV).
Vestibular Disorders Assn.                  *Phone:* 1-800-837-8428 or 503-229-7705
P.O. Box 4467                               *Fax:* 503-229-8064
Portland, OR 97208-4467                     *E-mail:* veda@vestibular.org
                                            *Website:* http://www.vestibular.org

## VITILIGO

**National Vitiligo Foundation**                                        **National**
*14 affiliated groups. Founded 1985.* Mutual help and education for persons with vitiligo, a
skin disorder affecting pigmentation. Fund-raising for research. Semi-annual newsletter.
Telephone network.
Nat'l Vitiligo Fdn.                         *Phone:* 903-531-0074; *Fax:* 903-525-1234
611 S. Fleishel Ave.                        *E-mail:* vitiligo@tmfhs.org
Tyler, TX 75701                             *Website:* http://www.vitilgofoundation.org

## VOMITING, CYCLIC

**Cyclic Vomiting Syndrome Association**                             **International**
*19 affiliated groups. Founded 1993.* Mutual support and information for families and
professionals dealing with cyclic vomiting syndrome. Networking, phone support,
educational materials, and research support. Newsletter.
CVSA                                        *Phone:* Debra Waites 614-837-2586
3585 Cedar Hill Rd. NW                      *E-mail:* waites@cvsonline.org
Canal Winchester, Ohio 43110                *Website:* http://www.cvsonline.org

## VON HIPPEL-LINDAU SYNDROME

**VHL Family Alliance**                                    **International network**
*28 US chapters; 11 foreign affiliates. Founded 1993.* (Multilingual) Opportunity for families affected by VHL to share their knowledge and experiences. Goal is to improve diagnosis, treatment and quality of life for VHL families. Newsletter, phone support and education, tissue bank, and handbook. Funds research. Literature in several languages. Assistance in starting local chapters.

VHL Family Alliance            *Phone:* 1-800-767-4845 or 617-277-5667
171 Clinton Rd.                *Fax:* 617-734-8233; *E-mail:* info@vhl.org
Brookline, MA 02245-5815       *Website:* http://www.vhl.org

## VULVODYNIA

**National Vulvodynia Association, Inc.**                              **National**
*100 affiliated groups. Founded 1994.* Provides information and support to women with vulvodynia. Educates health care professionals and the public about this condition. Newsletter, literature, information and referrals, phone support, and advocacy.

NVA                            *Phone:* 301-299-0775; *Fax:* 301-299-3999
P.O. Box 4491                  *E-mail:* mate@nva.org
Silver Spring, MD 20914-4491   *Website:* http://www.nva.org

**The Vulvar Pain Foundation**                                  **International**
*110 networks/30 support groups. Founded 1992.* Provides research, treatment information and emotional support to women experiencing vulvar pain and related disorders (fibromyalgia, interstitial cystitis, irritable bowel). Identifies interested health care professionals. Participates in research. Newsletter, phone support, pen pals, videos, seminars, The Low Oxalate Cookbook. Dues ($40-$70). Assistance in starting groups. For information send $2 with self-addressed stamped envelope when writing.

The VP Fdn.                    *Phone:* 336-226-0704
P.O. Drawer 177                *Fax:* 336-226-8518
Graham, NC 27253               *Website:* http://www.vulvarpainfoundation.org

## WAGR SYNDROME / ANIRIDIA

**Reaching Out - The WAGR Network**                       **International network**
*3 affiliated groups. Founded 2000.* Provides information and support to persons with WAGR Syndrome or aniridia, and their families. Literature, networking, information and referral, and phone support. Newsletter. Encourages research. Email group.

Reaching Out                   *Phone:* 313-381-4302
2063 Regina                    *E-mail:* WAGR@yahoogroups.com
Lincoln Park, MI 48146         *Website:* http://www.wagr.org or
                               members.aol.com/ReachingOutNet/index.html

## WALDENSTROM'S MACROGLOBULINEMIA

**International Waldenstrom's Macroglobulinemia Foundation**        **International**
*16 affiliated groups. Founded 1994.* Provides support and information to persons with
Waldenstrom macroglobulinemia, their families and caregivers. Information and referrals,
phone support, conferences, newsletter, and literature. Regular support group meetings.
Assistance in starting new groups.

Int'l Waldenstrom's                          *Phone:* 941-927-IWMF
  Macroglobulinemia Fdn.           *Fax:* 941-927-4467
2300 Bee Ridge Rd., Suite 301               *E-mail:* iwmf1@juno.com
Sarasota, FL 34239                          *Website:* http://www.iwmf.com

### WEAVER SYNDROME

**Support for Families with Weaver Syndrome**                    **National network**
*Founded 1995.* Grassroots group of parents interested in networking with other families
affected by Weaver syndrome. Phone support, pen pals.

Support for Families w/Weaver Synd.   *Phone:* Patty Mayer 425-747-5382
4357 153rd Ave., SE                   *Fax:* 425-235-6225
Bellevue, WA 98006                    *E-mail:* dpmayer@msn.com

### WEGENER'S GRANULOMATOSIS

**Wegener's Granulomatosis Association**                          **International**
*Many affiliated groups. Founded 1986.* Emotional support and information for patients with
life-threatening uncommon Wegener's granulomatosis and related vascular illnesses.
Provides information to patients and physicians about this disorder and educates families,
friends and general public about the devastating effects of Wegener's, it's symptoms and
treatment. Dues $20/U.S.; $25/Int'l (includes bi-monthly newsletter).

Wegener's Granulomatosis Assn.   *Phone:* 1-800-277-9474; *Fax:* 816-436-8211
P.O. Box 28660                   *E-mail:* wgsg@wgsg.org
Kansas City, MO 64188-8660       *Website:* http://www.wgsg.org

### WHITE LUNG / ASBESTOSITITS
*(Also see Respiratory)*

**White Lung Association**                                      **National network**
*Founded 1979.* Educational support and advocacy for asbestos victims and their families.
Provides public education on health hazards of asbestos and the education of workers on
safe work practices. Dues $25/yr.

White Lung Assn.          *Phone:* 410-282-4300; *Fax:* 410-254-4602
P.O. Box 1483             *E-mail:* jfite@whitelung.org
Baltimore, MD 21203       *Website:* http://www.whitelung.org

## WILLIAMS SYNDROME

**Williams Syndrome Association**                        **National network**
*11 chapters. Founded 1982.* To encourage research related to Williams syndrome, find and support families with Williams syndrome, and share information among parents and professionals re: educational, medical and behavioral experiences. Newsletter.
Williams Syndrome Assn.          *Phone:* 248-541-3630; *Fax:* 248-541-3631
P.O. Box 297                     *E-mail:* TMonkaba@aol.com
Clawson, MI 48017-0297           *Website:* http://www.williams-syndrome.org

## WILSON'S DISEASE

**Wilson's Disease Association**                    **International network**
*Founded 1979.* Provides information and referrals about Wilson's disease, a genetic disorder that causes excessive amounts of copper accumulation in the body, affecting the liver and brain. Provides mutual support and aid for those affected by the disease and their families. Promotes research into treatment and cure. Quarterly newsletter. Pphone support network.
Wilson's Disease Assn.           *Phone:* 1-800-399-0266 or 203-775-9666
4 Navaho Dr.                     *E-mail:* hasellner@worldnet.att.net
Brookfield, CT 06804             *Website:* http://www.wilsonsdisease.org

## WOLF-HIRSCHHORN / 4P- SYNDROME

**4P- Support Group**                                    **National network**
*1 group in England. Founded 1984.* Provides support and information exclusivley to families of children with Wolf-Hirschhorn syndrome. Offers phone support, biographies on other children with this syndrome. Newsletter.
4P- Support Group                *Phone:* 954-476-9345
c/o Bonnie Radtke                *E-mail:* bbr@juno.com
1874 NW 108th Ave.               *E-mail:* 4pminus@4p-supportgroup.org
Plantation, FL 33322             *Website:* http:www.4psupportgroup.org

## WOMEN'S HEALTH
*(Also see specific disorder)*

**National Black Women's Health Project International**
**/Self-Help Division**                                       **National**
*15 chapters. Founded 1981.* Grassroots organization aimed at improving the health of Black women by providing wellness education, services, self-help group development, health information and advocacy. Self-help brochure, quarterly newsletter, and annual news magazine. Membership dues vary.
NBWHP                            *Phone:* 202-543-9311
600 Pennsylvania Ave. SE, #310   *Fax:* 202-543-9743
Washington, DC 20003
320

**National Latina Health Organization**                    **National network**
*Founded 1986.* Works toward bilingual access to quality health care for women through self-empowerment, education, advocacy, outreach and developing public policy specifically aimed at Latinas. Information and referrals, phone support, literature. Self-help facilitator trainings, maintains a Latina health resource library, school-based youth programs and mentorship program.

Nat'l Latina Health Org.          *Phone:* 510-534-1362
P.O. Box 7567                     *Fax:* 510-534-1364
Oakland, CA 94601                 *E-mail:* latinahlth@aol.com

**AllHealth Message Boards**                                          **Online**
Various message boards, mailing lists and chat rooms dealing with all aspects of health including menopause, breast cancer, addictions, arthritis, heart, disabilities, caregivers, infertility, respiratory, mental health, parenting, medications. Newsletters.
                          *Website:* http://allhealth.com

**Women's Health Forums**                                            **Online**
Offers a large variety of message boards concerning women's health including: cancer, gynecological disorders, menopause, mental health, fitness, eating disorders, breast health and family.                     *Website:* http://womenshealth.org

## XERODERMA PIGMENTOSUM

**Xeroderma Pigmentosum Society**                      **International network**
*Founded 1995.* Provides sharing of support, information and coping skills for families affected by xeroderma pigmentosum. Newsletter. Promotes research into finding a cure. Information and referrals, phone support, conferences, pen pals, literature, advocacy in community, education and protection. Camp Sundown for patients and their families.

XP Society                      *Phone:* 518-851-2612 (Voice/Fax)
Box 4759                        *E-mail:* caren@xps.org
Poughkeepsie, NY 12602          *Website:* http://www.xps.org

## X-LINKED HYPOPHOSPHATEMIA RICKETS

**XLH Network**                                                      **Online**
*Founded 1996.* Support and information for families affected by x-linked hypophosphatemia (aka x-linked hypophosphatemic rickets, familial hypophosphatemic rickets, or vitamin d-resistant rickets), and interested professionals. Exchanges and disseminates information. Online flyer, member listserv.

Colin Steeksma                  E-mail: Larry.Winger@ncl.ac.uk
34640 Devon Crescent            E-mail: Colin_Steeksma@telus.net
Abbotsford, BC V2S 2X6 Canada   Website: http://xlhnetwork.ncl.ac.uk

Elaine Jacobson                          E-mail: emj@super.org
3517 Mase Lane                           *Website:* http://georgia.ncl.ac.uk/VitaminD/
Bowie, MD 20715                          vitaminD.html

# WORSTER-DROUGHT /
# CONGENITAL SUPRABULBAR PARESIS
*(Also see Cerebral Palsy)*

**Worster-Drought Syndrome Support Group**                          **Model**
Provides support and information for families of children with Worster-Drought syndrome
(aka congenital suprabulbar paresis), a form of cerebral palsy. The main problems occur
with the mouth, tongue and swallowing muscles. Phone support in the United Kingdom,
pen pals, networking of families, literature, newsletter, and occasional national meetings.
Worster-Drought Synd. Group        *Phone:* 020 7383 3555; *Fax:* 020 7383 0259
c/o Contact-a-Family               *E-mail:* W.D.S.P.G@btinternet.com
170 Tottenham Court Rd.            *Website:* http://www.wdssg.org.uk/
London W1T 7HA UK

CB EO

# A Couple of Research Studies..."Self-Help Groups
# and Alternative/Complementary Medicine"

Few people realize that the **use of self-help groups is a major form of alternative or
complementary medicine practiced today by Americans.** In the first famous study
documenting the growth of alternative health methods that appeared in the New England
Journal of Medicine ("Unconventional Medicine in the United States" by D.M. Eisenberg,
R.C. Kessler, et al., January, **1993**, pp. 246-252) **the "use of self-help groups" was one of
the 16 alternative health approaches** that were identified and studied.

The major follow-up study published in 1998 in the Journal of the American Medical
Association ("Trends in Alternative Medicine Use in the United States, 1990-1997" by
D.M. Eisenberg, et al., Nov. 11, **1998**, pp. 1569-1575), examined Americans' use of those
original 16 alternative medicine therapies and found that of the **seven therapies that had
increased in use from 1990 to 1997, one was "self-help groups," with the percentage of
Americans reporting they had participated in a self-help group more than doubling**
from 2.3% to 4.8%.

While these national studies reflect the **importance and growing role of self-help groups
in alternative and complementary medicine,** unfortunately it is still rare to see self-help
support groups even mentioned in any of the many published guides to alternative
medicine!

# MENTAL HEALTH

*Be who you are and say what you feel,*
*because those who mind don't matter, and those who matter don't mind.*
*- Dr. Seuss*

## ANXIETY / PHOBIA / AGORAPHOBIA
### *(Also see Mental Health General)*

**ABIL (Agoraphobics Building Independent Lives), Inc.**                    **National**
*50+ groups/contacts. Founded 1986.* Mutual support, encouragement, hope, goal setting, and education for persons with agoraphobia, anxiety or panic-related disorders and their families and friends. Provides information and referrals, phone support, newsletter, assistance in starting new groups.
ABIL, Inc.                          *Phone:* 804-353-3964 or 804-547-5040
3805 Cutshaw Ave., #415             *E-mail:* answers@anxietysupport.org
Richmond, VA 23230                  *Website:* http://www.anxietysupport.org

**AIM (Agoraphobics In Motion)**                                          **National**
*13 groups. Founded 1983.* Self-help group that uses specific behavioral and cognitive techniques to help people recover from anxiety disorders. Relaxation techniques and small group discussions, field trips. Newsletter, pen pals. Group Development guidelines ($27).
AIM                                 *Phone:* 248-547-0400 or 248-547-5040
1719 Crooks                         *E-mail:* anny@ameritech.net
Royal Oak, MI 48067-1306            *Website:* http://www.aim-hq.org

**Anxiety Disorders Association of America**                          **National network**
*Founded 1980.* Promotes welfare of people with phobias and related anxiety disorders. An organization for consumers, health care professionals and other concerned individuals. Publishes membership directory, self-help group directory, ADAA Reporter, newsletter.
ADAA                                *Phone:* 301-231-9350; *Fax:* 301-231-7392
11900 Parklawn Dr., Suite 100       *E-mail:* anxdis@adaa.org
Rockville, MD 20852-2624            *Website:* http://www.adaa.org

**Fear of Success Anonymous**                                             **National**
*3 affiliated groups. Founded 1989.* Gathering of men and women who are committed to obtaining and enjoying the benefits of success, as we individually define it, in all areas of our lives. Follows the 12-steps to overcome fears, avoid self-sabotaging behavior and take action. Newsletter, phone lists, workshops, assistance in starting groups.
FSA                                 *Phone:* 818-907-3953
16161 Ventura Blvd., Suite 727      *E-mail:* info@fasonline.org
Encino, CA 91436                    *Website:* http://www.fosaonline.org

**International Paruresis Association, Inc**                    **International network**
*15 affiliated groups. Founded 1996.* Provides emotional support and information for persons with paruresis (shy or bashful bladder). Supports research to develop effective treatments. Information and referrals, literature, phone support, workshops, conferences, advocacy. Assistance in starting similar groups.
Int'l Paruresis Assn.                           *Phone:* 1-800-247-3864; *Fax:* 410-706-6046
P.O. Box 26225                                  *E-mail:* ssoifer@ssw.umaryland.edu
Baltimore, MD 21210                             *Website:* http://www.paruresis.org

**Selective Mutism Foundation, Inc.**                               **National network**
*Founded 1992.* Mutual support for parents of children with selective mutism, a psychiatric anxiety disorder in which children are unable to speak in social situations. Open to adults who have, or outgrew, the disorder. Information, phone support, newsletter.
Sue Newman                                      Carolyn Miller
P.O. 450632                                     P.O. Box 13133
Sunrise, FL 33345-0632                          Sissonville, WV 25360
                                                *Website:* http://selectivemutism.org

**Open Door Outreach, Inc.**                                              **Model**
*7 groups in Minnesota. Founded 1986.* Support and information fro persons suffering from anxiety disorders, and their families. Offers strategies in anxiety management. Literature, referrals, phone support, pen pals, conferences, newsletter. Assistance in starting groups.
Open Door Outreach, Inc.                         *Phone:* 612-377-2467 (eve)
c/o Judith Bemis                                 *Fax:* 612-928-6716
608 Russell Ave. S.                              *E-mail:* nelsonh@usfamily.net
Minneapolis, MN 55405                            *Website:* http://www.anxietysupport.net

🖥 **Alt.Support.Shyness.FAQ**                                           **Online**
Supportive message board and newsgroup for shy persons. Information to help overcome shyness. Tips on job hunting, assertiveness, dating, children and shyness
                                *Web:* members.aol.com/cybernettr/shyness.html

🖥 **SMG Support Center**                                                **Online**
Devoted to educating and promoting awareness on selective mutism and other related childhood anxiety disorders. Online support group for parents, teachers and professionals dealing with selective mutism.
SMG Support Center                              *Phone:* Shelly Heckman 570-546-7103
1848 John Brady Dr.                             *E-mail:* shellyheckman@aol.com
Muncy, PA 17756                                 *Website:* selectivemutism.org/smg/smsup.htm

🖥 **Social Anxiety Group**                                             **Online**
Mutual support and education for persons with anxiety disorders. Exchange of coping skills. Education about anxiety disorders. Several online support group meetings for persons with social phobias.                        *Website:* http://anxietynetwork.com

# ATTACHMENT DISORDER

**Attachment Disorder Network**                                          **National network**
*Founded 1988.* Support and information for parents and professionals dealing with children with attachment disorder. Newsletter, phone support, information and referrals. Dues $15 (includes newsletter). Information package ($20).
Attachment Disorder Network          *Phone:* Peggy Thompson 913-432-0823
7501 W. 71st St.                              *E-mail:* GailADPN@aol.com
Overland Park, KS 66204               *Website:* http://www.radzebra.org

**Parent Network for the**
**Post-Institutionalized Child**                          **International network**
*Founded 1993.* Connects families who have children who came from maternity hospitals, orphanages, or institutions for the irrecuperable or "street children" of economically deprived countries. Helps parents deal with the variety of problems (such as aggressive or autistic-like behaviors, learning disabilities, attachment disorders, etc) that can be created by an infant history of deprivation. Newsletter.
PNPIC                                          *Phone:* 724-222-1766; *Fax:* 770-979-3140
P.O. Box 613                                 *E-mail:* info@pnpic.org
Meadow Lands, PA 15347               *Website:* http://PNPIC.org

# BORDERLINE PERSONALITY
*(Also see Mental Health Patients)*

💻 **BPD Central**                                          **Online**
Provides links to online groups for persons dealing with a loved one with borderline personality disorder. Several mailing lists given for parents, siblings, grandparents, and others close to someone with BPD, and one group for persons with BPD themselves.
BPD Central                                 *Phone:* 1-888-357-4355
P.O. Box 07016                             *E-mail:* BPDCentral@aol.com
Milwaukee, WI 53207-0106            *Website:* http://www.bpdcentral.com

💻 **Helen's World of BPD Resources**                          **Online**
Resources for those living with someone with borderline personality disorder. Links to support services, information and educational material. Assists persons in creating and joining local, live support groups.          *E-mail:* helenbpd@yahoo.com
*Website:* http://voy.com/79827/          *Website:* http://home.hvc.rr.com/helenbpd

*"Mutual empathy is the great unsung human gift."*
*- Jean Baker Miller, MD & Iren Stiver, The Healing Connection*

325

# DEPRESSION / BIPOLAR (MANIC-DEPRESSION)
*(Also see Mental Health Patients, General Mental Health)*

**Dep-Anon**                                                                  **National**
*Founded 1999.* 12-step fellowship for men, women and children whose lives have been affected by a family members' depression. Members share hope, strength and experience in order to grow emotionally and spiritually.

Dep-Anon                                   *Phone:* Hugh S. 502-569-1989
P.O. Box 17414                             *E-mail:* info@depressedanon.com
Louisville, KY 40217                       *Website:* http://www.depressedanon.com

**Depressed Anonymous**                                                  **International**
*50 affiliated groups. Founded 1985.* 12-step program to help depressed persons believe and hope they can feel better. Newsletter, phone support, information and referrals, workshops, conferences and seminars. Information packet ($5).

D.A.                                       *Phone:* Hugh S. 502-569-1989.
Box 17414                                  *E-mail:* depanon@ka.net
Louisville, KY 40217                       *Website:* http://www.depressedanon.com

**Depression and Bipolar Support Alliance**                                 **National**
(formerly National Depression and Manic-Depression Association) *400+ chapters. Founded 1986.* Mutual support and information for persons with depressive and manic-depressive illness, and their families. Public education on the nature of depressive illnesses. Advocacy for research and improved access to care. Annual conference, chapter development guidelines. Quarterly newsletter. Catalog.

DBSA                                       *Phone:* 1-800-826-3632 or 312-642-0049
730 N. Franklin, Suite 501                 *Fax:* 312-642-7243
Chicago, IL 60610                          *Website:* http://www.ndmda.org

**DRADA (Depression and Related Affective Disorders Association)**      **International**
*82 affiliated groups in mid-Atlantic area. Founded 1986.* Aims to alleviate the suffering arising from depression and manic-depression by assisting self-help groups, providing education and information. Supports research. Newsletter, literature, phone support. Assistance in starting new groups, training for group leaders, peer support programs. Young People's Outreach Project.

DRADA                                      *Phone:* 410-955-4647 or 202-955-5800
Meyer 3-181                              .  *Fax:* 410-614-3241
600 N. Wolfe St.                           *E-mail:* drada@jhmi.edu
Baltimore, MD 21287-7381                   *Website:* http://www.med.jhu.edu/drada

**MDSG-NY (Mood Disorders Support Group), Inc.**                             **Model**
*3 affiliated groups in New York. Founded 1981.* Support and education for people with manic-depression or depression and their families and friends. Guest lectures, newsletter, rap groups, assistance in starting groups.

MDSG, Inc.                         *Phone:* 212-533-6374; *Fax:* 212-675-0218
P.O. Box 30377                     *E-mail:* info@mdsg.org
New York, NY 10011                 *Website:* http://www.mdsg.org

**BPSO (Bipolar Significant Others) Bulletin Board**                    Online
Provides support and information for families and friends of persons with bipolar disorder
(aka manic-depression). Opportunity to communicate online with others in similar
situations.                        *Website:* http://www.bpso.org

**Child and Adolescent BiPolar Foundation**                             Online
Opportunity to share information and support with families, children and teens with bi-polar
disorders. Message boards, support group information, community center and information.
                           *Website:* http://www.bpkids.org

## DEPRESSION AFTER DELIVERY (POST PARTUM)
*(Also see Childbirth, Parenting)*

**Depression After Delivery**                                        National
*100 affiliated groups. Founded 1985.* Support and information for women who have
suffered from postpartum depression. Volunteer telephone support in most states,
newsletter, group development guidelines.
D.A.D.                             *Phone:* 908-575-9121 or 1-800-944-4773
91 East Somerset St.               *Fax:* 908-541-9713
Raritan, NJ 08869                  *Website:* http://www.depressionafterdeliver.com

**Postpartum Support International**                             International
*300+ affiliated groups. Founded 1987.* To increase the awareness of the emotional changes
women often experience during pregnancy and after the birth of a baby. Information on
diagnosis and treatment of postpartum depression. Provides education, advocacy, and
annual conference. Encourages formation of support groups. Helps strengthen existing
groups. Phone support, referrals, literature, and newsletter.
Postpartum Support Int'l           *Phone:* 805-967-7636; *Fax:* 805-967-0608
927 N. Kellogg Ave.                *E-mail:* jhonikman@earthlink.net
Santa Barbara, CA 93111            *Website:* http://www.postpartum.net

## DISSOCIATIVE IDENTITY /
## MULTIPLE PERSONALITY DISORDER
*(Also see Mental Health Patients, Abuse, Trauma)*

**Amongst Ourselves and Amongst Others**                               Online
Mailing list communities for persons with dissociative identity disorder (multiple
personality disorder) or supporters of persons with dissociative identity disorder. All
subscriptions must be approved.    *Website:* http://foxfiremad.com/amongst/

327

⌨ **Healing Hopes**                                                **Online**
Offers large variety of interactive message forums and chat rooms for persons who are
diagnosed with dissociative identity disorder, and their families.
*Website:* http://www.healinghopes.org

⌨ **NEEDID (Network to Explore & Express DID)**                    **Online**
Support for individuals with a trauma-related dissociative disorder, including post-traumatic
stress disorder. Open to supportive others with patient's permission. For group activities,
members must be in therapy and adhere to confidentiality and safety contracts. Not open to
persons with a primary diagnosis of borderline personality. Online newsletter, discussion
forums. Small donation requested (but can be waived).
*Website:* http://www.needid.bizland.com/

## FAMILIES OF THE MENTALLY ILL
*(Also see specific disorder)*

**Dep-Anon**                                                       **National**
*Founded 1999.* 12-step fellowship for men, women and children whose lives have been
affected by a family members' depression. Members share hope, strength and experience in
order to grow emotionally and spiritually.
Dep-Anon                              *Phone:* Hugh S. 502-569-1989
P.O. Box 17414                        *E-mail:* depanon@ka.net
Louisville, KY 40217                  *Website:* http://www.depressedanon.com

**Federation of Families for Children's Mental Health**            **National**
*122 affiliated groups. Founded 1989.* Parent-run organization focused on the needs of
children and youth with emotional, behavioral or mental disorders and their families.
Provides information and advocacy; newsletter, conferences.
Fed. of Families for Children's MH    *Phone:* Barbara Huff 703-684-7710
1101 King St., Suite 420              *E-mail:* ffcmh@ffcmh.org; *Fax:* 703-836-1040
Alexandria, VA 22314                  *Website:* http://www.ffcmh.org

**National Alliance for the Mentally Ill**                         **National**
*1200+ affiliates. Founded 1979.* Grassroots, self-help groups for consumers and family
members affected by serious mental illness. Focuses on education, advocacy, research and
support. Quarterly newsletter.
NAMI                                  *Phone:* 1-800-950-6264 (helpline)
Colonial Place Three                  or 703-524-7600 (day)
2107 Wilson Blvd.                     *Fax:* 703-524-9094
Arlington, VA 22201-3042              *Website:* http://www.nami.org

**Relatives Project, The**                                         **National**
*3 affiliated groups. Founded 1994.* Offers self-help groups for families and friends of
persons with mental or emotional problems. Helps families and friends deal with

troublesome relationships. Teaches coping skills and techniques to manage stress in order to create a peaceful domestic environment. Assistance in starting new groups.

Relatives Project  
c/o Phyllis Berning  
Abraham A. Low Institute  
550 Frontage Rd., Suite 2797  
Northfield, IL 60093  

*Phone:* 847-441-0445  
*Fax:* 847-441-0446  
*E-mail:* lowinstitute@aol.com  
*Website:* http://lowinstitute.org  

**Parents Involved Network of Pennsylvania**                                    Model  
*Statewide in Pennsylvania. Founded 1984.* Parent-run, self-help advocacy organization for families of children and adolescents who have emotional or behavioral disorders. Provides support, telephone information and referrals, and linkage with other parents and parent organizations. Newsletter.

PIN of Pennsylvania  
1211 Chestnut St., 11th fl.  
Philadelphia, PA 19107  

*Phone:* 1-800-688-4226 or 215-751-1800  
*E-mail:* pin@pinofa.org  
*Website:* http://www.pinofpa.org  

**REACH ("Reassurance to Each")**                                    Model  
*10 groups in Minnesota. Founded 1939.* Mutual support, education and information for families and friends of persons with mental illness. Information and technical assistance available for starting REACH Groups.

REACH  
c/o MHA of MN  
205 W. 2nd St., Suite 412  
Duluth, MN 55802  

*Phone:* 218-726-0793  
or 1-800-862-1799 (in MN)  
*Fax:* 218-727-1468  
*E-mail:* info@mentalhealthmn.org  

## MENTAL HEALTH (GENERAL)
*(Also see specific disorder)*

**16 Steps of Empowerment**                                    National  
*100+ groups. Founded 1992.* Offers support for a wide variety of quality of life issues, such as addiction, codependency, abuse, empowerment, etc. The 16 Steps focus on a positive approach to help members celebrate personal strengths, have choices, stand up for themselves, heal physically, express love, and see themselves as part of the entire community, not just the recovery community.

16 Steps of Empowerment  
362 N. Cleveland Ave., Suite 1  
St. Paul, MN 55104  

*Phone:* 651-645-5782  
*E-mail:* empower16@yahoo.com  
*Web:* http://crosswinds.net/~empower16steps.htm  

**Emotions Anonymous**                                    International  
*1100 chapters. Founded 1971.* 12-step fellowship for people experiencing emotional difficulties. Members share experiences, strengths and hopes in order to improve emotional health. Books and literature available to new and existing groups.

E.A.                                    *Phone:* 651-647-9712; *Fax:* 651-647-1593
P.O. Box 4245                           *E-mail:* info@emotionsanonymous.org
St. Paul, MN 55104-0245                 *Website:* www.emotionsanonymous.org

### GROW, Inc.                                                      International
*143 groups in IL, NJ and RI. Founded in 1957.* 12-step mutual help program to provide
know-how for avoiding and recovering from depression, anxiety and other mental health
problems. Caring and sharing community to attain emotional maturity, personal
responsibility, and recovery from mental illness. Leadership training and consultation to
develop new groups.
GROW, Inc.                              *Phone:* 217-352-6989
2403 W. Springfield Ave.                *Fax:* 217-352-8530
Box 3667                                *E-mail:* programsec@growil.com
Champaign, IL 61826

### HESHE (Help Everyone Share Healthy Emotion) Anonymous            National
*Founded 1997.* 12-step fellowship that helps members recover from any addictive or
abusive behavior. Helps members stay emotionally sober. Groups for adults and
adolescents. Deals with any addiction, compulsion, abusive behavior, or dysfunction.
HE/SHE World Service                    *Phone:* 802-447-4736 (eve)
P.O. Box 1752                           *Website:* http://www.berks.com/12step
Keene, NH 03431                         or http://homepages.together.net/~heshe

### International Association for Clear Thinking                   International
*100 chapters. Founded 1970.* For people interested in living their lives more effectively and
satisfactorily. Uses principles of clear thinking and self-counseling. Offers group handbook,
chapter development kit, audio tapes, facilitator leadership training, and self-help materials.
IACT                                    *Phone:* 920-739-8311
P.O. Box 1011                           *Fax:* 920-582-9783
Appleton, WI 54912

### Pathways to Peace                                              International
*11 groups. Founded 1998.* Self-help program to help deal with anger management. Offers
peer support and education. Workbook ($24). Assistance in starting new groups.
Pathways to Peace                       *Phone:* 716-595-3884
P.O. Box 259                            *E-mail:* transfrm@netsync.net
Cassadaga, NY 14718                     *Website:* http://www.pathwaystopeachinc.com

### Recovery, Inc.                                                International
*700+ groups. Founded 1937.* A community mental health organization that offers a
self-help method of will training. Offers a system of techniques for controlling
temperamental behavior and changing attitudes toward nervous symptoms, anxiety,
depression, anger and fears. Program is based on medical model and group principles
parallel cognitive behavioral therapy. Publications. Information on starting groups.

Recovery, Inc.                    *Phone:* 312-337-5661; *Fax:* 312-337-5756
802 N. Dearborn St.              *E-mail:* inquiries@recovery-inc.com
Chicago, IL 60610                *Website:* http://www.recovery-inc.com

### CAIR (Changing Attitudes In Recovery)                    Model
*30 groups in California. Founded 1990.* Self-help "family" sharing a common commitment to gain healthy esteem. Includes persons with relationship problems, addictions, mental illness, etc. Offers new techniques and tools leading to better self-esteem. Assistance in starting groups. Handbook ($9.95), tapes, leader's manual.
CAIR                             *Phone:* 209-577-1667 (day)
c/o Psych. Assoc. Press          *Fax:* 209-577-3805
706 13th St.                     *E-mail:* CAIRforyou@aol.com
Modesto, CA 95354                *Website:* http://www.cairforyou.com

### 🖳 Anger Management Live Chat                    Online
Professionally-facilitated live chat that discusses the management and mismanagement of anger. Teaches techniques that aid in developing harmonious relationships. Chat room open everyday, 8pm-midnight (CT). Also has a message board.
*Website:* http://www.angermgmt.com

## MENTAL HEALTH PATIENTS / EX-PATIENTS
## PSYCHIATRIC SURVIVORS
*(Also see specific disorder)*

### CONTAC (Consumer Organization
### And Networking Technical Assistance Center)                    National
Center for mental health consumers and consumer-run organizations nationwide that promote self-help, recovery and empowerment. Technical assistance for organizing and maintaining self-help groups, and leadership training. Listserv, on-line peer support.
CONTAC                           *Phone:* 1-888-825-8324 or 304-346-9992
P.O. Box 11000                   *Fax:* 304-345-7303
Charleston, WV 25339             *E-mail:* usacontac@contac.org
                                 *Website:* http://www.contac.org

### Disabled Artists' Network                    National network
*Founded 1985.* Mutual support and exchange of information for professional visual artists with physical or mental disabilities. Provides information and referrals, pen pals, and reports to active members. Include self-addressed stamped envelope when writing.
Disabled Artists' Network
P.O. Box 20781
New York, NY 10025

*"Never doubt that a small group of thoughtful, committed citizens can change the world; indeed, it's the only thing that ever does."* — *Margaret Mead*

**NADD Association for Persons with**
**Developmental Disabilities and Mental Health Needs**                    **National**
*5 affiliated groups. Founded 1983.* Promotes the development of resources for persons with both mental retardation and a mental illness through education, advocacy, research and exchange of information. Conferences, national resource database, audio tapes and books available. Directory of members.

NADD                                     *Phone:* 845-331-4336; *Fax:* 914-331-4569
132 Fair St.                             *E-mail:* thenadd@aol.com
Kingston, NY 12401                       *Website:* http://www.thenadd.org

**National Empowerment Center**                                          **Resource**
*Founded 1992.* Consumer-run center that provides information on local self-help resources and upcoming conferences. Also provides networking, conference calls and workshops.

Nat'l Empowerment Ctr.                   *Phone:* 978-685-1518 or 1-800-769-3278
599 Canal St.                            *Fax:* 978-681-6426; *TTY:* 1-800-889-7693
Lawrence, MA 01840                       *Website:* http://www.power2u.org

**National Mental Health Consumers Self-Help Clearinghouse**             **Resource**
Consumer self-help resource information geared towards meeting the group needs of mental health consumers. Assistance in advocacy, listings of publications, on-site consultations, training, educational events.         *Phone:* 1-800-553-4-KEY

Nat'l MH Consumers SHC                   *TDD:* 215-751-9655; *Fax:* 215-636-6312
1211 Chestnut St., Suite 1207            *E-mail:* info@mhselfhelp.org
Philadelphia, PA 19107-4103              *Website:* http://www.mhselfhelp.org

**On Our Own, Inc.**                                                     **Model**
*3 groups in Maryland. Founded 1981.* Mutual support and advocacy for mental health consumers. Sponsors drop-in centers for educational, social and recreational activities.

On Our Own                               *Phone:* 1-800-553-9899 (MD) or 410-444-4500
P.O. Box 18899                           *Fax:* 410-444-8755
Baltimore, MD 21206                      *E-mail:* onourown@aol.com

**Reclamation, Inc.**                                                    **Model**
*1 group in Texas. Founded 1974.* Alliance of mentally restored people helping to reclaim the human dignity destroyed by the stigma of mental illness. Directs ex-patients in worthwhile, positively visible projects to improve image. Quarterly newsletter. Staffed and funded by ex-patients.

Reclamation, Inc.                        *Phone:* Don H. Cullwell, Dir. 210-822-3569
2502 Waterford Dr.
San Antonio, TX 78217

**Well Mind Association of Greater Washington**                          **Model**
*1 group in Maryland. Founded 1967.* Holistic medical information clearinghouse with an emphasis on mental health. Provides education about mental illness as principally a

metabolic or biochemical disorder. Explores the connection between mental illness and environmental, biological and physiological factors. Newsletter, information, referrals to practitioners, literature, books and tapes.

Well Mind Assn.                          *Phone:* 301-774-6617
P.O. Box 312                             *Fax:* 301-946-1402
Ashton, MD 20861-0312

## OBSESSIVE-COMPULSIVE DISORDER
*(Also see Mental Health General)*

**Obsessive-Compulsive Anonymous**                          **National**
*50 affiliated groups. Founded 1988.* 12-step self-help group for people with obsessive-compulsive disorders. Assistance available for starting groups.

O.C.A.                                   *Phone:* 516-739-0662
P.O. Box 215                             *Website:* http://members.aol.com/west24th/
New Hyde Park, NY 11040                  index.html

**Obsessive-Compulsive Foundation, Inc.**                    **International**
*11 chapters. Founded 1986.* Support and education for people with obsessive-compulsive and related disorders, their families, friends and professionals. Supports research into the causes and effective treatments of these disorders. Bi-monthly newsletter, referrals to support groups and treatment centers, annual conference, books, audio and video tapes. Trains mental health professionals in treatment techniques. Online chat room "Ask the Experts."

OCF                                      *Phone:* 203-315-2190
P.O. Box 9573                            *Fax:* 203-315-2196
New Haven, CT 06535                      *E-mail:* info@ocfoundation.org
                                         *Website:* http://www.ocfoundation.org

**Trichotillomania Learning Center**                         **International**
*Founded 1991.* Information and support to patients, families and professionals about trichotillomania (compulsive hair pulling). Newsletter, information and referrals, annual retreat, conferences, phone support, pen pals, and literature. Assistance in starting groups.

TLC                                      *Phone:* 831-457-1004; *Fax:* 831-426-4383
303 Potrero #51                          *E-mail:* trichster@aol.com
Santa Cruz, CA 95060                     *Website:* http://www.trich.org

**⌨ OC & Spectrum Disorders Association**                    **Online**
Forum and moderated and unmoderated support groups that provide support and information for anyone interested in obsessive-compulsive disorder. Topics include medications, family and relationships, obsessions, humor, therapy, teens with OCD, etc.
*E-mail:* chatadmin@ocdhelp.org     *Website:* http://www.ocdhelp.org/chatinfo.html

💻 **OCD Support Groups**                                                   **Online**
Offers a large variety of support groups dealing with obsessive-compulsive disorder
including body dysmorphia, hoarding and clutter, home schooling OCD children, OCD and
social phobia, skin picking and other minor self-injury, teens with OCD, survivors of sexual
abuse, gays and lesbians with OCD.     *Website:* http://groups.yahoo.com/group/

## SCHIZOPHRENIA
*(Also see Mental Health Patients)*

**Schizophrenics Anonymous**                                        **International**
*150+ chapters. Founded 1985.* Organized and run by people with a schizophrenia-related
disorder. Offers fellowship, support and information. Focuses on recovery, using a 6-step
program, along with medication and professional help. Weekly meetings, phone network,
and newsletter. Provides assistance in starting and maintaining groups.

Schizophrenics Anonymous          *Phone:* 517-485-7168
c/o Nat'l Schizophrenia Fdn.      *Fax:* 517-485-7180
403 Seymour St., Suite 202        *E-mail:* schizanon@aol.com
Lansing, MI 48933.                *Website:* http://www.sanonymous.org

**Schizophrenia Society of Canada**                                      **National**
*10 societies. Founded 1979.* Information, support and advocacy for families and friends of
persons with schizophrenia. Public awareness campaigns, advocacy and fund-raising.
Newsletters, guidelines and assistance for starting self-help groups. Information and
referrals, phone help, conferences, brochures, handbooks, videos.

Schizophrenia Soc. of Canada      *Phone:* 416-445-8204; *Fax:* 416-445-2270
75 The Donway W., #814            *E-mail:* info@schizophrenia.ca
Don Mills, ON Canada M3C 2E9      *Website:* http://www.schizophrenia.ca

## SELF-INJURY

💻 **Self-Injury**                                                          **Online**
Moderated message board that provides support and strength for persons who use self-
injurious behavior to deal with their intense emotions. To access boards, go to website
below, look under "psychology" and click on "self-injury."
                              *Website:* http://boards.ivillagehealth.com


*"Although the world is full of suffering...*
*It is also full of overcoming it."*
*- Helen Keller*

# MISCELLANEOUS

*"The only way to help people*
*is to give them a chance to help themselves."*
*- Elbert Hubbard*

## ACCIDENT VICTIMS
*(Also see Trauma)*

**ACCESS (AirCraft Casualty Emotional Support Services)**     **National network**
Matches persons who have lost a loved one in an aircraft accident to volunteers who previously experienced a similar loss. Aim is to help fill the void that occurs when the emergency and disaster relief organizations disband, the initial shock subsides, and the natural grieving process intensifies. Persons communicate through e-mail or by phone.

ACCESS                                      *Phone:* 1-877-227-6435
1594 York Ave., Suite 22              *E-mail:* info@accesshelp.org
New York, NY 10028                    *Website:* http://www.accesshelp.org

**Wings of Light, Inc.**                                         **National network**
*3 support networks. Founded 1995.* Support and information network for individuals whose lives have been touched by aviation accidents. Separate networks for: airplane accident survivors; families and friends of persons killed in airplane accidents; and persons involved in the rescue, recovery and investigation of crashes. Information and referrals, phone support.

Wings of Light                          *Phone:* 1-800-613-8531 or 623-516-1115
PMB 448, Suite 1                       *Website:* http://www.wingsoflight.org
16845 N. 29th Ave.
Phoenix, AZ 85053

⌨ **CRASH Foundation (Citizens for Reliable And Safe Highways)**        **Online**
Dedicated to providing immediate compassionate support to truck crash survivors and families of truck crash victims. Referrals to grief counseling, medical services and truck crash experts. Phone support, conferences, advocacy, First Response Program, and Survivors Network.

CRASH                                    *Phone:* 415-435-4994
1628 Tiburon Blvd.                      *Fax:* 415-435-4997
Tiburon, CA 94920                       *Website*: http://www.trucksafety.org/

*"Alone we can do so little; together we can do so much."*
*- Helen Keller*

## AGING / OLDER PERSONS

**AARP**                                                                **National**
*4000 chapters. Founded 1958.* Nonpartisan membership organization for people 50 and over. Provides information and resources. Advocates on legislative, consumer, and legal issues. Assists members to serve their communities. Offers a wide range of unique benefits, special products, and services for members. Modern Maturity and My Generation magazines and monthly AARP Bulletin. Celebrates the attitude that age isn't just a number--it's about how you live your life.

AARP                                    *Phone:* 202-434-2277; *TDD:* 1-877-434-7589
601 E St., NW                           *E-mail:* jdieterle@aarp.org
Washington, DC 20049                    *Website:* http://www.aarp.org

**Gray Panthers**                                                        **National**
*47 chapters. Founded 1970.* Multigenerational education and advocacy movement/organization which works to bring about fundamental social changes including a national health care system, elimination of all forms of discrimination, and economic justice. Newsletter, newspaper. Chapter development guidelines. Dues $20/US; $35/Org; $40/Int'l.

Gray Panthers                           *Phone:* 202-737-6637; *Fax:* 202-737-1160
733 15th St., NW, Suite 437             *E-mail:* info@graypanthers.org
Washington, DC 20005                    *Website:* http://www.graypanthers.org

**Older Women's League**                                                 **National**
*60+ chapters. Founded 1980.* Membership organization that advocates for various economic and social issues on behalf of midlife and older women (social security, pension rights, employment, caregiver support, elder abuse, etc.). Newsletter, chapter development guidelines. Dues $25.

OWL                                     *Phone:* 202-783-6686 or 1-800-825-3695
666 11th St., NW, Suite 700             *Fax:* 202-638-2356
Washington, DC 20001                    *E-mail:* info@owl-national.org
                                        *Website:* http://www.owl-national.com

**SOWN (Supportive Older Women's Network)**                              **Model**
*50 groups in Philadelphia area. Founded 1982.* Helps women (60+) cope with their specialized aging concerns. Support groups, leadership training, consultation, outreach and networking. Newsletter.

SOWN                                    *Phone:* 215-477-6000
2805 N. 47th St.                        *Fax:* 215-477-6555
Philadelphia, PA 19131                  *E-mail:* sown@erols.com

## ARTISTIC CREATIVITY

**ARTS Anonymous (Artists Recovering Through the 12-Steps)**        **International**
*150 affiliated groups. Founded 1984.* 12-step program for persons interested in fulfilling

their creative potential. Retreats, literature. Meeting start-up guidelines. Include self-addressed stamped envelope when writing. For referrals to groups outside of New York area, send $2 along with your address and a list of nearby cities.

ARTS Anon.                              *Phone:* 212-873-7075 (touch tone phone)
P.O. Box 230175                         *E-mail:* jaymark@accesshub.net
New York, NY 10023                      *Website:* http://www.pagehost.com/arts

## CAREGIVERS / FAMILIES OF NURSING HOME RESIDENTS
*(Also see specific illness)*

**Children of Aging Parents**                                                  **National**
*26 groups. Founded 1977.* Non-profit membership organization dedicated to the needs of caregivers of the elderly. National network of support and offers information, referral and counseling. Bi-monthly newsletter-capsule. Low cost materials available. Assistance in starting groups.

CAPS                                    *Phone:* 1-800-227-7294 or 215-945-6900
1609 Woodbourne Rd., #302A              *Fax:* 215-945-8720
Levittown, PA 19057                     *Website:* http://www.careguide.net

**National Family Caregivers Association**                                      **National**
*Founded 1992.* Dedicated to improving the quality of life for family caregivers through support and validation, education and information, public awareness and advocacy. Information and referrals, newsletter, resources and literature.

Nat'l Family Caregivers Assn.           *Phone:* 301-942-6430 or 1-800-896-3650
10400 Connecticut Ave., #500            *Fax:* 301-942-2302; *E-mail:* info@nfcacares.org
Kensington, MD 20895-3944               *Website:* http://www.nfcacares.org

**Well Spouse Foundation**                                                   **International**
*100+ support groups. Founded 1988.* Provides emotional support and information to the well spouses and children of the chronically ill. Informs educators, human service professionals and the public about the needs of spousal caregivers. Newsletter. Chat rooms and bulletin boards. Guidelines and assistance available for starting new groups.

Well Spouse Fdn.                        *Phone:* 1-800-838-0879 or 212-685-8815
30 E. 40th St., Suite PH                *E-mail:* dester@aol.com
New York, NY 10016                      *Website:* http://www.wellspouse.org

**Advocacy Center for Long-Term Care**                                           **Model**
*Statewide in MN. Founded 1972.* Provides services to consumer councils in nursing homes and their members through technical assistance and education to residents, families and staff. Workshops and training. Variety of printed resource materials on long-term care topics. How-to materials on starting nursing home family councils and resident councils.

Advoc. Ctr. for Long-Term Care         *Phone:* 952-854-7304
2626 E. 82nd St., Suite 220            *Fax:* 952-854-8535
Bloomington MN 55425                   *E-mail:* ac4ltc2cce@aol.com

**DEBUT (Daughters of Elderly Bridging the Unknown Together)**          **Model**
*1 group in Indiana. Founded 1981.* Support group designed by, and for, women struggling with the responsibilities, emotions, and decisions involved in the care of aging parents. Phone network, weekly meetings.
DEBUT                                          *Phone:* Pat Meier 812-339-2092
Area 10 Agency on Aging
7500 Reeves Rd.
Bloomington, IN 47404-9688


🖳 **Family Caregiver Alliance**                                         **Online**
Unmoderated listserv for caregivers to share support, strategies and ideas with each other. Includes gay, lesbian, bisexual and transgender caregivers group.
Family Caregiver Alliance          *Phone:* 1-800-445-8106
690 Market St., Suite 600          *E-mail:* info@caregiver.org
San Francisco, CA 94104            *Website:* http://www.caregiver.org


🖳 **Web of Care**                                                       **Online**
Offers support for family caregivers including online chats, discussion boards, healthcare information, and more. Also has a professional care provider's section.
                                   *Website:* http://www.webofcare.com

## CLUTTERERS / MESSINESS

**Clutterers Anonymous**                                                **National**
*28 affiliated chapters.* 12-step fellowship of individuals who share experience, strength, and hope with each other that they may solve their common problems with clutter and help others recover. The only requirement for membership is a desire to eliminate clutter and bring order to one's life.
CLA                                *E-mail:* admin@clutters-anonymous.org
P.O. Box 91413                     *Website:* http://www.clutterersanonymous.net
Los Angeles, CA 90009-1413


**Messies Anonymous**                                                   **National**
*25 groups. Founded 1981* (Multilingual) 12-step group that aims to improve the quality of life of disorganized homemakers. Provides motivation and a program for change to help members improve self-image as control of house and life is obtained. Optional donation at meetings. Quarterly newsletter ($16/two years). Interactive online group. Books and materials available in English, German and Spanish. Send a self-addressed stamped envelope when writing.
Messies Anonymous                  *Phone:* 1-800-MESS-AWAY or 305-271-8404
5025 SW 114th Ave.                 *Fax:* 305-273-7671; *E-mail:* SRFMA@aol.com
Miami, FL 33165                    *Website:* http://www.messies.com

# CRIME VICTIMS / OFFENDERS
## (Also see Bereavement, Trauma)

**MADD (Mothers Against Drunk Driving)**                          **National**
*600+ chapters. Founded 1980.* The mission of MADD is to stop drunk driving, support victims of this violent crime, and prevent underage drinking. Newsletter, chapter development guidelines.
MADD                                    *Phone:* 214-744-6233 or 1-800-GET-MADD
511 EJ Carpenter Freeway #700           *Fax:* 972-869-2206
Irving, TX 75062-8187                   *Website:* http://www.madd.org

**National Center for Victims of Crime**                          **National**
*Founded 1985.* Provides crime victims with information, resources, and referrals to existing victim assistance groups. Several newsletters. Acts as a national stalking resource center. Comprehensive services for crime victims. Information and referrals.
NCVC                                    *Phone:* 1-800-394-2255 or 202-467-8700
2000 M St., NW, Suite 480               *E-mail:* ncvc@ncvc.org
Washington, DC 20036                    *Website:* http://www.ncvc.org

**National Organization of Parents of Murdered Children**         **National**
*300 chapters and contact persons. Founded 1978.* Mutual support for persons who have survived the violent death of someone close, as they seek to recover. Newsletter. Court accompaniment also provided in many areas. Parole Block Program and Second Opinion Service also available.                     *Phone:* 1-888-818-POMC or 513-721-5683
NOPMC                                   *Fax:* 513-345-4489
100 E. 8th St., B-41                    *E-mail:* NatlPOMC@aol.com
Cincinnati, OH 45202                    *Website:* http://www.pomc.com

**NOVA (National Organization for Victim Assistance)**            **National**
*2300 members. Founded 1975.* Support and advocacy for victims and survivors of violent crimes and disaster. Newsletter, information and referrals, phone help, conferences, crisis response training, group development guidelines. Dues $35/ind; $125/org.
NOVA                                    *Phone:* 202-232-6682 or 1-800-TRY-NOVA
1730 Park Rd., NW                       *Fax:* 202-462-2255; *E-mail:* nova@try-nova.org
Washington, DC 20010                    *Website:* http://www.try-nova.org

**RID (Remove Intoxicated Drivers)**                              **National**
*152 chapters in 41 states. Founded 1978.* Citizens' project organized to advocate against drunk driving, educate the public, reform legislation and aid victims of drunk driving. Newsletter. Chapter information kit ($20). For pamphlet send self-addressed stamped envelope.
RID                                     *Phone:* 518-372-0034 or 518-370-4917
P.O.Box 520                             *Fax:* 518-370-4917; *E-mail:* info@rid-usa.org
Schenectady, NY 12301                   *Website:* http://www.rid-usa.org

**Shoplifters Anonymous**                                          **National**
*3 groups. Founded 1980.* 12-step fellowship for those wishing to stop their compulsive stealing or shoplifting. Offers support, advice and information.
Shoplifters Anonymous          *Phone:* 212-673-0392
P.O. Box 55                    *E-mail:* lion54@nyc.rr.com
New York, NY 10276

Shoplifters Anonymous          *Phone:* 612-925-4860
P.O. Box 24515
Minneapolis, MN 55424

**CASA (Cleptomaniacs And Shoplifters Anonymous)**                 **Model**
*Founded 1992.* Secular support group for recovering shoplifters, kleptomaniacs and other persons suffering from dishonesty related to fraud, stealing or cheating. Pen pals, information and referrals, phone support. Online chat room. Assistance in starting similar groups. Include self-addressed stamped envelope when writing.
CASA                           *Phone:* Terry S. 248-358-8508 (eve)
P.O. Box 250008                *E-mail:* shulmann@umich.edu
Franklin, MI 48205             *Website:* http://www.shopliftersanonymous.com

**Criminals and Gangmembers Anonymous, Inc.**                      **Model**
*6 affiliated groups. Founded 1996.* 12-step group for criminals and gang members who have a sincere desire to find relief from their addiction to all forms of criminality. For those with a desire for peace within themselves and a wish to live in harmony with others. Online groups.                          *Phone:* 916-973-8603
Criminals/Gangmembers Anon.    *E-mail:* CGAnonymous@usa.net
P.O. Box 255867                *Website:* http://www.angelfire.com/id/
Sacramento, CA 95865-5867      CGAnonymous/

**Fortune Society**                                                **Model**
*Founded 1967.* Support and education for ex-offenders. Provides substance abuse treatment, tutoring, employment assistance, AIDS/HIV education and services, counseling and court advocacy. Most of the counselors are ex-offenders and/or in recovery from drug addiction. Assistance available for starting similar groups.
Fortune Society                *Phone:* 212-206-7070
39 W. 19th St., 7th fl.        *Fax:* 212-633-6845
New York, NY 10011             *Website:* http://www.fortunesociety.org

**Seventh Step Society of Canada**                                 **Model**
*13 groups in Ontario. Founded 1978.* Sponsors groups in correctional facilities for inmates and street groups for at-risk individuals. Uses a process of reconciliation for offenders. Members help each other talk out their resentments and modify their thinking. Each group uses volunteers including non-con and ex-cons who have proven themselves by staying away from trouble.

Seventh Step Society Of Canada
10620 Waneta Crescent SE
Calgary, Alberta Canada T2J 1J6

*Phone:* 403-271-2278; *Fax:* 403-271-8907
E-mail: seventh@7thstep.ca
*Website:* http://www.7thstep.ca

## Save Our Sons And Daughters (SOSAD)     Model
*1 group in MI. Founded 1987.* Crisis intervention and violence prevention program that provides support and advocacy for survivors of homicide or other traumatic loss. Weekly groups, professional grief counseling and training, education on peace movement to youth, advocacy, public education. Newsletter, conferences, and assistance in starting groups.
SOSAD
2441 W. Grand Blvd.
Detroit, MI 48208-1210

*Phone:* 313-361-5200
*Fax:* 313-361-0055
*E-mail:* sosadb@aol.com

## 🖳 Families of Inmates     Online
E-mail list for people with loved ones in jail or prison. Members offer support to each other through the rough times.    *Web:* groups.yahoo.com/group/Families-of-inmates

## 🖳 Prison Talk Online     Online
Support for persons who are dealing with a loved one in prison. Opportunity to connect with others in the same situation. Aim is to bridge the communication barrier that exists in the criminal justice system, and to effect change in policy, prisoner rights, sentencing, etc.
Prison Talk Online    *Website:* http://www.prisontalk.com/
P.O. Box 10616
College Station, TX 77842-0616

## 🖳 Stalking Victim's Sanctuary     Online
Provides information on stalking and dealing with it. Chat group, ideas on dealing with stress, referrals to groups.    *Website:* http://www.stalkingvictims.com/

## CULT SURVIVORS

## reFOCUS (recovering FOrmer CUltists Support)     National network
*Founded 1984.* Support for former members of closed, high demand groups, relationships or cults. Referrals to other former cult members by group and/or area, support groups, therapists, and services. Literature, internet newsletter, recovery workshops, conferences.
reFOCUS
P.O. Box 2180
Flagler Beach, FL 32136

*Phone:* 904-439-7541; *Fax:* 904-439-7537
*E-mail:* torefocus@aol.com
*Website:* http://www.refocus.org

## DONOR'S OFFSPRING (ARTIFICIAL INSEMINATION)

## Donors' Offspring, Inc.     International
*Founded 1981.* Information, support and reunion registry forms for sperm donors and their

offspring. Assistance for adults searching for their donor families. Newsletter ($20 for 2 years), monthly national phone conference. Assistance in starting new groups.
*E-mail:* candace1@usa.net          *Phone:* 417-548-3320 (Voice/Fax)

# EMPLOYMENT

### 9 to 5, National Association of Working Women                    National
*24 chapters. Founded 1973.* Support, advocacy and legislative assistance on issues that affect women who work. Job-problem counselors can advise women on how to make changes on their jobs. Dues $25/yr. Phone support, conferences, newsletters. Group development guidelines.

9 to 5                             *Phone:* 1-800-522-0925 (hotline)
Nat'l Assn. of Working Women       *Office:* 414-274-0925
1430 W. Peachtree St., #610        *E-mail:* Hotline9to5@igc.org
Atlanta, GA 30309                  *Website:* http://www.9to5.org

### Business and Professional Women/USA                             National
*2800 chapters. Founded 1919.* Organization comprised of working women, to promote work place equity and provide networking opportunities. Lobbying efforts, tri-annual magazine, periodic publications, resource center, and grassroots community action projects. Annual national convention. Dues $31.

Business and Prof. Women/USA       *Phone:* 202-293-1100
2012 Massachusetts Ave., NW        *Fax:* 202-861-0298
Washington, DC 20036               *Website:* http://www.bpwusa.org

### Employment Support Center                                        Model
*7 groups in Washington, DC. Founded 1984.* Provides technical assistance for self-help groups for the unemployed, underemployed, and persons in transition. Provides leadership training for groups. Sets up new groups and coalitions of job clubs with training and materials. Newsletter. Extensive network of group leaders, employment professionals, job seekers. Offers job bank, consultations, network meetings and programs, small business seminars, self-help and job search sessions. Self-Help Bridge to Employment manual ($25).

ESC                                *Phone:* 202-628-2919; *Fax:* 202-628-2920
711 8th St., NW                    *E-mail:* jobclubs@hotmail.com
Washington, DC 20001               *Website:* http://www.angelfire.com/biz/jobclubs

### Job Transition Support Group                                     Model
*1 group in Minnesota. Founded 1976.* Support and encouragement for people laid off from their jobs or seeking a job change. Weekly meetings include speakers' presentations and small group discussions. Group development guidelines ($5).

Job Transition Support Group       *Phone:* 952-925-2711 (Church)
c/o Colonial Church of Edina       *Fax:* 952-925-1591
6200 Colonial Way
Edina, MN 55436

**MATCH (Mother's Access To Careers at Home)**                    Model
*2 affiliated groups (VA and MD). Founded 1990.* Provides networking, business and emotional support and advocacy for mothers who have, or wish to pursue, careers from home. Newsletter, information and referrals, phone support, special interest groups. Assistance in starting new groups.

MATCH                                 *Phone:* 703-205-9664
Fairfax County Gov. Ctr.              *Website:* http://www.mothersaccessto
12000 Government Ctr. Parkway         careersathome.org
Fairfax, VA 22035

**Women Employed**                                                Model
*1 group in Illinois. Founded 1973.* Promotes economic advancement for women through service, education and advocacy. Career development services, job bank, career counseling, networking, conferences to link women. Quarterly newsletter, publications list. Annual membership dues $50/year.

Women Employed                        *Phone:* 312-782-3902; *Fax:* 312-782-5249
111 N. Wabash, Suite 1300             *E-mail:* info@womenemployed.org
Chicago, IL 60602                     *Website:* http://www.womenemployed.org

## ENVIRONMENTAL CONCERNS
*(Also see Chemical Sensitivity)*

**Center for Health, Environment and Justice**                    National
*7,000 groups. Founded 1981.* Grassroots environmental crisis center, providing information and networking for people affected by toxic waste. Assists in organizing self-help groups, and provides scientific and technical backup. Conferences, information and referrals. Newsletters.

CHEJ                                  *Phone:* 703-237-2249
P.O. Box 6806                         *E-mail:* info@chej.org
Falls Church, VA 22040-6806           *Website:* http://www.chej.org

## FOOD SHARING

**World SHARE (Self-Help And Resource Exchange)**              International
*18 U.S. affiliates. Founded 1983.* Builds healthy communities by creating opportunities and incentives through self-help activities, to encourage people to participate together in solving community problems. Provides access to affordable food, and supplies volunteer services to communities. By donating volunteer time to a community activity, participants can save 50% on a monthly food package.

World SHARE                           *Phone:* 1-800-773-SHARE (CA) or 619-686-5818
1250 Delevan Dr.                      *E-mail:* info@worldshare.org
San Diego, CA 92102                   *Website:* http://www.worldshare.org

# HEIGHT ISSUES
*(Also see Growth Disorders, specific disorder)*

**Little People of America**                                        **National**
*54 chapters. Founded 1957.* (English/Spanish) Provides mutual support to people of short stature (4'10" and under), and their families. Information on physical and developmental concerns, employment, education, disability rights, medical issues, adaptive devices, etc. Newsletter. Educational scholarships and medical assistance grants, access to medical advisory board, assistance in adoption. Local, regional and national conferences and athletic events. Online chat room, list serve. Dues $30.

LPA                             *Phone:* 1-888-LPA-2001
P.O. Box 745                    *E-mail:* LPADataBase@juno.com
Lubbock, TX 79408               *Website:* http://www.lpaonline.org

**Tall Clubs International**                                        **International**
*65+ groups. Founded 1938.* Social support for tall persons, (men at least 6'2", women at least 5'10"). Advocacy for clothing and other special needs of tall people. Skywriters and TALLrific for persons under 21. Group development guidelines, information and referrals, conferences, newsletters, and socials.

Tall Clubs Int'l                *Phone:* 1-888-468-2552
Box 26515                       *Website:* http://www.tall.org
Los Vegas, NV 89126-0515

# LANDMINE SURVIVORS
*(Also see Amputation/Limb Deficiency)*

**Landmine Survivors Network**                            **International Network**
*Founded 1997.* Created by and for landmine survivors. Links victims in mine-affected countries to a range of rehabilitative services. Provides peer counseling and direct assistance. Promotes social and economic reintegration. Strives to protect future generations from the scourge of landmines. Maintains database of medical facilities, prosthetic clinics and rehabilitation projects who work with landmine survivors and their families.

Landmine Survivors Network      *Phone:* 202-464-0007; *Fax:* 202-464-0011
1420 K St., NW, Suite 650       *E-mail:* lsn@landminesurvivors.org
Washington, DC 20005            *Website:* http://www.landminesurvivors.org

# LIGHTNING / SHOCK VICTIMS

**Lightning Strike and Electric Shock Survivors**          **International network**
*Founded 1989.* Support for survivors of lightning or electric shock, their families, and families of non-survivors. Studies the long-term after-effects. Information and referrals, phone support, annual conferences, help in starting groups. Newsletter, books and tapes.

LS&ESSI Inc.                    *Phone:* Steve Marshburn Sr. 910-346-4708
P.O. Box 1156                  *Fax:* 910-346-4708; *E-mail:* lightnin@internet.net
Jacksonville, NC 28541-1156    *Website:* www.mindspring.com/~lightningstrike

## LITIGATION / MALPRACTICE

**Litigation Stress Support Group**                                    **Model**
*1 group in NJ. Founded 1986.* Peer support and networking for doctors and their families
going through malpractice suits. Phone network. Assistance in starting similar groups.
Litigation Stress Support Group        *Phone:* 609-896-1766 (day)
2 Princess Rd.
Lawrenceville, NJ 08648

## MEN'S ISSUES
*(Also see specific issue)*

**Bald-Headed Men of America**                                    **National**
*6 affiliated groups. Founded 1973.* Self-help group instilling pride in being bald.
Exchanging feelings and experiences through group discussions have led to acceptance of
being bald. "We believe the best cure for baldness is to promote a positive mental
attitude...with humor." Annual conference (usually in September), newsletter.
Bald Headed Men of America        *Phone:* 252-726-1855
102 Bald Dr.                      *Fax:* 252-726-6061
Morehead City, NC 28557          *E-mail:* jcapps4102@aol.com

**National Organization For Men**                                    **National**
*15 chapters. Founded 1983.* Seeks equal rights for men, uniform national divorce, custody,
property and visitation law. Educational seminars. Lawyer referral. Quarterly newsletter.
Nat'l Org. for Men               *Phone:* 212-686-MALE or 212-766-4030
11 Park Pl.                      *Website:* http://www.tnom.com
New York, NY 10007-2801

**NOHARMM (National Organization to Halt**
**the Abuse and Routine Mutilation of Males)**              **National network**
*Founded 1992.* Advocacy and education for men concerned about circumcision. Empowers
men to speak out for the rights of children to have body ownership. Information and
referrals, newsletter, literature.
NOHARMM                          *Phone:* 415-26-9351; *Fax:* 305-768-5967
P.O. Box 460795                  *E-mail:* info@noharmm.org
San Francisco, CA 94146          *Website:* http://www.noharmm.org

**NORM (National Organization of Restoring Men)**              **International**
*20 affiliated groups. Founded 1989.* (Meetings for men only; information for all) Provides a
safe environment in which men can, without fear of being ridiculed, share their concerns

about circumcision/restoration and for a desire to be intact and whole again. Confidential discussions on foreskin restoration. Referrals, phone support, assistance in starting groups.

NORM
c/o R. Wayne Griffiths
3205 Northwood Dr., #209
Concord, CA 94520-4506

*Phone:* 925-827-4077 (eve)
*Fax:* 925-827-4119
*E-mail:* waynerobb@aol.com
*Website:* http://www.norm.org

**National Men's Resource Center**                          Model
*1 group in California. Founded 1982.* Educational website with thousands of on-site men's book reviews, men's resources and links to hundreds of men's issues, events, periodicals and groups. Serves as a diverse men's community (men's rights, pro-feminist, recovery, and re-evaluation). Information on men's issues regarding positive changes in male roles and relationships (including abuse, aging, circumcision, divorce, fathers, health, isolation, kids, mid-life, multicultural, prostate, sexuality, spirituality, transition, violence, work, etc).

Nat'l Men's Resource Ctr.
P.O. Box 1080
Brookings, OR 97415

*E-mail:* menstuff@menstuff.org
*Website:* http://www.menstuff.org

## NEAR DEATH EXPERIENCE
*(Also see Accidents, Trauma)*

**International Association for Near-Death Studies**          International
*35 affiliated groups. Founded 1981.* Support group for anyone who has had a near-death experience, their families and the professionals working with them. Information and education for interested public. Promotes research. Newsletter; group development guidelines.

IANDS
P.O. Box 502
E. Windsor Hill, CT 06028-0502

*Phone:* 860-644-5216
*Fax:* 860-644-5759
*E-mail:* office@iands.org
*Website:* http://www.iands.org

## NETWORKING FOR ILL / DISABLED
*(Also see Disabilities, specific disorder)*

**CUSA**                                                    National
*120 correspondence groups. Founded 1947.* Correspondence support groups for persons of all faiths with any type of disability or chronic illness. Catholic in founding, but open to all. Emphasis on spiritual values and mutual support. Through group letters members find close relationships, understanding and courage. Dues $10/yr. (can be waived).

CUSA
176 W. 8th St.
Bayonne, NJ 07002

*E-mail:* ams4@juno.com
*Website:* http://www.Cusan.org

**Friends' Health Connection**                                          **National network**
A support network that connects people of all ages with any disorder, illness or handicap.
Also networks caretakers, families and friends. Members are networked with each other
based on health problem, symptoms, hobbies, lifestyle, interests, occupation, location and
other criteria, and communicate via letters, phone, tapes, e-mail, and face-to-face. Intended
for emotional support, not for romantic purposes. Fee $30 first yr., $15 yr. thereafter.

Friend's Health Connection            *Phone:* 1-800-483-7436
P.O. Box 114                          *E-mail:* info@ friendshealthconnection.org
New Brunswick, NJ 08903               *Website*: http://www.friendshealthconnection.org

**MUMS National Parent-to-Parent Network**                              **National**
*61 affiliated groups. Founded 1979.* Mutual support and networking for parents or care
providers of children with any disability, rare disorder, chromosomal abnormality or health
conditions using a database of over 17,000 families from 52 countries, covering 2700
disorders, very rare syndromes or undiagnosed conditions. Referrals to support groups and
provides assistance in starting groups. Newsletter ($15 parents/$25 professionals). Matching
services $5. Other literature available.

MUMS National                         *Phone:* 1-877-336-5333 (parents only)
  Parent-to-Parent Network     or 920-336-5333; *Fax:* 920-339-0995
150 Custer Court                      *E-mail:* mums@netnet.net
Green Bay, WI 54301-1243              *Website:* http://www.netnet.net/mums/

## PATIENTS' RIGHTS

**New England Patients' Rights Group**                                  **Model**
*Founded 1993.* Mutual support for health care consumers, many of whom are suffering
because of deficiencies or negligence in the system. Advocates for consumer empowerment,
quality, accurate information, informed consent, insurance needs, patients' rights and
protection. Newsletter.

NE Patients Rights Group              *Phone:* 781-769-5720
P.O. Box 141                          *Fax:* 781-769-0882
Norwood, MA 02062

## PREJUDICE / RACISM

**Recovering Racists Network**                                          **National**
*Groups in CA, MO and MI. Founded 1997.* Mutual support to help people overcome their
everyday racism and prejudice. Newsletter, literature, phone support, conferences,
advocacy, anti-racism training, high school Race Awareness Program, online support,
information and referral. Assistance in helping others to start similar groups.

RRN                                   *Phone:* 925-682-4959
670 W. Washington Ave.                *Fax:* 925-687-4437
Kirkwood, MO 63122                    *Website:* http://www.rrnet.org

# SEX INDUSTRY / PROSTITUTION

**PRIDE (from Prostitution to Independence, Dignity and Equality)**          **Model**
*1 group in Minnesota. Founded 1978.* Provides PRIDE support groups and other services to assist women and children in escaping the sex industry (including prostitution, pornography and stripping). Collect calls accepted.

PRIDE                                   *Phone:* 612-728-2064
c/o Family & Children Service            or 612-728-2062 (24 hr. crisis line)
4123 E. Lake St.                         *Fax:* 612-729-2616
Minneapolis, MN 55406                    *E-mail:* FCSPRIDE@aol.com

**Sex Workers Anonymous**                                                **Model**
(formerly Prostitutes Anonymous)   12-step group for persons of all ages, races, sexualities, religions, or backgrounds to find recover from any aspect of the sex industry. Meetings available in a few cities. Phone support. Publishes book of member's recovery ($20).                          *E-mail:* recoveryfromsexwork@hotmail.com
                                    *Website*: http://prostitutesanonymous.com

# SEXUAL ORIENTATION

**COLAGE (Children Of Lesbians And Gays Everywhere)**               **International**
*30 affiliated groups. Founded 1990.* Support and advocacy group run by and for children of lesbian, gay, bisexual and transgendered parents. Provides help with custody cases. Information and referrals, phone support, conferences, pen pals, literature, newsletter. Membership $35. Assistance in starting new groups.

COLAGE                                   *Phone:* 415-861-5437; *Fax:* 415-255-8345
3543 18th St., Suite 1                   *E-mail:* Collage@colage.org
San Francisco, CA 94110                  *Website:* http://www.colage.org

**COURAGE**                                                        **International**
*95 groups. Founded 1980.* Provides spiritual support and fellowship for men and women with same-sex attractions who are striving to live chaste lives in accordance with the Roman Catholic Church's teachings. The companion group, EnCourage, is for families and friends of persons with same-sex attractions. Newsletter, phone help, conferences, assistance in starting groups.

COURAGE                                  *Phone:* 212-268-1010
c/o St. John the Baptist                 *E-mail:* NYCourage@aol.com
210 W. 31st St.                          *Website:* http://www.couragerc.net
New York, NY 10001

**Dignity/USA**                                                        **National**
*59 chapters. Founded 1969.* Organization of gay, lesbian, bisexual and transgendered Catholics, their families and friends. Concerned with spiritual development, feminism, education and advocacy. Newsletter "Dignity Journal." Chapter development guidelines.

348

Dignity/USA
1500 Massachusetts Ave NW #11
Washington, DC 20005

*Phone:* 1-800-877-8797; *Fax:* 202-429-9808
*E-mail:* dignity@aol.com
*Website:* http://www.dignityusa.org

## Family Pride Coalition                                    National

*160+ local groups. Founded 1979.* Support, education and advocacy for gay and lesbian parents and prospective parents, and their families. Information and referrals, phone support, family events, literature. Newsletter. Assistance in starting groups.

Family Pride Coalition
P.O. Box 65327
Washington, DC 20035-5327

*Phone:* 202-331-5015; *Fax:* 202-331-0080
*E-mail:* prede@familypride.org
*Website:* http://www.familypride.org

## International Foundation for Gender Education              International

*300+ affiliates. Founded 1987.* Support and educational services for and about gender variant persons (including transsexuals, cross-dressers, intersex, androgynies, non-gendered and multi-gendered persons). Services include referrals to local support groups and to medical and psychological professionals. Speakers program, publication of "Transgender Tapestry" magazine, synchronicity bookstore, and national outreach.

IFGE
P.O. Box 540229
Waltham, MA 02454-0229

*Phone:* 781-899-2212 or 781-894-8340
*Fax:* 781-899-5703; *E-mail:* info@ifge.org
*Website:* http://www.ifge.org

## Intersex Society of North America                         International

*3 affiliated chapters. Founded 1993.* Peer support for intersexuals to overcome the stigma of the condition. Education for parents and professionals to provide better care. Newsletter, information and referrals, literature, and advocacy. Internet networking mailing list.

ISNA
P.O. Box 301
Petalluma, CA 94953

*Phone:* 707-283-0036; *Fax:* 707-293-0030
*E-mail:* info@isna.org
*Website:* http://www.isna.org

## National Gay and Lesbian Task Force                       National

*Founded 1973.* Advocates and organizes for the rights of gay, lesbian, bisexual and transgendered people. Technical assistance for state and local organizers. Publications and materials for organizers. Newsletter.

Nat'l Gay & Lesbian Task Force
1700 Kalorama Rd., NW
Washington, DC 20009

*Phone:* 202-332-6483; *TTY:* 202-332-6219
*Fax:* 702-332-0207; *E-mail:* ngltf@ngltf.org
*Website:* http://www.ngltf.org

## P-FLAG (Parents, Families and Friends of Lesbians and Gays)    International

*450 chapters worldwide. Founded 1981.* Helps families understand and accept gay, lesbian, intersexual and transgendered family members. Offers help in strengthening families, support groups for families and friends, educational outreach, newsletter, chapter development guidelines, grassroots advocacy, information and referrals.

P-FLAG                              *Phone:* 202-467-8180; *Fax:* 202-467-8194
1726 M Street, NW, Suite 400        *E-mail:* info@pflag.org
Washington, DC 20036                *Website:* http://www.pflag.org

**Renaissance Transgender Association, Inc.**                    **National**
*6 chapters and 6 affiliates. Founded 1987.* Mutual support for both transvestites and transsexuals. Provides education about transgender issues for the public and the transgender community. Networking with other support groups, information and referrals, phone support, pen pals. Monthly magazine, "Transgender Community News ($45/yr). Assistance in starting new groups.
Renaissance Transgender Assn.       *Phone:* 610-975-9119
987 Old Eagle School Rd., #719      *Fax:* 610-971-0144; *E-mail:* info@ren.org
Wayne, PA 19087                     *Website:* http://www.ren.org

**Society for the Second Self (Tri-Ess International)**          **National**
*31 chapters. Founded 1976.* Provides informational and educational resources to promote the understanding of crossdressing. Offers support equally for heterosexual crossdressers and their spouses, partners and families. Emphasizes security and confidentiality, full expression of both masculine and feminine elements, the balance and integration of these traits into the whole personality, and relationship-building. Pen pals and Big Sister programs, journal, newsletter, membership directory. online forums. Annual conventions.
Society for Second Self             *Phone:* 713-349-8969 (eve)
8880 Bellaire B2, PMB 104           *E-mail:* TRIESSINFO@aol.com
Houston, TX 77036                   *Website:* http://www.tri-ess.net

**Straight Spouse Network**                        **International network**
*50 groups and 58 state/country contacts. Founded 1991.* Confidential support network of current or former heterosexual spouses or partners of gay, lesbian, bisexual or transgender mates. Helps straight spouses or partners cope constructively with the coming-out crisis and assists mixed-orientation couples and their children build bridges of understanding. Resource information and referrals. Newsletter.
SSN                                 *Phone:* 510-525-0200
c/o Amity Pierce Buxto, PhD         *E-mail:* dir@ssnetwk.org
8215 Terrace Dr.                    *Website:* http://www.ssnetwk.org
El Cerrito, CA 94530-3058

**Family Pride Coalition**                                       **National**
*160+ local groups. Founded 1979.* Support, education and advocacy for gay and lesbian parents and prospective parents, and their families. Information and referrals, phone support, family events, literature. Newsletter. Assistance in starting groups.
Family Pride Coalition              *Phone:* 202-331-5015; *Fax:* 202-331-0080
P.O. Box 5326                       *E-mail:* info@familypride.org
Washington, DC 20035-5327           *Website:* http://www.familypride.org

**Rainbow Room**                                                        **Model**
*Founded 1979.* Adult facilitated support group for gay, lesbian, bisexual, transgender and questioning youth (16-21). Provides a safe space for youth to talk about the issues that effect their daily lives.

| | |
|---|---|
| Rainbow Room | *Phone:* 860-278-4163 |
| Hartford Gay/Lesbian Hlth Coll. | *TTY:* 860-278-4163; *Fax:* 860-278-5995 |
| P.O. Box 2094 | *E-mail:* info@hglhc.org |
| Hartford, CT 06145-2094 | *Website:* http://www.hglhc.org |

## SPEECH / STUTTERING
*(Also see Apraxia, Anxiety, specific disorder)*

**International Foundation for Stutterers, Inc.**                    **International**
*Founded 1980. 6 chapters* Aims to eliminate stuttering through speech therapy in conjunction with self-help groups. Education for public and professionals. Newsletter, speakers, phone help, guidelines on forming self-help groups.

Int'l Fdn. for Stutterers            *Phone:* Elliot Dennis 609-275-3806 (eve)
P.O. Box 462
Belle Mead, NJ 08502

**National Stuttering Association**                                    **National**
*80 groups. Founded 1977.* Provides information about stuttering. Self-help chapter meetings provide supportive environment where people who stutter can learn to communicate more effectively. Network of groups. Referrals, advocacy, monthly newsletter, group development guidelines. Dues $20-35.

| | |
|---|---|
| Nat'l Stuttering Assn. | *Phone:* 1-800-364-1677; *Fax:* 714-630-7707 |
| 4071 E. LaPalma, Suite A | *E-mail:* nsastutter@aol.com |
| Anaheim, CA 92807 | *Website:* http://www.nsastutter.org |

**Speak Easy International Foundation, Inc.**                        **International**
*6 chapters. Founded 1977.* Self-help group for adult and adolescent stutterers. Must have speech dysfunction or phobia. Phone network, peer counseling, newsletter. Annual national symposium. Dues $70/year.

Speak Easy Int'l                     *Phone:* Antoinette or Bob 201-262-0895
233 Concord Dr.                      *E-mail:* bob-antoinette@worldnet.att.net
Paramus, NJ 07652

**Toastmasters International**                                        **International**
*8800 chapters. Founded 1924.* Mutual help for people to improve speaking skills, express themselves more effectively and to gain confidence. For those who are hesitant to speak before an audience. Leadership training. Membership fees. Monthly magazine.

| | |
|---|---|
| Toastmasters Int'l | *Phone:* 949-858-8255; *Fax:* 949-858-1207 |
| P.O. Box 9052 | *E-mail:* tminfo@toastmasters.org |
| Mission Viejo, CA 92690-7052 | *Website:* http://www.toastmasters.org |

**U.S. Society for Augmentative and Alternative Communication**          **National**
*30 affiliated groups. Founded 1986.* Addresses the needs of persons who are severely
speech impaired or unable to speak. Works to improve services and products. Dues $53
(includes newsletter). Information, referrals, conferences, advocacy, literature, networking.
USSAAC                                   *Phone:* 941-312-0992 (Voice/fax)
P.O. Box 21418                           *E-mail:* USSAAC@aol.com
Sarasota, FL 34276

## TRAUMA
*(Also see Accidents, specific event)*

🖳 **Gift from Within**                                                    **Online**
One-on-one post-traumatic stress disorder survivor network, where victims of specific
trauma are matches with veteran survivors of similar trauma.
                                         *Website:* http://www.giftfromwithin.org

🖳 **Trauma Anonymous**                                                    **Online**
Information on trauma and post-traumatic stress disorder. Information on symptoms and
treatment. Chat rooms for veterans, victims of domestic violence, and survivors of sexual
abuse. Message board for victims.       *Website*: http://www.bein.com/trauma/index.html

## VETERANS / MILITARY

**Blinded Veterans Association**                                          **National**
*52 regional groups. Founded 1945.* Information, support and outreach to blinded veterans.
Assistance with finding jobs, information on benefits and rehabilitation programs.
Newsletter. Chapter development guidelines. Regional meetings.
BVA                                      *Phone:* 202-371-8880 or 1-800-669-7079
477 H St., NW                            *Fax:* 202-371-8258 *E-mail:* bva@bva.org
Washington, DC 20001                     *Website:* http://www.bva.org

**Disabled American Veterans**                                            **National**
*2221 chapters. Founded 1920.* Assists veterans in gaining benefits earned in military
service. Sponsors self-help groups for all disabled veterans and their families. Bimonthly
magazine. Guidelines for developing chapters.
Disabled American Veterans               *Phone:* 859-441-7300; *Fax:* 859-442-2090
P.O. Box 14301                           *E-mail:* feedback@davmail.org
Cincinnati, OH 45259-0301                *Website:* http://www.dav.org

*"Who then can so softly bind up the wound of another*
*as he who has felt the same wound himself."– Thomas Jefferson*

**National Gulf War Resource Center, Inc.**                **National**
*61 affiliated groups. Founded 1995.* Supports the efforts of grassroots organizations that assist veterans affected by the Persian Gulf war illnesses. Conducts research into the causes of Gulf war syndrome. Information and referrals, media assistance, provides congressional testimony, advocacy, literature, self-help guides.

Nat'l Gulf War Resource Ctr.        *Phone:* 1-800-882-1316 ext. 162
P.O. Box 11131                      *E-mail:* hq@ngwrc.org
McLean, VA 22102-7131              *Website:* http://www.ngwrc.org

**Paralyzed Veterans of America**                          **National**
*Various chapters. Founded 1947.* To ensure that spinal cord injured or diseased veterans achieve the highest quality of life possible. Membership available to individuals who are American citizens who suffer from spinal cord dysfunction as a result of trauma or disease. Must have served on active duty and had an other than dishonorable discharge. Information and referrals, magazine.

PVA                                *Phone:* 202-872-1300
801 18th St. NW                    *E-mail:* info@pva.org
Washington, DC 20006              *Website:* http://www.pva.org

**Society of Military Widows**                             **National**
*27 chapters. Founded 1968.* Support and assistance for widows/widowers of members of all U.S. uniformed services. Help in coping with adjustment to life on their own. Promotes public awareness. Magazine/journal. Dues $12. Chapter development guidelines.

Soc. of Military Widows            *Phone:* 703-750-1342
5535 Hempstead Way                 *E-mail:* naus@ix.netcom.com
Springfield, VA 22151             *Website:* http://www.militarywidows.org

**TAPS (Tragedy Assistance Program for Survivors**        **National network**
Provides support for persons who have lost a love one while serving in the armed forces (army, air force, navy, marine corps, national guard, reserves, service academies or coast guard). Networking, crisis information, problem solving assistance and liaison with military agencies. Kids programs, seminars.

TAPS                               *Phone:* 1-800-959-TAPS or 202-588-8277
2001 S St., NW, Suite 300          *Fax:* 202-638-5312
Washington, DC 20009              *Website*: http://www.taps.org

**Vietnam Veterans of America, Inc.**                      **National**
*600 chapters. Founded 1978.* Devoted to the needs and concerns of Vietnam era veterans and their families. Leadership and advocacy in all areas that have an impact on veterans, with an emphasis on agent orange related problems and post traumatic stress disorder. Monthly newspaper, group development guidelines.

VVA                                *Phone:* 1-800-VVA-1316 or 301-585-4000
8605 Cameron St., Suite 400        *E-mail:* communications@vva.org
Silver Spring, MD 20910-3710      *Website:* http://www.vva.org

# WOMEN'S ISSUES
*(Also see specific issue)*

**Love-N-Addiction**                                                    **International**
*73 chapters. Founded 1986.* Explores how loving can become an addiction. Builds a healthy support system to aid in recovery from addictive love into healthy love. Uses ideas from book <u>Women Who Love Too Much</u> by Robin Norwood. Chapter development guidelines ($15). Calls returned collect or leave address for information.)
Love-N-Addiction                          *Phone:* Carolyn Meister 860-423-2344
P.O. Box 759
Willimantic, CT 06226

**National Organization for Women**                                    **National**
*500 chapters. Founded 1966.* NOW is an action organization that seeks social, political, economic and legal equity between women and men through grassroots organizing, lobbying, litigation, protests and demonstrations. Educational meetings, national newsletter. Chapter development guidelines.
NOW                                   *Phone:* 202-628-8669
733 15th St., NW, 2nd fl.             *E-mail:* now@www.now.org
Washington, DC 20005                  *Website:* http://now.org

🖥 **Women.com Message Boards**                                        **Online**
Alarge variety of message boards for women including: careers, family, pregnancy, health, relationships, and health.              *Website:* http://messages.women.com/

# YOUTH / STUDENTS

**SADD (Students Against Destructive Decisions)**                      **National**
*25,000 groups. Founded 1982.* To help eliminate impaired driving, end underage drinking, drug abuse, and other destructive decisions. Alerts students to dangers of alcohol use and its resulting consequences, and to organize peer counseling programs for students. Newsletter, group development guidelines. Special programs: "Student Athletes Detest Drugs."
SADD                                  *Phone:* 1-877-SADD-INC or 508-481-3568
P.O. Box 800                          *Fax:* 508-481-5759
Marlboro, MA 01752                    *Website:* http://www.saddonline.com

**National Association of Students Against Violence Everywhere**        **National**
1000 affiliated chapters. Youth group that focuses on crime prevention, conflict management and community service. The groups are student initiated and student directed and are developed in elementary, middle and high schools, as well as other community agencies. Promotes positive peer influence and student support.
Nat'l Assn of SAVE                    *Phone:* Dr. Riley 1-866-343-7283 or 919-661-7800
322 Chapanoke Rd., Suite 110          *E-mail:* drpriley@nationalsave.org
Raleigh, NC 27603                     *Website:* http://www.nationalsave.org

**Chapter 7**

# TOLL–FREE SPECIALTY HELPLINES

The following toll-free numbers may be a helpful, cost-free resource for persons seeking additional information about a particular subject. Many of these non-profit agencies provide information and referral, literature and other services regarding specific topics.

TDD and TTY refer to telecommunication devices for the deaf and hard-of-hearing and cannot be accessed by a regular phone unless "Voice" is indicated. Also, toll-free numbers start with 800, 888, 877 and 866 exchanges.

## ADOPTION / FOSTER CARE

**National Adoption Center**                                    1-800-TO-ADOPT
Information on adoption agencies and support groups. Network for matching parents and children with special needs.        *Fax:* 215-735-9410
*E-mail:* NAC@adopt.org                    *Website:* http://www.adopt.org/adopt

**National Adoption Information Clearinghouse**                 1-888-251-0075
Provides professionals and the general public information on all aspects of the adoption process. Offers literature and referrals.    *Phone:* 703-352-3488
                              *Website:* http://www.calib.com/naic

## AGING / SENIOR CITIZENS

**Alliance for Aging Research**                                 1-800-639-2421
Citizen advocacy organization that strives to improve the health and independence of older Americans through public and private research. Promotes healthy aging. Provides statistics on the health and well-being of older persons. Advocacy. Conducts information campaigns.

**Eldercare Locator**                                          1-800-677-1116
Provides information for families & friends of the elderly. Referrals to area agencies on aging for information on insurance, Medicaid, taxes, respite care, etc. (Mon-Fri, 9am-8pm EST)                    *Website:* http://www.aoa.dhhs.gov

**National Council on the Aging**                              1-800-424-9046
Information on resources for the aged, their families and professionals.
*Fax:* 202-479-0735                    *Website:* http://www.ncoa.org

**National Institute on Aging**                    **1-800-222-2225**
Provides publications on topics of interest to older adults, doctors, nurses, social activities directors, health educators, and the public. Sponsored by federal government.
*Phone*: 301-587-2528 (day)          *E-mail:* niaic@jds1.com; *Fax:* 301-589-3014
*TDD:* 1-800-222-4225                 *Website:* http://www.nih.gov/nia

# AIDS

**AIDS Clinical Trials Information Service**                    **1-800-874-2572**
*(Bilingual)* Provides information on clinical trials and drugs for HIV infections & AIDS and referrals to testing sites. Free materials (English & Spanish). (Mon-Fri, 12noon-5pm)
*TDD:* 1-888-480-3739                 *E-mail:* actis@actis.org
*Phone:* 301-519-0459 (Int'l)        *Website:* http://www.actis.org

**CDC National AIDS/HIV+ Hotline**                    **1-800-342-AIDS**
*(Bilingual)* Answers basic questions about AIDS/HIV (prevention, transmission, testing, health care). Referrals. Free literature. Sponsored by Amer. Soc. Health Assn. (24 hrs)
*Spanish:* 1-800-344-7432            *Website:* http://www.ashastd.org
*TDD:* 1-800-AID-7889 (day/eve)

**CDC National Prevention Information Network**                    **1-800-458-5231**
Provides information on resources and support groups, educational materials, and business and labor responses to AIDS. With touch-tone phone, can get information on different services, publications.          *Phone:* 1-800-243-7012
*E-mail:* info@cdcnpin.org           *Website:* http://www.cdcnpin.org

**CDC National STD/AIDS Hotline**           **1-800-342-2437 or 1-800-227-8922**
*(Bilingual)* Provides information sexually transmitted diseases (including yeast, AIDS, cancroids, herpes, genital warts, syphilis and gonorrhea). Referrals, information on prevention, free pamphlets.          *E-mail:* hivnet@ashastd.org
*Spanish:* 1-800-344-7432 (24 hr)    *Website:* http://www.ashastd.org
*TTY:* 1-800-243-7889                *Website:* http://www.iwannaknow.org (teens)

**Gay Men's Health Crisis**                    **1-800-243-7692**
Provides information and referrals for persons affected by AIDS.
                            *Website:* http://www.gmhc.org

**HIV/AIDS Treatment Information Service**                    **1-800-448-0440**
*(Bilingual)* Information on federally-approved treatments for HIV infection and AIDS.
*TDD:* 1-888-480-3739                 *Website:* http://www.hivatis.org

**Project Inform**                    **1-800-822-7422**
*(Bilingual)* Information about experimental drugs, treatment of AIDS, volunteer training programs. Quarterly newsletter, journal. *Website:* http://www.projectinform.org

**Teen AIDS Line**                                        **1-800-234-TEEN**
Provides information for teens on AIDS and other sexually transmitted disease.

## ALCOHOL

**American Academy of Family Physicians**                 **1-800-274-2237**
*(Bilingual)* Provides free handouts on many health concerns, illnesses, mental health disorders, addictions, disabilities, etc.)    *Phone:* 913-906-6000 ext. 5175
                                        *Website:* http://www.familydoctor.org

**National Association for Children of Alcoholics**       **1-888-554-2627**
Advocates for children and families affected by alcoholism and other drug dependencies. Newsletter, advocacy, literature, educational materials.
*E-mail:* nacoa@nacoa.org          *Website:* http://www.nacoa.org

**National Clearinghouse**                                **1-800-729-6686**
**for Alcohol and Drug Information**              *Spanish:* **1-877-767-8432**
*(Bilingual)* Information on alcohol, tobacco and drug abuse and prevention. Referrals to treatment centers, research, groups, drugs in the work place, community programs, AIDS and drug abuse.          *TTY:* 1-800-487-4889; *Phone:* 301-468-2600
*Website:* http://www.health.org      *E-mail:* info@health.org; *Fax:* 301-468-6433

**National Council on Alcoholism & Drug Dependence**      **1-800-622-2255**
Information on counseling and treatment services for alcohol or drug abuse. Prevention and education programs. Newsletter.          *Website:* http://www.ncadd.org

**National Organization on Fetal Alcohol Syndrome**       **1-800-666-6327**
Provides information and referrals on fetal alcohol syndrome. Can speak with a clinician or get free packet of information.          *Website:* http://www.nofas.org

## ALLERGY / ASTHMA

**Asthma & Allergy Network - Mothers of Asthmatics**      **1-800-878-4403**
Provides emotional support and patient education resources for persons with asthma and allergies. Newsletter.          *E-mail:* aanma@aol.com

**Asthma & Allergy Referral Line**                        **1-800-822-2762**
Provides pamphlets on asthma and allergies. Referrals to doctors.
*Phone:* 414-272-6071          *Website:* http://www.aaaai.org

**National Institute of Allergy & Infectious Disease**    **1-800-243-7644**
Provides information on clinical trials being conducted on allergic and infectious diseases.
                                        *Website:* http://www.niaid.nih.gov

# ALOPECIA AREATA

**Locks of Love**                                                              **1-888-896-1588**
Provides custom hairpieces to financially disadvantaged children with long-term medical
hair loss. Uses donated hair.          *Phone:* 561-963-1677
*E-mail:* info@loksoflove.org             *Website:* http://www.locksoflove.org/

# ALZHEIMER'S DISEASE

**American Health Assistance Foundation**                                       **1-800-437-2423**
Provides educational information and funds research for Alzheimer's disease, glaucoma,
heart disease and macular degeneration.   *Website:* http://www.ahaf.org

**Alzheimer's Disease Education & Referral Center**                             **1-800-438-4380**
Provides information and publications on Alzheimer's disease to health and service
professionals, patients and their families, caregivers and public.
*Phone:* 301-495-3311                      *E-mail:* adear@alzheimers.org
*Fax:* 301-495-3334                        *Website:* http://www.alzheimers.org

# ANXIETY

**NIH Anxiety Information Line**                                                **1-888-826-9438**
Provides information and literature on anxiety via mail.
*Phone:* 301-443-4513                      *Website:* http://www.nimh.nih.gov

# ATTORNEY

**Attorney Referral Network**                                                  **1-800-624-8846**
Computerized legal service that recommends attorneys in callers' area. Does not make
referrals to pro-bono or legal aid attorneys.

**National Organization of Social Security Claimant's Reps**                    **1-800-431-2804**
Provides referrals to social security lawyers who assist claimants in getting social security.

# BLIND / VISUALLY IMPAIRED

**American Foundation for the Blind**                                           **1-800-232-5463**
Information and referral for agencies, catalog of publications. (Mon-Fri, 8:30am-4:30pm)
*TDD:* 212-502-7662                        *Website:* http://www.afb.org

**American Health Assistance Foundation**                                       **1-800-437-2423**
Provides educational information and funds research for Alzheimer's disease, glaucoma,
heart disease and macular degeneration.   *Website:* http://www.ahaf.org

358

**Braille Institute**                                              **1-800-272-4553**
Provides publications, cassettes, and free books for visually impaired children. Free Braille calendar. Referrals to resources. Tapes on vision loss available.
*E-mail*: info@brailleinstitute.org          *Website:* http://www.brailleinstitute.org

**DB-Link**                                                       **1-800-438-9376**
Information and referral on education, health, employment, technology, communication, recreation, etc. for children who are deaf-blind. Newsletter.
*TTY:* 1-800-854-7013                 *Website:* http://www.tr.wou.edu/dblink

**Glaucoma Research Foundation**                                  **1-800-826-6693**
Non-profit, phone support network for persons with glaucoma. Literature. Funds research.
*Phone:* 415-986-3162                 *Website:* http://www.glaucoma.org

**Guide Dog Foundation**                                          **1-800-548-4337**
Provides seeing eye dogs to the blind free of charge.
*Fax:* 631-361-5192                   *Website:* http://www.guidedog.org

**Guiding Eyes for the Blind**                                    **1-800-942-0149**
Dedicated to enriching the lives of blind and visually impaired men and women by providing them with guide dogs free of charge.
*Phone:* 914-245-4024                 *E-mail:* student@guidingeyes.org (teach dogs)
*E-mail:* info@guidingeyes.org        *Website:* http://www.guidingeyes.org

**Hadley School for the Blind**                                   **1-800-323-4238**
Provides free distance education to blind and visually impaired persons using brailed materials, large print or audiocassettes.
*Phone:* 847-446-8111                 *E-mail:* info@Hadley-School.org
*TTY:* 847-446-4111                   *Website:* http://www.hadley-school.org

**Library of Congress National Library**                          **1-800-424-8567**
Refers callers to libraries that have information on books on tapes and in Braille available for qualified blind or handicapped persons who cannot read standard print.
*TTY:* 202-707-0744                   *E-mail:* nls@loc.gov
*Fax:* 202-707-0712                   *Website:* http://www.loc.gov/nls

**National Braille Press**                                        **1-800-548-7323**
Provides books and publications in Braille at cost. Will do brailing for contractors and textbooks.                        *Website:* http://www.braille.com

**National Family Association for Deaf-Blind**            **1-800-255-0411 ext. 275**
Information and advocacy for families of persons who are deaf-blind. Newsletter.
*Fax:* 516-944-7302                   *E-mail:* nfadb@aol.com
                                      *Website:* http://www.NFADB.org

359

**Prevent Blindness America**                  **1-800-331-2020 or 1-800-221-3004**
Fights vision loss through research, education and direct services. Provides referrals to local services. Offers literature on vision, eye health, and safety.
*E-mail:* info@preventblindness.org     *Website:* http://www.preventblindness.org

**Recording For The Blind and Dyslexic**                          **1-800-221-4792**
Provides information on free cassettes, recorded textbooks and consumer publications to eligible handicapped persons. Information on volunteer programs for recording tapes. Worldwide services. $75 to join; $25/yearly thereafter.
*E-mail:* custserv@rfbd.org          *Website:* http://www.rfbd.org

**Research to Prevent Blindness**                                 **1-800-621-0026**
Publications and information on various eye diseases including macular degeneration, cataracts, glaucoma, diabetic retinopathy, corneal disease, retinitis pigmentosa, amblyopic/strabismus, uveitis, as well as general information. Funds research.
*Phone:* 212-752-4333          *Website:* http://www.rpbusa.org

**Retinitis Pigmentosa International**                            **1-800-344-4877**
Provides support and information for persons affected by retinitis pigmentosa, and their families. Supports research.          *Website:* http://www.rpinternational.org

**Vision World Wide**                                             **1-800-431-1739**
Information and referrals for blind and low vision persons. Publications.
*Phone:* 317-254-1332          *E-mail:* info@visionww.org
*Fax:* 317-251-6588          *Website:* http://www.visionww.org

# BONE MARROW TRANSPLANT

**Caitlin Raymond International Bone Marrow Registry**            **1-800-726-2824**
Comprehensive international resource for patients and physicians conducting a search for unrelated bone marrow or cord blood donor.
*Phone:* 508-334-8969          *E-mail:* info@crir.org
*Fax:* 508-334-8972          *Website:* http://www.crir.org

**National BMT LINK**                                             **1-800-LINK BMT**
Provides information and referral for bone marrow transplants. Referrals to support groups. Peer-support, one-on-one counseling, information on becoming a donor, and educational booklets.          *Website:* http://comnet.org/nbmtlink

**National Marrow Donor Program**     **1-800-627-7692; 1-800-654-1247; 1-800-526-7809**
Provides information on bone marrow and stem cell transplants and information on becoming a marrow donor. Maintains computerized data bank of available tissue-typed marrow donors nationwide. Provides patient advocacy to assist patients through the donor search and transplant process.          *Website:* http://www.marrow.org

# BRAIN TUMOR

**Pediatric Brain Tumor Foundation**                                    1-800-253-6530
Support and education concerning pediatric brain tumors. Seeks to find the cause and cure by supporting research. Encourages interaction among affected families.
*E-mail:* pbtfus@pbtfus.org                    *Website:* http://www.pbtfus.org

# BUSINESS

**American Association of Home-Based Business**                    1-800-447-9710
Provides information on starting home-based businesses.
*Fax:* 301-963-7042                    *Website:* http://www.aahbb.org

**SCORE (Service Corp of Retired Executives)**                    1-800-634-0245
Provides counseling for starting or maintaining businesses. Referrals to local chapters.
                                    *Website:* http://score.org

**U.S. Small Business Administration**                    1-800-827-5722
Provides information, training and literature on starting and financing small businesses.
                                    *Website:* http://www.sba.gov

# CANCER

**Alliance for Lung Cancer Advocacy, Support and Education**        1-800-298-2436
Operates a national "phone buddies" program, hotline, comprehensive helpline, in addition to other services.                    *Website:* http://www.alcase.org

**AMC Cancer Information and Counseling Line**                    1-800-525-3777
Provides current medical information and counseling for cancer patients.
                                    *Website:* http://www.amc.org

**American Cancer Society**                                    1-800-227-2345
*(Multilingual)* Information and referrals on various issues related to cancer (treatment, services, literature, transportation, equipment, encouragement and support). English, Spanish and Chinese speaking.                    *Website:* http://www.cancer.org

**Anderson Network**                                    1-800-345-6324
Emotional support for cancer. Matches cancer patients with others with exact diagnoses.
*Fax:* 713-745-3762                    *Website:* http://www.manderson.org

**Bloch Cancer Hotline**                                    1-800-433-0464
Networks persons with cancer with home volunteers with same type of cancer. Free books about cancer.                    *Website:* http://www.blochcancer.org

**Cancer Care, Inc.**                                          **1-800-813-HOPE**
Free counseling for cancer patients and their families. Financial assistance, information and referrals, community and professional education. Teleconference programs. On-going telephone and in-person support groups. *Website:* http://www.cancercare.org

**Cancer Hope Network**                                        **1-877-HOPE-NET**
One-on-one support to cancer patients and their families undergoing cancer treatment from trained volunteers who have survived cancer themselves.
*E-mail:* info@cancerhopenetwork.org    *Website:* http://www.cancerhopenetwork.org

**Cancer Information Service**                                 **1-800-4-CANCER**
*(Bilingual)* Provides information about cancer and cancer-related resources to patients, the public and health professionals. Free publications on smoking cessation.
*TTY:* 1-800-332-8615                  *Website:* http://cancer.gov

**Cancer Research Institute**                                 **1-800-99-CANCER**
Provides general cancer resource directory. Supports leading-edge research aimed at developing immunologic methods of preventing, treating and curing cancer.
*Phone:* 212-688-7515                  *Website:* http://www.cancerreseaarch.org

**Family Studies Cancer Risk Line**                           **1-800-828-6622**
Provides information on familial cancers. Sponsored by Dana-Farber Cancer Institute.
                                       *Website:* http://www.partners.org

**Gilda Radner Familial Ovarian Cancer Registry**             **1-800-OVARIAN**
Information on the warning signs of cancer, diagnostic tests and family history.
                                       *Website:* http://www.ovariancancer.com

**Gynecologic Cancer Foundation**                             **1-800-444-4441**
Makes referrals to physicians who specialize in the treatment of gynecological cancer.
*E-mail:* gcs@sba.com                  *Website:* http://www.wcn.org

**Hereditary Cancer Institute**                               **1-800-648-8133**
Studies family-linked cancer. Counseling, information on clinical trials, cancer and hereditary factors.                 *Website:* http://www.medicine.creighton.edu/
*E-mail:* tinley@creighton.edu         medschool/PrevMed/

**International Cancer Alliance**                              **1-800-I-CARE-61**
Provides information on descriptions, treatment, detection and clinical trials on specific types of cancer. Newsletter.   *Website:* http://www.icare.org/icare

**International Myeloma Foundation**                           **1-800-452-2873**
Information, seminars, grants and newsletter on myeloma.
*E-mail:* info@myeloma.org             *Website:* http://www.myeloma.org

**Look Good...Feel Better**                    **1-800-227-2345**
Helps cancer patients improve their appearance during treatment. Free workshops across the country.                    *Website:* http://www.cancer.org

**National Alliance of Breast Cancer Organizations**                    **1-888-80-NABCO**
Collaborates with public and corporate partners on educational and medical programs that heighten awareness of breast cancer. Connects women with services. Advocacy.
*Phone:* 212-889-0606                    *Website:* http://www.nabco.org

**National Childhood Cancer Foundation**                    **1-800-458-6223**
Advocates for the needs of children with cancer and their families. Information, newsletter.
*E-mail:* rrodriguez@nccf.org                    *Website:* http://www.nccf.org/

**Ovarian Cancer Research Fund**                    **1-800-873-9569**
Dedicated to advancing and supporting research that promotes the development of new therapies and techniques for early detection, screening and treatment of ovarian cancer. Educational outreach and public awareness projects, videos and resource materials.
*Fax:* 212-947-5652                    *Website:* http://www.ocrf.org

**Patient Advocate Foundation**                    **1-800-532-5274**
Provides education and legal counseling to cancer patients (relative to a diagnosis) concerning managed care, discrimination, insurance and financial issues.
*Phone:* 757-873-6668                    *E-mail:* info@patientadvocate.org
*Fax:* 757-873-8999                    *Website:* http://www.patientadvocate.org

**Skin Cancer Foundation**                    **1-800-SKIN-490**
Provides free packets of information on skin cancer and treatment. (Mon-Fri, 9-5 ET)
*Phone:* 212-725-5176 (Admin)                    *Website*: http://www.skincancer.org

**S. Koman Breast Cancer Foundation**                    **1-800-462-9273**
Information on breast cancer and breast health. (Mon-Fri, 9am-4:30pm)
*Website:* http://www.breastcancerinfo.com

## CAREERS

**Goodwill Industries**                    **1-800-741-0186**
Provides employment and training services for people with disabilities and other disadvantaging conditions (welfare, illiteracy, criminal history, homelessness).
*Phone:* 301-530-6500                    *Website:* http://www.goodwill.org

**National Job Corps Information Line**                    **1-800-733-5627**
*(Bilingual)* Referrals to job corps training (persons 16-24). Helps persons to earn high school equivalency diplomas. (24 hrs)    *Website:* http://www.jobscorps.org

## CHARITY / SERVICE ORGANIZATIONS

**Alternative Gifts International**                    **1-800-842-2243**
Works with non-profit agencies that provide gifts to impoverished persons worldwide.
*Website:* http://www.altgifts.org

**America's Second Harvest**                    **1-800-771-2303**
Provides hunger relief through a network over 200 food banks and food-rescue programs.
*Website:* http://www.secondharvest.org

**AmVets**                    **1-800-244-6350**
Makes referrals to used clothing collection agencies and provides pick-up information.
*Website:* http://www.amvets-ny.org

## CHILD ABUSE

**American Humane Association**                    **1-800-227-4645**
Protects children and animals from abuse, neglect and cruelty. Advocates on behalf of children (firearms, capital/corporal punishment, child protective services, medical neglect, etc) and animals.          *Website:* http://www.americanhumane.org

**ARCH National Respite Locator Service**                    **1-800-677-1116**
Referrals to respite care services for caregivers and families of children with disabilities or illness. Helps children at risk of abuse.     *Website:* http://www.chtop.com/locator.htm

**Child Help USA Hotline**                    **1-800-422-4453**
General information on child abuse and related issues. Referrals to local agencies for child abuse reporting. Crisis counseling. (24 hrs)

**National Clearinghouse on Child Abuse and Neglect Information**     **1-800-FYI-3366**
Provides information on all aspects of child maltreatment. (Mon-Fri, 8:30-5:30)
*E-mail:* nccanch@calib.com          *Website:* http://www.calib.com/nccanch/

**Prevent Child Abuse America**                    **1-800-CHILDREN**
Provides a large variety of topics including: neglect, adult survivors of child abuse, discipline, sexual abuse, etc.          *Website:* http://www.preventchildabuse.org

**U.S. Customs Service**                    **1-800-BE-ALERT**
Takes reports on child internet pornography. Aim is to stop this form of child sexual abuse.

## CHILD CARE

**National Association for Family Child Care**                    **1-800-359-3817**
Provides information and training for in-home care providers.

**National Child Care Information Center**                    **1-800-616-2242**
Provides information to enhance and promote quality childcare.
*E-mail:* info@nccic.org                    *Website:* http://nccic.org

## CHOLESTEROL

**UAB Eat Right**                    **1-800-231-3438**
Information on nutrition & related topics (weight loss & cholesterol). (Mon-, 8-4)

## CONSUMER

**FDA Consumer Affairs**                    **1-888-463-6332**
Information on any FDA-regulated product (food and drugs). Has information on rare illnesses, starting businesses, freedom of information act, health and medical issues. Free literature. Referrals to toll-free numbers. Assists in emergencies.
*Phone:* 301-827-4573 or 301-827-6242 *Website:* http://www.fda.gov

**Opt Out**                    **1-888-567-8688**
Removes your name and address from all mailing lists offered by the main consumer credit reporting agencies (Trans Union, Experian, Equifax and Innovis) which send out new charge card offers.

**Toy Safety Hotline**                    **1-877-486-9723**
Provides information on toy safety and best selling age-appropriate toys. Brochures.
                    *Website:* http://www.toyhotline.org

**U.S. Consumer Product Safety Commission**                    **1-800-638-2772**
*(Bilingual)* Recorded information on product safety. Takes reports on unsafe products.
*TTY:* 1-800-638-8270                    *E-mail:* info@cpsc.gov
*Fax:* 301-504-0281                    *Website:* http://www.cpsc.gov

## CREDIT COUNSELING

**Consumer Credit Counseling Services**                    **1-800-388-2227**
With touch-tone phone, callers can find out about local credit counseling services.
                    *Website:* http://www.nscc.org

## CRIME VICTIMS

**Consumer Response Center**                    **1-877-FTC-HELP**
Federal Trade Commission's aid for people who are victims of fraud. Complaints are shared with law enforcement agencies. Does not resolve individual disputes.
                    *Website:* http://www.ftc.gov

**Fight Crime Invest in Kids**                                      **1-800-245-6476**
Provides access to educational childcare and after-school programs in order to prevent crime. Provides crime fighting events and prevention programs. Research and advocacy.
*Phone:* 202-776-0027                    *Website:* http://www.fightcrime.org/

**GAINS Center**                                                  **1-800-311-4246**
Information and technical assistance on services for people with co-occurring mental health and substance abuse disorders who come in contact with the justice system.
*E-mail:* gains@prainc.com                *Website:* http://www.rrainc.com

**Juvenile Justice Clearinghouse**                                **1-800-638-8736**
Information and referrals re: juvenile justice programs and department of justices.

**National Institute of Corrections**                    **1-800-995-6423 ext. 70147**
Provides information and technical assistance re: mentally ill persons in prison.
*E-mail:* aault@bob.gov                   *Website:* http://www.nicic.org

**National Institute of Justice Clearinghouse**                   **1-800-851-3420**
Provides information on all aspects of the criminal justice system and support for victims.
                                          *Website:* http://www.ncjrs.org

**We Tip Hotlines**                          **1-800-78-CRIME or 1-800-87-FRAUD**
Takes reports on crimes or felonies.

## CYSTIC FIBROSIS

**Cystic Fibrosis Foundation**                                    **1-800-344-4823**
Information, brochures, insurance information, pharmaceutical services, research.
*E-mail:* info@cff.org                    *Website:* http://www.cff.org

## DEAF / HEARING IMPAIRED

**ASHA Hearing & Speech Helpline**               **1-800-638-8255 (Voice/TDD)**
*(Bilingual)* Information on speech, hearing and language disabilities. Referrals to speech and language and hearing clinics. Information on listening devices. (day)
*E-mail:* actioncenter@asha.org           *Website:* http://www.asha.org

**Better Hearing Institute**                                      **1-800-327-9355**
Information and literature on any hearing-related issue. (Mon-Fri, 9am-5pm EST)
*Phone:* 703-684-3391                     *Website:* http://www.betterhearing.org

**Captioned Media Program**                                       **1-800-237-6213**
Provides free loan program of open captioned media for the deaf or hearing impaired.
*TTY:* 1-800-237-6819                     *Website:* http://www.cfv.org

366

**DB-Link**                                            **1-800-438-9376**
Information & referral on education, health, employment, technology, communication, recreation, etc. for children who are deaf-blind. Newsletter.
*TTY:* 1-800-854-7013                    *Website:* http://www.tr.wou.edu/dblink

**Dial-A-Hearing Screening Test**                      **1-800-222-EARS**
Conducts hearing test over the phone. Provides information and referral to services.
*E-mail:* dahst@aol.com                  *Website:* http://www.dialatest.com

**HEAR Now**                                           **1-800-648-4327**
Helps financially needy individuals obtain hearing aids. Collects used hearing aids for recycling. Newsletter, information and referrals. (Mon-Fri, 8am-5pm)
*Fax:* (952)828-6946                     *E-mail:* nonprofit@starkey.com

**Hearing Aid**                                        **1-800-521-5247**
Provides general literature on hearing aids and hearing loss. Referrals to doctors.
                          *Website:* http://www.ihsinfo.org

**John Tracy Clinic for Preschool Deaf Children**      **1-800-522-4582**
Information and support for parents and preschool deaf children. Free correspondence course for parents.        *Website:* http://www.jtc.org

**National Cued Speech Association**          **1-800-459-3529 (Voice/TTY)**
Supports the use of cued speech for communication, language development, and literacy. Networking, literature, advocacy, information and referrals, phone support, conferences, family camps.                 *Website:* http://www.cuedspeech.org

**National Family Association for Deaf-Blind**     **1-800-255-0411 ext. 224**
Information and advocacy for families of persons who are deaf-blind. Newsletter.
*Fax:* 516-944-7302                      *Website:* http://www.NFADB.org

**National Institutes. on Deafness and Other Communication Disorders  1-800-241-1044**
Information on hearing, speech, language, smell and taste, voice and balance disorders. Fact sheets, brochures, information packets, newsletters. Referrals to national agencies dealing with hearing, speech, language, smell and taste, voice and balance.
*TTY:* 1-800-241-1055                    *Website:* http://www.nidcd.nih.gov

## DENTAL

**Donated Dental Services**                            **1-888-471-6334**
Information on free dental care for qualified elderly or disabled patients. Services include dentures, crowns, or other significant dental work.

# DEPRESSION

**National Foundation for Depressive Illness**                     1-800-248-4344
Recorded message on the signs of depression and manic-depression.

**National Institute of Mental Health Information Line**          1-800-421-4211
Automated phone system that takes orders for free brochures on depression.
*Phone:* 301-443-4513 (Info & Referral)  *Website:* http://www.nimh.nih.gov

# DIABETES

**National Diabetes Education Program**        1-800-438-5383 or 1-800-860-8747
(Bilingual) Provides educational information on diabetes. Publishes "Do Your Level Best"
kit and diabetes kit to public and health care professionals.

**National Institute of Diabetes & Digestive & Kidney Diseases**    1-800-860-8747
Referrals and literature on diabetes, digestive, endocrine, urologic disorders, etc.
*E-mail:* nkudic@info.niddk.nih.gov      *Website:* http://www.niddk.nih.gov

# DIABETES INSIPIDUS

**Nephrogenic Diabetes Insipidus Foundation**                     1-888-376-6343
Provides information and support to persons affected by nephrogenic diabetes insipidus.
*E-mail:* info@ndif.org                    *Website:* http://www.ndif.org

# DIET / NUTRITION

**American Dietetic Association**                                  1-800-366-1655
*(Bilingual)* Recorded information on diet. Referrals to local dietitians. Some brochures
available.                          *Website:* http://www.eatright.org

**Eat Right Hotline**                                             1-800-231-3438
Provides information on all aspects of nutrition, exercise and diet. Can talk with a
nutritionist or have information mailed to you. Will research questions.

# DISABILITIES

**Abledata**                                                     1-800-227-0216
Provides information, publications and consumer reviews of all types of assistive
technologies for persons with disabilities. *Website:* http://www.abledata.com/

**Access Board**                                                 1-800-872-2253
Advocates for accessibility.  Forms to press charges against agencies that are not accessible.

**ADA Technical Assistance Line**                    **1-800-514-0301**
Provides free publications on the American Disabilities Act. A new publication will be available each month in a limited supply.
*TDD:* 1-800-514-0383              *Website:* http://www.ada.govm

**Alliance for Technology Access**                    **1-800-455-7970**
Referrals to centers that provide information on computer hardware, software and other assistive technology designed for disabled persons. Helps identify funding resources. Works with school systems.              *Website:* http://www.ataccess.org

**American Academy of Family Physicians**                    **1-800-274-2237**
*(Bilingual)* Provides free handouts on many health concerns, illnesses, mental health disorders, addictions, disabilities, etc.)    *Website:* http://www.familydoctor.org

**American Disability Benefit Group**                    **1-800-300-7545**
Offers assistance to persons seeking to obtain social security disability benefits. Goal is to make the process easier by assisting with filing of paperwork and court appearances.
*E-mail:* disabilitycase@hotmail.com    *Website:* http://www.disabilitycase.com

**Canine Companions for Independence**                    **1-800-572-BARK**
Trains dogs to assist people with physical and developmental disabilities. Trains volunteers to raise puppies.              *Website:* http://www.caninecompanions.org

**Childcare Plus**                    **1-800-235-4122**
Information and referrals to families of children (birth to 5) with disabilities. Inclusion training for professionals.              *Website:* http://www.ccplus.org

**Delta Society**                    **1-800-869-6898**
Trains volunteers and pets for visiting animal programs in hospitals, nursing homes, rehabilitation centers and schools. Provides immediate assistance to people with service dogs who are denied access to public places. Online bereavement support for pet loss.
*Phone:* 425-226-7357              *E-mail:* info@deltasociety.org
*TTY:* 1-800-809-2714              *Website:* http://www.deltasociety.org

**Disabled and Alone**                    **1-800-995-0066**
Helps families and caretakers of disabled persons make lifetime plans for the care of their loved one after they are gone. One time membership fee.
*Phone:* 212-532-6740              *Website:* www.disabledandalone.org

**Easter Seals National Headquarters Disability Helpline**                    **1-800-221-6827**
*(Bilingual)* Provides disability resource packets for children and adults with disabilities. Online directory available.              *Website:* http://www.easter-seals.org

**Families and Advocates Partnership for Education**          **1-888-248-0822**
Support and education for families with children with any disability. Advocates for the Individuals with Disabilities Education Act. Literature, training, information and referrals.
*TTY:* 952-838-0190                    *Website:* http://www.fape.org

**HEATH Resource Center**                    **1-800-544-3284** (Voice/TDD)
Information and referrals on post-secondary education and adult training programs for people with disabilities. Sponsored by U.S. Dept. of Education.
*E-mail:* askheath@heath.gwu.edu        *Website:* http://www.heath.gwu.edu

**Job Accommodation Network**          **1-800-526-7234 or 1-800-ADA-WORK**
Information on accommodations for people with any disability. Sponsored by Office of Disability Employment Policy & Dept. of Labor. (day/eve)
*E-mail:* jan@jan.icdi.wvu.edu          *Website:* http://www.jan.wvu.edu.com

**Library of Congress National Library**
**Blind and Physically Handicapped**                              **1-800-424-8567**
Refers callers to libraries that have information on books on tapes and in Braille available for qualified blind or handicapped persons who cannot read standard print.
*TTY:* 202-707-0744                    *Website:* http://www.loc.gov/nls

**National Accessible Apartment Clearinghouse**                  **1-800-421-1221**
Maintains a database of over 46,000 accessible apartments nationwide. Helps people with disabilities find accessible apartments. Owners and managers may also use this service to register their accessible units.        *Website:* http://www.aptsforrrent.com/naac

**National Information Center for Children/Youth with Disabilities**     **1-800-695-0285**
Provides information on disabilities with a special focus on children (birth to 22). Services include responses to questions, referrals, and technical assistance to parents, educators, caregivers and advocates. Referrals to support groups.
*Phone:* 202-884-8200 (Voice/TTY)      *Website:* http://www.nichcy.org

**National Institute for Rehab Engineering**                     **1-800-736-2216**
Provides information, advice and referrals to people with disabilities about assistive technology equipment to help them to be more independent and self-sufficient.

**PRIDE (Promote Real Independence for Disabled and Elderly)**          **1-800-332-9122**
Provides assistance for disabled and elderly persons, and their families in the area of homemaking, independence in dressing, personal grooming and fashionable apparel.
                              *Web:* members.aol.com/SEWTIQUE/pride.htm

**Rural Institute on Disabilities**                              **1-800-732-0323**
Provides assistance for disabled children and adults who live in rural areas. Technological services, early intervention, and services for the elderly.

**SNAP (Special Needs Advocate for Parents)**                    **1-888-310-9889**
Support for parents of special needs children. Referrals to educational advocates, support groups, attorneys, other resources. Assistance with estate planning. Newsletter, speaker's bureau. Interactive bulletin boards.    *Website:* http://www.snapinfo.org

**Through the Looking Glass**                    **1-800-644-2666**
Information and referrals for disabled parents or parents of disabled children. Newsletter, phone support.    *Website:* http://www.lookingglass.org

**U.S. Equal Employment Opportunity Commission**                    **1-800-669-4000**
Information, speakers, technical assistance, training and referrals re: enforcing ADA and prohibiting discrimination in employment of disabled persons.
*Website:* http://www.eeoc.gov

## DOMESTIC VIOLENCE

**National Domestic Violence Hotline**                    **1-800-799-7233**
Information and referrals for victims of domestic violence.
*TDD:* 1-800-787-3224                    *Website:* http://www.ndvh.org

## DOWN SYNDROME

**Down Syndrome Hotline**                    **1-800-221-4602**
Provides information and referral, packets for new parents, information on education, support groups, medical research, newsletter, phone support, information on conferences.
*Phone:* 212-460-9330                    *Website:* http://www.ndss.org

## DRUG ABUSE

**American Academy of Family Physicians**                    **1-800-274-2237**
*(Bilingual)* Provides free handouts on many health concerns, illnesses, mental health disorders, addictions, disabilities, etc.)    *Website:* http://www.familydoctor.org

**American Council for Drug Education**                    **1-800-488-DRUG**
*(Bilingual)* Provides general information on drug abuse and treatment. Brochures. Referrals to crisis counseling. Publications. (24 hrs)

**Drug Policy Information Clearinghouse**                    **1-800-666-3332**
Sends out information on drug abuse, and publications on national drug policies.
*E-mail:* ondcp@ncjrs.org                    *Website:* http://www.whitehousedrugpolicy.gov

**National Association for Children of Alcoholics**                      **1-888-554-2627**
Advocates for children and families affected by alcoholism and other drug dependencies.
Helps children hurt by parental substance abuse. Newsletter, advocacy, policy making,
literature, videos, educational materials. *Website:* http://nacoa.org

**National Clearinghouse**                                              **1-800-729-6686**
**for Alcohol and Drug Information**                        *Spanish:* **1-877-767-8432**
*(Bilingual)* Information on alcohol, tobacco and drug abuse and prevention. Referrals to
treatment centers, research, groups, and community programs.
*TTY:* 1-800-487-4889                        *Website:* http://www.health.org

**National Council on Alcoholism and**                          **1-800-622-2255 or**
**and Drug Dependence**                                         **1-800-654-HOPE**
Provides information on counseling and treatment services for substance abuse. Prevention
and education programs. Newsletter.     *Website:* http://www.ncadd.org

**National Helpline**                                              **1-800-662-HELP**
*(Bilingual)* Referrals to treatment centers. Sponsored by Phoenix House. (24 hrs)
                                        *Website:* http://www.drughelp.org

**National Inhalant Prevention Center**                          **1-800-269-4237**
Provides information and referrals to persons concerned about inhalants. Literature, training
and technical assistance. Newsletter.     *Website:* http://www.inhalants.org

**National PRIDE (Parents' Resource Inst. for Drug Education)**      **1-800-668-9277**
Trains youth volunteers on how to conduct drug prevention education.

## DWARFISM

**Little People's Research Fund**                                **1-800-232-5773**
Referrals (primarily research) and literature on dwarfism. Networks parents together.

## EATING DISORDERS

**National Eating Disorders Association**                        **1-800-931-2237**
Information on professional services and support groups for persons with eating disorders.
Literature, training conferences.     *Website:* http://www.nationaleatingdisorders.org

## EDUCATION

**ERIC Clearinghouse on Disabilities and Gifted Education**      **1-800-328-0272**
Information regarding special/gifted education including: ADD, gifted children, behavior
disorders, inclusion, etc.     *Website:* http://ericec.org

**Federal Student Aid Information Center**                    1-800-433-3243
Information on federal student aid.        *Website:* http://www.fafsa.ed.gov

**Goodwill Industries**                                        1-800-741-0186
Provides employment and training services for people with disabilities and other disadvantaging conditions (welfare, illiteracy, criminal history, homelessness).
*Phone:* 301-530-6500                *Website:* http://www.goodwill.org

**National Association for the Education of Young Children**    1-800-424-2460
Information and referrals re: early childhood education (infancy – 8 years of age).
*Phone:* 202-232-8777                *Website:* http://www.naeyc.org

**National Job Corps Information Line**                        1-800-733-5627
*(Bilingual)* Referrals to job corps training (persons 16-24). Helps persons to earn high school equivalency diplomas. (24 hrs)    *Website:* http://www.jobscorps.doleta.gov

**Sallie Mae**                                                 1-800-428-9250
Information on student loans for eligible persons.

## ENERGY / UTILITIES

**Energy Efficiency and Renewable Energy Clearinghouse**       1-800-363-3732
Free information on energy efficiency & renewable energy. Answers technical questions. Provides referral to other organizations.  *Website:* http://www.eren.doe.gov

## ENVIRONMENT

**American Public Information on Environment**                 1-800-320-2743
Information, education and aid to families with environmental concerns.
*E-mail:* info@americdnpie.org        *Website:* http://www.americanpie.org

**Chemical Information Referral Center**                       1-800-424-9300
Takes reports on chemical spills.        *Website:* http://www.chemtrec.org

**Environmental Protection Agency Safe Drinking Water**        1-800-426-4791
Provides information and policy regulations on a variety of environmental concerns.
*E-mail:* hotline-spwa@epa.gov        *Website:* http://www.epa.gov

**Indoor Air Quality Information Clearinghouse**              1-800-438-4318
Information and referral on indoor air quality, pollutants, health effects, control methods, commercial building maintenance.    *Website:* http://www.epa.gov/iaq/

**National Lead Information Center & Clearinghouse**     **1-800-424-LEAD**
Provides information on lead-based paint and safe work practices for renovating. Distributes
EPA literature.       *Website:* http://www.epa.gov/lead

## EPILEPSY

**Epilepsy Information Service**     **1-800-642-0500**
Answers general questions on epilepsy. Free literature. Conducts workshops, conferences.
      *E-mail:* pgibson@wfubmc.edu

## EXERCISE / FITNESS

**Aerobics & Fitness Association of America**     **1-800-445-5950**
Information on non-medical aspects of fitness programs (injuries, low-impact aerobics and
video referrals.       *Website:* http://www.afaa.com

**American Running Association**     **1-800-776-2732**
Information on aerobic sports. Referrals to sports medicine clinics, podiatrists and
orthopedists.       *Website:* http://www.americanrunning.org/

## EYE CARE

**Eye Care America**     **1-800-222-3937**
Assists financially disadvantaged persons (65+) in obtaining medical eye care.
      *Website:* http://www.eyenet.org

## FACIAL DISFIGUREMENT

**Children's Craniofacial Association**     **1-800-535-3643**
Information and support for children with craniofacial disfigurement and their families.
Referrals to doctors and support groups. Educational booklets. Information on free medical
clinics, retreats, advocacy.       *Website:* http://www.ccakids.com

**FACES: The Nat'l Craniofacial Assn.**     **1-800-332-2373**
Assists children and adults with craniofacial disorders resulting from disease, accident or
birth. Financial assistance, referrals to support groups, newsletter, information & referrals to
services and medical professionals.    *Website:* http://www.faces-cranio.org

## FOOD HANDLING / SHARING

**Center for Food Safety and Applied Nutrition**     **1-888-SAFE-FOOD**
Information on food safety, cosmetics and colors, seafood, and women's health nutritional
information. Sponsored by FDA.     *Website:* http://www.cfsan.fda.gov

**Meat and Poultry Hotline**                                    **1-800-535-4555**
Answers questions on safe handling of food for the consumer at home. Helps persons understand labels on meat and poultry. Sponsored by US Dept of Agriculture.
*E-mail:* mphotline.fsis@usda.gov          *Website:* http://www.fsis.usda.gov

## FOOT CARE

**Foot Care Information Center**                                **1-800-366-8227**
Provides literature and referrals on foot care and podiatric medicine. Referrals to podiatrists.
*Website*: http://www.apma.org

## GAMBLING

**National Council on Problem Gambling**                        **1-800-522-4700**
Information, referrals to support groups, and counseling for compulsive gamblers.
*Phone:* 202-547-9204          *Website:* http://www.ncpgambling.org

## GASTROINTESTINAL DISORDERS

**National Institute of Diabetes & Digestive & Kidney Diseases**    **1-800-891-5389**
Provides referrals and literature on various subjects concerning diabetes, digestive disorders, kidney disease, metabolic and endocrine disorders, urologic disorders, etc
*Kidney:* 1-800-891-5390          *E-mail:* nkudic@info.niddk.nih.gov
*Diabetes:* 1-800-860-8747          *Website:* http://www.niddk.nih.gov

## GRANTS / FUNDING

**Foundation Center Customer Service**                          **1-800-424-9836**
Information on grant providers and funders, and grant writing for non-profit projects. Offers course on proposal writing. Free library.  *Website:* http://fdncenter.org

## HEALTH

**Agency for Health Care Research & Quality**                   **1-800-358-9295**
Provides research-based information to enhance consumer and clinical decision-making, improve health care quality, and promote efficiency in public and private systems of health care delivery. Pamphlets.          *Website:* http://www.ahrq.gov

**American Academy of Family Physicians**                       **1-800-274-2237**
*(Bilingual)* Provides free handouts on many health concerns, illnesses, mental health disorders, addictions, disabilities, etc.)    *Website:* http://www.familydoctor.org

**American Board of Medical Specialties**                    **1-866-275-2267**
Will tell you if your physician is board certified. (Mon-Fri, 9am-6pm)
*Phone:* 847-491-9091                    *Website:* http://www.abms.org

**Center for Patient Advocacy**                    **1-800-846-7444**
Tries to ensure that all persons have timely access to the highest quality medical care. Educates patients on how to deal with managed care agencies. Newsletter, legislative actions alerts, advocacy.

**Center for the Study of Inherited & Neurological Disorders**    **1-800-283-4316**
Provides information on disorders currently under study by the Center for Human Genetics. These include: macular degeneration, Alzheimer's, ALS, autism, Bethlem myopathy, Charcot Marie Tooth disease, Chiari malformations, syringomyelia, cardiovascular disease, muscular dystrophies, familial focal segmental glomerulosclerosis, familial spastic paraparesis, hereditary benign intraepithelial dyskeratosis, MS, neural tube defects, osteoarthritis, Parkinson's and tuberous sclerosis. *Website:* http://wwwchg.mc.duke.edu

**Centers for Disease Control and Prevention**                    **1-800-311-3435**
Provides information over the phone on specific diseases.
*E-mail:* inquiry@edc.gov                    *Website:* http://www.cdc.gov

**Genetic Alliance Information**                    **1-800-336-GENE**
Coalition of consumer advocates, health professionals, researchers, and policy makers that provides individuals and families with quality genetics resources so that they may make quality healthcare decisions. Provides information, support resources, research findings and referrals. (Mon-Fri, 8am-5pm)            *E-mail:* jlewis@geneticalliance.org

**March of Dimes**                    **1-888-663-4637**
Dedicated to decreasing the incidence of birth defects, infant mortality, low birth weight and lack of prenatal care. Provides information, referrals and literature.
                                        *Website:* http://www.modimes.org

**Minority Health Resource Center**                    **1-800-444-6472**
Federally-funded library service that provides information and referral to sources on health problems for minorities.            *TTY:* 301-230-7199
*Fax:* 301-230-7198                    *Website:* http://www.omhrc.gov

**National Alliance for Hispanic Health**                    **1-800-504-7081**
*(Bilingual)* Provides referrals to clinics and doctors, and prenatal care. Information on pregnancy and childcare.            *Website:* http://www.hispanichealth.org

**National Center on Complementary & Alternative Medicine**    **1-888-644-6226**
Information on clinical trials and research being conducted on alternative medicine.
*E-mail:* info@nccam.nih.gov            *Website:* http://nccam.nih.gov

376

**National Health Information Center**                    **1-800-336-4797**
Helps locate health information through resources, information and referrals. Publications and directories on health promotion and disease prevention topics.
*Phone:* 301-565-4167                    *E-mail:* info@nhic.org
*Fax:* 301-984-4256                    *Website:* http://www.health..gov/nhic

**National Immunizations Information Hotline**                    **1-800-232-2522**
*(Bilingual)* Information and referrals on immunizations for infants, adults and health care professionals.                    *E-mail:* nipinfo@cdc.gov
*Spanish:* 1-800-232-0233                    *Website:* http://www.cdc.gov/nip

**National Institute of Allergy & Infectious Disease**                    **1-800-243-7644**
Provides information on clinical trials being conducted on allergic and infectious diseases.
*Website:* http://www.niaid.nih.gov

**National Institute for Occupational Safety and Health**                    **1-800-356-4674**
Information on all aspects of occupational health and safety.
*Phone:* 513-533-8326                    *Website:* http://www.cdc.gov/niosh

**National Library of Medicine**                    **1-888-346-3656**
Information and referrals to help callers research health questions.
*E-mail:* custserv@nlm.nih.gov                    *Website:* http://www.nlm.nih.gov

**National Reference Center for Bioethics Literature**                    **1-800-633-3849**
Provides information via e-mail or mail on bioethical topics. Does limited searches on special topics except legal issues.                    *Website:* http://bioethic.georgetown.edu

**National Women's Health Information Center**                    **1-800-994-9662**
*(Bilingual)* Provides information and referrals for all women's health questions.
*TTY:* 1-888-220-5446                    *Website:* http://www.4woman.gov/

**National Women's Health Resource Center**                    **1-877-986-9472**
Provides information on women's health issues. Dedicated to helping women make informed decisions about their health.                    *Website:* http://www.healthwoman.org

# HEART

**American Health Assistance Foundation**                    **1-800-437-2423**
Provides educational information and funds research for heart disease and other disorders.
*Website:* http://www.ahaf.org

**American Heart Association**                    **1-800-242-8721**
Information on heart health and support groups. (Mon-Fri, 6am-12 midnight)
*Website:* http://www.americanheart.org

**Arrhythmogenic Right Ventricular Dysplasia Registry**        **1-800-483-2662**
Nurse coordinators answer questions about arrhythmogenic right ventricular dysplasia and help with the diagnosis. Funds research. *Website:* http://www.arvd.org

**Cardiac Arrhythmias Research and Education Foundation, Inc.**        **1-800-404-9500**
Support, education and registry for individuals and families affected by long QT syndrome and other genetic arrhythmias. Helps to create community forums for mutual support.
*E-mail:* care@longqt.org          *Website:* http://www.longqt.org

**NIH National Heart, Lung & Blood Inst. Helpline**        **1-800-575-WELL**
Provides information on the prevention and treatment of high blood pressure and high blood cholesterol.

**Texas Heart Institute Heart Information Service**        **1-800-292-2221**
Answers questions on cardiovascular via phone, mail, or e-mail. Literature on aneurisms, cholesterol, heart transplants, stroke patients, women and heart disease. Information on support groups.          *Website:* http://www.texasheartinstitute.org

## HOMOSEXUALITY

**Gay & Lesbian National Hotline**        **1-888-843-4564**
Provides information and referrals for gays, lesbians, transgendered, and persons with questions about their sexuality.        *Website*: http://www.glnh.org

## HOSPICE

**Children's Hospice International**        **1-800-242-4453**
Refers patients to hospices & specialists in their areas. Bibliography, manuals.
*Volunteer Info:* 703-684-0330          *Website:* http://www.chionline.org

**Hospice Education Institute**        **1-800-331-1620**
Provides information and referrals re: hospice care.
*E-mail:* hospiceall@aol.com          *Website:* http://www.hospiceworld.org

**Hospice Foundation of America**        **1-800-854-3402**
Provides education and information on hospice care. Sponsors research. Offers teleconference series "Living with Grief," for bereaved families. Audiotapes for clergy.
          *Website:* http://www.hospicefoundation.org

**National Hospice Helpline**        **1-800-658-8898**
Information for hospice care for terminally ill persons. Referrals to hospice programs nationwide. (Mon-Fri. 8:30am-5pm)        *Website:* http://www.nhpco.org

## HOSPITAL

**Hill Burton Hotline**                                    **1-800-638-0742**
Information about free hospital care for eligible persons (low income). Directories of medical centers that are part of Hill Burton program throughout US.
*Phone:* 1-800-492-0359 (in MD)          *Website:* http://www.hrsa.gov/osp/dfcr

**National Association of Hospital Hospitality Houses**          **1-800-542-9730**
Referrals to hospital hospitality housing that provide lodging for families of hospital patients and/or hospital outpatients.      *Website:* http://www.nahhh.org

**Shriner's Hospital**                                    **1-800-237-5055**
Information on free hospital care available to children under the age of 18 needing treatment for burns, spinal cord injury, cleft palate, or orthopedic care.
                              *Website:* http://www.shrinershq.org

## HOUSING

**Community Connections**                                **1-800-998-9999**
Provides information about housing and community development, homeless prevention, first-time homebuyer programs, veterans, and low-income housing, and HUD.
*TDD:* 1-800-483-2209          *Website:* http://www.comcon.org

**HUD Center for Faith-Based & Community Initiative**          **1-800-308-0395**
Acts as liaison between religious organizations and Housing and Urban Development.

**Public Housing Drug Elimination Support Center**          **1-800-955-2232**
Has information and publications on public housing, welfare to work, and drug prevention program (drug use and violence in public housing).
*Fax:* 301-585-6271          *Website:* http://www.hud.gov

## IMMIGRANTS

**Immigration and Naturalization Services**                **1-800-375-5283**
Comprehensive information for immigrants including naturalization processes, adjustment of status for permanent residency, travel documents. Also has information on international services and border patrols.          *Website:* http://www.ins.usdoj.gov

## IMPOTENCY

**Impotence "Information Center"**                        **1-800-843-4315**
Provides information about the causes and treatments of impotence. Referrals to local physicians.          *Website:* http://www.visitams.com

# INCONTINENCE

**Incontinence "Information Center "**                    **1-800-843-4315**
Provides information about the causes and treatments of incontinence. Referrals to local physicians.                    *Website:* http://www.visitams.com

**National Association for Continence**                    **1-800-252-3337**
Clearinghouse of information on incontinence. Referrals to physicians.
*Phone:* 864-579-7900                    *Website:* http://www.nafc.org

# INSURANCE

**Insurance Information Institute**                    **1-800-331-9146**
Provides information on homeowners and auto insurance. Also provides hints and literature on preventing theft and accidents.                    *Website:* http://www.iii.org

**National Insurance Consumer Helpline**                    **1-800-942-4242**
Provides general information on homeowners and auto insurance. (Mon-Fri, 8am-8pm)
                    *Website:* http://www.iii.org

# KIDNEY

**American Kidney Fund**                    **1-800-638-8299**
Provides information and referrals, and financial assistance to kidney patients. (Mon-Fri, 9am-5pm ET)                    *Website:* http://www.kidneyfund.org

**National Institute of Diabetes & Digestive & Kidney Diseases**                    **1-800-891-5390**
Provides referrals and literature on a broad range of subjects including kidney disease.
                    *Website:* http://www.niddk.nih.gov/

**National Kidney Foundation**                    **1-800-622-9010 or 1-800-WAKE-DRY**
Education and research information on kidney disease. Referrals to local affiliates.
*Phone:* 212-889-2210                    *Website:* http://www.kidney.org

# LEARNING DISABILITIES

**ADHD Experts on Call**                    **1-888-275-2343**
Can speak with experts in the field of attention deficit hyperactivity disorder. Information on symptoms, diagnosis and treatment options.

**International Dyslexia Association**                    **1-800-ABCD-123**
Provides information and referrals for persons with dyslexia. (Mon-Fri, 8:30am-4:30pm)
*Phone:* 410-296-0232 (in MD)                    *Website:* http://www.interdys.org

**National Center for Learning Disabilities**                    **1-888-575-7373**
Provides information and referrals for learning disabled adults and children.
*Phone:* 212-545-7510                    *Website:* http://www.ld.org

**Recording For The Blind and Dyslexic**                    **1-800-221-4792**
Information on free cassettes, recorded textbooks, and consumer publications to eligible handicapped persons. Information on volunteer programs for recording tapes.
*E-mail:* custserv@rfbd.org                    *Website:* http://www.rfbd.org

## LEGISLATION

**Project Vote Smart**                    **1-888-868-3762**
Non-partisan information about all elected officials and candidates for Federal, state, local and gubernatorial offices.                    *Website:* http://www.vote-smart.org

**U.S. Government Federal Information Center**                    **1-800-688-9889**
*(Bilingual)* Information about federal programs and agencies (patents, taxes, jobs, social security, rules and regulations, passports, visas, dept. of states, and veteran affairs.)
*TDD:* 1-800-326-2996                    *Website:* http://fic.info.gov

## LEPROSY

**American Leprosy Missions**                    **1-800-LEPROSY or 1-800-543-3135**
Provides information on projects and programs that fight leprosy in 23 countries.
*E-mail:* amlep@leprosy.org                    *Website:* http://www.leprosy.org

## LIFE THREATENING ILLNESS

**Funeral Service Consumer Assistance Program**                    **1-800-662-7666**
Assists consumers in matters involving funeral services. Information, resources and help in resolving complaints. Literature on funerals, grief, and pre-need funeral planning.

**Medical Escrow Society**                    **1-800-422-1314**
Provides information on obtaining advance cash from life insurance policies for persons with a life threatening illness.                    *Website:* http://medicalescrow.com

**Partnership for Caring**                    **1-800-989-9455**
Information and education concerning end-of-life issues. Includes caregiver questions.
*Phone:* 202-296-8071                    *Phone:* 1-800-406-8345 (emergencies)
*E-mail:* pfc@partnershipforcaring.org                    *Website:* http://www.partnershipforcaring.org

# LITERACY

**National Literacy Hotline**                                    **1-800-228-8813**
Information and referrals to local literacy programs. Referrals for both volunteers and people needing literacy services.        *Website:* http://www.nifl.gov/nifl/HLindex.htm

# LYME DISEASE

**American Lyme Disease Foundation**                             **1-800-876-5963**
Provides information on Lyme disease. Referrals to doctors. Brochures.
*E-mail:* Inquire@aldf.com                    *Website:* http://www.adlf.com

**National Lyme Disease Foundation**                            **1-800-886-LYME**
Provides information and referrals for Lyme disease. Education, literature, advocacy. Need touch-tone phone.                    *Website:* http://www.patientadvocacy.org

# MEDICARE

**Medicare**                                            **1-800-MEDICARE**
*(Bilingual)* Provides information on Medicare, Medigap, and health plan options.
*TDD:* 1-877-486-2048                    *Website:* http://www.medicare.gov

# MENINGITIS

**Meningitis Foundation**                                        **1-800-668-1129**
Support for persons with spinal meningitis and their families. Provides information, education, and supports research. Chat rooms.
*Phone:* 317-595-6383 (international)      *Website:* http://www.musa.org

# MENOPAUSE

**North American Menopause Society**                             **1-800-774-5342**
Provides free packets of information on menopause. Referrals to clinicians and discussions groups.                            *Website:* http://www.menopause.org

# MENTAL HEALTH

**American Academy of Family Physicians**                        **1-800-274-2237**
*(Bilingual)* Provides free handouts on many health concerns, illnesses, mental health disorders, addictions, disabilities, etc.)      *Phone:* 913-906-6000 ext. 5175
                                        *Website:* http://www.familydoctor.org

**Compeer**                                          **1-800-836-0475**
Provides volunteer "friends" for children and adults who receive mental health treatment.

**National Alliance for Research on Schizophrenia & Depression**    **1-800-829-8289**
Information on schizophrenia, depression, and bi-polar disorder. Information on current research. Newsletter, literature.        *Website:* http://www.narsad.org

**National Institute of Mental Health Information Line**        **1-800-647-2642**
Provides information and literature on anxiety, phobias, obsessive-compulsive and depression.            *Website:* http://www.nimh.nih.gov

**National Mental Health Association**                    **1-800-969-6642**
Free literature on over 200 mental health topics including bipolar, depression, bereavement, post-traumatic stress disorder, and warning signs of mental illness. Referrals to local mental health services. Free national directory of local mental health associations, and offers low-cost materials. Advocacy.        *TDD:* 1-800-433-5959
*E-mail:* infoctr@nmha.org        *Website:* http://www.nmha.org

**National Mental Health Services Knowledge Exchange Network**    **1-800-789-CMHS**
Refers callers to many mental health organizations nationwide.
*E-mail:* ken@mentalhealth.org        *Website:* http://www.mentalhealth.org

**TARA**                                          **1-888-482-7227**
Provides information on borderline personality. Referrals to clinicians, treatment programs, and self-help groups. Publishes journal, speaker's bureau. Conferences, advocacy.
*Phone:* (212-966-6514        *E-mail:* taraapd@aol.com

## MENTAL RETARDATION

**American Association on Mental Retardation**            **1-800-424-3688**
Information on mental retardation.        *Website:* http://www.aamr.org

**Best Buddies**                                     **1-800-89-BUDDY**
One-on-one friendships and integrated employment opportunities for people with mental retardation (pre-teens through adults). Opportunity for developmentally disabled persons to interact with non-disabled peers.        *Website:* http://www.bestbuddies.org/

**Training Center on Aging with Mental Retardation**        **1-800-996-8845**
Aim is to promote independence, productivity, inclusion and self-determination of older adults with mental retardation. Provides training, technical assistance and materials to patients, families and professionals.        *TTY:* 312-413-0453

## METABOLIC DISORDERS

**National Institute of Diabetes & Digestive & Kidney Diseases**          **Various**
1-800-891-5390 (kidney); 1-800-860-8747 (diabetes); 1-800-891-5389 (digestive diseases)
Provides referrals and literature on a broad range of subjects concerning diabetes, digestive disorders, kidney disease, metabolic and endocrine disorders, hematological diseases, urologic disorders.                    *Website:* http://www.niddk.nih.gov

**World Life Foundation**                               **1-800-289-5433**
Support, research, information and referrals for rare metabolic disorders. Offers air transportation for ambulatory patients who need non-emergency treatment.

## MILITARY / VETERANS

**Department of Veterans Affairs**                        **1-800-827-1000**
Comprehensive information on available programs and services for veterans including pensions, vocational rehab, and education. Special programs for disabled, homeless, minority and women veterans.          *Website:* http://www.va.gov/

**National Veterans Service Fund, Inc.**                   **1-800-521-0198**
Provides social services for Vietnam and Persian Gulf war veterans, and their families, focusing on those with disabled children. Publications.
*Phone:* 203-656-0003              *Website:* http://www.vvnw.org/

**VA Persian Gulf and Agent Orange Veterans Helpline**        **1-800-749-8387**
Refers Gulf war veterans and veterans affected by agent orange with medical problems to local Gulf war coordinators at local VA medical centers.

**Veterans of the Vietnam War, Inc.**                        **1-800-VIETNAM**
Membership organization for veterans and their supporters. Educates public about post-traumatic stress disorder, veteran health issues, agent orange, and POW/MIA issues. Find-a-Vet locator service, newsletter. Works with homeless/incarcerated vets.
*Phone:* 570-603-9740 (general info)      *E-mail:* HHennen555@aol.com
*Phone:* 1-800-843-8626 (legal)          *Website:* http://www.vvnw.org

## MISSING CHILDREN

**Child Find of America Hotline**                        **1-800-I-AM-LOST**
Helps parents locate children and aids lost children who need assistance (Mon-Fri, 9-5).
*Phone:* 845-255-1848              *Website:* http://www.childfindofamerica.org

**National Center for Missing & Exploited Children**          **1-800-843-5678**
Information re: missing and exploited youth. Helps parents locate missing children.
                    *Website:* http://www.missingkids.com

384

**Vanished Children Alliance**                    **1-800-VANISHED**
Provides emotional support and technical assistance to families of missing children. Offers educational training and materials. Speaker's bureau, parent's support group, in-house legal assistance. (24 hrs)                    *Admin:* 408-296-1113 (8am-4pm)
*E-mail:* info@vca.org                    *Website:* http://www.vca.org

## MULTIPLE SCLEROSIS

**Multiple Sclerosis Foundation**                    **1-800-441-7055**
Support services for those with multiple sclerosis. Grants for research, information and referrals on traditional and alternative treatments. Newsletter. Phone support.
                    *Website:* http://www.msfacts.org

## MUSCULAR DYSTROPHY

**Muscular Dystrophy Family Foundation, Inc.**                    **1-800-544-1213**
Provides services, resources, home medical equipment and adaptive devices to help people with muscular dystrophy and their families. Comprehensive direct services.
*Phone:* 317-443-2054 (eve)                    *Website:* http://www.mdff.org

## NEUROLOGICAL IMPAIRMENT

**National Institute of Neurological Disorders**                    **1-800-352-9424**
Provides information on neurological disorders and stroke. Sponsored by NIH.
*Fax:* 301-402-2186                    *Website:* http://www.ninds.nih.gov

## NICOTINE

**Office on Smoking and Health**                    **1-800-232-1311**
Provides information on the affects of tobacco on health, how to stop smoking, second hand smoke, and other current topics relating to tobacco
*E-mail:* tobaccoinfo@cdc.gov                    *Website:* http://www.cdc.gov/tobacco

## ORGAN DONATION

**Children's Organ Transplant Association**                    **1-800-366-2682**
Public education on organ transplants. Assists families in fund-raising for transplant and transplant-related expenses. Aids children and adults who are U.S. citizens in need of an organ transplant.                    *Website:* http://www.cota.org

**The Living Bank - National Organ & Transplant Registry**                    **1-800-528-2971**
Donor cards, educational materials and referrals to medical schools for persons wishing to donate their bodies after death.                    *Website:* http://www.livingbank.org

**Minority Organ Tissue Transplant Education Program**    **1-800-393-2839**
Provides educational information re: organ transplants. Referrals to physicians.
*Website:* http://www.nationalmottep.org

**National Foundation for Transplants**    **1-800-489-3863**
Provides support services, financial assistance and advocacy to adult and child organ and bone marrow transplant candidates and recipients. Assists in fund-raising activities.
*Phone:* 901-684-1697    *Website:* http://www.transplants.org

## OSTEOPOROSIS

**NIH Osteoporosis & Related Bone Diseases Resource Center**    **1-800-624-BONE**
Resources and information on metabolic bone diseases such as osteoporosis.
*TDD:* 202-466-4315    *Website:* http://www.osteo.org

**Osteoporosis Helpline**    **1-888-934-2663**
General information and fact sheets on the symptoms, causes and treatment of osteoporosis.

## PAGET'S DISEASE

**Paget's Foundation**    **1-800-237-2438**
Information, brochures, patient's guide, doctor referrals, professional packets and newsletter on Paget's disease of the bone, as well as primary hyperparathyroidism.
*Phone:* 212-509-5335    *ebsite:* http://www.paget.org

## PARKINSON'S DISEASE

**National Parkinson's Foundation**    **1-800-327-4545**
Professional will answer any question on Parkinson disease. (Mon-Fri, 8:30am-5pm)
*Phone:* 1-800-433-7022 (FL)    *E-mail:* mailbox@parkinson.org
*Phone:* 305-547-6666 (in Miami)    *Website:* http://www.parkinson.org

## PEDICULOSIS

**National Pediculosis Association**    **1-800-446-4672**
Provides information and materials concerning head lice. Books, videos, literature.
*Website:* http://www.headlice.org

## PESTICIDES

**National Pesticide Information Network**    **1-800-858-7378**
Information on most aspects of pesticides. Sponsored by EPA.
*E-mail:* npic@ace.orst.edu    *Website:* http://npic.orst.edu

## PLASTIC SURGERY

**American Society of Plastic and Reconstructive Surgeons**          **1-888-475-2784**
Referrals to plastic surgeons, information on particular plastic surgeons as to qualifications.
*Website:* http://www.plasticsurgery.org

## PREGNANCY / CHILDBIRTH

**Antiepileptic Drug Pregnancy Registry**          **1-888-233-2334**
*(Multilingual)* Registry of women who are taking antiepileptic drugs and who are pregnant.
Helps to determine which therapies are associated with increased risks.

**March of Dimes**          **1-888-663-4637**
Dedicated to decreasing the incidence of birth defects, infant mortality, low birth weight and
lack of prenatal care. Provides information, referrals and literature.

**National Abortion Federation**          **1-800-772-9100**
Information and referrals regarding abortions. Financial aid.
*Website:* http://www.prochoice.org

**National Alliance for Hispanic Health**          **1-800-504-7081**
*(Bilingual)* Provides referrals to clinics and doctors, and prenatal care. Information on
pregnancy and childcare.          *Website:* http://www.hispanichealth.org

**National Life Center, Inc.**          **1-800-848-LOVE**
Provides counseling and information for pregnant women. Referrals to testing sites, free
maternity and baby clothes, and formula.

**OTIS (Organization of Teratology Information Services)**          **1-888-285-3410**
*(Multilingual)* Provides local referrals to agencies that provide information concerning
prenatal drug, medication, chemical and other potentially harmful exposures. Literature.
(Mon-Fri, 8:30am-4pm)          *Website:* http://www.otispregnancy.org/

**Planned Parenthood**          **1-800-230-7526**
Connects callers to local planned parenthood clinics nationwide.
*Admin:* 1-800-829-7732          *Website:* http://www.plannedparenthood.org/

**Pregnancy Hotline**          **1-800-848-5683**
Free, confidential information for pregnant women, shelters for women and girls, baby
clothes, adoption referrals. (24 hrs)          *Website:* http://www.nationallifecenter.com

**Pregnancy Hotline**          **1-800-238-4269**
Information and counseling to pregnant women. Referrals to free pregnancy test facilities,
foster and adoption centers. (24 hrs)          *Website:* http://www.bethany.org

387

## PRESCRIPTIONS, LOW COST

**Pharmaceutical Patient Assistance Directory Line**          1-800-762-4636
Provides a directory of pharmaceutical assistance programs for persons who cannot afford prescriptions on their own.          *Website:* http://www.pharma.org/patients

## PRIMARY IMMUNE DEFICIENCY

**Jeffrey Modell Foundation**                                 1-800-JEFF-844
Information on primary immune deficiency diseases. Referrals to major medical centers and psychiatric and social support services. Information on insurance reimbursement.
*E-mail:* info@jmfworld.org          *Website:* http://www.jmfworld.org

## PROSTATE PROBLEMS

**Prostatitis Foundation**                                    1-888-891-4200
Support, information, referrals and education to men with prostatitis. Encourages research funding.          *Website:* http://www.prostate.org

**Prostate Information Center**                               1-800-543-9632
General information about prostate disease. Brochures, physicians referrals. Answers "Information Center."          *Website:* http://www.visitams.com

## PROSTITUTION

**HIPS Hotline**                                              1-800-676-HIPS
Peer crisis peer counseling and support for persons involved in, or affected by, the sex industry. Provides information  for sex workers and their families in a non-judgmental, supportive atmosphere.

## PROZAC

**Prozac Survivors Support Group, Inc.**                      1-800-392-0640
Information and brochures on symptoms of adverse reactions to Prozac.
*Website:* http://www.pssg.org

## RADIATION SURVIVORS

**National Association of Radiation Survivors**              1-800-798-5102
Provides information for persons exposed to ionizing radiation from the development, production, testing, use or storage of nuclear weapons and nuclear waste. Advocacy, research, and public education.          *Website:* http://www.radiationsurvivors.org/

## RARE / GENETIC DISORDERS

**FDA Office on Orphan Product Development**                1-800-300-7469
Provides referrals for persons who need a rare orphan drug.
*Website:* http://www.fda.gov/orphan

**NORD (National Organization for Rare Disorders)**          1-800-999-6673
Information and networking for persons with rare disorders. Literature.
*Phone:* 203-744-0100 (in CT)          *Website:* http://www.rarediseases.org

## REHABILITATION

**American Medical Rehab Providers Assn.**      1-800-368-3513 or 1-888-346-4624
Refers callers to rehabilitation hospitals or centers.

**Center for Rehab Technologies**                      1-800-726-9119
Information on products, technology, resources and services for persons with disabilities.
*Phone:* 404-894-0240          *TTY:* 404-894-4960
*Website:* http://www.assistivetech.net      *Website:* http://techconnections.org/

**National Rehabilitation Information Center**      1-800-346-2742 *(Voice/TTY)*
Library and information center on disability and rehabilitation of all types.
*Phone:* 301-459-5900 (Voice/TTY)      *Website:* http://www.naric.com

## RESPIRATORY

**Asthma & Allergy Network - Mothers of Asthmatics**          1-800-878-4403
Provides emotional support and  educational resources for persons with asthma and
allergies. Newsletter.          *E-mail:* aanma@aol.com

**Asthma & Allergy Referral Line**                      1-800-822-2762
Provides pamphlets on asthma and allergies. Referrals to doctors.
*Phone:* 414-272-6071          *Website:* http://www.aaaai.org

**National Institute of Allergy & Infectious Disease**          1-800-243-7644
Information on clinical trials being conducted on allergic and infectious diseases.
*Website:* http://www.niaid.nih.gov

**National Jewish Lung Line**                          1-800-222-5864
Information and referrals. Registered nurses answer questions on all types of lung diseases.
Referrals to doctors, free literature.      *Website:* http://www.njc.org

# REYE'S SYNDROME

**National Reye's Syndrome**                                    **1-800-233-7393**
Guidance to families affected by Reye's Syndrome. Helps increase public awareness.
*E-mail:* nrsf@reyessyndrome.org     *Website:* http://www.reyessyndrome.org

# ROSACEA

**National Rosacea Society**                                    **1-888-NO-BLUSH**
Information and educational materials on rosacea (a chronic condition of the facial skin).
*E-mail:* rosaceas@aol.com

# RUNAWAYS

**National Runaway Switchboard**                              **1-800-621-4000**
Crisis intervention and information and referrals for runaways re: shelter, counseling, food
pantries, and transportation. Greyhound bus tickets available for qualifying kids. (24 hrs)
*Phone:* 858-292-5683                  *Website:* http://www.nrscrisisline.org

**National Youth Crisis Hotline**                              **1-800-HIT-HOME**
Crisis hotline and information and referral for runaways or youth (18 and younger) and their
parents. (24 hrs)                  *Website:* http://www.1800hithome.com

# RURAL ISSUES

**Rural Information Center**                                    **1-800-633-7701**
Information on rural issues. Provides brief database searches for free.
*E-mail:* rric@nal.usda.gov          *Website:* http://www.nalusda.gov/ric

# SCLERODERMA

**Scleroderma Research Foundation**                          **1-800-441-2873**
Referrals to doctors and clinics nationwide who treat scleroderma. Conducts research into
the cause and cure of scleroderma.     *Website:* http://www.srfcure.org

# SELF-ABUSE

**SAFE (Self-Abuse Finally Ends) Alternative Info Line**     **1-800-DONT-CUT**
Provides recorded information on dealing with self-abuse and self-mutilation and treatment
options.                  *Website:* http://www.selfinjury.com

## SEXUAL ABUSE / RAPE

**RAINN (Rape, Abuse and Incest National Network)**          **1-800-656-HOPE**
Support and confidential crisis counseling for victims of sexual assault. Callers are automatically routed to their local center. *Website:* http://www.rainn.org

## SEXUALLY TRANSMITTED DISEASE

**CDC National STD/AIDS Hotline**          **1-800-342-2437 or 1-800-227-8922**
Education and research about sexually transmitted diseases (including yeast, AIDS, cancroids, herpes, genital warts, syphilis and gonorrhea). Referrals, information on prevention, free pamphlets.
*Spanish:* 1-800-344-7432 (24 hrs)          *TTY:* 1-800-243-7889 (day/eve)
*Website:* http://www.ashastd.org          *Website:* http://www.iwannaknow.org (teens)

**Teen AIDS Line**          **1-800-234-TEEN** (Mon-Fri) or **1-800-440-TEEN** (weekends)
Provides information on AIDS and sexually transmitted disease.

## SOCIAL SECURITY

**National Organization of Social Security Claimant's Reps**          **1-800-431-2804**
Provides referrals to social security lawyers who assist claimants in getting social security.
*Website:* http://www.nosscr.org

**Social Security**          **1-800-772-1213**
Provides information on all aspects of social security, supplemental security income and Medicare.          *Website:* http://www.ssa.gov

## SPINAL CORD INJURY

**Christopher Reeves Paralysis Foundation**          **1-800-539-7309**
Information and referrals about research into the cure for paralysis.
*E-mail:* info@paralysis.org          *Website:* http://www.paralysis.org

**Foundation for Spinal Cord Injury**          **1-800-342-0330**
Dedicated to the prevention, care and cure of spinal cord injuries through public awareness, education and research. Free counseling. Networking.
*E-mail:* info@fscip.org          *Website:* http://www.fscip.org/

**Kent Waldrup National Paralysis Foundation**          **1-877-724-2873**
Aim is to find the cure for paralysis. Provides education, implements community-based service programs for spinal cord injured persons, and supports medical research.
*E-mail:* kwpf@kwpf.org          *Website:* http://www.spinalvictory.org

**National Spinal Cord Injury Hotline** 1-800-962-9629
*(Bilingual)* Information, referral and peer support for spinal cord injured persons and their families. (Mon-Fri, 9am-5pm EST; 24 hrs. for new injuries)
*E-mail:* scihotline@aol.com *Website:* http://www.spinalcord.org

**Paralyzed Vets of America** 1-800-424-8200
Information, referral and advocacy for disabilities, paralyzed vets
*E-mail:* info@pva.org7 *Website:* http://www.pva.org

## STUTTERING

**Stuttering Foundation of America** 1-800-992-9392 or 1-800-967-7780
Information and referrals for stutterers and those who treat stutterers. Phone support, conferences. Referral list of speech pathologist who specialize in stuttering. (24 hrs)
*E-mail:* stutter@stutteringhelp.org *Website:* http://www.stutteringhelp.org

## SUDDEN INFANT DEATH

**American SIDS Institute** 1-800-232-SIDS
Dedicated to the prevention of sudden infant death syndrome. Promotes infant health through research and education. *Website:* http://www.sids.org

**SIDS Alliance** 1-800-221-7437
Information on medical research, referrals to support groups, referrals to community services, education. (24 hrs). *Website:* http://sidsalliance.org

## SUICIDE PREVENTION

**1-800-SUICIDE** 1-800-784-2433
Suicide intervention counsels callers immediately, then connect them to their closest community suicide crisis resource. *Website:* http://www.suicidology.org

## TAXES

**IRS Federal Tax Information** 1-800-829-1040
Information regarding federal tax questions & problems (30 day waiting period for written requests.) (24 hours) *Website:* http://www.irs.gov

## THERAPIST / COUNSELOR REFERRAL

**Int'l Assn. for Marriage and Family Counselors** 1-800-545-AACD
Provides referrals to professionals working in the area of marriage counseling, marital therapy, divorce counseling, mediation, and family counseling and therapy.

**Therapist Network**                                    **1-800-THERAPIST**
Referrals to mental health associations, mental health professionals, and other resources.

## THYROID

**Thyroid Foundation of America**                        **1-800-832-8321**
Answers general questions on the thyroid. Information, referrals, literature. Membership
dues $15-25 (includes a quarterly newsletter and free book).
*E-mail:* info@tsh.org                    *Website:* http://www.allthyroid.org

**Thyroid Society for Education and Research**           **1-800-THYROID**
Has recorded information on thyroid disease.
*Phone:* 713-799-9909                     *Website:* http://the-thyroid-society.org

## TRANSPORTATION, MEDICAL

**Air Ambulance Central**                **1-800-262-8526 or 1-800-843-8418**
Will fly patients from anywhere for needed medical services.
                              *E-mail:* airmedusa@aol.com

**Air Life Line**                        **1-800-446-1231 or 1-877-AIR-LIFE**
Provides referrals to volunteer pilots who will fly needy patients for medical care. (24 hrs)
                              *Website:* http://www.airlifeline.com

**Miracle Flights for Kids**                             **1-800-FLY-1711**
Arranges airplane travel for children and adults with healthcare problems. Need doctors note
and 16 days notice.                     *Website:* http://www.miracleflights.org

**National Patient Travel Center**                       **1-800-296-1217**
Information and referral for persons who need cost effective transportation for specialized
treatment after an illness or accident.    *Website:* http://www.mercymedical.org

## TRAUMA

**American Red Cross**                                   **1-800-375-2040**
Provides disaster relief, emergency, health, safety, and community services.
                              *Website:* http://www.redcross.org

**American Trauma Society**                              **1-800-556-7890**
Provides referrals and educational materials on the prevention of physical traumas.
*Phone:* 301-420-1109 (in MD)            *E-mail:* info@amtrauma.org
*Fax:* 301-420-0617                      *Website:* http://www.amtrauma.org

**Think First Foundation**                                    **1-800-844-6556**
Aims to prevent brain, spinal cord and other traumatic injuries through education and training.                    *Website:* http://www.thinkfirst.org

## UROLOGICAL DISEASE

**American Foundation for Urologic Disease**              **1-800-828-7866**
Information for patients and others interested about urological diseases.
*Phone:* 1-800-242-2383 (booklets)        *Website:* http://www.afud.org/

**National Institute of Diabetes & Digestive & Kidney Diseases**    **1-800-891-5390**
Referrals and literature on diabetes, digestive disorders, kidney disease, metabolic and endocrine disorders, hematological diseases, urologic disorders.
*E-mail:* nkudic@info.niddk.nih.gov        *Website:* http://www.niddk.nih.gov

## VARICELLO ZOSTER VIRUS

**VZV Info Line**                                           **1-800-472-VIRUS**
Recorded information on varicello zoster virus. Free packets of information available for chicken pox, shingles and post-herpetic neuralgia.
*Phone:* 212-472-3181        *Website:* http://www.vzvfoundation.org

## VISITING NURSES

**Visiting Nurse Assn. of America**                        **1-888-866-8773**
Referrals to Visiting Nurse Associations. *Website:* www.vnaa.org

## VOLUNTEERING
**Peace Corps**                                             **1-800-424-8580**
Provides information on overseas volunteer opportunities to work with third world countries. Helps with agriculture, business, environmental, etc.) Volunteer tours are two years each. (Mon-Fri, 8:30am-5pm)        *Website:* http://www.peacecorps.gov

**Volunteers of America**                                   **1-800-281-4354**
Provides local human service programs and opportunities for individual and community involvement in volunteer programs that deal with social problems. Also has Retiree Volunteer Coalition.                    *Website:* http://www.voa.org

**Volunteer Connection**                                    **1-800-VOLUNTEER**
*(Bilingual)* Connects callers to local volunteer centers, Points of Light Foundation, Unity in the Spirit of America, and other resources.

## WISH GRANTING FOR CHILDREN

**Believe in Tomorrow**                                    1-800-933-5470
Provides programs and services for children with life threatening illnesses.
*Website:* http://www.believeintomorrow.org

**Brass Ring Society**                                     1-800-666-9474
Has trips to Disney World for children with cystic fibrosis or other life-threatening illnesses.

**Children's Wish Foundation Int'l**                       1-800-323-9474
Grants wishes to terminally ill children up to age of 18.
*E-mail:* wish@childrenswish.org          *Website:* http://www.childrenswish.org

**Dream Factory**                                          1-800-456-7556
Grants dreams for children with a life threatening or critical chronic illness.

**Give Kids the World Foundation**                         1-800-995-KIDS
Working in partnership with Wish organizations, offers a resort facility in Florida for families with terminally ill children.     *Phone:* 407-396-1114

**Make-A-Wish Foundation**                                 1-800-722-9474
Grants wishes to children with serious illnesses.
*E-mail:* mawf@wish.org               *Website:* http://www.wish.org

**A Special Wish Foundation**                              1-800-486-9474
Grants wishes to children with terminal illnesses or life threatening disorders.
*E-mail:* spwish@coil.com             *Website:* http://www.spwish.org

**Starlight Children's Foundation**                        1-800-274-7827
Grants wishes for seriously ill children.   *Website*: http://www.starlight.org

**Sunshine Foundation**                                    1-800-767-1976
Grants the dreams and wishes of seriously ill, physically challenged, and abused children ages 3 to 21.                     *Website:* http://sunshinefoundation.org

## YOUTH

**Action, Parent and Teen Support**                        1-800-367-8336
Referrals to all types of agencies and services for troubled teens and their parents.  (24 hrs)

**Children's Defense Fund**                                1-800-233-1200
Advocates for children with a emphasis on low income and disabled children. Prevention programs, training seminars, Confident Kids Support Groups.
*Website:* http://www.childrensdefense.org

---

**Girl's and Boy's Town National Hotline**                    **1-800-448-3000**
*(Bilingual)* Provides crisis intervention, information and referrals children and their families. Free, confidential. Short-term crisis intervention. (24 hours)
                                         *Website:* http://www.boystown.org

**KID SAVE**                         **1-800-543-7283 or 1-800-334-4KID**
Information and referrals to public and private services for children and adolescents in crisis. Referrals to: shelters, mental health services, sexual abuse treatment, substance abuse, family counseling, residential care, adoption/foster care, etc. (24 hrs)
*E-mail:* kidsave@kidspeace.org          *Website:* http://www.kidspeace.org
                                         *Website:* http://www.teencentral.net

**NineLine**                                                 **1-800-999-9999**
Crisis/suicide hotline. Referrals for youth or parents re: drugs, domestic violence, homelessness, runaways, etc. Message relays, reports of abuse. Helps parents with problems with their kids. (24 hours)          *Website:* http://www.convenanthouse.org/

**Safe Sitter**                                              **1-800-255-4089**
Trains adolescents 11-13 on how to be effective baby sitters.
*E-mail:* safesitter@inet_direct.net      *Website:* http://www.safesitter.org


**Research on Groups for Parents of Children with Disabilities...**
A study reporting on parents' perceptions of the effect of parent-led support groups: *"Results of the study indicated that the effects of belonging to a parent-led parent support group were substantial. Through these groups, parents gain increased skills, an increased sense of power and a sense of belonging. Participants are able to connect with each other and provide support and skills to deal with the day-to-day issues of raising a child with disabilities."* - "The Perceived Effects of Parent-Led Support Groups for Parents of Children with Disabilities" by M. Law, S. King, D. Stewart, & G. King, Physical & Occupational Therapy in Pediatrics, vol. 21, no. 2/3, pp. 29-48, 2001.

**Research on Groups for Families Caring for Elderly Relatives...**
An experimental study, published June, 2002, compared the effectiveness of providing a member-run mutual support group for family caregivers of a relative with dementia, with that of conventional family service available to this group in Hong Kong. Fifty-two caregivers were involved in the study. *"Significant differences were found for distress levels and quality of life, with the mutual support group having greater improvements than the control group. The results of this study show the importance of psychosocial support beyond conventional services generally offered to family caregivers in dementia."* It's interesting to note that these results were found in a country where family traditions for caring for elderly parents are so strong. - "The Effectiveness of a Mutual Support Group for Family Caregivers of a Relative with Dementia." by W. Y. Fung & W. T. Chien, in Archives of Psychiatric Nursing, 16(3):134-44, June, 2002.

# GROUP NAMES

CRASH Fdn.*, 335
Creative Grandparenting, 167
Creutzfeldt-Jakob Fdn., Inc. 217
Criminals & Gangmembers Anonymous, 340
Crohn's and Colitis Fdn of Amer., 217, 253
Crystal Meth Anonymous, 127
CUB (Concerned United Birthparents), 166
CUSA, 36
Cushing's Help and Support, 218
Cushing's Support and Research Fdn., 218
Cutis Laxa Int'l, 218
Cyclic Vomiting Syndrome Association, 317
Cystic Fibrosis Fdn., 219
Cystinosis Fdn., Inc., 219
Cystinuria Support Network, 219
DAD (Depression After Delivery), 327
DAD-to-DAD, 169
Dancing Eye Syndrome, 219
Dandy-Walker Syndrome Network, 220
Daughters of Elderly Bridging Unknown
    Together (DEBUT), 338
Deaf-Blind Division/Nat'l Fed of the
    Blind, 148 , 154
DEBRA of American, 224
Debtors Anonymous, 132
DEBUT, 338
Delta Society Pet Bereavement Support*, 141
Dentatorubral Pallidoluysian Atrophy
    Network, 220
Dentists Concerned for Dentists, 123
Dep-Anon, 326, 328
Depressed Anonymous, 326
Depression After Delivery (DAD), 327
Depression & Related Affected Dis., 326
Depressive & Bipolar Support Alliance, 326
Dercum's Disease*, 220
DES Cancer Network, 201, 221
DES-Action U.S.A. , 201, 221
Diabetes Insipidus Fdn., Inc,. 222
Diabetic Mommies*, 222
Diabetics Anonymous , 221
Dignity/USA, 348
Disabled American Veterans, 157, 352
Disabled Artists' Network, 157, 331
Disorders of Chromosome 16 Fdn., 210
DivorceCare, 176
Domestic Violence Anonymous, 116
Donors' Offspring, Inc., 341

Double Trouble in Recovery, Inc. , 131
DRADA , 326
Dual Disorders Anonymous, 131
Dubowitz Synd. Info & Parent Support, 223
Dysautonomia Fdn, Inc., the, 223
Dystonia Medical Research Foundation, 224
Dystrophic Epidermolysis Bullosa Research
    Assn., 224
EA/TEF Child/Family Sprt. Connection, 310
EAR (Ear Anomalies Reconstructed), 195
Eating Addictions Anonymous, 129, 224
Eating Disorders Anonymous, 129, 225
ECMO Moms and Dads, 228
ECMO Support*, 229
EFFORTS*, 296
Ehlers-Danlos National Fdn., 226
ELASTIC, 186
Ellis Van Creveld Support Group, 226
Emotions Anonymous, 329
Emphysema Fdn. For Our Rights to Survive
    (EFFORTS), 296
Employment Support Center, 342
Encephalitis Global*, 226
Encephalitis Support Group, 226
Endometriosis Assn., 227
Endometriosis Research Center*, 227
Epilepsy Foundation , 228
Erb's Place*, 198
Ex-Partners of Servicemembers, 176
EX-POSE, 176
Facing Our Risk of Cancer Empowered*, 205
FACT (Fostered Abandoned Children), 167
Factor V Leiden Mailing List & Digest*, 230
False Memory Syndrome Foundation, 112
Families Anonymous, 119, 173
Families of Inmates*, 341
Families of S.M.A. , 304
Family Caregiver Alliance*, 338
Family Empowerment Network, 231
Family of COPD Support Programs*, 296
Family Pride Coalition , 169, 349
Family Ties of Nevada, 220
Family Village*, 157
Family Voices, 158
FAMYL Organization., The, 188
Fanconi Anemia Research Fund, 190
Fathers' Network, The, 172
Fdn. for Ichthyosis & Rel. Skin Types, 248

401

Parents/Researchers Interested in Smith-Magenis (PRISMS), 302
Parkinson's Disease Fdn., Inc. 283
Pathways to Peace, 117, 330
Patient Advocates for Advanced Cancer Treatment, 203
Pediatric/Adolescent Gastroesophageal Reflux Assn. (PAGER), 234
People First, 163
People Living Through Cancer, 205
PEP , 172
Periodic Paralysis Association *, 284
Perthes Association Message Board*, 285
Pet Loss Grief Support Website*, 141
Peter's Anomaly Support Group*, 285
Peters' Partners , 285
Peutz Jeghers Syndrome Online Group*, 285
P-FLAG, 349
PHCentral*, 294
Phenochromocytoma Group Site*, 286
Phoenix Society for Burn Survivors, 152
Pick's Disease Network*, 286
Pick's Disease Support Group*, 286
Pierre Robin Network  , 286
Pill Addicts Anonymous, 128
Pills Anonymous, 128
Pink Disease Support Group, 287
Pituitary Network Association, 287
Pityriasis Rubra Pilaris Online Support Group, 287
PKD Fdn for Research in Polycystic Kidney Disease, 256
PKIDs, 251
Platelet Disorder Support Assn.,* 248
PLS Friends*, 290
Pneumoworld *, 304
Polycystic Ovarian Syndrome Assn, 258
Positive Partners*, 116
Postpartum Education for Parents (PEP) , 172
Postpartum Support International, 327
Power Surge*, 264
Prader-Willi Syndrome Association , 289
Precocious Puberty Support Network, 289
Preemie-List * , 175
Premature Ovarian Failure Support Group, 289
Prescription Parents, Inc., 212
Prescriptions Anonymous, 128

PRIDE , 348
Primary Immune Deficiencies Online Group*, 249
PRISMS, 302
Prison Talk Online*, 341
Progressive Osseous Heteroplasia Assn, 290
Project DOCC , 157
PROMM Discussion List Group, 291
Prostatitis Chat Room*, 291
Prostitution to Independence, Dignity and Equality, 348
Proteus Syndrome Foundation, 291
Proximal Femoral Focal Deficiency Virtual Support Group, 291
Prozac Survivors Support Group, 292
Pseudotumor Cerebri Society , 292
Pseudotumor Cerebri Support Network, 292
Psychologists Helping Psychologists, 121
Pull-Thru Network, 191, 250, 279
Pulmonary Fibrosis Assn., 293
Pulmonary Hypertension Association, 293
Purine Research Society, 265
PVL Resource Center*, 285
PXE International, Inc., 293
Pyridoxine Dependent Kids, 294
QUAD-LIST Discussion Group*, 164
Rainbow Alliance of the Deaf, 155
Rainbow Room, 351
RAINBOWS, 136, 178
Raising Our Celiac Kids, 208
Rational Recovery Systems, 122
Ray of Hope, 141
Raynaud's Association, Inc., 294 '
REACH , 329
Reach to Recovery, 200
Reaching Out - The WAGR Network, 318
Realtors Concerned for Realtors, 124
Reclamation, Inc., 332
Recovered Alcoholic Clergy Assn., 126
Recovering Couples Anonymous, 169
Recovering Racists Network, 347
Recovery, Inc., 330
Recurrent Respiratory Papillomatosis Foundation, 283
Reflex Sympathetic Dystrophy Syndrome Assn., 295
reFOCUS, 341
Relatives Project, The, 328

* Denotes an  online group

# A Triumph of the Human Spirit...

*"The human spirit remains one of the amazing aspects of life. Just like trick candles on a birthday cake, the unfairness of life temporarily blows out the flame, in spite of this, the fire refuses to be extinguished. I have unlimited gratitude for the courageous men and women in 12 step groups who have displayed that inextinguishable fire known as the human spirit."* - James S., in his Forward to The Step Study Workshop for Depressed Anonymous, copyright 1999 (used here with permission), Depressed Anonymous Publications, Louisville, KY.

The number of different self-help groups continues to grow. The first Edition of this Sourcebook in 1986 was only 120 pages long. From church basements and other community sites, to the newer mutual support networks woven on the Internet, individuals are always starting needed new groups that provide the support, understanding and help that only those who "have been there" can give one another.

Within days of sending each new edition of the Sourcebook to the printer, we usually learn of yet another new type of self-help group that has developed. So if you don't find a group for your particular concern within these pages, you may want to check with us either by phone (973-326-6789) or at our website database (www.selfhelpgroups.org). A few people may want to consider the possibility of starting that needed new type of group. You can contact us for free help with that, too.

While self-help groups are powerful resources for helping people, they can still be relatively hidden resources when it comes to community, social and even health services. For example, self-help groups are rarely thought of when community volunteer efforts are discussed. Yet, in communities across the country, self-help groups represent a major way that Americans help one another purely as volunteers. As another example, people are using self-help groups as a form of complementary or alternative medicine (see p. 322), yet information on self-help support groups is missing from almost all published guides to alternative medicine. There's much work to do to see that these "hidden resources" are better known and tapped.

The true potential of self-help groups is just being realized. It's a very hopeful sign that so many mutual aid groups continue to develop to help people better cope with life adversities and reduce suffering. We hope that this Sourcebook helps inspire and aid you in the part you play in advancing and enriching those self-help group efforts.

*- Ed Madara and Barbara White*

# INDEX

# D

extracorporeal membrane oxygenation, 228-229
extramarital affair, 169
eye disease, 148

# F

Fabry syndrome, 229
facial disfigurement, 229-230
facial paralysis (see Bell's palsy), 196
facioscapulohumeral disease, 230
factor V leiden, 230
fainting diseases (see Fainting List), 274
false memory syndrome, 112
familial adenomatous polyposis (if cancer, see ACOR), 205
familial erythrophagocytic lymphohistiocytosis, 244
familial hypophosphatemic rickets, 321
familial spastic paraparesis, 303
families of addicted, 118-123, 125-128, 129-130, 132-134
families of alcoholics, 124-125
families of autistic, 146
families of cocaine addicted, 126
families of coma victims, 151
families of disabled, 158-160
families of food addicts, 130
families of gamblers, 130
families of homicide victims, 139-140, 339, 341
families of homosexuals/bisexual/transgendered, 348-350
families of in-mates, 341
families of organ donors, 136
families of persons with borderline personality, 325, 328-329
families of persons with depression/bipolar, 326-327, 328-329
families of persons with dissociative identity disorder, 327-329
families of persons with schizophrenia, 328-329, 334
families of persons with trichotillomania, 333
families of persons with vision loss, 147-150
families of sex addicts, 132-133
families of sexually-abused, 114-116
families of sexually-abused, 114-116
families of suicide attempters (see SOLOS), 142
families of the mentally ill, 328-329
families, bereaved, 135-144
family, 165-180
Fanconi anemia, 190
farmers, disabled, 156
fat discrimination, 280
fathers of disabled children, 160
father's rights (divorce), 176-177
fathers, 169-170, 172, 346

# H

# I

# M

overweight, 280
oxalosis, 280

# P

Paget's disease, 281
pain care and life-threatening illness, 259
pain, chronic, 281-282
pain, vulvar, 318
pallid infantile syncope, 295
PAN, 212
pancreatic cancer, 200, 202, (see ACOR), 205, 206
PANDAS (see MGH Neurology WebForums), 275
panhypopituitarism (see growth disorder), 238, 282
panic attacks, 323-324, 329-331
panniculitis disorders, 282
papillomatosis, 282-283
paralysis, 164
paralyzed veterans, 352-353
parental stress, 111
parenting (general), 169-172
parents abused by adult child, 172
parents of addicted, 172-173
parents of autistic children, 146
parents of blind children, 147-150
parents of children on gluten-free diet, 208
parents of children with behavioral problems, 329
parents of children with cancer, 200
parents of children with emotional problems, 329
parents of children with heart defects, 239-240
parents of children with limb deficiency, 145
parents of children with mental illness, 327-328
parents of chronically-ill children, 158-160
parents of deaf children, 153, 155
parents of disabled, 158-160, 175
parents of disabled/ill, networking of, 346-347
parents of ill children, 158-160
parents of multiples, 179-180
parents of murdered children, 339, 341
parents of premature, 175
parents of sexually-abused children, 114, 116
parents of suicide attempters (see SOLOS), 142
parents of uncontrollable children, 172
parents, bereaved, 138-140
parents, disabled, 172
parents, gay/lesbian, 169, 349-350
parents, single, 178-179
Parkinson's disease, 283

rape, prisoner, 116
rare cancers (see ACOR), 205
rare disorders (general), 294
Raynaud's phenomenon, 294
realtors, addicted, 124
recovery personnel, aircraft accidents, 335
recovery/rescue workers, 137
recruitment (see hyperacusis), 246
recurrent respiratory papillomatosis, 283
reflex anoxic seizure, 295
reflex sympathetic dystrophy, 295
relaxation techniques (see anxiety), 323
religious leaders, abused by, 113-114
religious order, addicted women in, 119
renal disorders, 255-256
repetitive motion injury, 206
reproductive anomaly (see growth disorder), 238
rescue personnel, 137
rescue personnel, aircraft accidents, 335
respiratory disorders, 296
restless legs syndrome, 296
restoring circumcision, 345-346
retinitis pigmentosa, 148
retinoblastoma  (see ACOR) 205, 297
retinopathy of prematurity, 151
Rett syndrome, 297
Reye's syndrome, 297
rhabdomyosarcoma (see ACOR), 205
rheumatic diseases (see arthritis), 193-194
rickets, x-linked hypophosphatemic, 321
ring 9, 181
ritual sexual abuse, 114
RLS, 296
Robinow syndrome, 297
rod monochromacy (see achromatopsia), 182
Romberg disorder (see MGH Neurology WebForums), 275, 283
rotator cuff injuries, 278
RRP, 283
RSDS, 295
RSH, 302
Rubinstein-Taybi syndrome, 298
Russell Silver syndrome (see growth disorder), 238, 298

## S

saline implants, adversely affected by, 301
sand spinal tumor (see brain tumor), 198-199
sarcoidosis, 298

# T

## U

## V

# W